COMPETITION

COMPETITION
A Feminist Taboo?

Edited by Valerie Miner and Helen E. Longino

Foreword by Nell Irvin Painter

THE FEMINIST PRESS
at The City University of New York
New York

90 89 88 87 5 4 3 2 1

Lines from the poem "Afterimages" are from *Chosen Poems Old and New* by Audre Lorde. Copyright © 1982 by Audre Lorde. Reprinted by permission of W. W. Norton and Company.

Library of Congress Catalog-in-Publication Data

Competition, a feminist taboo?

1. Women—Psychology. 2. Competition (Psychology)
3. Feminism—Psychological aspects. I. Miner, Valerie.
II. Longino, Helen E.
HQ1206.C69   1987   305.4'2   87-8515
ISBN 0-935312-75-7
ISBN 0-935312-74-9 (pbk)

Cover design by Gilda Hannah
Text design by Paula Martinac

For Natalie Lando who has done so much,
behind the scenes, for women readers and writers.

Contents

Foreword

NELL IRVIN PAINTER

Until quite recently in Western society, none of the prime settings for competition in the big time—sports, war, politics, academia, and business—welcomed women. Non-Western societies have known the phenomena of market women and Amazon warriors, but when we in North America imagined the arenas in which women competed, we were more likely to think along the lines of beauty pageants, those degrading symbols of objectification that feminism rejects.

Before contemporary feminism, competition among women delimited and defined women's competition as a whole. It seemed as unnatural for women to compete with men (though some hardy women did it, thereby virtually desexing themselves) as it would be unthinkable for them to compete for something other than men's approval. Women entered the sweepstakes of dating, marriage, and beauty contests, which the greatest beauties won. Thorstein Veblen had long ago revealed the class basis of beauty standards, yet women still made the effort to appear alluring on those terms. Even black, yellow, and red women, who did not qualify for the Miss America pageants, tried to measure up against an inappropriate standard of physical beauty that in the case of black women, at least, had been designed with their bodies as a negative object. Only in women's schools and colleges or the sex-segregated hierarchies of Catholic schools might women compete with attributes other than beauty for prizes unrelated to the rivalry for men. But awards that only women could win lacked the prestige of those associated with the so-called best and brightest, that is, white men.

A quarter of a century ago, many sorts of people, including women, did not qualify for pursuing society's major prizes, which were reserved for our equivalent of warriors: middle- and upper-class white men. Barred from the warrior ranks and thereby eliminated from their contests, the rest of us could merely serve the warriors' needs, hoping through their success to satisfy our own ambitions. By the mid-1960s, however, reflected glory, like second-class citizenship and segregation, no longer sufficed. After much agitation, some of us entered the races hitherto reserved for white men. But we took our places with misgivings.

Just as the civil rights movement and feminism widened the course, many of us shrank from it, in word if not deed, having discovered the realities of competition. What society touted as meritocracy we recognized as contests that had been fixed from the beginning—crooked, elitist undertakings that violated our nonhierarchical, egalitarian, feminist/black/Third World values. We found that the competition for success had been limited by more than sex and race, that individuals form working-class backgrounds and from the provinces also bore handicaps. Even though many of us now competed openly with women and men for the sorts of prizes whose pursuit had once seemed unwomanly and continued to seem unsisterly, we pretended not to compete. Realizing how unlikely we tokens were to win, few of us broadcast satisfaction with having been admitted to the race. Competition, except for the title of most oppressed, was anathema to feminists. In reality, two things were occurring at once. Feminists began to speak of the need to replace competition with cooperation at the same time that women, some of whom were feminists, began competing for every prize society offers.

In sports (an arena that the Civil Rights Act of 1964 helped to open) women embrace competition and relish victory. Here there is no agonizing over defeating rivals, and women savor winning without misgivings. After arduous training and stiff competition, losing hurts and winning satisfies. Women in sports—in open competition with clear criteria and stopwatches—enjoy the luxury of untainted victories. In intellectual pursuits, however, where men also compete, the phrases "good enough" or, more usually, "not good enough" haunt women who win or lose the fellowships, tenure, book contracts, and favorable reviews that sketch out victory in lines that are not fixed. In the purported meritocracy of the intellect, enormous numbers of women are made to feel not-good-enough.

Unlike the winner of a marathon, the tenured woman may not reap satisfaction from having won one round or surmounted a barrier. She probably continues to be haunted by the fear of being-not-good-enough, a quality that may never be pinned down. Not-good-enough may be a matter of style, personal or literary, or it may signify the absence of the approval of a powerful judge, even though male judges usually find only one woman at a time to be good-enough. The designation of not-good-enough may come from one's sex/race/class, together or separately, or from one's perceived shortcomings as an individual. The quality of being-not-good-enough attaches to the person, so that mere achievement may not necessarily erase its stigma. When a not-good-enough person produces a book stuffed with research, it is called "plodding," while a work of imagination may be termed "flimsy." The same books by good-enough people would be said to rest on a solid foundation of research or to display stunning insight. The work of a not-good-enough person can rarely be considered good-enough.

The judgment of not-good-enough seldom needs to be articulated or explained, because omitting mention of not-good-enoughs usually suffices. But if named, not-good-enoughs may be dismissed with a brief gesture or phrase. Not surprisingly, the newcomers to big-time competition, minorities and women, particularly those from working-class backgrounds, most commonly become not-good-enoughs, a process that subtly restores the status quo ante by removing them from the competition.

Purveyors of not-good-enoughism are the frightened and the threatened, who need not necessarily be white or male. Any vulnerable competitor can seek to eliminate competition. Such attempts spring from the same source as the kind of needless competition sometimes fostered among newcomers. One essay in this collection deals with middle-class, white housewives competing with their working-class, black women employees; another, a middle-class, white woman competing with a young, working-class Asian-American, much to the latter's surprise. "I [had] never thought myself intimidating," says Debra Matsumoto, "and it was a new experience for me to be viewed as a threat as well as a member of the elite."

At some point, just about every woman realizes that she is seen not only as not-good-enough but also as a threat, that some person wishes to eliminate her from competition while another seeks to engage her in it—both situations indicating pernicious rivalry. Unwelcome competition satisfies neither the inventor of the competition nor its object, neither of whom probably feels strong. If ever cooperation should be substituted for competition, it should be in such a situation. Sadly, lack of self-confidence, which engenders senseless competition, also renders collaboration difficult.

Without self-confidence, both competition and collaboration sour. But the self-confidence that is crucial to both relationships often eludes women who have long been stigmatized as not-good-enough. Happily, women are not locked in a vicious circle of not-good-enough, undermined self-confidence, and frustrating rivalries. Healthy competition is the key because competing in races one can win, however limited, breaks the circle. The big time may break hearts, but many other arenas of fruitful competition exist. Competing, whether against men or women, brings experience, and experience strengthens. Strength breeds confidence. Appropriate competition encourages the experience, strength, and confidence that nourish the cooperation that feminists prize.

Contributors

Martha A. Ackelsberg is professor of government at Smith College and author of a number of articles on urban politics, families and public policy, and anarchism. She is at work on a book on the Spanish anarchist women's organization, *Mujeres Libres*.

Kathryn Pyne Addelson teaches at Smith College in the philosophy department and the program in the history of the sciences. She has worked with community organizing groups and has a special interest in building alternative institutions. She is author of the forthcoming book *Moral Passages*, in which she offers a philosophy of morality and society that is compatible with a decentralized, nonhierarchical political approach.

Sandra Butler, author of the internationally respected *Conspiracy of Silence: The Trauma of Incest*, is a speaker, trainer, lecturer, counselor, workshop leader, and writer.

Erika Duncan's latest novel, *Those Giants: Let Them Rise*, published by Schocken Books in February 1986, is the story of a woman's search for her own largeness among the "giants" of her present and her past. Her other two books are *A Wreath of Pale Roses* (1977) and *Unless Soul Clap Its Hands: Portraits and Passages* (1985). She was co-founder of the Woman's Salon, is a contributing editor for *Book Forum*, and teaches fiction writing in her home while working on a writing-teaching project at New York University which ranges into connections with mathematics and philosophy.

Michèle Farrell is an assistant professor of French at Rice University. Her areas of interest include seventeenth-century French literature, the epistolary genre, and feminist theory. She explores the relationships between gender and genre in seventeenth-century French texts, and also studies those texts with regard to the sociohistorical implications they hold for women.

Rosabeth Moss Kanter is author of *Men and Women of the Corporation* (Basic

Books, 1977) and co-editor of *Another Voice* (Doubleday, 1975). She is the chair of Goodmeasure, Inc.

Elaine Bell Kaplan is a doctoral candidate in sociology at the University of California, Berkeley. Her work has been published in *Feminist Issues*, and she is preparing a dissertation on the impact of public policy (AFDC) on the lives of black single mothers.

Evelyn Fox Keller, trained in theoretical physics and molecular biology, has worked in mathematical biology and, more recently, in the history, philosophy, and psychology of science. She is professor of mathematics and humanities at Northeastern University, and a visiting scholar in science, technology, and society at M.I.T. Keller is best known for her two recent books, *A Feeling for the Organism: The Life and Work of Barbara McClintock* (W. H. Freeman, 1983), and *Reflections on Gender and Science* (Yale University Press, 1985).

Myrna Kostash is a second-generation Ukrainian-Canadian, born and educated in Edmonton, Alberta. Her books include *All of Baba's Children* (Hurtig, 1977) and *Long Way from Home* (Lorimer, 1980).

Grace Lichtenstein is a journalist and author of *Machisma*. She has written widely about women in sports and was executive editor of *World Tennis* magazine. For 10 years she was a reporter and national correspondent for *The New York Times*. She is co-author of *Sonny Bloch's Inside Real Estate* (Weidenfeld and Nicholson, 1987).

Joyce P. Lindenbaum is a licensed clinical social worker in private practice in Berkeley, California. She is also on the consulting staff of Family Guidance Services, Children's Hospital, Oakland, California.

Helen E. Longino teaches philosophy at Mills College, has published essays in the philosophy of science and in feminist theory, and is currently completing a book entitled *The Idea of a Value-Free Science*. She is one of the founding editors of *Hypatia: A Journal of Feminist Philosophy* and is politically active in and out of the academy.

María Cristina Lugones came to the United States from Argentina in 1967. She is a teacher of philosophy (at Carleton College) and community organizer, and is currently working on play and playfulness among women across cultural and racial boundaries.

Toni A. H. McNaron teaches English literature and women's studies at the University of Minnesota. She is editor of *Women in the Night: Women Speaking about Incest* (Cleis Press, 1982) and *The Sister Bond: A Timeless Connection* (Pergamon, 1985) and is on the editorial board of *Hurricane Alice*.

Debra A. Matsumoto graduated from the University of California, Berkeley with a B.A. in English Literature. She is a free-lance editor and proofreader and works on a variety of manuscripts for publishing companies both in the United States and abroad. She currently resides in Berkeley.

Marjorie Mbilinyi was born in the United States in 1943 and became a citizen of Tanzania and the Third World in 1967. She has borne four children, one of whom died an infant like so many other infants of the Third World. She is a full professor at the University of Dar es Salaam. She is currently on leave and writing two books in Brussels. She is co-author, with Ophelia Mascarenhas, of *Women in Tanzania* (1983).

Valerie Miner's novels include *Blood Sisters, Winter's Edge, Movement, Murder in the English Department*, and the forthcoming *All Good Women*. Her fiction focuses on cross-class and cross-cultural movement among women. Her collaborative work includes being co-author of *Her Own Woman, Tales I Tell My Mother*, and *More Tales*. She has won the P.E.N. Syndicated Fiction Prize and other literary awards. For the last 10 years she has taught at the University of California, Berkeley.

Helene Moglen is chair of women's studies and professor of English literature and history of consciousness at the University of California at Santa Cruz. She is author of *The Philosophical Irony of Laurence Sterne* (University of Florida Press, 1975) and of *Charlotte Bronte, The Self Conceived* (University of Wisconsin Press, 1984), and co-author of *Sexual and Gender Harassment in the Academy: A Guide for Faculty, Students, and Administrators* (Modern Language Association of America, 1981).

Daphne Muse is an author of children's books and the assistant editor for Children's Advocate, a California-based newspaper that focuses on children's rights and issues at the state, national, and international levels.

Nell Irvin Painter is the author of three books on U.S. history. She teaches at the University of North Carolina at Chapel Hill and has been seen simultaneously as not-good-enough and as a threat.

Letty Cottin Pogrebin, an editor of *Ms.* magazine, is the author of six books, including *Growing Up Free, Family Politics*, and, most recently, *Among Friends*. She is also a free-lance writer and lectures widely on women's issues.

Jennifer Ring received her doctorate from the University of California, Berkeley, in 1979. She teaches political theory at Stanford and the University of California, Davis, and is writing a book. She lives in Berkeley with her husband and daughter, and windsurfs, runs, and lifts weights at every free moment.

Barbara Rosenblum is a professor of sociology and author of books and articles too numerous to cite here. She is a protean intellectual with wide-ranging expertise. Eight-page vita available upon request.

Paula Ross, born in Detroit, Michigan, in 1947, has never played team sports and therefore has a very individual sense of what it means to compete. She is editor of two anthologies, *Across the Generations* (Educators' Improvement Incorporated, 1985) and *My Story's On! Ordinary Women/Extraordinary Lives* (Common Differences Press, 1985). Her fiction has appeared in *Conditions: Nine,* and *IKON.* Currently on leave as co-director of Women's Voices Creative Writing Workshop, she lives and writes in Berkeley, California.

Elizabeth V. Spelman has been teaching philosophy and living in western Massachusetts since 1973. She currently teaches at Smith College and is at work on *Inessential Woman,* forthcoming from Beacon Press.

Yvonne is a poet and filmmaker and former poetry editor at *Ms.* Her media arts company, Chameleon Productions, Inc., has published two volumes of her epic trilogy: *Iwilla/Soil* (1985) and *Iwilla/Scourge* (1986).

A Feminist Taboo?

HELEN E. LONGINO and VALERIE MINER

Why is it so hard for women to talk about competition? This book offers various voices—in contradiction and in agreement—about an issue that has been simmering for years. Feminists have long been fiercely critical of male power games, yet we have often ignored or concealed our own conflicts over money, control, position, and recognition. As women have moved into the cultural and economic mainstream and as poor women's problems have grown more visible, these conflicts have become ever more pressing. It is time to end the silence. We hope this book will expand the feminist discussion of "difference" by focusing on our interactions with one another as well as on our identities and self-definitions.

The editors of this anthology approach competition as a complex issue that elicits emotional distress and creates political wariness. Both of us are radical feminists and socialists and thus have two traditions behind us that seem antithetical to competition. We are often faced with a conflict between our commitment to, indeed our longing for, solidarity with other women and our need to compete in the marketplace for work. Without a better understanding of the competitive structures in which we work and play and of our own responses to these structures, we believe most women will remain frustrated, guilty, angry, and divided.

The first step toward understanding is to acknowledge the existence of competition in our family lives and in our public spheres. It is painful to admit the deep rivalries we have had with sisters and mothers, just as it is embarrassing to point to our competition with other women in workplaces, neighborhoods, and political groups. If we could stop feeling defensive and fearful long enough to consider how we compete not only for money but also for attention and affection and righteousness, we might be better able to eliminate the negative elements of competitiveness from our lives. If we could muster the courage to examine the functions that competitiveness serves under both capitalism and patriarchy, we might feel less guilty about being caught in its web. Only after acknowledging the behavior and recognizing its part in our lives and our culture will we be able to find a way out of this dark, silent, suffocating room.

The time is ripe for this subject because we—the individuals who sparked the current wave of feminism and the women's movement itself—have grown older. Many of us who were active in the late 1960s and early 1970s are now in the uneasy middle of careers or families or political battles (or all three) rather than on the margins. Many of us face competition with other women for promotions or grants or awards. In the old days we didn't dream of such predicaments. The ideals of sisterhood ruled out rivalry, or so we thought. Many feminists believed that the antagonism we expressed toward each other in the business of manhunting would dissolve when we stopped stalking men. Then, we often imagined feminism as an arena filled with loving light and right. Now, most of us no longer look to the women's movement as the mother who will make it all better. We have learned that the fallible movement is a place of stimulation, support, and vitality, but that it is not the long-lost womb. Meanwhile, within the women's movement we have noticed that some women are more visible than others. In the United States, especially, we have made the mistake of creating a new star system whereby some of us have become spokespersons for the movement and then used our positions to further our careers or to assume the mantle of leader. Within the movement one finds competition for recognition from a feminist audience as well as competition for the reputation of being more feminist than thou.

Perhaps one of the greatest obstacles to an honest examination of competition is our fear. Fear of failure and fear of success in the areas in which we compete. Fear of facing the internal contradictions between our behavior and our principles. Fear of being morally wrong or of being moralistically paralyzed in mediocrity. Fear of being gossiped about or trashed or put on a pedestal which can metamorphose into public stocks. Fear of risking and losing. Fear of winning unfairly.

One reason we have been alarmed by competition is that we are unprepared for it. Women have been socialized to avoid overt conflict. The assertive self-confidence required is trained out of us (or it was when we, the editors, were growing up) at an early age. Some people think that women are innately noncompetitive. This book does not pursue the wild goose of the nature versus nurture debate with regard to competitiveness. We wish rather to view the experience of women in competitive structures through feminist eyes, eyes in which sisterhood is still an ideal.

The definition of competition is approached in various ways by our contributors. Several of them begin at the Latin root, *competitus*, which means "to strive together toward." It is as useful to discuss what competition is *not* as to find a precise definition of it, because major problems arise from the confusion of competitive feelings with emotions like envy, jealousy, and resentment. What is the difference between conflict and competition? How do we distinguish between overt and covert forms of competition? Is one fair and the other not?

We began this project with a deep suspicion about the way competition has been embedded in our social system and, consequently, into our psychology. This led us to ask such questions as: How has the Puritan ethic promoted competitiveness? What is the relation of our faith in competition to the credibility we lend the U.S. voting system? How many of us are laboring under the need to prove ourselves fit in an outmoded form of social Darwinism? How have biology and economics combined under capitalism to graft competitiveness onto the popular face of human nature? Whatever the answers to these questions, our understanding of competition needs to be tempered by an awareness of the social structures within which it takes place and an understanding of what the stakes are in any given competitive situation. What is the goal of competition? What are we trying to win? Can more than one of us win? Can we each win in different ways? Let's consider three examples.

Two women sit in a living room arguing vehemently about a topic of mutual concern: competition among women. Each has thought about the issue at great length. One contends that competition can sharpen skills and awareness. The other argues that competition is always destructive. They are both committed to the women's movement. They know each other well, respect each other's ideas, and feel safe with one another. They are competing for the "right" answer. Finding the right answer is almost as important to them as being the person who walked into the room with that answer. They will even entertain the possibility of compromise.

Two women stand before a community group. They engage in heated debate about a familiar topic of intense concern. Each cares passionately about her ideas. As feminists they want to contribute to the women's movement with the analysis they have prepared for tonight's debate. Yet each is open-minded and has considerable respect for the other. What is at stake here? The women's reputations as public speakers? The audience's response and possible commitment to one or the other side of the debate? The "right" answer?

Two women sit on a stage before a university audience. Each is a prominent scholar, noted for her insight and acerbity. They are debating about our favorite topic. Previously, they have argued with each other about it in the press, on a radio talk show, on another platform. Each has given considerable thought to the issue and has agreed to come to the university tonight because there is a tenured position available. What are they competing for? The academic post? A reputation as the better public speaker or "feminist thinker"? The audience's allegiance? The "right" answer? All of the above?

Before we examine the dialectical potential of competition, it's worth noting some of the dissonant interests within the structures of competition. In the first scene, the women may enter the room with the interest of learning from one another. But their pride may obviate that possibility. Each may become so intent on winning the argument that she loses the possibility of developing her ideas. In the second scene, issues of pride become magnified as the exchange moves from private to public; the women may get so seduced by the audience that they forget that they have come to engage in a debate about which they wish to find an answer. The third scene is more complex still. Are the women competing as old rivals, as job seekers, as sisters who are interested in getting to the bottom of a fascinating controversy? These identities compete with each other.

Considering the potential of competition to contribute to dialectical process requires the imagination of a goal attainable by multiple competitors. Isn't competition among ideas better distinguished from other forms of competition, such as electoral politics or horse races where only one entrant can win? When we compete on behalf of ideas, are we competing to persuade or to learn? If the goal is to learn, certainly everyone benefits by the best efforts of the others. If one could envision a cooperative sociality, it would be a world where the course is not set, the direction not predetermined by inaccessible goals. The focus of competitive discussion in such a culture would be on increasing understanding, not on honoring particular routes to understanding or various speeds at which to approach understanding. Presumably a number of people could, through different channels and different perspectives, meet to vitalize and deepen a mutual enlightenment. Certainly the women's movement could do with more honest arguing and more generous listening. If we all did our best and stimulated one another's excellence, then perhaps competition could benefit everyone.

The very work of imagining, editing, and submitting this book has raised our consciousness about competition in surprising ways. We began the anthology because we wanted to air the issue. Little did we know what a competitive adventure it would become. When we first proposed the topic, a literary agent advised us to drop the anthology form and write the book ourselves. Better yet, she said, one of you should write it alone, because it would be more marketable in an individual voice. Since we had both worked on the issue and talked about it at length and since we have a close personal relationship that we did not want to destroy, we declined her suggestion. Then came other reports. Great idea, but it would be better from one voice. Best-seller, we were told. Lots of possibilities. Like Alvin Toffler's *Future Shock* or Gail Sheehy's *Passages*. Get a personality behind the message. But, we replied falteringly, we are talking about competition *among* women. We have no message. We want to elicit a chorus of women's experiences from different classes and races and cultures. We want to spark a dialogue. It would be more feminist as an anthology. Feminist, schmeminist, said the reports. Think commercial. But it would be more interesting with a variety of voices. . . . We persisted, despite the temptations of fame and fortune, not to mention mass publication. This history is presented not as testimony to our high caliber, but as evidence of the kind of competition we encountered in the very process of making the book.

Other examples are more revealing. When we sent out a call for papers, we received many enthusiastic replies and a few bewildered ones. Most respondents sent proposals that opened up intriguing areas of investigation. In some cases, despite discussion and correspondence, the proposed essays never materialized. Competition is easier to chat about than to write about, we told ourselves. An agitated colleague wrote to us saying that although she had noticed that women inexplicably sought to compete with her, she herself did not engage in such behavior. She had nothing to contribute to the discussion except a barrage of criticism about other feminists. We had hoped to include a piece about competition in couples. We asked one lesbian couple who were both writers. They were delighted. They missed the first deadline. But, they insisted, they were working on it. They missed the second deadline. Then they split up. Although their separation was unconnected with this book per se, it was related to rivalry in their relationship. We invited another couple to write the essay. How did you know we were talking about this very issue in therapy? one of them wrote back. They also split up. Finally a third couple submitted a piece on their own.

Likewise, as co-editors, we encounter conflicts. Helen is a philosopher; Valerie is a novelist. We have vastly different approaches to thinking and writing. We are both stubborn. As you might imagine, the very composition of this introduction became a point of contention. Helen tells Valerie that philosophers are trained to think about thinking. Valerie says that's all very well, but she would be insulted if what she did all day wasn't considered thinking. Helen argues for precision, sometimes in convoluted sentences that Valerie says may be accurate but are incomprehensible. Valerie argues for clarity. She prefers short sentences. Helen says a certain conceptual complexity is lost in what she calls choppy writing. As a scholar, Helen is eager to include studies by her colleagues in the academy. As a narrative writer, Valerie wants to have people tell tales from their own lives. But somehow we came together in these various areas. We have remained together. This book represents a dialectical discovery through our competition about ideas and approaches as well as a certain amount of commonsense concession; we flipped a coin to determine whose name would appear first on the title page and on the joint essays.

We have organized the forum in three parts. Letty Cottin Pogrebin's "Competing with Women," which appeared in the first issue of *Ms.* magazine, July 1972, constitutes Part I. Pogrebin's essay considers competition a pivotal feminist issue. Clearly, many of us are still twirling. Part II exposes "Daily Realities." Here contributors write about overt and covert competition in public settings and rivalry in the family. Part III, "Feminist Transformations," considers the social functions of competition and offers some new visions.

Essays in the second section detail personal encounters with competition. Evelyn Fox Keller and Helene Moglen discuss competition among academic women. Myrna Kostash and Marjorie Mbilinyi write about international competition from their homes in Canada and Tanzania, respectively. Grace Lichtenstein and Jennifer Ring study women who learn through a sport how to compete with others and with themselves. Rosabeth Moss Kanter, Debra A. Matsumoto, and Elaine Bell Kaplan discuss competition in the workplace, the latter two from cross-class and cross-race perspectives. Toni A. H. McNaron tells us about the insights she gathered while editing *The Sister Bond*. Erika Duncan writes about mothers and daughters from her experience in both positions. Michèle Farrell considers the celebrated epistolary relationship between Madame de Sévigné and her daughter, The Countess of Guignan, in seventeenth-century France. Barbara Rosenblum and Sandra Butler volley about their competition as lesbian partners. Daphne Muse examines girls who compete for male attention at the expense of their own friendship. Yvonne returns to her childhood, revealing her competition with girls in Catholic school.

The moral and political significances of competition differ markedly depending on whether the stakes are blue ribbons and gold medals or a meal ticket, education, or a job. Labor and community organizers often show how conflicts among oppressed groups serve the interest of the oppressor. Our contributors suggest that something similar is true of certain forms of competition among women. They also caution us against generalizing that competition is good or bad. Some competition does foster excellence. Competition whose outcome is "fitness" for life and a sociobiological stamp of approval, however, is a dangerous myth. And competition that undermines our efforts to gain equality—of rights and of respect—is downright self-sabotage.

While not offering conclusions, Part III shows that there are other approaches, that solidarity and cooperation are possible and not necessarily antithetical to conflict and difference. Our intent is not to be didactic but to empower readers through a variety of contributions to come to their own conclusions.

Feminists, as intellectuals and activists, engage in a kind of archaeology. That is, in our conceptual, analytic, and visionary work as scholars and writers as well as in our shaking and remaking the conditions of women's lives as activists, we lay bare the determinants of the female world. Each critical foray—theoretical or practical— is a dig that reveals the dynamics underlying some experienced reality. But unlike traditional archaeologists, we do not work in a static world. We excavate in a continually changing system. We dig in shifting ground.

Feminist archaeology does share with traditional forms the temptations of hasty generalization. One dig does not a world history reveal. Early in the current wave of U.S. feminism, white, middle-class women whose greater access to media gave them louder voices than those less privileged spoke as if their discoveries about their own lives represented the experiences of all women. The great majority of us remained unseen. In this volume, women from different cultures discuss a variety of social roles and positions. As Asian, black, Latina, native-American, working-class, lesbian, and other women have made their voices heard, the idea that there could be any easy comprehension of female experience has lost its hold over our imaginations. Therefore we have sought out diverse voices. This book does not present a classically harmonious chorus. Here, rather, is the sound of women vigorously and honestly thinking, chipping away at the layers of tradition and social practice that interact to keep us in our places.

Each essay in the collection reveals different conceptual, experiential, or analytic points of view. Each offers answers to the questions that prompted us to explore the topic: How does competition motivate us? Do we feel more competitive with women than with men? What are the intersections between competition and co-operation? What are the differences between our internal and external experiences of competition? How can we distinguish between striving for excellence, striving for success, and striving for control? The answers sometimes complement and sometimes confound one another.

Our hope is that these questions and answers will provide a fulcrum for self-examination, a point of departure for greater individual and collective self-knowledge. Perhaps the anthology will lead to articles, conferences, classes, or more books. The ripples have already begun since some of our contributors, impatient with the pace of book publishing, have already published the pieces we assigned them in such feminist journals as *Signs, Sojourner, Feminist Studies,* and *Women's Studies International Forum.* In addition, a number of women have contemplated facets of this subject in essays they haven't yet completed. We want this anthology to stimulate readers to reconsider how we think and feel about other women. The multidimensionality of competition revealed by this contribution to feminist archaeology is a challenge to our talents. We do not need to be paralyzed by feelings of personal immorality or political incorrectness. By directly addressing the issue of competition with one another, by analyzing these feelings and the situations and culture that provoke them, we can take that much more power in our lives. Feminists have recognized that our social systems need to change drastically in order to accommodate women as full human beings. By focusing clearly on the many aspects of one hallmark of Western social organization, we hope this book will contribute to a better understanding of that necessary change.

Part I

A LIBERATING VISION

Competing with Women

LETTY COTTIN POGREBIN

I have this fantasy, see. It came to me a few years ago in the weblike half-sleep of morning. Today, if anything, it has a more absurd clarity than when it first unfolded.

For openers, there's this subway train stuck in a tunnel. (Analysts, keep still!) It's rush hour, and the train is jammed with commuters. Like most New Yorkers, I am a hardy masochist. I wait, uncomplaining, among the other pressed bodies. It's silent as only a self conscious mob can be silent—just coughs and shuffling packages and rustling newspapers.

Then the word spreads. This is no ordinary breakdown. There will be no exodus along the tracks. We are sealed within locked doors and immovable windows. It will be at least 36 hours before we are rescued.

Now it so happens that at the time of this imagined melodrama I am a nursing mother. And since I am breast feeding my real-life twins, I am quite a prodigious producer of that mystical substance known as mother's milk. My breasts fill as the hours pass. My nipples begin to leak. But instead of feeling embarrassed by the wet splotches on my chest, I am triumphant. They are proud badges of my life-giving power.

Because participants in an urban catastrophe—blackouts, stalled elevators, garbage strikes—relinquish their usual anonymity in a kind of human bonding effort, I tell the woman beside me about my mammary abundance. She tells the person next to her, and before long the eyes of a carload of people are riveted to my

Reprinted from *Ms.* 1 (July 1972): 78–81, by permission. Copyright 1972 by Letty Cottin Pogrebin.

breasts. As the second day dawns, tempers flare, patience wanes, fear surfaces, and people are hungry and thirsty. Thirsty. THIRSTY.

As the fantasy fades out, I am nursing my parched and grateful companions—one by one.

Psychoanalysts will have a field day decoding the rather obvious symbolism. But I'll never be persuaded that my fantasy has anything to do with phallic trains, womblike tunnels, or sexual liquids. For me, this elaborate scenario is my apocalyptic put-down of all the women with whom I have ever competed. In this semidream at last I have something no other woman has. It is my psychic catharsis—the reaffirmation of my womanly worth. No matter what my inadequacies, no matter how glaring my flaws, no matter about the admirable, accomplished, or beautiful women beside whom I may pale—in this fantasy I am superwoman.

Whether by virtue of full breasts (literally or figuratively) or a devastating hostess gown, we women have long been engaged in the enervating game of going every other woman one better. While this invidious habit is more widespread than name-dropping or nail-biting, until recently it has been every woman's dirty little secret. Now, the lid is off. Women are trading secrets with one another. And the real revelation is that our competitiveness is not a dirty act of treachery but the survival tactic of a second-class human being. Lacking confidence, bereft of self-esteem, we play the only game in town that seems to offer a payoff.

The rules are simple.

• If you feel depressed, don't examine your discontent—find a woman who's worse off than you are.

• If you doubt your attractiveness, don't question the standards of beauty—outdo and outdress every woman in sight.

• If you feel your "femininity" under attack, don't jettison the label once and for all—point a finger at some tough cookie and call yourself a powder puff by comparison.

• If you believe that you're intellectually lacking, don't embark on the Harvard Classics—ridicule other women for sublimating their frustrations in affairs of the mind.

That was the old way. Raising ourselves by standing on the crushed remains of our sisters. Measuring ourselves against a merciless yardstick whose notches are not concrete ideals and goals but rather women to be surpassed. Putting them down to hoist us up. Creative despair.

Competing. There's another set of rules, too: a formula for self-definition that is tested not in the laboratory of the self but via experiments in learning to please. It began long ago for all of us. No matter how different our childhood experiences or economic backgrounds, there is a remarkable sameness about the way we learned to think.

Boys were praised for what they did and made. We were praised for what we looked like. Having the prettiest dress or the best hairdo meant competing. Attracting compliments meant competing. Getting attention meant competing. And so it went through our developing years until the pattern was set.

Men compete for rewards and achievements; we compete for men. Men vie for worldly approval and status; we vie for husbands. Men measure themselves against standards of excellence and an established level of performance; we measure ourselves against one another. Our options are limited and our possibilities inhibited by that great leveling force which seeks to make only wives and mothers out of us all. The great diversity of worldly goals and all the routes to personal satisfaction are expected to merge into one prime dedication: join the race, get a man, and may the best woman win.

We can all remember when we were little girls on the starting line of this lifelong race against an unseen herd of "other girls" or "other women."

I happen to remember piano lessons. I was given them with a vengeance. Not to develop a love of music or a gratifying personal competence—but because "you'll be so popular at parties if you can play piano for everybody." (Read: "and the *other girls* can't.")

Or dancing school. No one hoped I would become a ballerina or even a ballet-omane. I went because "it will help you keep in shape." (Read: "while the *other girls* get fat.")

Or college. It was automatic for a middle-class girl in the fifties. In fact it was unthinkable to drop out. But not because college was a place for exploration or personal growth or the development of mental acumen. Being educated meant "you'll catch a better class of husband." (Read: "than *other women* in this teeming marriage market.")

Part of the indoctrination cost money—lessons, clothes, the diploma, whatever the budget would allow. The rest was communicated by an attitude—and from that we learned the real catechism of femininity.

In my house, it was epitomized by our family's farewell cheer. Whenever my sisters or I were leaving for a party or a date, we were a given a kiss and a flat: "Be charming." Not "Have fun" or "Be yourself," but "Be charming."

Every honest sorcerer will admit that one can't "charm" or captivate without knowing the formula. So we learned it because we couldn't trust ourselves and because we weren't taught to have a self we could define without outside help. To be charming (to please boys, win their approval, and beat out all those *other girls*) we had to look pretty, be clever and witty (but never smarter than he was), and— most important—*learn about what interests him.* That was a part of the formula I mastered best. If the truth be known (and I'm just now coming to terms with it), I mastered it only too well. In a profound sense, I am the sum of the boys and men whose interests I made my own.

For the back-court man I pursued in high school, I learned about the zone defense, and he boasted that I was the only girl who knew the basketball team's record by heart. In college and in the years before my marriage, there were men for whom I learned tennis, became a jazz buff, invested in the stock market, cut my hair, endured lacrosse matches, read the metaphysical poets, conccaled my real political opinions, learned to drive a motor scooter, and developed a notable tolerance for Bix Beiderbecke records, Zen Buddhism, and draft beer.

Sure, it's nice to learn from others, and we all expand our horizons that way to some extent. But for me and many other women, the formula became our only source of self-actualization. What were we really worth without it? We could never be sure. So we believed we had to move with each man's tide or some other woman would swim away with him. We *might* end up with honest enthusiasm for our adopted interests, but then again we might waste a lot of time falsifying zeal for someone else's passion. Always, it was someone else's passion that started us off. And that's a circuitous route to self-enrichment at best. Moreover, we tended to lose sight of who we were and what we cared about. Values were externally imposed. Self-esteem was a gift men bestowed by choosing us over all the others. Self-image was something we defined by fitting the mold and crowding our sisters out. Cram that foot into the glass slipper, honey, or the Prince will ride to the next girl's house.

But the shoe is pinching us too tightly and has been for too long. And now, in our own voices, we are admitting how uncomfortable we have been.

One friend of mine describes her involved competitive ritual. When she arrives at a cocktail party and before she seeks the attention of any man, she runs an elimination tournament in her head.

"Well, I'm thinner than most of the other women, but I'm certainly not as sophisticated as that one in the chain belt," the interior monologue might begin. "The woman at the window seems confident and gregarious, but my voice is sexier. None of them looks as hip as I. Matter of fact, they all look pretty square."

Like a contestant at a Pillsbury Bake-Off, my friend continues her survey of the party, checking out the competition until she has satisfied (or deluded) herself about her position. "I've got to feel I'm the best in *some* category if I'm going to function at a party at all," she admits.

Another friend has come to grips with her own brand of one-upswomanship. "Anytime I feel threatened by a more snazzy woman, I promote my kids," says this housewife. "They're my product. And I guess I've used them to compensate for my own lack of productivity."

How does she use her children as a tool of competition?

"By letting a woman know how gorgeous and brilliant my kids are and by making the point that whatever any woman has going for her, nothing beats my glorious motherhood."

One minor problem, she adds: It only works with single or childless women.

When we first arrived in New York, my roommate and I agreed immediately on a *modus operandi:* no matter what we had planned to do or see together, all bets were off if a man asked either of us for a date. We resolved not to let one another get in the way of our social lives. Our friendship could take it. We understood that our feelings didn't count; our interests were subordinated. *Männer uber alles.*

Wounding women to win men is an old story. Just as capitalizing on the credentials of a lover, husband, or offspring is almost a cliché of consciousness-raising. Acquiring vicarious status by the house we live in, the jewelry he gives us, the better sex we're getting, the vacations, the paintings, the classier car—these are universal competitive vices which even have their counterparts among men.

What has differentiated us as women are the root causes of our competitiveness, which go deep into the vortex where human identity is born and nourished. When that identity is deprived of nourishment, it fights; and the most convenient target is another victim. Woman against woman—a struggle programmed by cultural computers, an exercise in the squandering of the spirit, a battle that we lose even if we win.

And now that we are beginning to gain our own identities, we see the futility of dueling with our own sex. We have come to understand why the honor and the spoils have gone elsewhere. We've begun the long process of disengaging our foils.

"I have to apologize to you for something I said seven years ago," burst out a friend over lunch recently. She recalled a long-forgotten conversation in which I had proudly announced that I'd "caught up" with her family in one fell swoop. She had two children, and I had just given birth to twins. Her reply had been: "But yours are both girls. You won't match me until you've had two boys."

An actress friend told me of a similarly enlightening exchange between herself and a young woman playing the ingenue role in the same play. The ingenue brightly reported that the leading man found my friend "really sexy." My friend was flattered (some women *still* like the word) but said nothing. To which the ingenue replied incredulously: "Well, don't you think that's hysterical. Imagine *you*, sexy?!"

Instead of retreating with her frayed ego, my friend confronted the other actress. They talked about gratuitous insults, humor that hurts, fading youth, and show-business backstabbing. An act of minor bitchiness had become a rite of passage. They came to understand one another as women.

This understanding—this gut empathy—is what happens to us when we stop competing. It's the new feeling we have about buying clothes, for example.

"I hate it, now," says a onetime shopping addict. "But I used to comb the boutiques religiously. If a saleswoman said, 'everybody's wearing it this season,' it wasn't for me. I had a reputation to live up to. My way-out wardrobe was my identity."

Another former clotheshorse now resents the time required to buy even the basic necessities. "I don't need the shopping orgy any more," she says. "The flirting with new styles, the foreplay of making a selection, the climax of buying something new. It's all a rip-off."

For me, shopping has taken on a whole new dimension in feminist terms. Whereas I often was intimidated or annoyed by saleswomen whom I felt to be supercilious,

I now see the job through their eyes. I don't get into a power trip. I've lost the need to win points over a saleswoman.

Is this the cathartic belch of an uptight middle-class white liberal? Is it condescending? Then ask my far-from-affluent black friend about her "saleslady problem." Until very recently she rode the scapegoat to market, too. "After all," she remarked, "it wasn't every day I could give white women orders and get away with it."

In the same sense I am no longer impatient with telephone operators, washroom attendants, supermarket cashiers, bank tellers, charge-account adjusters, order clerks—the whole range of bottom-rank bureaucrats, inevitably women, inevitably underpaid, and inevitably bone-tired and bitter.

"Madam, you must pay ten cents to use the toilet even if the door *is* open. I don't make the rules, y'know." No wonder they are rigidly obedient to their faceless employers. They can't afford to lose their jobs.

"Move along." "Get on line." "Dial again." No wonder they are vacuous and ill-tempered. Try standing on your feet or sitting in one place and repeating a deadening routine, every day, every week, year after year.

These women are *us* as we would be if we were living in their skins. As long as there is a class system within our sex caste, we must all be Untouchables together if we cannot be Brahmins together.

Once you kick the competition habit, prepare for a new high: liking women. Really liking women. Finding out that we have a lot to say to one another. That we're not embarrassed to be seen with groups of women because we know we're not doing the old number about diaper rash, girlish gossip, or hired help. (Did we *ever*? Or was that just a ruse to keep us from talking about our deeper discontents?)

Finding out that dinner parties don't have to be planned by pairs—opting out of the gourmet olympics altogether. ("I didn't *enjoy* making gnocchi. I enjoyed everyone *knowing* I could make gnocchi," admits a drop-out competitive cook.) Discovering that we're smart and savvy as well as sensitive. That men aren't the only people with global concerns and heady insights. That we're doing important things, working at interesting jobs, changing ourselves, and making changes in our world. That we can now assume the best about one another until proven otherwise, instead of doing it the other way around. That we aren't judged by what we look like and that we've forgotten to notice what the other woman is wearing.

My breakthrough had something to do with that last item. It wasn't a glass-shattering shriek of recognition. I didn't go cold turkey to cure myself of competing. It happened gradually and without fanfare. But one day last winter I looked into the mirror and I marveled at the sight. The plain fact was that I had let my eyebrows grow in.

No trumpets for you, perhaps. But for me, a clarion call to announce a major act of liberation. These eyebrows that I had plucked relentlessly for 20 years served as my ticket to the merry-go-round. If they were neat and arched, I could go round and round with other women, reaching for the brass ring, holding my own. As soon as the stubble appeared, it had to be routed out with a magnifying glass, tweezers, and assorted balms. Keeping my eyebrows kempt meant keeping up with the competition. Conversely, a lapse in the plucking vigil meant chaos and disaster. Eyebrows growing toward the hairline, eyebrows across the bridge of the nose—the end of the illusion.

Yet here they were, fully grown and I hadn't even noticed when or what had made me give up grooming-by-harassment. Maybe it was around the time when a very dear, very tall friend stopped using a phony little voice in order to sound like one of the petite girls in her office. ("Talk softly and marry a big prick just doesn't work," she said.) Or maybe it was when I saw one of the so-called stars of the Women's Movement doing the drudgework of a conference at 3 A.M. with no one around to appreciate her. Or it could have been when my husband remarked on the sudden influx of terrific women among our friends. Or when one of my children asked: "Who was that pretty lady you were arguing with last night?" And I answered: "That was no lady, that was a Humphrey delegate."

It might be useful to figure out precisely when I got hooked on not competing with women. But, frankly, I can't spend any more time speculating about it. I, like you, have more important things to do.

Part II

DAILY REALITIES

Competition: A Problem
for Academic Women

EVELYN FOX KELLER and HELENE MOGLEN

PROLOGUE

We undertook this project knowing that the topic was experienced as threatening, and that others who had also been asked to address it had, perhaps wisely, refused. We decided to accept the challenge because we believed that the subject was too important to ignore, and we thought that we were cool and detached enough—secure enough also in our friendship—to handle it with equanimity.

We were naive. Although we feel that we have only begun to tap into some of the issues that make the topic of competition among academic women so disturbing, we know that we did tap deeply enough into hidden roots of competition to experience substantial fear—both in what we wrote about, and in our relation to each other as we wrote. Sifting through our own experiences in the academy, telling each other stories of our students, friends, and colleagues, deciding what to include and how to include it, attempting to establish theoretical and interpretive contexts, we discovered that our goals were not the same, and that they did, at times, come into conflict. As these conflicts surfaced, they brought with them echoes of the complex

Helene Moglen is grateful for faculty research funds granted by the University of California, Santa Cruz, and the Santa Cruz Feminist Studies Organized Research Activity. The authors wish to thank Marge Frantz, Lorraine Kahn, Caren Kaplan, Pamela Roby, and Debbie Wright, who helped to define the problems, and Judith Aissen, who participated in the early stages and was invaluable at the end. We are also grateful to Roberta Apfel, Marianne Hirsch, Amy Lang, and Gail Reimer for their insightful responses to the manuscript. A slightly different version of this essay appears in *Signs: Journal of Women in Culture and Society* 12, no. 3 (Spring 1987). Copyright 1987 by the University of Chicago.

ways in which our personal and professional lives had touched and tangled, but had never been discussed or understood. Like many women, we had not allowed our disagreements to reach the point of confrontation, and had been so expert at developing strategies to avoid competition that we had been able to say with real conviction, "You and I? Of course we don't compete."

Caught in the midst of conflicting needs to "tell the truth," to justify ourselves, to maintain friendship, and to keep secure our places in the women's communities in which we live and work, disagreement did become confrontation. There were moments when we thought of abandoning our project; more important, we recognized that our friendship was at risk.

We had then to speak—differently than we had before—of the roles that we had played with one another: the too-good mother, the never-grateful-enough daughter, rivalrous but loving sisters. We had to face the ways in which we have competed as teachers, scholars, colleagues, friends, mothers, women.

Out of our anger and our pain grew compromises about our work, and a better although necessarily imperfect understanding of one another and our relationship. In the most important way, this experience seems to us to speak directly to both the subject and the hope of this chapter.

INTRODUCTION

Historically, women have been outsiders in the academy: marginal as students, scholars, teachers, and administrators. In fact, marginality has been, in part, the strategy that we ourselves devised in response to the forces that threatened to exclude if not subsume us. We discovered ways to utilize indirection, unobtrusiveness, and even invisibility to survive. Because our attempts were seldom experienced as threatening—and were, in fact, often ineffectual—we were believed and believed ourselves to be, like women generally, immune to the problems of competition that seemed to characterize the male world. But as the doors to the ivory tower have swung open, as positions of influence and power have become available to women, we have lost both innocence and purity. Recognizing the strategies of marginality to be adaptive (although not devoid of the critical potential for subversion), we rushed openly to seize the opportunities offered and claimed territory in those bastions of privilege from which we had been barred. Fallen creatures now, we look at one another's nakedness in dismay.

We can no longer deny that competition is a reality for women working in the academy in precisely the same institutional terms that it has always been a reality for men. As universities are presently constituted, influence and power are by definition in limited supply; in accordance with larger social assumptions the entire motivational structure is seen as organized around these limitations. In addition, however, we have come to recognize that competition creates special problems for women; for feminists most of all. The fact is that women seem to experience different, deeper, and more painful forms of competition with one another than they do with their male peers. As colleagues have repeatedly told us, "We compare ourselves with women, not with men"; "The success of men doesn't threaten me, but the success of women does"; "Men can take it. They really ask for it because they already have so much"; and, most commonly, "Competition with women gets close to things that are really very scary."

Indeed, the stories that women tell about competition among women in the academy are full of grievance, and it is this sense of grievance that provides the focus of our chapter. It seems that just as women are never good enough mothers or, for that matter, grateful enough daughters, neither are we good enough mentors or colleagues or students. It is evident that wherever there is a threat to survival, be it emotional or material; wherever there is the possibility of reward, be it in recognition, influence, money, jobs—or sympathy and love, so too is there competition. The feminist dream of a sisterhood capable of triumphing over personal conflict has failed us in our real lives, much as the sentimentalized ideal of loving siblings has often failed real sisters. Not only have feminists inherited a mythology of sisterhood that fits poorly into a world of scarce material and emotional resources, we have found that sisterhood itself—real or mythic—is often inappropriate to our circumstances. Sometimes we are mothers, sometimes daughters, sometimes lovers, sometimes friends. Each of these roles is split into good and bad. None of these relationships can be cleansed of the threatening feelings of envy and resentment—even of the "killer instinct"— that we associate with competition and have tried so hard for so long to banish from our images of ourselves.

Although all of us are aware of these problems, we seldom discuss them openly with one another and have rarely attempted to write about them. Yet they threaten to destroy much of what we have in recent years accomplished as feminists in the academy. It is for this reason that we have decided to attempt an analysis of some of the ambiguities and ambivalences that define competitive relationships among academic women, especially among academic women doing feminist scholarship. Because of the intense pain frequently experienced by women around issues of competition, and because of our confidence in the transformative potential of self-understanding, we have chosen to focus our attention on some of the psychological dimensions of the problem, attempting to explore residual elements of intrafamily conflicts in these more public dilemmas. We realize, however, the limitations such a choice imposes. We also recognize that our perspective is further limited by our situations. Although we have been mothers, sisters, daughters, lovers, friends, teachers, students, junior and senior colleagues, nontenured and tenured faculty in public and private colleges and universities, we are now tenured professors in respectable institutions. We are also white and middle class and have achieved status in a world that is unlike us only to the extent that it is predominantly male. Indeed, we have chosen our examples to illustrate the kinds of conflict with which we're most familiar; as a consequence, many problems such as those introduced by the addition of race and class differences, or by the appearance of older women at junior levels, remain to be explored. Even our analytic framework rests upon theoretical assumptions conceived (and revised by feminists) in terms appropriate to the mainstream culture that has served as both its context and its reference. We understand, therefore, that we might be accused of writing our history of competition among academic women from the top down rather than from the bottom up. It is for just this reason that we hope that our tentative analysis will stimulate debate, that others will be encouraged by our partiality to tell their own stories and to offer their revisions. Only then will we all be able to work together constructively to consider strategies for change.

INTERGENERATIONAL INTERACTIONS

Thirty years ago, women entering the academy as graduate students and junior faculty appropriately saw themselves as functioning in a world of the fathers. Those older women who had been able to escape marginality and achieve secure positions of seniority in the university appeared to their students and younger colleagues to be either irrelevant in their impotence or anomalous in their strength. Because there were then so few tenured women in the academy, and because those few tended to be isolated and without access to the centers of power, younger women seeking avenues to success begged their maps or bought them—with their bodies, if necessary—from the males who agreed to be their mentors.

That situation has now changed dramatically. Politicized by the feminist movement, the academy no longer provides a neutral space for women. Many of those who had held senior positions have been given new kinds of power, and all are more visible than they might once have been. Seen as "representing women," they mediate between the fathers and the daughters from privileged positions, exercising special authority in the processes of hiring and firing and in determining the shape of curricula. Even when refusing their new authority, these senior faculty cannot deny their institutional power. In whatever ways they choose to act—indeed, even if they choose *not* to act—they find themselves accountable to other women. They are beset by difficulties whichever way they turn, for, at the center of the maze in which they stand, the daughters watch and judge.

The same dilemma is experienced by a slightly younger generation of senior women who have come to positions of power and influence on the heels of the feminist movement. Often feminists themselves, they are equally implicated in the gender politics of the academy; and as closely watched as were their predecessors. Indeed, the fact is that for all women in positions of academic power, relations with younger, less powerful women remain problematic, as problematic as relations to those in power are to the younger women themselves. In the section that follows, we present four stories—drawn, as are all our stories, from our own and colleagues' experiences—that suggest the kinds of intergenerational conflicts that are often encountered by the haves and the have-nots. In the fifth story, a real rather than a figurative mother appears as the focus of conflict.

Story 1
Hilda, a well-known scholar, has been for twenty years a dominant figure in the history department of a prestigious Eastern university. Although many historians have been hired in recent years, not one of those appointed as a senior professor has been a woman, and none of the women appointed at the junior level has been granted tenure. The members of the junior faculty who have been fired blame Hilda

for the termination of their contracts, claiming that she is seeking to preserve her long-valued singular position as evidence of her distinction: a woman smart and tough enough to make it in an elite male world. Many members of the women's caucus of the professional organization over which Hilda has twice presided share this perception. They fear that the feminist movement has intensified Hilda's now-defensive hostility toward women at the same time that it has, indirectly, given her more power over their fates. While Hilda herself confesses to skepticism about the value of social history, including women's history, she denies any other bias that could adversely affect her treatment of the women in her department. Aware of the perceptions that many have of her, she feels increasingly embattled, and victimized by academic feminism. She knows that the position of women will not be strengthened if poor work is presented as the best scholarship of which women are capable, and she believes that she is trying to protect the reputation of women scholars, as well as of her department and university, by working to maintain the same high standards that have always been upheld in the past.

Story 2

Liz, a graduate who has just completed her Ph.D., asks Barbara, a former teacher and a senior scholar in her field, to write a letter of recommendation for her dossier. Barbara says that she would be pleased to comply, but asks to read Liz's dissertation so that her letter will be better informed. She finds the dissertation disappointing, however, and tells Liz that while she remains willing to recommend her, she thinks that Liz would do better to approach someone who could be more enthusiastic about her work. Liz is hurt, angry, and confirmed in her view of Barbara as a male identified woman who, although a feminist scholar, has remained fundamentally unsympathetic to the needs and aspirations of women who are less powerful than she. Other graduate students doing feminist scholarship hear Liz's story and, wishing not to be subject to Barbara's "masculine" judgments, decide not to work with her. Barbara, in turn, finds a way of rationalizing their rejection, deciding that the students engaged in feminist scholarship are intimidated by her because they are either incompetent or wary of working with women scholars in general, for fear that women will be less helpful to them than men in advancing their careers.

Story 3

Margaret, a senior philosopher, has acted for several years as a mentor for Jennie, for whom she feels personal concern and genuine respect. When Jennie completes her dissertation, Margaret uses her professional and personal connections to help get Jennie a prestigious job at a major university. After Jennie has accepted the position, she sends Margaret a polite thank-you note, but declines Margaret's invitation to a celebration dinner and leaves town without saying good-bye. Margaret is devastated, feeling used and personally rejected. On her side, Jennie feels simultaneously guilty and unable to respond appropriately. Experiencing herself as disempowered by Margaret's generosity, afraid that she is perceived as unable to succeed on her own, Jennie avoids confronting her own ambivalence by withdrawing altogether.

Competition

Story 4

A meeting of doctoral candidates in women's studies turns into a gripe session. The students feel betrayed by the apparent refusal of their mentors to mentor. They believe that the women on the faculty are unable to accept the power they have both within the university and in their professions. "They have access to resources and belong to influential networks," one asserts. "They publish papers, participate in conferences, write book reviews, hire, and fire. And still they cling to their images of themselves as oppressed victims, courting us as friends by identifying with our impotence!" These students believe that they need mentors and even, in their own words, "moms who are adults, able to act as well as to care for us. If they won't help us, who the hell will?"

The problem is that their mentors do not actually experience themselves as powerful. Over the years they have internalized the patronizing judgments made by scornful male teachers and colleagues. Thus, even when they achieve positions of authority, they continue to feel the oppression of past struggles and the ongoing burdens of tokenism. How can they effectively assert power if they actually feel impotent?

Story 5

Clara, a graduate student, observes: "I'm very, very close to my mother. For me to finish my dissertation puts me in competition with her—even my conversations with my father—and the interests we share. It puts me in competition with her also because she didn't have the opportunity to finish her own dissertation. In finishing mine I have to surpass her, and that's a really hard thing to do, especially if you like your mother. I feel really sympathetic with her, and I identify with her a lot. The idea of surpassing her doesn't give me pleasure. On a superficial level, it would give me pleasure to include her in my success, but really it's horrible. It makes me feel absolutely horrible. It's very, very hard for me. I know there's an element of competition there—I can feel it, between us, around us—because I've had more privileges than she did. I never had to go through what she did."

Interpretations

Although clearly inappropriate in some ways, the recurrent analogy of mother-daughter relations suggests a framework for thinking about relations between senior and junior women in the academy that may be instructive. Indeed, the very frequency with which that analogy is invoked attests to the extent to which our relations with older women who are not in fact our mothers, and with younger women who are not in fact our daughters, remain haunted by the residue of unresolved conflicts from another domain.

Consider, for example, the familiar conflict between mothers and daughters arising from the difficulty mothers have in valuing the accomplishments of their daughters, especially when these accomplishments are at odds with or simply different from their own. Whether from jealousy or from an attempt to hold on to an attachment appropriate to an earlier time, a truly independent (or possibly even rebellious) daughter poses for many mothers a severe emotional challenge or, worse, a vitally felt threat. It is much easier and much safer to have a daughter who continues to abide by her mother's own values, who remains willing to accept guidance and help, whose passivity neutralizes the threat of incipient competition. In this spirit, one senior faculty woman indicated her wish that her department would hire, instead of a radical feminist, "a pensive young woman," who would be a desirable colleague for her.

On the other side, it must be said that daughters are notoriously sensitive to the failings of their mothers. Though traditional orthodox psychoanalytic theory has it that only sons desire to murder their same-sex parent, the mother-daughter relation also has its dark underside. In spite of the fact that its consequences are abundantly visible in practice, an account of the overtly and covertly aggressive components in the dynamics of the mother-daughter relationship still remains largely unwritten. Indeed, one of the principal themes that emerge in the stories just presented is that of women's failure to deal effectively with their anger. This failure surely has at least some of its roots in the widespread and often deeply felt need to deny or minimize anger and aggression in mother-daughter relations.

The same failure may also be implicated in the preoccupation throughout psychological literature with identification as the principle feature of mother-daughter relations. Identification itself, however, has two faces. In the traditional writings, it is seen as interfering with the development of ego boundaries, while in the feminist literature, it is seen as fostering relational abilities. Indeed, in much of the feminist writing on this subject, identification is regarded as relatively unproblematic. It is believed to provide a critical basis for cooperation and altruism, and a safeguard against the kinds of competition and self-interest that arise from the excessively sharp differentiation said to be fundamental to male personality development.

The fact that remains inadequately credited in both traditional and feminist accounts, however, is that no matter how strong their biological and psychological bonds, mothers and daughters are also separate individuals. They neither are same selves, nor share the same interests. Furthermore, the common association made between identification and cooperation on the one hand, and between separation and competition on the other, is too simple. Under certain circumstances, cooperation may actually be facilitated by differentiation and autonomy. Conversely, all of us are familiar with the many kinds of conflict that emerge from too strong an identification between mothers and daughters. The most dramatic general expression of the ambivalence of mother-daughter identification can be seen in the splitting of mothers into good and bad—the fairy godmother and the wicked stepmother—and, simultaneously, in the splitting of daughters into grateful and ungrateful. Both forms of splitting surface in the expectations that both older and younger women have of one another. Add to this the perception of scarce resources—in the realm of jobs, ideas, or male approval—and the tensions between good and bad mothers (or daughters), and between individuality and collectivity often become unbearable.

All of these themes are in evidence in the stories we have cited. In Story 1 and Story 2 we see a phenomenon that suggests, from one point of view, the denial of filiality and the exclusion of daughters and, from another view, the assertion of self and principle. If a good mother is defined as one with infinite largess, unstintingly bestowed, then both Hilda and Barbara are bad mothers. If a grateful daughter is one who respects the standards and wisdom of the mother, then Liz is an ungrateful daughter. The bad mother may indeed view the world as one of scarce resources, insufficient to share with an unlimited number of others who identify themselves as daughters. The ungrateful daughter, on the other hand, tends to deny the principle of scarcity, attributing all deprivation to withholding by a bad mother. Behavior that, in a more neutral "other," might be understood and forgiven as ordinary self-protection, perhaps even healthy competition, is recast as unforgivable hostility. A stance that might in other contexts be seen as merely different, even uninteresting by virtue of its difference, is recast as objectionable, less than worthless, requiring exclusion.

Margaret, in Story 3, tries hard indeed to be the good mother whom no one would wish to repudiate, and, acting as though she had infinite resources at her disposal, she puts her seniority and power to the use of her adopted daughter. But alas, now it is the daughter who repudiates the filial connection, feeling compromised by Margaret's very generosity. This story could be interpreted as the rebellion of a daughter who asserts her autonomy in the face of a potentially overwhelming mother. It is also possible that Jennie feels in Margaret's generosity a use of power that is in fact compromising; that, in denying the unpleasant side of a power inequity, seeks to employ power itself to secure a bond of love and gratitude into which conflict and competition will never intrude.

Other women employ different strategies to secure the same ends. They might unconsciously seek to avoid the resentment and envy they themselves experience in competitive situations by eschewing power and privilege altogether. Indeed, many of the women about whom the graduate students complain in Story 4 do not experience themselves as powerful. True, they have jobs, networks, influential books, but they do not experience *themselves* as influential or powerful. When pressed, they might acknowledge, "Yes, sure, I have three books in print and I'm an editor of *Diacritics*, but look at the mess my life is in," or, "Look at how badly the establishment continues to treat me, ignoring my accomplishments and failing to acknowledge my reputation." In short, they claim the sympathy of others, even of their graduate students, thereby denying any substantive advantage that might drive a wedge between them or that might disqualify their right to friendship and sympathy. The graduate students quite understandably resent such denial, particularly if it deprives them of a much-needed kind of support. But they too engage in a kind of denial: in their eyes, relative advantage in one area tends to be translated into invulnerability. They attribute to those older women whom they dub "mothers" a kind of power that even well-connected mothers often do not have.

For all of these women complex issues of love, identification, and separation are problematically interconnected, evoking the needs and anxieties of that primary relationship of which these are the obscure reflection. It is for this reason that younger women, like Clara in Story 5, might feel extremely ambivalent about their own success when it places them in a position that they perceive to be superior to the one occupied by their actual mothers. Success for them might indeed be more painful than failure, and they might even subvert their own potential achievements in order to remain in filial relationships that they value. Ironically, the resentment they fear might reflect their own projected feelings rather than the attitudes of the beloved "other."

INTRAGENERATIONAL INTERACTIONS

If as daughters we have found it difficult to resolve—indeed, even directly to engage—our conflicts with bad and good mothers, we have found it equally difficult to deal with the competitive feelings we experience with one another. What we do know and are able to discuss is that the morality of the women's movement, with its emphasis upon mutuality, concern, and support, seems tremendously difficult to implement in the real-world situations of the current academic marketplace. Graduate students doing feminist scholarship find themselves competing first for the approval of the same faculty mentors, and then for the same pitifully few positions within their own disciplines or in women's studies programs. Junior faculty members find themselves in similar conflicts: jobs are always scarce, and approval is never quite sufficient. If they are feminist scholars, they continually find themselves in competitive situations with other women with whom they feel intellectually and often emotionally bonded. Additionally, intragenerational competition is exacerbated by complex forms of bias pertaining to race, sexual orientation, and age. Women who are doubly or triply marginalized in these ways feel particularly vulnerable to their peers and colleagues as well as to the establishment in which they seek a place. Furthermore, given that tenure is awarded to only a fraction of the faculty at an institution, women might well discover that conventional peer competition is further intensified by the prevalent attitude that one resident feminist is enough for any department, that all feminists are similar and therefore roughly interchangeable. Finally, anyone who loses the competition endures more than temporary humiliation. Many good scholars and effective teachers are forced to seek "alternate careers," virtually abandoning decades of study and aspiration. In such situations the price exacted for not "making it" is probably even higher for junior faculty than it is for graduate students, since more energy and ego have been invested in professional accomplishment. How do women respond to these stresses? Undoubtedly in a variety of ways, many of them familiar in the conventional male world. We offer two stories to illustrate responses that might be seen as conforming more to women's than to men's conventions.

Story 1

Several graduate students doing feminist work in different departments have been meeting together as a support group. The primary task they have set themselves is to neutralize the painful feelings they all experience about competition. "In order not to have any trade secrets from one another," they explain, "we share our work as much as possible in writing groups and informal seminars. Those of us who have the closest connection, and are likely to feel the heaviest competition, are the most careful about keeping in touch about job possibilities and calls for papers. Of course, you feel your stomach sinking when you phone a friend whose work you think is terrific, and you say, 'I just found out about a job that's right up your alley.' And even while you say, 'I'm going to apply for it, too,' you're thinking, 'There goes that job. Now I've screwed myself.' But we've all agreed that we have to adopt the philosophy that what goes around, comes around—and that someone's going to hand you a possibility if you offer her one. Sure it's idealistic; but, for us, it's survival with honor."

Story 2

Karen and Harriet are assistant professors of English at a state college in the Midwest. Overwhelmed by heavy teaching loads and advisory responsibilities, with little time to do their own research, each has been a mainstay for the other: confidante, adviser, and guide. Because their areas of competence overlap, they find themselves applying for the same positions at universities that will offer them the professional opportunities they crave. In a short time, Karen receives an offer of a tenure-track position at the institution from which Harriet received her undergraduate and graduate degrees, and to which she longs to return as a professor. Although Karen wants this position very much and knows that she has every reason to accept it (even Harriet urges her to do so, although not without ambivalence), she cannot bring herself to "betray" her friend. She declines the offer.

Making It in the 1980s

Intragenerational conflict among academic women does not end with tenure. Indeed, it is in the community of established feminist scholars where conflicts aroused by competition—real or threatened—often appear to be most acute, perhaps because the rewards are most tangible. Those of us who were engaged in the development of feminist scholarship in the early to mid-1970s experienced ourselves as radical innovators, operating outside conventional structures. We bought time for our feminist research with our more mainstream scholarship. It became possible only gradually to claim actual academic credit for such work during our struggles for jobs and promotions, in both traditional departments and the newly emerging women's studies programs. Over the last few years all that has changed. Feminist scholarship has moved into the conventional reward system; or, rather, the conventional reward system has (at least in some fields) discovered feminist scholarship. And along with this transformation has come another, less welcome kind of change. From an early belief in collectivity as an ideal that, as feminists, we thought we were uniquely situated to put into practice, we have come to recognize collectivity as a myth that seems ever more remote from our actual experience. With the advent of conventional rewards (money, grants, publication, reputation, prestigious jobs) came the realization that collectivity may have had more to do with our status as outsiders than it did with feminism. The fact is that only some of us have landed prestigious jobs; reputation and money have also been inequitably distributed. And those of us who have in some sense "made it" have found it necessary to deal with unwelcome feelings of envy, resentment, and spite, as well as with an entire range of notably unsisterly forms of behavior. The two stories that follow provide examples.

Story 3

A highly desirable position in women's history is created at a major Midwestern university. Lucy, a full professor of American history, chairs the search committee. Although several good candidates emerge, there is general agreement among members of the department that Ann, another American historian, is the most distinguished of the applicants. Lucy argues vehemently against Ann's candidacy—although they have, in the past, been friends—and ultimately uses her influence successfully to subvert the appointment. Lucy offers two reasons for her position: (1) hiring Ann would fail to serve departmental needs, particularly the needs of the graduate students, because Lucy's and Ann's work is so similar. Someone working in European women's history would clearly be preferable to another Americanist, (2) the differences between their perspectives—one focuses on domestic history and emphasizes the continuity and value of women's culture, while the other is concerned with the history of women in the public sphere and is dedicated to the abolition of intellectual and political separatism—are so great that peaceful coexistence would be impossible. Although Lucy's arguments are not at all unreasonable, some believe she has in fact been motivated by envy and resentment, that she seeks to defend her turf against a possibly powerful intruder.

Ann is shocked by the reports of Lucy's opposition. She had trusted Lucy as an ally, had perceived their work as complementary, and had thought that together they could offer the university the opportunity to establish itself as a leader in American women's history. She is hurt and bewildered, but doesn't feel able to discuss the matter openly with Lucy. The result is that collegiality between them has been destroyed. Both, one perhaps because of guilt and the other from anger, fear subsequent encounters of any kind. They attempt to avoid conferences and other professional meetings that would bring them together. Other feminist historians, hearing the story, feel it necessary to declare loyalty to one side or the other.

Story 4

In one field where the influx of rewards has been truly dramatic, three women have been identified as *the* outstanding feminist scholars in the discipline. Dozens of other scholars, although undoubtedly benefiting in small ways from the increase in their subject's prestige, have felt themselves barred from the magical inner circle. With the scant possibility of success writ large, an early sense of collectivity has given way to a clearly demarcated hierarchy, which precisely parallels the conventional ordering in the major universities. Greta is one of three women at the top. Her feminist colleagues watch her closely for the first signs of unsisterly behavior— manifest evidence that she has been corrupted by "male" success—and, indeed, such indications are soon abundantly forthcoming. Everyone, it seems, has a story: one scholar's work that should have been cited was not; another was overlooked in the organization of a conference; a third describes a gratuitously dismissive insult;

a fourth is denied help in advancing her own career, and so on. The conclusion: Greta is ungenerous in her victory.

For her part, Greta feels betrayed by a begrudging sisterhood. Achievement, instead of constituting a value, has come to be seen as a kind of failure. As Valerie Miner has said, "It seems more sisterly to struggle than to be successful."[1] Yet wasn't it precisely *for* the recognition of their enterprise and the success of their ideas that they have all been struggling? How can they expect academic rewards to be evenly distributed? Is everyone's work of equal value, and has public recognition ever been an adequate indication of quality?

Interpretations

Even though the rallying cry of the feminist movement has been "sisterhood is powerful," feminists have not analyzed the relationship between sisters in their attempts to define the politics of gender. We have written about mother-daughter attachment; we have rewritten, in several versions, the romance of the bourgeois family; we have sought to understand our needs and obligations as lovers, both of other women and of men. Even in the face of disquieting contradictions, we have assumed sisterhood alone to be benevolent and harmonious. The tortuous knots of its ambivalent conflicts—rooted in close bonding and identification, in profound envy and resentment—have still to be untied.

Indeed, so fraught is much of our experience with our own biological sisters that we may well wonder what the origin could be of this myth of harmonious sisterhood. Relationships between real sisters are frequently very close, fostering considerable mutual dependency and deep love. But those relationships also foster intense antagonisms, so much so that the success of a sister is often equated with the failure of oneself. Indeed, envy (and their intense discomfort with it) seems to be the emotion talked about with the most urgency by the women with whom we have spoken. It is this primarily, they say, that makes competition with women so much more acute and painful ("close to things that are really very scary") than competition with men.

But the psychological anatomy of envy seems to us to remain fundamentally mysterious. The usual interpretation of sibling rivalry is based on a model of siblings as well-demarcated individuals, competing for the love of a mother—or father— which itself is assumed to be a scarce resource. But that love is not a pre-established resource, fixed in its magnitude. Even when parents display clear preferences for one child over another, which they undoubtedly often do, the bestowal of their love cannot (even under these circumstances) be objectively described as a zero-sum game. Even less can it be described in the all-or-nothing terms in which children often experience it. Indeed, it frequently seems that it is not the parent's love that is competed for, but the parent herself or himself. When one attempts to trace envy between siblings (perhaps, given the intensity of the mother-daughter bond, especially the envy between sisters) to the quest for a parent's love, it is almost as if that love (whatever its quantity) is seen as capable of supporting the life of only one child. Rivalry then can feel deadly indeed.

But sibling rivalry cannot be traced entirely to the parent-child relationship. The fact is that sisters are rarely if ever as clearly demarcated from each other as any of the models just given imply. The description of sibling rivalry as a competition for a parent's love (imagined either as a fixed resource or as an all-or-nothing source of vitality) ignores the complex bonding and mutual dependencies that arise between siblings, again perhaps especially between sisters. The very closeness of the relationship seems to compel comparison of the partners—a comparison that can produce severe narcissistic injury when it reflects badly on oneself, and, conversely, particular narcissistic pleasure when it reflects well. Instead of promoting the ease of sharing pleasure in each other's success, the very closeness of the sister-sister relation appears under certain circumstances to exacerbate the tendency to equate the other's success with one own's failure, and vice versa.[2]

A second complication is the fear of abandonment that can be provoked by unequal success in a relationship of strong mutual dependency. This is an issue that may be even more conspicuous between best friends than between sisters, and is certainly a theme that lurks in the background of many of our stories. But if unequal success is seen as a threat to the bond between sisters or best friends, we must ask why. Perhaps an examination of experiences of intragenerational conflict may shed some light on these dynamics.

All four of the stories presented in this section revolve around the threat to sisterly bonding posed by the need or desire for external resources and rewards. The graduate students in Story 1 created a culture of mutual support in which conflict appears kept to a minimum. But all of these young women are being trained for jobs that may not in fact be plentiful enough to go around. Painfully aware of the disruptiveness of envy and competition to both their ideals and their relations, they want desperately to find ways to maintain both in the face of their inescapable competition for available jobs. Their strategy is to commit themselves to a philosophy of trust—"what goes around, comes around"—knowing all the while just how idealistic their principle is. Their commitment is an act of faith. The question is, What happens to this faith when, for all their mutual aid, some do not get jobs or, at least, not the jobs they want? Will the preservation of honor be enough to protect them against the inevitable disappointment they will feel? And finally, how well will their friendships survive the increasing disparity in their fortunes?

Karen, in Story 2, faces a similar bind and—concerned, she says, for her friendship with Harriet—decides against her own professional self-interest. In fact, she has probably been motivated not by a desire to avoid competition but by her own inability to deal with the resentment that she believes Harriet would feel. She presumes such feeling because she thinks that she would be resentful if the circumstances were reversed. Of course, if she believes that other opportunities will be readily forthcoming, her decision is relatively easy. If they are not, however, the friendship will somehow have to absorb the costs (and the implicit expectations) that attend her sacrifice.

Both of these accounts are notable in the degree to which they focus entirely on the avoidance of competition, the underlying assumption being that competition, conflict, and envy can be avoided if only we are good enough. The complex psychological roots of competition are not recognized; conflict is seen as originating entirely from external sources. The presumption is that in a world of infinite resources, love and cooperation will prevail.

In Stories 3 and 4, it is not academic survival that is at stake, but something simultaneously lesser and accordingly more complicated. To the extent that the conflict in these stories can be seen as competition for scarce resources, it must be emphasized that though the resources in question may be scarce, they are also new; prior to the women's movement, they did not exist at all. Indeed, both these stories appear to corroborate the view that competition increases with the magnitude of the stakes—in other words, it is not so much poverty that creates the breeding ground for competition, as it is the possibility of wealth. But not all conflict can be reduced to such simple terms. There is competition for nonmaterial stakes—power, influence, love—and there are real differences in our goals, values, and strategies that can never be resolved or banished. In these two stories the idealism of the graduate students and the sisterly altruism of Karen have given way to precisely those demons that had been feared. With the advent of status and power, women have begun to exhibit the kinds of behavior previously thought of as male, but perhaps with a difference. The dream of harmonious sisterhood has not vanished, but neither has it softened the edge of sisterly rivalry when conflict and competition do erupt. Indeed, in some ways, it seems to make it worse. Competition denied in principle, but unavoidable in practice, surfaces in forms that may be far more wounding, and perhaps even fiercer and more destructive, than competition that is ideologically sanctioned. Conversely, the equation between conflict and competition lends all differences in goals and values the subjective character of a life-and-death struggle.

In Story 3 Lucy may well feel threatened, as might anyone in her situation. But given the taboo that feminists (and sisters) place on such feelings of threat, they can hardly be acknowledged, even to oneself. One consequence of such denial is that private fears and desires infuse a more public discussion of political, institutional, and intellectual differences, and this in turn leads to a more rigid defensiveness than might otherwise be necessary. From Ann's perspective, all such differences are subordinated to the subjective dimensions of Lucy's conflict. The fact that Lucy and Ann both collude (each in her own way) in the denial of the reality of what is at least a potential turf conflict does not prevent them from enacting that conflict, however different their roles might be in the drama. What it does prevent is the recognition of an intrinsically ambivalent situation: Yes, the proximity of their interests does incur some costs and entail some potential conflicts, but it also promises certain gains that would not be available to either of them alone. Denial here delimits not the conflict but the possibilities of a creative solution to the conflict. It simultaneously precludes the possibility of nurturing friendship (or collegiality) through actual conflict—something at which most men are in fact far more accomplished.

In Story 4, we see perhaps the saddest consequence of the denial of envy and competition. Here, in the new contests that have emerged, the ideology of sisterhood has itself become a weapon. Although not usually in a position to grant material rewards, the feminists left in the background are claiming the authority to dispense moral rewards: "Great is (or is not) a good feminist!" But what does it mean to be a good feminist in a real world where real power, real issues of professional survival, and real opportunities to exert influence are at stake; where the need for some standards of excellence—however drastically they must be revised—survives as a necessary source of motivation; where neither power, excellence, nor the capacity or the ability to influence is ever distributed equally? How, finally, as feminists, are we to deal with inequality without allowing it to disrupt our friendships and community?

CONCLUSION

Feminists frequently claim that academic resources are organized and distributed in ways that discourage cooperation and guarantee competition, and that competition among women in the academy is caused by institutional structures that are designed to foster it. We believe the first part of this claim to be both just and in serious need of further elaboration, but we think the second part is too simple.

In the prevailing nonfeminist view of human nature and the world that dominates organizational, economic, and evolutionary thought, individuals are assumed to be essentially autonomous units and the world a finite reservoir of inexpandable and accordingly scarce resources. In the struggle for survival that inevitably ensues, in which each individual is motivated primarily by self-interest, competition (either tacit or overt) is obligatory. Indeed, so entrenched is this view of animate and inanimate nature that, in most of the economic and biological literature, scarcity has come to be effectively synonymous with competition. In such a view, it is cooperation that is seen as anomalous, that becomes the problem in need of explanation.

Feminists have quite rightly taken exception to this formulation, pointing out repeatedly and in many different ways that human beings are not autonomous units; indeed, that the assumption that they are is itself a masculinist projection. They have also tended to take issue with the premise of fixed, scarce resources. And it is unquestionably true that this assumption, which *prima facie* defines a kind of competition, is badly in need of critical evaluation. In particular, its inadequacy lies in the fact that it precludes precisely those kinds of interactions that, through mutual dependencies, can effectively increase the available resources.

But to reject scarcity altogether as a problem—as, for example, merely an artifact of masculinist or capitalist culture—is also unrealistic. Even though competition is not, as our culture tends to assume it is, a necessary incentive for performance, the problem of scarcity cannot be wished away. To pose cooperation as a given and competition as the problem in need of explanation (as the romance of women's culture does) is as unrealistic and as ideologically problematic as the more conventional, converse stance.

It may in the end be neither necessary nor possible to unravel the full psychological complexities of either mother-daughter or sister-sister relations, but this much seems clear: The belief that women can, if only we are good enough, avoid conflict and competition among ourselves reflects a highly idealized view of both women and nature. On the contrary, it seems to us that conflict and competition are inescapable facts of both the inner and outer realities of women's lives. These realities seem to argue that:

- Resources are not infinite.
- It is neither possible nor advantageous for women to avoid the dilemmas of power, be it power in the interests of another or power over others.
- The continuum of identification versus separation/individuation in the description of self-other relations does not map onto a continuum of cooperation versus competition. Rather, identification is fraught with its own kind of conflict, and individuation contains its own possibilities of harmonious and mutually constructive coexistence.

However, the same realities also argue that:

- Because we are not autonomous individuals but fundamentally relational beings, self can never be totally separated from other nor self-interest from altruism.
- Resources are not fixed, predetermined givens, but are in fact functions of human need and ingenuity. To take the example most pertinent to the present discussion, the availability of jobs for women in the academy has significantly expanded in response to the demands of the women's movement. While some of these may in fact have been at the cost of men's jobs, others—entirely new kinds of positions and programs—have been created in response to the efforts of feminists working collectively.
- Just as institutional structures help shape our interactions, so too do our own expectations. The equation of one's success with another's failure is not only an expression of bad faith, it is a stance that compels competition. Conversely, the commitment to the view that "what goes around, comes around" may be an unrealistic expression of good faith but, insofar as such faith fosters cooperation and mutual responsibility, it is a commitment with real consequences. For one, it provides an important spur to the kinds of efforts that can and do promote an expansion of existing resources.
- Finally, however formative our family experiences, our relationships as colleagues are not in fact those of mothers and daughters or of sisters. Short of resolving residual conflicts in the domestic arena and reforming our expectations as mothers, daughters, and sisters, we can at the very least recognize the inappropriateness of those expectations of each other as colleagues in a world beyond the family.

Given the fact that neither competition nor cooperation alone can adequately describe real interaction between people in a real world—be they men or women—we would like to end by asking: How many of our difficulties are exacerbated by the acceptance of a bifurcation between these two modes of interaction? All of us, it seems, would be aided by an entirely new perspective on both inner and outer nature that posits an *a priori* dialectical relation between competition and cooperation that might differently shape our development in both the private and the public spheres. The romance of women's culture has been extremely helpful in baring some of the roots of masculinist liberal capitalism, but its own mythology of difference and separation has worked to obstruct the recognition of fundamental interconnection that is essential to dialogic engagement. It is only after we have understood and acknowledged the realities of our own condition that we can begin searching for new strategies to deal cooperatively with competition and conflict. Perhaps our best hope lies with our willingness to examine the assumptions and practices of cultural traditions other than our own.

NOTES

1. Valerie Miner, "Rumors from the Cauldron: Competition among Feminist Writers," this volume.
2. The very parallel (if not identical) proximity between envy and intimacy in some lesbian relationships has been insightfully written about by Joyce Lindenbaum in "The Shattering of an Illusion: The Problem of Competition in Lesbian Relationships" (this volume). Lindenbaum offers a useful distinction between envy and competition. The latter, she claims, depends on a prior differentiation between selves, and, in turn, carries the potential for promoting differentiation and even "detoxifying" envy.

Feminism and Nationalism

MYRNA KOSTASH

Like Saul on the road to Damascus, I too was a traveler when I was first illuminated. I had been traveling for a year when in early 1971 I visited a Canadian friend living in England. One evening, thinking I would be interested, she handed me a packet of materials sent to her by a friend in California and suggested I read them. Except for Anne Koedt's "The Myth of the Vaginal Orgasm," I no longer remember what the articles were, but, when I had finished reading them, I knew without doubt or irresolution that I was a feminist and that once back home in Canada I would work in the women's liberation movement.

In retrospect I see this moment of my illumination as characterizing the movement itself: its internationalism, its fertile interfusion of ideas and experience and vision from the dispersed communities of feminists in the Western world, its apparently happy communication across borders. In retrospect I also see it contained all that is problematic in that dispersion.

Back in Toronto, I encountered a movement in full tilt. The headiness of it! The Toronto Women's Liberation Movement, the Radical Feminists, the feminists in the Canadian Liberation Movement and in the sects of the Left. This exhilarating hodgepodge of veterans of the Committee to End the War in Vietnam and of the cane-cutting brigades to Cuba; of anti-imperialist Trotskyists and Communists; of Canadian nationalists and francophone separatists; of dissident Americans; of the acolytes of Ti-Grace Atkinson and adherents of the S.C.U.M. (Society for Cutting Up Men) manifesto. Not to mention women involved in film, literature, journalism, sculpture, theater, publishing, academia. I remember being drunk with it, this inebriating grog of ideas and influences, everything from Simone de Beauvoir and Germaine Greer, to Bernadette Devlin and Leila Khaled, to Emma Goldman and Evelyn Reed, to Shulamith Firestone and Kate Millett, to our own Margaret Atwood and Maryon Kantaroff and Joyce Wieland. Truly, I thought, women have no country: we are each other's, and if I have a nationality it is my femaleness, and if I have a government it is the leadership of this movement in which I am voluntarily inscripted; and if I am a patriot (matriot?) it is to the idea of the primordial loyalty of sisters.

I traveled some more. To Boston, Seattle, Berkeley. And up and down and back and forth across Canada. Back to England and Spain. Confirming each time the seeming equality of citizens hip in the feminist "nation": We are women and there is for us no higher law than that of our own revolution. I settled down in Alberta and learned that feminism had emigrated from western Ukraine to western Canada along with social democrats at the beginning of the century; that feminists were engaged in the agony of dissidence in the Soviet Union and eastern Europe; that native American women were struggling against the patriarchal inheritance of the Indian Act; that ethnic women were struggling to define the border where ethnic group solidarity leaves off and the community of women outside the ghetto begins. And I have felt the most intense identifications with all these women: Where you have been, I too have been, in dream, in spirit, in desire.

Finally, I went to Greece, for six months, and, after peeling off layers of relationships with local playboys, foreign women, socialist men, I eventually found what I was looking for—Greek feminists—and felt at home.

Sort of.

By the time I got to Greece, I had been exactly ten years a feminist, ten years a traveler across the borderlands that divide and quarter woman-nation (I think of the tribes of the Great Plains, their kinship arbitrarily transformed into opposing "nationalities" by the white man's 49th parallel: the conceit of the property owner!), ten years a witness to the ambition of gender solidarity we had all perfervidly willed into being. It has not been simple. Our will has not shown us yet the way. In spite of the indisputable invigoration of our movement by means of the cross-references and cross-fertilizations of ideas and experiences among women of disparate cultures, nationalities, and allegiances, our solidarity remains tenuous. Over ten years, I have been witness to and participant in the cleavages of our unity: competition for feminist validity among the components of our splendid diversity, the distressingly familiar hierarchial ordering of authority according to political "authenticity."

Montreal, 1973. We are packed like sardines in the basement of a bistro to see an Angolan film. The filmmaker is among us. She and her film tell us of the grievous brutality of the Portuguese regime in Angola and of the sorrow and resistance of the Angolan women. We are moved, and we are angry, and we flinch as though the gloved hand of the Portuguese soldier is striking our own faces. A Quebeçoise filmmaker starts to speak. Yes, she says, we know something of your struggle, for here, too, in Quebec, we struggle . . . for independence, self-determination, cultural integrity. Ah, yes, replies the Angolan, but are your men imprisoned in work camps, are your children dying of starvation, are your women tramping barefoot to seek redress? Well, no, says the Quebeçoise, but our men are unemployed and our children undernourished and our women. . . . And so they carry on, the two of them,

Quebeçoise and the Angolan, women, warriors, artists, in common, competing for the authenticity of the colonialized, as though deprivation were a sweepstakes. And I sit, mournfully, thinking: Do I have to choose between these women?

Over ten years there has been a whole catalogue of such contradictions between women presented as political choices to be made. Between Quebec separatists and Canadian nationalists; between ethnics and WASPs; between Third World women and metropolitans; between regions and centers; between Canadians and Americans;[1] between Greeks and Canadians. Let me speak of these last two divisions, as they subsume so many others.

I was not there, but someone who was told me of the visit to Canada in the early 1970s of a delegation of women from North Vietnam. Canadian women had organized it, with the idea that American women in the antiwar movement meet with their Vietnamese counterparts (this being impossible on U.S. soil). The Americans arrived and closeted themselves with the Vietnamese. The Canadian women made sandwiches.

1972. I help organize a Women's Arts Festival at the University of Toronto. Casting about for a "drawing card," we decide upon the Chicago Women's Rock Band who duly arrive, along with a group of fans from Albany, Buffalo, and Detroit, all of them awe-inspiring in their sheer bulk and their stentorian voice. While they make themselves at home in the auditorium lounge, we Canadians haul their considerable equipment from the van. Experiencing myself, in an instant, as a "coolie" laboring on behalf of my colonial "masters," I approach the rock band, asking for some extra "manpower." "Ain't no *man*power around *here,*" they reply, and return to their conversation.

1975. On my study wall: photographs of Joan Baez, Angela Davis, Janis Joplin, and Jane Fonda. On my bookshelves: Robin Morgan, Kate Millett, Shulamith Firestone, Alix Kates Shulman, Betty Friedan, Adrienne Rich, Marge Piercy, Phyllis Chesler. In my head: a familiarity with U.S. feminist opinion regarding racism, socialism, rape, pornography, representation of women in the media, sexist anthropology, women in literature, suffragism, NOW, Weatherwomen, alternative presses, psychoanalysis, mothering, orgasm, lesbian separatism, and Bella Abzug.

1978. In Berkeley I notice that the books I have written are not in the feminist bookstores.

1980. A group of antirape activists in my city organize a weekend conference on sexual violence against women and invite a keynote speaker, Andrea Dworkin, from the United States.

1981. As book columnist for the local newspaper, I observe from publishers' catalogues and review copies that American feminists write books, Canadian feminists edit anthologies.

What is going on here? There is no doubt that, from the perspective of the Canadian[2] feminist, the U.S. women's liberation movement has enormous authority; indeed, it is seen as the original movement from which all others have taken their inspiration and justification. Never mind that feminism in Canada has historical roots in British and continental feminism as well as in indigenous movements for social reform; the point is we do not tend to perceive this as anything half as consequential as feminism in the United States. When U.S. women demonstrate against beauty pageants, when they publish Redstocking manifestoes and organize rape crisis centers and make video films about female genitals and run candidates for political office—well, the whole world knows something is afoot. In the most powerful country in the world, the women are rising up angry, and the rest of us, dazzled, awed, inspired, provoked, and feeling a genuine kinship, can only follow suit: we imitate them and call it "sisterhood."

This is not to call into question the very substantial achievements of U.S. feminism and its role in evoking our own courage and imagination as Canadian feminists. But, as we do with so much else in U.S. culture, the authority we ascribe to its feminism has the effect of at once idealizing that movement (women in the United States are so gutsy, so innovative, so sophisticated) and trivializing our own (Canadians are timid, conformist, naive). By exaggerating the influence and accomplishments of U.S. women relative to our own, we underestimate the work of our own foremothers and sisters and consign it to relative obscurity. It is no surprise, then, that we become invisible to one another, that we find form and function only in the light of the U.S. movement. We do not see in our own community, an authority on pornography: we invite a woman from the United States to speak and are flattered when she accepts. We believe our own propaganda about U.S. chutzpah and Canadian deference; and so we celebrate Mary Daly's *Gyn/Ecology* and, for ourselves (who else would be interested?), we invite submissions to a modest anthology on domestic labor and circulate it among a small circle of Marxist academics.

Concomitant with this is the ethnocentrism of the people in the United States. By my own observation they, even the feminists among them, consider themselves to live at the center of the civilized world; the rest of us, then, live at points on the concentric circles that radiate at increasing distance from that center. If Canadian feminists view their work as relatively inconsequential and localized, it is also the case that they see this confirmed in the attitudes of women in the United States. Where is the Canadian who has not experienced the maddening and sometimes humiliating ignorance of even educated and well-traveled U.S. women on the subject of Canada? We are painfully aware that we are of no more interest to them than is, say, Belgium, while we, of course, continue to be fascinated, appalled, intrigued, excited by them. (Quebec holds rather more interest for them because, it would seem, of the rather exotic fact that the Quebeçois speak French.) If this is a relationship of sisters, it is very much like that of the nine-year-old girl who both admires her teen-age sister and is infuriated by her privileges, her status, and her patronizing attitude toward her sibling's inferiority. Competition on the younger sister's part for that same privilege and status would be seen as risible.

There would be no more to say about that if it were not for the historical fact of Canadian nationalism. In its most recent manifestation, it has emerged, parallel with the women's movement, from the declining forces of the New Left where it had been sparked by the campaign against the U.S. imperalist incursion into Vietnam. As we studied their ways of war and colonialist entrepreneurship, we became ever more sensitive to the hegemonistic presence of their capital and culture in our own society. We began to dream, along with the Vietnamese, of "national liberation" and chafed at the U.S. presumption (even among radicals) that we were to be regarded as no more than some largish extension of the Midwest—Iowa, say. In Canadian feminists, the two ambitions—for international sisterhood and for national solidarity—coexisted peacefully for a while; we granted exemption from imperalist guilt to our sisters in the United States. After all, they too were oppressed by Wall Street and CBS. But after one too many consignments to the metaphorical sandwich brigade, we found our loyalties sorely tried.

U.S. parochialism provokes in Canadian feminists defensiveness about our own cultural and political achievements and resentment of U.S. power. That we have a double allegiance—to the notion of transnational feminism and to Canadian self-determination—divides our loyalties and energies as feminists. Our movement is in constant danger of being captured either by the male-dominated nationalist movement or by U.S.-dominated sisterhood: in either case we feel powerless as Canadian women, incapacitated in any genuine competition of ideas and experience.

As I have suggested, the reasons for this incapacitation are to be found in part in the colonialization of the Canadian economy and culture (both popular and intellectual) by U.S. institutions. There is a large literature on this subject which I do not need to detail here; suffice it to say that, as a consequence, the Canadian "mentality" is under great pressure at all times to identify U.S. interests as our own and to define purely Canadian interests as, at best, particular of a region and, at worst, divisive of continental alliance. This pressure is exacerbated by blithe disregard in the United States of Canadian nationalist sentiment and by the imperatives of liberal ideology among the Canadian ruling class. To them, cooperation with the United States is a good thing; it ensures, so the argument goes, a high standard of living, peace along the "world's longest undefended border," a common cause against our mutual enemies and, not least, access to the highest achievements of Western culture.

Needless to say, not even Canadian feminists are exempt from such pressures. We are simultaneously victims and perpetrators of the myth of U.S. superiority: in accepting uncritically so many U.S. feminists' conviction of the centrality and decisiveness of their own struggles, we make it impossible for any of us to compete as partners in the arena of feminism.

There is this, too, to consider. As feminists we have experienced ourselves and our movement rather differently than have the U.S. feminists theirs, and so even were all things equal between us there would still be this: our sisterhood would be attenuated by our respective feminist histories, and our competition in the arena would be inevitable.

For a variety of reasons, the autonomous women's liberation movement has not been nearly so autonomous in Canada as in the United States. As in the United

States, the Canadian women's movement emerged from women who had been active in the New Left, but the Canadian repudiation of male-dominated politics was not nearly so violent or neat. The ideology of the Cold War had penetrated and disrupted the Old Left and the social democratic and trade union movements, but it had not, in Canada, cleaved them. For almost two generations there has been a tradition of continuous socialist activity in the mainstream of Canadian political life and the New Left was another form of it. The emergent women's liberation movement situated itself not so much in opposition to this tradition as in advance of it: women's liberation was the future of the working class.[3]

While feminists have organized separately from left-wing and trade union organizations, they have not excluded themselves from them, particularly when it has been a question of working for such "pro-Canadian" issues as the organization of independent unions (independent of the AFL-CIO) or the publication of left-wing nationalist newspapers. Such collaborative activity with male-dominated groups has its own contradictions, of course, but the point I want to make here is that for very many Canadian feminists the notion of an "autonomous" women's movement that would group women irrespective of class loyalty or class interest smacks of bourgeois reformist feminism, herein included radical feminism with its theory of the primary social contradiction being located in gender, not class. The Canadian perception of a deep-rooted ambivalence within U.S. feminism about the politics of class struggle means, even in the best of possible worlds, that there is still the competition that will have to be taken up by women on either side of that politic.

During the winter and spring of 1981–1982 I lived in Nafplion, Greece. As a freelance writer, unmarried and childless, I was free to do this. I'd dreamed of living in Europe since my university days. For the first six weeks I was miserably lonely. I had no friends. More to the point, I had no women friends. Every day I visited the town's cafés, bars, parks, seaside paths, and tavernas, and every day I met men: the public spaces belong to them and they speak English, a language they learned from the foreign women who preceded me. But the vast mass of women in Nafplion do not speak English, and I didn't speak Greek. Nor do they sit alone in tavernas and cafés; after dark they do not go to them at all. Whenever I saw them, they were either in the shops, trailing children behind them, or in the company of men to whose flanks they were stuck even though excluded from the males' conversation. If they looked around and noticed me, and I smiled, they gave back a cold and suspicious regard. They did not like me.

The reason became clear as I got to know their men. Greek men "prefer" foreign women. According to them, Greek women are "bossy" and quickly run to fat. They haggle and whine and nag about money. They refuse sex until marriage and, after marriage, refuse it for money. They are ignorant and unworldly and have no opinions. And so on. In a town like Nafplion, with much tourist traffic, the security of the Greek woman is constantly threatened. The men I met made no attempt to conceal the fact they were married, nor any apology that they were spending their free time at the taverna in the company of foreign women. Occasionally, a Greek man marries a foreigner: each time this happens, of course, one Greek woman loses out on finding a husband. Thus, the competition that Greek women feel toward foreign women is very concrete. But for a foreign woman like me who has no material interest in their men, this competition is painful for its consequences of estrangement among women.

Eventually I did make friends with some Greek women: feminists and socialists grouped around the women's movement and the Panhellenic Socialist Party (PASOK), the governing party of Greece. And here another competition took place.

"Ah, you're from America [sic]!" Then the wistful sigh, the furtive glance around the room and the questions, sotto voce: "Tell me, how do you do things in your women's movement?" I am, for instance, talking with Ada, a twenty-two-year-old student who works for one of the PASOK committees. I have just complained, loudly, about the PASOK May Day posters currently festooning Athens: posters of male faces, male masses, male clenched fists. "I know, I detest this too," says Ada, "but . . ." and her voice trails off in a whisper. I follow her glance as it lights on the men at the desks and telephones. "But our men, they are not so liberated as yours." Such defensiveness!

I visit the newly opened Women's Café in the student district of Athens. A charming place. Lace curtains, potted plants, a bit of a library, a small bar, round, marble-topped tables, groups of women of all ages in earnest conversation. And three men. Intrigued, I ask one of the women working at the bar why there are men here. She blushes and stammers in answer: "We had a long argument about it. We decided it would be, well, fascistic, to keep them out. They mustn't feel we hate men."

I drop in on a meeting of the Multi-National Women's Liberation Group, a group of mainly American and English feminists. I am told that they have "learned their lesson" and henceforth will become publicly involved in feminist campaigns only if invited to do so by the Greek women's organizations. Their earlier initiatives in campaigns against rape and pornography, for instance, had not been appreciated. Such campaigns must seem to be Greek, or not take place at all.

Anna D. and Anna K. both live in Nafplion. The former is a Socialist, the latter a Communist. I have come to know them separately. In spite of the fact that they know each other, neither mentions the other to me.

Anna D. tells me of the main success of the local Union of Greek Women (Socialist). Together with members of the engineers, merchants, labor, cultural, and municipal government associations, the women have succeeded in halting a major hotel development on a local beach. "This was a revolutionary action for the women of Nafplion," Anna explains. "Imagine women carrying placards and shouting slogans! The men in the street called us 'whores.' " I ask her if the Union plans any explicitly feminist campaigns. "Ah, well, we have to be very careful about using that word—feminism—in the provinces. After all, we're not against men. Someday, perhaps, we won't be afraid of the word but for now. . . ."

Anna K. takes me to the meeting room of the Social and Cultural Center of Women (Communist). It is just before Christmas and the Center has put up a book display. Children's books. And books by Gorky, Brecht, Neruda, Mayakovsky, Lenin, Engels, Ritsos—and Edna O'Brien. (Edna O'Brien?) "The first task," says Anna, "is to raise women's cultural level. They are not used to getting anything more for themselves than raising children and watching T.V. Of course, it's not easy for working men either."

Soula M., Anna K.'s sister, is very suspicious of the New Left. She's read a Soviet sociologist's critique of Daniel Cohn-Bendit but she has not read Cohn-Bendit. She is also suspicious of the Women's Café. "Why do we need such a thing?" she asks. "I can go anytime I like to an ordinary café." Soula's husband, meanwhile, does not "allow" her to get a driver's license.

I have been invited to Easter dinner at Anna K.'s house. The whole family—Socialists and Communists all—have also been invited. The women serve the men, from cooking to clean-up, and then sit, warily, patiently waiting for their drunk and guffawing mates to decide when they can leave. In all the months I spent in Greece, I did not once see a man lift a finger to participate in housework or child care. Not even a Socialist finger.

Catherine S. is fed up. A Greek-Australian who is going back to Australia, she says: "Greeks think they are the only people ever to have suffered." She is discouraged. "I have, on my initiative, been twice to Geneva to attend conferences on women's health. Do you think I can get the feminists here in Athens to care? No!"

I have a confession to make. After six months of this, I began to believe I really was a representative of an "advanced" form of feminism. I took a certain smug satisfaction in being able to inform Greek feminists of the debates and issues raging in my country. To enlighten them about the books that have not yet been translated into Greek. To commiserate with them about how awful Greek men are compared to North American men. To nod my assent in apologetic discussions about how "underdeveloped" Greek feminism is. To point out that in my country feminists would not tolerate this and that, have gone beyond it. To assert that, inevitably, Greek feminists will have to separate out from the men on the Left, just as we did, in my country. In short, I was becoming, in relation to Greek feminists, an "American." In the competition for feminist authenticity, I had, this time, reversed the roles. It was a revelation to me.

It has been humbling to put that experience into perspective. To seek behind the immediate dynamic of my political "superiority" the nature of the problem. I have had to acknowledge the privilege that attaches to my relative economic independence and social mobility and to admit that, for all the distress and anger I felt on behalf of Greek women—the identification, the sisterhood across the borders of national and cultural difference—just by living among Greeks, I exploited the advantage of my situation in middle-class Canada. I earn my own money, I can travel, I can challenge machismo.

The fact is, I come from a society (including its women's movement) that is everywhere glamorized, everywhere envied, even as it is feared or deplored. America! (The distinction between the United States and Canada was meaningful only to me, it seemed). Territory of wealth, possibility, transformation. Big cars on the highway, dishwashers in the kitchen, a woman alone in her apartment, a profession, appointments with a psychiatrist, sex in the singles bars. A razzle-dazzle, irreverent, brazen, and noisy women's liberation movement turning men into putty.

The fact is, I was both envied and resented in Nafplion. Compared to Greek women, my right to bold rhetoric had been easily won: the struggle with the Church, with patriarchs, with women's own self-abnegation—not to mention the eternal struggle with a harsh soil—had been engaged in Canada by two generations of feminists before me. I stood on their shoulders to look Greek women in the eye.

The fact is, the economic and political preeminence of the United States has relegated Greece to the periphery of capitalist and democratic projects; and well these women knew it, their defensiveness and parochialism and self-depreciation serving as a mask for this economic inferiority.

The fact is, for Greek women and men the "national" question is *the* question. A question of the liberation of a whole society from its masters abroad in order that its particular genius may be released, including the genius of its women. As a Canadian, I understood some of this, but not all of it. I did not understand that one's history can go back two thousand years, can include generations and genera-tions of people hounded and despised by Roman, Byzantine, Turkish, Italian, Ger-man, and U.S. overlords. I did not understand the *passion* fructified by the blood spilled in civil war, nor the strength of the appeal to women to hold fast to their Greekness—their mothering, nurturing Greekness—in the face of assaults upon it. The fact is, both the Left and the Right have taken this up, and women must have a very independent consciousness indeed to assert the primacy of the liberation of their own sex while the nation as a whole is imperiled. (There is, to be sure, a small group of separatist feminists active in Athens.) The fact is that for the simple act of self-assertion, Greek women can be beaten, sequestered, thrown out of the house, or pauperized, almost with impunity.

I began to understand these women, and slowly realized how unequal is the competition for *the* feminist idea across the Great Divide that separates the capitalist, industrialist heartland from its periphery. At the periphery, the sexual double stan-dard is only now being tentatively challenged by the greater education and worka-day experience of women. The relative underdevelopment of Greek society is painfully obvious to anyone who crosses over from Canada. The work to be done! Educational and medical services to be extended, the economy to be repatriated, civil relations modernized, agriculture mechanized, labor laws strengthened, bu-reaucracy humanized, and, throughout the cells of civil society, the virus of defer-ence to authoritarian, corrupt, even brutal administration expunged. Not to mention the liberation of women into full citizenship. Even middle-class women like Anna K. and Anna D. felt that the advancement of women could not leap ahead of the least developed sectors: working-class and rural men *and* women.

"In the future," Calliope B., a feminist activist, said to me, "there will be no difference between the Greek and Western women's movements. But for now there is the difference of our retardation. The Metaxas dictatorship in the 1930s, the war and fascist occupation, the civil war, the postwar witch hunts, the junta from 1967 to 1973—all this has not exactly been fertile ground for feminism!"

Europe had the Renaissance; the Greeks had the Ottoman Empire sitting on their backs. We had industrialization; they had emigration. We had the revolutionary struggle for democracy; they had a war of independence, followed by a monarchy. We colonized; they were colonized. We had suffragism; they had a government by the army. We had the New Left; they had a junta, and they lived and died in prisons while we ran through the streets.

To each of these catastrophes, however, the Greeks have put up magnificent resistance. And if Greek women cannot or will not separate their struggle for liberation from the patriarchy from the national struggle for independence and social justice, it is because of the tremendous moral authority of the male-dominated Nationalist and Socialist movements in the campaign for this independence and social justice. Who was I, the representative of Coca-Cola-ization, to tell them they were strategically incorrect? Who was I, the "American," to lecture them on transnational sisterhood? Who was I, the Canadian from a society that itself structurally separates rich and poor women, the educated and the illiterate, the well and the sick to pretend that all women are created equal?

In the competition for the hearts and minds of women, feminism[4] is not necessarily a disinterested ideology, innocent of the pollutions of the society within which it was engendered. It is naive to believe, for instance, that feminists who live in a racist or authoritarian culture somehow transcend these generative forces through sheer femaleness. In the competition for feminist authenticity, then, not all women are free to associate as economic, social, and moral equals. We are constrained by all the disfigurements of the body politic: poverty, racism, corruption, and despair. To this extent, feminism as the association of free and equal com-matriots is a utopian idea.

But we are on our way there. Canadian feminists have labored prodigiously and with considerable success to establish our own institutions of collective female achievement, in the arts, in political parties of our own, in all-women trade unions, in professional associations, and in militant actions. Greek women have asserted female pride and female anger, through the medium of their own experiences. Canadian, Greek, and American women have struggled in our histories to be, after all, women among women.

NOTES

1. I use the term *American* to denote those who live in the United States.
2. I use the term *Canadian* to denote Canadians outside Quebec. I do not speak for the Quebeçoises whose political, cultural, and intellectual perspective is their own.
3. It has been argued that the vast majority of women are working class, by virtue of their relationship to the economy as housewives or waged workers or both.
4. I use the word *feminism* in the singular here to stand for that single feminist idea that women are oppressed *qua* women.

Competition in Women's Athletics

GRACE LICHTENSTEIN

More and more women want to be winners in sports—whether on the playing fields of a college, in big-money pro tennis tournaments, or in their local road-runners club. Once, in the Dark Ages before fitness and feminism, we pooh-poohed the idea of women as athletic champions. Now, we turn over the issues of competition, aggressiveness, and femininity, searching for a pattern as if they were sections of a Rubik's Cube.

Yet the link between "woman" and "athletic champion" often eludes us. After struggling to ski down an intermediate slope with some semblance of coordination, we have difficulty imagining how Debby Armstrong feels whooshing down a far steeper slope with confidence and abandon to win an Olympic medal. It is one thing to be strong and tough. But that strong? That tough? Is this kind of skill really compatible with a feminine personality? What can the rest of us learn from female athletes that will help us be winners in sports, at home, at work, in relationships, in our own eyes?

Over the past 13 years I have tried to address those questions for both personal and professional reasons. As a tomboy, a lifetime sports fan, and a weekend athlete, I have always loved watching athletes, but my early heroes were men. There were few women in the sports limelight when I grew up in the 1950s.

Although I became a newspaper reporter, my sportswriting was at first limited to freelance work, since even as late as 1973 there were no full-time female reporters in the sports department of my paper, the *New York Times*. That year, while writing a book about the then-budding women's pro tennis circuit, I got my first chance to meet women athletes. After the book, *A Long Way, Baby*,[1] was published, I was asked to write dozens of magazine articles about all kinds of female athletes. Later,

I became executive editor of *World Tennis* magazine. Thanks to Billie Jean King and other pioneers, the barriers that had kept so many talented athletes hidden finally began to crumble.

Many of the women athletes I have interviewed over the years retain an ambivalence about being heroes, perhaps because that role was once reserved for men. But what they say is less important than how they perform. In their guts, they've got the rest of us beat two sets to love.

Nevertheless, as world-class[2] female competitors have come to be accepted and recognized by the general public, they have become more comfortable with their role. Today, fans can name dozens of women—Martina Navratilova, Chris Evert Lloyd, Mary Decker Slaney, Nancy Lopez, Mary Lou Retton, Tiffany Chin, Cheryl Miller—who typify the new "lady jocks." They are all quite unique, yet they share certain characteristics as competitors. And some of those characteristics are quite different from those of their male counterparts.

The first noticeable characteristic among women athletes is their emotionalism. Within the professional ranks, I have seen golfer Nancy Lopez and sprinter Valerie Brisco-Hooks cry with an openness that one rarely sees among men, including the husbands of these two stars, who happen to be pro athletes too.

In tennis, the demeanor of the women pros is a 180-degree turnaround from that of the men. Navratilova and Evert Lloyd, who have maintained one of the fiercest rivalries in sports for over a decade, embrace each other after a tough match—even at Wimbledon, the tennis equivalent of the Super Bowl. An even more extraordinary event occurred a few years ago at the U.S. Open. After defeating Navratilova and ending her chances for her first American championship, Pam Shriver, Navratilova's doubles partner, put an arm around Navratilova to comfort her. In similar situations among men, the victor would simply shake his opponent's hand.

And who can forget Mary Decker's howl of anguish (followed by anger) after her Olympic collision with Zola Budd in 1984? Sure, men get emotional in sports, but their feelings tend to vent themselves in high-fives or fistfights rather than in hugs or tears.

Among amateurs as well as among pros, women often employ gestures of friendship to mask their competitive fire. Before one of their memorable battles, Navratilova and Evert Lloyd sat in the women's locker room together, sharing a bagel. It's hard to imagine any male pros speaking even a single friendly word to one another at such a time. (The ultimate male posture in such an instance is baiting, the way boxing opponents insult one another at the weigh-in before a fight.) I discovered the same need for friendship among the members of the U.S. women's ski team when I watched them do their dry-land training one summer in Hawaii. The younger members of the "team" in this individual sport looked to their senior member, Cindy Nelson, for leadership in everything from leisure time activities to lunch, even though throughout the winter they would all hope to beat her in World Cup races.

A typical scene of friendship among competitors in amateur road racing was used in an advertisement by Avon, the cosmetics company, when it was sponsoring many runs. The ad showed three women jogging hand in hand during a race. The copy began, "Whether you run for fun, fitness or competition. . . ."

The Avon ad highlights another aspect of women's sports. Perhaps the reason emotionalism and friendship play a major part is that for so many women, participation begins at the *non*competitive level. The ad had the order almost right: fitness usually comes first, especially among adult women taking up a sport, then fun, then competition. A huge number of women get involved in a "sport" like running, swimming, or aerobics as an exercise they hope will help them look and feel good. It is only when they find that they want to improve, do better than their friends, or "win" as well that they view exercise as competition.

A January 1986 survey of 1,700 readers of the magazine *Women's Sports and Fitness* bore out this evolution. The study, commissioned by Miller Lite and the Women's Sports Foundation, was called "The New American Athlete." When asked, "Why do you work out?" 54 percent of the respondents cited "improved health." The second most frequent answer was "stress reduction," cited by 15 percent. Then came "improved skills and accomplishment," 14 percent, followed by friendship and sociability, 9 percent. Only 8 percent of the respondents said "competition," and only 2 percent each checked "being on the team" and "winning." (The figures were rounded off to the nearest 1 percent.)

The same pattern prevailed in the survey when it came to a choice of sports. More than half (55 percent) of "very active women" picked as their first sport jogging/running and calisthenics/aerobics, both fitness-oriented rather than competition-oriented activities. Next came weight lifting (46 percent), another essentially "look-good" form of athletics. The top-ranked sport that can truly be called competitive was softball or baseball (43 percent).

How do these numbers really add up? The survey clearly emphasizes that young women today are becoming far more active than were their older sisters, not to mention their mothers. But that's not the same as being competitive.

Little boys are socialized to accept, and are taught, competitiveness, aggression, and sports at an early age. Despite Title IX, the women's movement, and the stardom of Evert Lloyd, that's still not as true for girls. When asked, "What keeps women out of sports?" a whopping 45 percent replied "lack of involvement and training as a child."

In this supposedly liberated age in which girls play Little League baseball and try out for their high school football team, boys continue to get more encouragement to play competitive sports. And when they play, they are rewarded more than their sisters.

As a consequence, even the most accomplished "lady jocks" have not been able entirely to escape the negative connotations that that phrase once carried. Years ago, Evert Lloyd, the woman who did more than anyone else to promote the acceptance of athleticism among "girls" (as opposed to tomboys), told me she would not fall down for a point. She was determined to be ladylike. Now she thinks the comment was naive, but she candidly acknowledges that it took her years to see herself as a hero rather than a freak.

Her sister tennis pros, whether American, European, Latin, Australian, South African, or Asian, have faced a similar battle. Nor is it any different in international sports, such as track or skiing. Christin Cooper, now in her mid-twenties, was a silver medalist in the 1984 Olympics. Yet when I asked about her athleticism, she insisted on relating it to health.

"If you exercise, you're more liable to eat better, you're spending your time outdoors, you're getting yourself in shape, you'll live longer, you'll feel wonderful. God, if there's something unfeminine about being healthy, I'd love to know about it," said Cooper in a 1981 interview.

But competition? Quite a different matter, in her eyes. "One thing I like about skiing is that you're working against yourself and not directly against anyone else," she said. Indeed, ski races are rarely head to head; and they are always against a clock. Cooper went further by admitting, "that's why I dislike tennis. I get very uptight in a direct confrontation with someone else."

This kind of problem crops up often when women athletes talk about their goals. Ask any boy involved in competitive athletics what he wants to accomplish, and he's likely to answer, "I want to be number one." Remember Mohammed Ali, an athlete without peer in the most confrontational sport on earth, braying, "I'm the greatest"?

Ask a girl what she's after, and she's more likely to answer, "I want to be the best I can be," or "to reach my potential." Even in the 1980s, cultural conditioning—in the United States but not in eastern European countries such as East Germany—seems to include the dictum, "nice girls don't brag." A youngster on the way up often still has a deep need to be accepted by more established stars in her sport, and she might be afraid of being considered "uppity" if she voices competitive goals. Inside, she may burn with longing for first place, but rarely will she express it quite so nakedly.

Before victory, however, comes desire. No studies, to my knowledge, deny that a burning desire to win lurks in women athletes around the globe.

In the United States, many women get involved in sports via an athletic brother or father. (The influence of mothers on world-class female athletes is less visible.) Valerie Brisco-Hooks first took up running at Locke High School in Los Angeles not only because her brother had run there before her but because one of her brothers had been killed there in a random shooting. "The field was named after him and I was a Brisco, so everybody thought I could run," she explained in a recent magazine interview. Cheryl Miller, basketball's dominant female player of the 1980s, began shooting hoops with her father and her brothers long before she became famous as a four-year All-American at the University of Southern California.

Chris Evert Lloyd and Nancy Lopez are the prototypical Daddy's girls, having both been schooled in their games by their fathers. Billie Jean King originally took up tennis at her father's urging—he didn't want her to stay heavily involved in "boys' games." Her brother became a major league baseball pitcher. Even when parents or siblings don't encourage kids to play a game, there is often a teacher or school coach to urge a young girl to take advantage of her height by playing basketball or her speed by running track.

If athletic women happen to be born in East Germany or Czechoslovakia, they grow up in a society that encourages them early, often, sometimes relentlessly. But competitiveness seems to evolve regardless of culture. Otherwise, how could Rosa Mota, the world-class marathoner, have emerged from the Latin chauvinism of Portugal; or Gabriela Sabatini, the sensation teenage Argentine tennis phenomenon; or Nawal El Moutawakel, the Olympic medalist runner from Muslim Morocco?

Somehow their burning desire was fanned, fed, reinforced. With reinforcement— a trophy, a trip to a foreign country for a track meet, a college scholarship—comes renewed dedication, a prerequisite for turning desire and talent into champion-level competitiveness.

With any luck, the dedication is rewarded with victory, the best kind of reinforcement there is. The wonderful thing about sports is that achievement is *measurable*, be it in points, lap times, or strikeouts. If you start with desire and talent, then add dedication, measurable results will follow, surely as night follows day. For nearly every competitor, male or female, winning can be as addictive as heroin, as necessary as food. Didn't we learn in high school that certain foods supply protein, "the building blocks of the body"? For an athlete, competition is the nourishment that supplies self-confidence, the building blocks of victories. Cindy Nelson won her first major ski race when she was 16 years old. Ten years later, she still hungered for more. Why?

"What makes you want to have a sandwich when you're stomach's growling? What makes you want to go have a beer when you're thirsty?" she retorted, in an interview we did several years ago. Competition, for Nelson and other full-time athletes, can become a means to an end, a way of feeding one's addiction to the delicious taste of victory.

But the need to win is not the exclusive motivation of full-time athletes. Like those of us who are weekend athletes, they enjoy the "feeling-good" part of sports: the heightened color in the cheeks and tingle along the surface of the skin, the sensation of mastering a skill, whether it is a backhand swing, a slalom turn, or a smooth stride. The need to win can eventually become a detriment, if a top performer such as Nelson continues to yearn for first place despite limbs weakened by injuries or advancing age. As long as the addiction to winning is understood to be a "positive" addiction and is kept within reasonable boundaries, however, it helps athletes strive for new goals.

What's more, in sports, unlike other aspects of a woman's life, competitiveness is always good. Among women in business, "being too competitive" may be a derogatory phrase. Not so in sports. There is no such thing as being too competitive, unless you have promised your best friend that the two of you will cross the finish line of your local 10K race hand in hand, and then you betray her by dashing out in front in the final strides. Or, like Mary Decker in that Olympic race, you have been so fixated upon finishing first that a mishap causes you to lash out mean-spiritedly at the unwitting agent of your failure.

From victories flow confidence. In numerous psychological studies, women athletes have scored higher than the general female population in self-esteem, self-confidence, optimism, and related traits.[3] When you act like a winner, you feel like one. (Interestingly, academic studies of successful businesswomen, such as those done for the Babson College publication "Frontiers of Entrepreneurial Research,"[4] and *The Managerial Woman* by Margaret Hennig and Ann Jardim, turn up strikingly similar findings.)[5]

The reason for this? Competition, at its most exalted level, is one surefire method of striving toward our potential for excellence.

Novelist and swimmer Jennifer Levin writes:

> At its most positive, competing creates a situation of high demand which requires that we give our very best. It provides a framework for coming to know ourselves as *human* beings (rather than merely "feminine" beings)—our strengths, possibilities, and limitations. It teaches us, at its most positive, to deal creatively with fear, to proceed with dignity, and to be equal to greater challenge in the future.[6]

Some women, especially those who did not grow up with participant or spectator sports as part of their personal history, misunderstand the nature of sports competition itself. The very word *compete* can sound threatening to them. Some nonathletic women picture a duel to the death, a life-and-death struggle. Others see sports as a trivial pursuit, as weekly or nightly televised orgies of violence that bring out the worst in men.

On the other hand, sports-oriented women know that each game is nothing more than a game—anything *but* a life-and-death struggle. Every sport is set within boundaries, it has a beginning and an end, a time limit, a context, rules that must be obeyed. That's why Evert Lloyd and Navratilova can battle so fiercely between the white lines of a tennis court but not carry any enmity beyond those lines.

The most accomplished female athletes know a secret. Your opponent, in the end, is never really the player on the other side of the net, or the swimmer in the next lane, or the team on the other side of the field, or even the bar you must high-jump. Your opponent is yourself, your negative internal voices, your level of determination.

Whether you are Evelyn Ashford getting back on the track after yet another hamstring injury, or Hana Mandlikova diving for a backhand volley seemingly out of her reach, or a Chinese gymnast chalking her hands for yet another practice, or a working single mother with three children who has resolved to enter next year's triathlon, you will win by overcoming your own inner qualms.

Furthermore, sports can teach women a significant lesson that applies to other aspects of life: the race (or match or game) goes not to the swiftest, but to the toughest. At the world-class level in swimming, for example, every competitor is spectacularly talented. The key that makes a Tracy Caulkins win consistently is mental, not physical. It is the ability to concentrate throughout a competition, to focus so completely on this one event, moment by moment, stroke by stroke, that gives the athlete the tiny edge she needs to beat an equally talented rival, whose attention might wander. Evert Lloyd, a Zen Master when it comes to concentration, always cites this quality as the key to her game. Yes, she is that strong, that tough. It has nothing to with muscles.

At the recreational level, women athletes have a harder time keeping their minds on a race or a match. But anyone who has taken a serious interest in a sport can tell you about those moments when she feels relaxed yet alert and everything starts to flow smoothly. It happens, occasionally, for each of us. At last, the muscles are correctly executing the orders programmed by the mind. The computer system is on target; the glitches disappear, and we are, as athletes like to say, "in the zone."

Male athletes, of course, know this secret as well. That's what they mean when they talk about "mental toughness," about "gutting it out," and "putting in the hours." Ultimately, then, the skills found in the best competitors are neither masculine (that is, a trait primarily found in men) nor feminine. The main difference is that women are only just beginning to come to grips with these secrets.

Where will the secrets lead women? One arena might be coed sports and another, contact sports like football. In the Miller Lite/Women's Sports Foundation survey (of both men and women), women under the age of 30 were the most enthusiastic about coed sports, while an overwhelming majority of all respondents were in favor of girls playing contact sports.

A sticky wicket, coed sports. In 1985 the Harlem Globetrotters basketball team added its first woman to the squad. Lynette Woodard was certainly qualified; she had been a member of the 1984 U.S. Olympic women's basketball team. But there seemed to be no question that the Globetrotters signed her less for her dribbling ability than for her marquee value. Woodard is really just another token, a sideshow.

Many schools have integrated teams in sports such as soccer, fencing, and tennis. But it's hard for me to imagine women competing in sports such as football or basketball on equal terms with men who, genetically, are bigger and stronger. A more likely scenario would be a two-tiered school sports system, similar to the outdated football arrangement in which smaller boys played on the 150-pounds-or-less team. In a two-tiered coed sport, the slower, smaller boys would play with girls at their level, while the quickest, most talented girls would have a chance to play on the top-level, mostly male team.

Certain noncontact sports, such as squash, lend themselves to an equal coed competition. In May 1983 Frank Satterthwaite, a squash club champion, published a provocative essay in *Esquire* exploring the subject. "In the old days (six years ago?) the accepted notion was, only weak men lose to women," wrote Satterthwaite. "The update on that seems to be, only weak men are bothered by losing to women—psychologically weak." Men who had never played sports with girls were the most inclined to be upset when discovering their opponent was a woman, he found.

But Satterthwaite himself noted that one part of him was "drawn" to the idea. "Some of my earliest memories involve throwing things at my sister—baseballs, footballs, the occasional bat," he explained, adding that, later in life, "I could never be serious about any girl who couldn't throw like a boy." Satterthwaite believes that "most athletic guys like athletic women. They are intrigued by what women can do . . . by the fact that they, too, have a feeling for sport. They want to include women in their games, and watch them keep up. But there's the rub. So far, most women cannot keep up at a higher level of coed competition."[7]

The same can be said of contact sports. Most women basketball players are not in Lynette Woodard's league, let alone in Magic Johnson's. Furthermore, outstanding women get understandably annoyed when they reach such a high level of play that they are touted as being *too* good for other women. That's what happened to Martina Navratilova in the mid-1980s. It was suggested that she leave women's tennis and play men instead. Martina was the first to point out that in singles, because of strength differentials, she would not have a chance against a top male pro. Behind her annoyance, I sensed that she felt, too, a slur on her personal femininity: Sexists in the stands might whisper that she had muscles "like a man" and that she played like one. Both charges would be ridiculous, but they shed light on what I hope is a fading popular myth: that the more developed a female competitor becomes, the more masculine she grows.

I would like to see a different attitude evolve. I expect to see greater accomplishments in sports for women, and a greater appreciation of women athletes in their own right, within their own single-sex competitions. Being an optimist, I think U.S. society has already made immense strides. The adulation showered upon our Olympic champions such as Joan Benoit, Evelyn Ashford, Valerie Brisco-Hooks, Mary Lou Retton, and company is surely proof that our culture is more prepared than ever to accept women as winners.

But even more important is the unique contribution made by the fitness movement, in concert with the feminist movement. Together they have conspired to bring out the athletic competitor in all of us, for health and fun as well as for medals and dollars. It's great that Mary Lou Retton keeps up with "the big boys," her grin stretched across a box of Wheaties. It's even greater, though, that tens of thousands of women have found how liberating it can be to run a mile one day, push for two after a while, and enter a local race not long after that. By discovering sports, women who might once have thought of themselves as losers or victims can see themselves as every bit as much a winner as Mary Lou. That's something to cheer about.

NOTES

1. *A Long Way Baby* (New York: William Morrow, 1974).

2. By *world-class*, I mean full-time athletes, including professionals, most Olympians, college all-Americans, and those in sports such as track and field, which are in theory amateur but in fact professional. By *amateur*, I mean part-time athletes, including those of us who participate on a recreational level.

3. See Carole A. Oglesby, ed., *Women and Sport: From Myth to Reality* (Philadelphia:

Lea and Febiger, 1978); and March I.. Krotee, ed., *The Dimensions of Sport Sociology* (West Point, N.Y.: Leisure Press, 1979).

4. Karl H. Vesper, Frontiers of Entrepreneurial Research (Wellesley, Mass.: Babson College, 1981).

5. Margaret Hennig and Ann Jardin, *The Managerial Woman* (New York: Pocket Books, 1976).

6. Jennifer Levin, "When Winning Takes All," *Ms.* (May 1983): 139.

7. Frank Satterthwaite, "Men Competing with Women," *Esquire* (May 1983): 102.

Perfection on the Wing

JENNIFER RING

I don't compete in athletics. I have never entered a running race or a bicycle race. I have participated in sailboat races, but always as crew, never as skipper, and not even the sailboard I bought has tempted me to try my skills against another sailor. This is not very odd. My life's work is scholarly, not athletic. I don't seem to have much trouble competing in academic life, although I haven't had occasion to analyze that corner of my soul. But my athletic life is a puzzle to me. There would be no reason for my concern and curiosity were it not for the fact that in my own eyes—and I am sure that any random sampling of friends and acquaintances would agree—I am one of the most competitive people I know, and have one of the most obsessive athletic spirits as well. The two simply do not seem to come together at the same time for me.

My interest in sports was a source of joy and embarrassment to me when I was growing up. The sexual conventions of the 1950s and 1960s were enough to crush the exuberance of any athletic girl, to saddle her with the patronizing title of tomboy, and to make her apologetic rather than proud of strength, speed, and aggressiveness. I was as obsessed as any boy with baseball, but I had to cultivate elaborate fantasies of a girls' Little League being organized by the time I would turn nine and be old enough to play in it. I was pretty good in pick-up street games: a slugger who could also pitch. But by the time I entered junior high school it was difficult to find other girls interested in playing baseball, and nobody thought my continued interest in the sport was a good thing.

The next time the athlete in me emerged, I found myself swimming laps for short distances while an undergraduate at UCLA. Early in my graduate career at Berkeley, my daily swim had lengthened to a mile or more, and I was feeling waterlogged. I began running at the track to dry out, and the distance grew each year. By the time

I started work on my doctoral dissertation, I was running the toughest trails in the Berkeley hills. The sweeping panorama of San Francisco Bay took my mind off my lungs and legs, although on my favorite run there was no avoiding "the connector," a stretch straight up the side of a hill connecting the steepest segments of the trail. As my dissertation progressed, my distances grew. During the last year of work I ran the entire trail several times a week, with shorter runs on my "easy" days. During the last few months, I couldn't live with myself whenever I had to walk up part of the connector.

My compulsion for distance has abated somewhat since then. But still, if a day passes without a workout that has left me drenched in sweat and groping for energy for an hour or so afterward, I spend the evening distracted by nervous energy and a hair-trigger temper. I have expanded the activities that fulfill my need for a daily dose of pain and exhaustion to include weight lifting, and reintroduced an occasional swim. I became interested in windsurfing because it looked like it might provide me with a *relaxing* occasional substitute for the usual daily exercise grind. But it turned out to be more "my" type of sport than I had imagined. The winds increase with each month of summer in the San Francisco Bay, and the challenge is now to stay with the 20- to 25-knot blows of August as they threaten to wrench the sail out of my hands and launch me into the chilly water. I come home aching, exhausted and exhilarated (and wet), and spend the following morning working out with weights to strengthen my upper body, determined to last longer the next time out. Addiction to tests of physical endurance has become a way of life, and still I don't compete. I can't say that my competitive spirit has actually broken somewhere along the line, but, as often happens with thwarted aggressive energy, it has turned inward.

I am tempted to think of this as a woman's problem. But it also reflects an aspect of life in the United States that, while perhaps more characteristic of the way women must live, is not confined to feminine experience. There exists a group of men and women who are reluctant to acknowledge the role played by competition in their lives. Those engaged in the genteel occupations of the middle class—academia, the arts, the professions—are likely to downplay the mandate to compete and win. The tendency is to renounce the crude desire to better one's opponents, to speak rather, of a community of peers, of "colleagues" rather than "rivals," denying the embarrassing ambition and competitiveness required to become a member of the "team" in the first place. The needs of this elite class parallel those of the competitive woman who has been taught that it is unbecoming to lust after overt victory and has been discouraged from pitting her strength against rivals. Members of this class strive for personal excellence, often regarding themselves as exceptional in one way or another. But they are reluctant to admit that their superiority comes at the price of victory over their peers. They experience the full force of the contradiction between the clashing U.S. ideals of liberty and equality. This is not an entirely new phenomenon,[1] but it has characterized a segment of life in the United States since the early 1970s. This happens to coincide with efforts during the late 1960s to understand "manhood" as not necessarily warlike. And of course it coincides with the emergence of the contemporary women's movement.

Endurance sports—long-distance running, marathons, triathlons[2]—which have so recently emerged seem to serve the needs of women and "new men" to compete athletically, but not in the traditional ways. Many women are competing in athletics for the first time through long-distance running and other endurance sports. Such competition is a solitary business. Even in a race, competitors provide as much comfort as challenge, lend as much energy as they take, serve as excuses to fire up the real competition, the one with oneself. The actual victories are subtle and momentary: seconds or minutes off previous personal records, which are soon accepted as complacently as if they had always been possible. Best times are rapidly converted into challenges for the future. Or—Spartan voluptuousness—pleasure is taken in each newly displayed definition of muscle, as the body hardens beyond what had previously been accepted as hard. As these achievements are absorbed into what endurance athletes come to expect of themselves, they need something more to bring the next rush of pride. Long-distance runners exemplify the restlessness of this competitive spirit. In their striving for elusive perfection, a humble two or three miles a day grow to five or six, to an obsession with eight, ten, and fifteen—and the rest of life becomes subordinated to the demands of so much daily energy expenditure. When the switch is made from running to racing, one would think that the concrete results of the race would satisfy the need for acknowledgment of excellence. But they don't necessarily, and the challenges continue: to finish well in shorter distances, to move on to marathons. Eventually, even several marathons a year can be taken in stride, and it is apparent once again that there is no victory against others that can finally satisfy, because there is no final victory over the self.

It is the educated middle class that seems to find these obsessive physical tests most compelling.[3] They often describe the pleasures of endurance sports in terms of getting "high" on the discipline of workouts, on oxygen, on scenery, and on solitude. But pushing one's physical limits to the point of thorough collapse, driving away all but pure physical sensation, the sweet opium of complete exhaustion, seems to fill a more profound need than the one created by boredom, or than the search for a new high. Addiction to oxygen depletion signifies a deeper yearning in the souls of those who crave it.

Could this be a new vision of competition in the United States, one that, precisely because it is private rather than openly aggressive, is more acceptable for women? Perhaps it's a new form of masochism, a tendency that has been regarded as peculiarly feminine, at least since the time Freud suggested it.[4] Or is it simply an avoidance of the overt competition from which women have been discouraged for so long? Team sports is one way boys in the United States are taught about democratic participation. Perhaps girls also need experience on teams so that women will not be bereft of a certain sort of effectiveness in U.S. life. Excelling in individual sports may circumvent access to the social, economic, and political skills which call for teamwork. Do women have to learn to compete in the traditional ways before they can have the luxury of withdrawing?

There are aspects of endurance sports that harken back to early U.S. history, to the necessity for hardness and independence faced by the settlers of the North American continent. Feminist historians refer to the tests of physical bravery and endurance experienced by pioneer women. From an 1838 diary: "We had some frightful places to pass. . . . We passed along the steep sides of mountains where every step the loose earth slid from beneath our horses' feet. . . . My horse fell and tumbled me over his head. Did not hurt me. . . . Left the campground half past four in the morning after a sleepless night with a toothache."[5] It may be that this ideal of hardened independence has been lost in the United States, replaced by a corporate ideal for which team sports provides a better metaphor.[6] Perhaps the emergence of endurance sports evokes a nostalgia for the rugged individualism of frontier America, which is missed most poignantly by middle-class corporate men and by women who were discouraged from ruggedness as soon as men became urbanized. The attraction these sports hold for women gives the appearance of picking up their history where it left off, before the comforts of urban life could impose a feminine ideal that was soft and dependent. The "new men" attracted to endurance sports might also be striving for a lost ideal of toughness, a genuine strength that does not rely on a dependent woman for verification, or on the destruction of a rival or an enemy for a sense of self-worth.

The recent prominence of endurance sports may also tacitly acknowledge that the mandate to succeed in this country is impossible to fulfill. Success is the imperative, sure enough, but it is so ill-defined that no one can ever be confident that it is securely within his or her grasp. Whoever "succeeds" in the United States often makes more enemies than friends, and faces the prospect of continually fighting off the next comer and of deciding that that particular success was not sufficient protection against mediocrity anyway. The next comer emerges, after all, from within. And nothing disintegrates more quickly than satisfaction with one's own achievements.[7] Perhaps it is best to acknowledge that the only possible victory is private, psychological, a victory over the self. The hardest part of such an admission is relinquishing clear-cut victory for anybody. But the promise is a sense of community *within* the competition. Striving for excellence without having to destroy a field of competitors seems a worthy vision for athletes and citizens in the United States, an effort to embrace freedom and equality at one and the same time.

But I get ahead of myself with this vision of an American people at peace with themselves, finally coming to grips with the difficult standards they have set, refusing any longer to use scapegoats to shore up crumbling self-confidence. If only all Americans were endurance athletes, there would be an end to exploitation, sexism, bigotry, aggressive wars. . . .

On a less speculative note, let us consider firsthand the brand of competitive energy that characterizes world-class women athletes in the United States. Not surprisingly, the most prominent women athletes in the world are not members of teams but participate in individual sports: running and track, tennis, swimming and gymnastics. It will fall to another discussion to analyze in detail the differences between, for example, competition in track and tennis. Also important, but not possible within the confines of this chapter, is an analysis of the competitive attitudes of male compared to female endurance athletes. Perhaps the discussion that follows will invite some hypotheses on the part of the reader. For now our question is, Given that there are some women in the United States who have managed to avoid the inability I share with many others to compete overtly in athletics, what are their attitudes about winning? What are their thoughts about themselves as athletes and women? For the purpose of symmetry and conciseness, I will present a sample of U.S. world-class runners: marathoner Joan Benoit, middle-distance champion Mary Decker,[8] and sprinter Evelyn Ashford.

Men and women have been racing together in marathons at least since Kathy Switzer disguised herself as a man (a hooded sweatshirt and an entry of "K. Switzer" did the trick) and crashed the 1966 Boston Marathon.[9] When Boston marathon organizer Jock Semple saw Switzer running, he was so outraged by her female presence in "his" traditionally male race that he charged her, tore her number off, and tried to remove her. Two friends who were running with her tackled Semple, and Switzer escaped, completing the race in a respectable time. But her pioneering feat was effective, and most distance races in the United States today include men and women. The International Olympic Committee, however, insisted on remaining behind the times until recently, clinging to the superstition that women are too weak to run in marathons, in spite of the fact that in the past decade or so the gap between the men's and women's records has narrowed to less than 14 minutes. Nineteen eighty-four marked the first year in which a women's Olympic marathon was scheduled.[10]

Joan Benoit, the top U.S. woman marathoner, fits the ideal of extreme ruggedness called for by endurance athletics. Benoit spent the winter before the 1984 Olympic trial in a house under reconstruction on the coast of her native Maine. She had bought the house partly because its need of total refurbishing made it affordable. But another part of the appeal had been that it required that she chop wood for heating, occupy just two rooms, use a bathroom open to the elements on one side, and make do frequently in midwinter without hot water. Such Spartan living quarters did not hamper the rigor of her training runs. From mid-May to the end of November 1983 she did at least one 20-mile run a week and maintained her regular regimen of 100-plus miles a week, in spite of a demanding fall racing season. Benoit regularly extends her runs with extra loops, wide turns, additional detours, so that her 10-mile runs are really 11, 12, or 14 miles; her 20-mile course is closer to 23.

Her chief competition for the top ranking in the world has been Grete Waitz, the great Norwegian marathoner and distance runner. Before the 1984 Olympics, Waitz had been rated first, even though Benoit had actually run a faster marathon when she shattered the women's world record by nearly three minutes in the 1983 Boston Marathon. Benoit's gold medal in Los Angeles the following year, however, finally gave her the formal satisfaction of a number-one ranking.

Despite the fact that Benoit is one of the top competitive athletes in the world, one who clearly has no problem with winning, it is interesting to note the private quality of her rivalry with Waitz. She had expressed resentment at Waitz's top ranking in 1983, the year she herself broke the women's marathon record, but until the Los Angeles Olympics Benoit had never raced against Waitz and won. She had accumulated the times to beat Waitz in a variety of races, and sometimes considered her rival's superior ranking a handicap to Waitz herself: "That's OK. I'd rather let her have the pressure. It'll just get me more fired up. But it does bother me that I ran 2-1/2 minutes faster than Grete and they still give her No. 1. What am I supposed to do? Run in hightops?" The rivalry also involves a touching element of identification. In the course of conversation, Benoit will find herself making comparisons with Waitz and stop herself, a little embarrassed at the open curiosity about her Scandinavian counterpart. Thinking about the preparation for toughness provided by her New England childhood, she remarks, "By the time I was 4 years old, I was spending all day outside on skis in the freezing cold. I——" Then, realizing that she could just as well be describing Waitz, she muses, "What's Grete really like? I bet she's a lot like me."[11]

In fact, both women do seem to share their most remarkable qualities. Both are essentially private people, having expressed the feeling that there is nothing particularly remarkable about their lives. The combination of unassuming personal modesty in tandem with true athletic greatness restores one's faith in the meaning of graciousness in competition, in both victory and defeat. Benoit ran a remarkably strong race to claim the gold medal in the first women's Olympic marathon. She took an early lead and maintained it; the other runners let her go because they thought she would fade late in the race, a thought that crossed her mind also for a while. But she finished with a time that would have won 13 of the 20 men's Olympic marathons—but did not quite beat her own 1983 world record. After her victory lap, she went up to Waitz on the infield and said, "I took a chance. And I lucked out." Waitz responded, "Hey, I'm glad to get second."[12]

America's leading female middle-distance runner is Mary Decker Slaney. She holds all seven American records, from the 800 through the 10,000 meters. During 1982 and 1983 she broke seven world records, an unprecedented feat in terms of both absolute number and range of distances. She currently (1985) holds the women's world records for the 3,000-meter and the mile.

In the *Sports Illustrated* article that names her Sportswoman of the Year[13] for 1983 there is ample discussion of the reason for Decker's (as she was then known) compelling drive for athletic superiority. "Decker is moved by a competitive yearning that rises from so deep in her character that it connects with her will to be loved. Since she was a child, she has tried to transform her hunger for comforting approval into dominating athletic performance." She talks of troubled times with her parents when she was a girl, and confesses: "It *was* a means to early approval. . . . It was therapy in the rough times, but mainly it was just such a great physical joy that I know I was born to run. . . . I don't think I did what I did for anyone but me."[14] It is odd that such a public competitor, in her moment of being chosen as the most formidable athlete of the year by America's top sports weekly, would talk neither about vanquished competitors nor victories on the track, but about her feelings about running and about her emotional life. The point is not whether a man would do the same.[15] For our purposes, the point is simply that an enormously effective woman athlete finds it natural to focus on the difficulty of satisfying herself, rather than on the difficulty of beating an opponent.

Her Olympic "test" was postponed until 1984 because of an injury in 1976 and the U.S. Olympic boycott in 1980. But in 1984, world politics seemed to converge on Mary Decker in a way that heightened the drama that has haunted her career from the start. The Soviets chose to boycott the 1984 games in retaliation for the 1980 U.S. boycott. The pending absence of her powerful Soviet and East German rivals raised the question of whether a gold medal in Los Angeles would "mean anything." But in fact, Decker had already beaten Zamira Zaitseva, the Soviet champion, at Helsinki in the 1983 World Championships of Track and Field. At that time, Zaitseva ran a fiercely aggressive race, brushing elbows with Decker, touching shoes at practically every stride. Decker said, "I thought about taking a swing at her, but then I worried about being disqualified, too. I was conscious of the U.S. vs. U.S.S.R. thing there a little." Zaitseva nearly crowded Decker into the rail with 170 meters left in the race, forcing Decker to back off and lose two yards. She finally drew even with only 10 meters to go, and both women charged for the finish. Decker says, "I lost my temper. I caught her because I was so angry."[16] Zaitseva threw herself at the finish line and fell, spectacularly, before she reached it. Decker also lunged for the finish, and only realized that she had won, having left Zaitseva sprawled on the ground behind her, when she opened her eyes after thundering across the line. But even after beating the best Soviet runner, she seemed neither to consider her challenge over, for having beaten Zaitseva once, nor to consider that the absence of her Soviet rivals would tarnish the gleam of an Olympic gold medal. Of the U.S.S.R. boycott, she commented, "I'm not going to L.A. to beat the Russians. I'm going to win a gold medal."[17]

Primed for the 1984 Olympics at last, Decker was not left to compete in peace. A new rival appeared on the scene, and unwillingly brought to bear the pressures of world politics once more. Zola Budd, a white teenager from South Africa, was being heralded as a barefoot phenomenon. She would, the world press predicted, beat Mary Decker, whom she had idolized from childhood, in the 3000-meter race. Since South Africa has been banned from international competition until apartheid is abolished, Budd took up residence and citizenship in England to be able to compete on Great Britain's Olympic team.

The encounter between the two women in Los Angeles was tragic. Publicity for the drama had, by race time, made the event seem more like a private duel between Decker and Budd than a race among eight runners. Decker moved out front quickly at the start, maintaining her lead, but easing the pace with each lap to reserve energy for a final kick. Budd's strategy was to run a fast pace throughout, so that she would not have to sprint against Decker and Maricica Puică of Romania (another favored runner and the eventual winner) at the end of the race. She thus stayed close to Decker, seeking an opportunity to pass her, squeeze into the inside lane, and set the pace herself.

As Budd closed in on Decker, her left foot touched Decker's right thigh. Decker shortened her stride rather than push back and risk, she later said, looking villainous for playing rough with the young runner. Budd continued on, slightly off balance. As she struggled to regain control, she drifted left, made contact again, and threw out her left leg to keep from falling. Decker tripped over Budd's extended leg and tumbled into the infield, before a horrified audience of millions. She tried to get up, said she felt "tied to the ground," and had in fact torn her gluteus muscle and injured her hip socket so badly that she wouldn't be able to race for months afterward. As she watched the race pass by, realizing that the Olympic gold had eluded her yet again, she writhed on the grass of the infield, holding her injured leg and screaming in pain, rage, and frustration. Budd looked back to see the horror, heard the thunderous boos raining down on her, carried on with tears streaming down her face, and finally dropped back to finish seventh.

Decker was ungracious in defeat, spurning Budd's effort to apologize and attacking her error and inexperience at a tearful press conference. When the initial finding of the trackside umpire, disqualifying Budd for obstructing Decker, was reversed following a protest by the British team, Decker looked less than Olympian in stature. Decker had once said, "If it comes down to a choice between causing pain or taking it, I'll take it."[18] In the moment at Los Angeles when Decker decided to take the pain rather than cause it, she set the scene for a new dimension of self-contained competition. She had to rise above a wave of unpopularity that turned on her after her treatment of Budd. She had to postpone once again the Olympic culmination to her career, a prize that becomes weightier the longer it eludes her.

Budd and Decker finally had their rematch a year later in London. Decker had written Budd with regrets for the harshness of her words after the Olympic race, and wished Budd luck before the rematch. She said, "I don't want her to be afraid of me. Not as a person. As an athlete, sure." Decker ran away with the race with a time that cut three seconds off Puică's Olympic time that fateful summer. She has established her mastery over the 3,000-meter, and Budd is not currently a threat in that arena. But Decker's only remark about the rematch was, "This doesn't prove anything. Puică is the Olympic champion and nothing can change that."[19]

Decker, Puică, and Budd were reunited in Zurich in 1985. The three ran a very tight mile race, finishing first, second, and third, respectively, and pushing Decker to break Puică's world record. Only in the last 200 yards was the race decided. Decker said to herself, "I better get going," and Kenny Moore, reporting the race for *Sports Illustrated*, observed, "She dipped her head for an instant. When it came up again, there was no expression there, nothing but a running animal." After the race she remarked, "So rare to get a race like today. You have to have that competition to push yourself."[20]

* * *

As far as running goes, sprinters seem to have little in common with long-distance runners. Sixty-, 100-, 200-meter dashes call for explosive strength, a burst of nerve and energy, and the will to train strenuously for a race that lasts only seconds. Distance runners may use training and racing meditatively; sprinters also train for hours each day, but in a race they must learn the paradoxical art of relaxing while running at full speed for a short distance. Distance runners must strengthen themselves for a sustained drive; sprinters need driving strength in hips, thighs, and upper body.

Evelyn Ashford is the world's fastest woman, holding the world record in the 100-meter dash. Watching Ashford run has been likened to watching a blur. One observer comments, "She appears less to run than to flow fast."[21] Ashford has agreed with an interviewer that she is, like most sprinters, "very high-strung." She describes the 100-meter dash, in which she set an Olympic record in 1984, as "just 100 meters of pressure, just go-go-go. You don't have any time to relax." In fact, she noted that in her Olympic race she felt slightly out of control—as though her legs were moving too fast for her body. (It was observed, however, that her body kept up quite nicely.) At one time she expressed preference for the 200-meter dash, although a pulled hamstring muscle before the Olympics forced her to limit her events and she chose the 100.[22] The 200, she said, gave her "time" (21.83 seconds) to stretch out and express herself as a runner. "You have time to get your act together—I think it allows me to express myself more fully as a runner. I like coming off that turn."[23]

Clearly, when we talk about the self-expression involved in a race that lasts 20 seconds and in one that lasts over two hours, there must be important differences. There are elements of Ashford's thoughts about herself as a champion, however, that parallel those of Benoit and Decker. All three, of course, spend hours each day in training. And training involves some slightly longer distance running for Ashford and some speed work for Benoit. Decker is the most versatile runner of the three. Weight training is also an important part of Ashford's weekly routine. It is the extended solitary workouts in preparation for performance that define the similarity in the running sports and provide the potential for self-discovery. If it takes six months to get in shape for a marathon, even the two hours of the race is but a brief moment. Ashford must train for hours each day, month after month, and then simply relax and let herself burst to the finish line during the actual race, which becomes the briefest moment suspended in time. "Time stands still when you're racing. . . . When I'm free-flowing and just everything's working, it feels like nothing. It's effortless. You don't feel the track, you don't feel your arms moving, you don't feel the wind going by. It's just nothing. It's perfect."[24]

Although one might think that a perfect moment of nothingness hardly describes an opportunity for introspection or self-expression, such a conclusion is unwarranted. The racing moment is the moment of truth, the response to the hours of solitude in training. A sprint may seem like raw, unselfconscious competition with others, thus having little in common with the endurance sports that invite introspective, private competition. but Ashford describes the key to her success as "curiosity." She is simply curious to know how fast she can go. She actually defines the effectiveness of her training in terms of that phenomenon. "My training is going very well and mentally, I'm still curious. I've always been an inquisitive sort of runner, wanting to know how fast I can go . . . and I still have that curiosity. So I'm feeling very positive." She spends a lot of time thinking about running, but she doesn't like to talk about it, doesn't like to read about it, tries not to analyze her races—whether they are successful or not. She claims she does what she does, and if it works it works—let others analyze why. But there is no question that running is the key to self-knowledge for her. "Running is really me and I spend most of my time thinking about running . . . and running . . . and getting ready to run . . . and coming back home from running." Ashford, like Benoit, is ambivalent about the pressure of being rated number one in the world, but finds it tolerable to accept second place. "Sometimes I can sit back and say, 'Evelyn, you're in a good position here. You know that the worst you can be is second. You will be no worse than second.' And that gives me confidence. I think, 'Wow I'm up there, I'm pretty good.' Then again, if you turn it around and say, 'I don't want to be second, I want to be first,' that puts the pressure on you."[25]

But the difference between first and second place is measured for sprinters in terms of hundredths of a second, and for marathoners in terms of seconds. It is difficult to avoid the conclusion that "first" is a psychological more than an athletic victory, that it is a symbol, and, that even when it is as clearly defined as the difference between Olympic gold and silver, the satisfaction it brings has more to do with one's opinion of oneself than with the world's judgment.

Two photographs of Ashford at the Olympics are particularly memorable. Her exultation when she learned she had set an Olympic record in the 100 meters—arms flung high, head thrown back, face grinning to the heavens—is the classic image of the victorious athlete. But on the victory stand she wept, and during the playing of the national anthem her face expressed a remarkable combination of wonder and apparent humility: the vision of a woman who has faced and tested herself, gotten what she demanded, and is humbled by it.

"Competition with self" plays a major part in what Benoit, Decker, and Ashford have to say about their competitive lives. The nature of endurance sports, of the three kinds of running, is most obviously geared toward an introspective sort of competition: training aside, the races are drawn-out solitary events. In contrast, the competition in a middle-distance race is more aggressive and usually more dramatic than what takes place in a marathon. Evelyn Ashford's sport seems the least introspective of the three, and thus may provide the ultimate statement about the inner complexity of victory in individual sport. At first glance, one would think winning a sprint is the whole point of the event. It must be impossible to enjoy running so fast for such a brief time without a "real" competitor: the race must be the focus of the sprinter's life, and that race is too short to provide space for private competition. But we saw that the sprinter has more in common with the endurance runner than may at first appear true. The sprinter also has the hours and months and years of private training. There is no team—only herself and a coach. The 100-meter dash is but a culmination of that solitary training, and it is the solitude that provides the time to set a private contest with one's own dreams.

A sprinter who says she's motivated by curiosity is placing the center of her athletic life in her head, in questions about herself. That curiosity is the common thread that binds endurance athletes with sprinters—and probably also with swimmers, bicyclists, and tennis players, whether they compete or not. "Just how good am I?" is the central question in their lives. Athletes who enter contests have a set of specific answers to that question, but it is left to them to interpret the results for themselves. What *is* the difference between number one and number two in the world?

NOTES

1. As early as the 1830s, visitors to the new American democracy observed its citizens driving themselves beyond anything Europeans had ever witnessed. Instead of the old European class structure defining limits to what was possible in life, the United States was already manifesting symptoms of endurance addiction, signs of things to come. Alexis de Tocqueville, the French aristocrat who visited this country in 1831 and wrote a book describing "Democracy in America," noted: "In proportion as castes disappear and the classes of society approximate, . . . the image of ideal perfection, forever on the wing, presents itself to the human mind." Americans, he wrote, displayed a "strange unrest . . . as old as the world; the novelty is to see a whole people furnish an exemplification of it." Americans were "forever brooding over advantages they do not possess. It is strange to see with what feverish ardor the Americans pursue their own welfare; and to watch the vague dread that constantly torments them." *Democracy in America* (New York: Vintage, 1945), vol. 2, 144.

2. The triathlon is a race that combines long-distance swimming, 100-plus miles of bicycle riding, and a marathon in a single day. Best times for the entire event average about nine hours.

3. The average age of triathletes is thirty; 65 percent are college graduates; and their average annual income is $32,000, according to *Tri-Athlete* 1, no. 1 (May 1983).

4. See Sigmund Freud, "Femininity," in *New Introductory Lectures on Psychoanalysis*, ed. James Strachey (New York: Norton, 1964; originally published in 1933): "The suppression of women's aggressiveness which is prescribed for them constitutionally and imposed on them socially favors the development of powerful masochistic impulses, which succeed, as we know, in binding erotically the destructive trends which have been diverted inwards. Thus masochism, as people say, is truly feminine" (p. 102).

5. Diary of Mary Richardson Walker, June 10 to December 21, 1838, quoted in Eleanor Flexner, *Century of Struggle, The Women's Rights Movement in the United States* (Cambridge: Harvard Belknap, 1975), 159.

6. Barbara Ehrenreich, in *The Hearts of Men* (New York: Anchor Doubleday, 1983), discusses the pressure for men in the 1950s to conform to the standards of corporate capitalism, and the consequent rage that was directed onto a "safe" target—women. Not until the 1960s did men begin to question both the definition of aggressive, competitive manhood that had grown out of American history, and its contradiction as manifested in "gray flannel" conformity.

7. For a fuller commentary on this phenomenon as a theme of life in the United States, see Richard Sennett and Jonathan Cobb, *The Hidden Injuries of Class* (New York: Vintage, 1973). The relationship between celebrity and U.S. class structure—the American abhorrence of mediocrity represented by anonymity—was actually remarked upon by John Adams, as early as 1791, in his*Discourses on Davila.*

8. Decker married Richard Slaney in 1984 and now goes by the name of Mary Decker Slaney. For most of her career she has been Mary Decker, however, and it seems simplest to use that name throughout this discussion.

9. Some people might date the first female entry in that race to the previous year, when Roberta Gibb simply joined the race without bothering to enter or get a number.

10. The irony is that women seem more naturally built for stamina and endurance than for a sprinting sort of strength. Giving birth is the obvious metaphor, even the most unathletic women are then called upon to perform for hours under the most strenuous physical duress. Perhaps the feeling that women are better suited for short rather than long races has disguised an apprehension about just how well women would do in long races, given the chance.

11. Amby Burfoot, "Simple Values Keep Joan Benoit's Life Under Control," *Runner's World* 19, no. 3 (March 1984): 86.

12. Kenny Moore, "They Got Off on the Right Track," *Sports Illustrated* 61, no. 8 (August 13, 1984).

13. In fact, the award should be *Sportsperson* or *Athlete* of the Year, because each year only one athlete is selected. Mary Decker's selection in 1983 meant that there was no "Sportsman of the Year."

14. Kenny Moore, "She Runs and We Are Lifted," *Sports Illustrated* 59, no. 27 (December 26, 1983/January 2, 1984): 35. Moore himself is an accomplished competition runner.

15. A random check through the December issues of *Sports Illustrated* (the month of the Sportsman/Sportswoman of the Year awards) down through the years reveals that the men who win the award (the last woman to win was Chris Evert in 1976) usually have much less to say about themselves, and more to say about their actual performances and rivals.

16. Moore, "She Runs and We Are Lifted," 36.

17. "Oh, For the Days of the County Fair," *Sports Illustrated* 60, no. 20 (May 21, 1984): 31.

18. Kenny Moore, "Tragedy and Triumph in Los Angeles," *Sports Illustrated* 61, no. 9 (August 20, 1984): 28.

19. Kenny Moore, "Sweet, Sweet Revenge," *Sports Illustrated* 63, no. 5 (July 29, 1985): 36.

20. Kenny Moore, "Banner Week in the Record Business," *Sports Illustrated* 63, no. 10 (September 2, 1985): 24.

21. Sarah Pileggi, 'The Lady Vanquishes," *Sports Illustrated* 55, no. 13 (September 21, 1981).

22. Valerie Brisco-Hooks won the Olympic gold in the 200 and 400 meters, and has since compiled an impressive record of victories over the East Germans, formerly considered Ashford's rivals only. The birth of her daughter kept Ashford off the racing circuit in the 1985 season, but the United States can probably look forward to a little healthy competition between Ashford and Brisco-Hooks, who are now the two fastest women in the country and threaten to establish themselves as the best women sprinters in the world in a range of events. When Marita Koch saw her teammate Marlies Göhr beaten by Brisco-Hooks in July

1985, she marveled, "We were thinking the fat one is at home with her baby. Then I saw Brisco-Hooks in the 100" (Moore, "Banner Week in the Record Business,"26).

23. "Runner's World Gold Medal Exclusive: Evelyn Ashford Talks about Her Training and Going for the Gold," *Runner's World* 19, no. 4 (April 1984): 34.

24. Ibid., 38.

25. Ibid., 27, 37.

Performance Pressures: Life in the Limelight

ROSABETH MOSS KANTER

During the 1970s sociologist Rosabeth Moss Kanter studied the work experiences and behavior of the women and men administering a large multinational industrial corporation, to which she gave the name Industrial Supply Company (Indsco). One of the conclusions of her study is that so-called masculine and feminine behaviors are a function neither of inherent characteristics of men or women nor of the particular tasks they perform. Masculinity and femininity are instead related to one's position in the organization and are best understood as responses to the structures of power and opportunity within the corporation. When Kanter was studying organizational behavior at Indsco, women were just beginning to enter its managerial ranks. The representation of women in corporate management has not changed much since her study. Women are still tokens, and therefore, still experience the pressures described in the following excerpt from her book.

—Editors' Note

Indsco's upper-level women, especially those in sales, were highly visible, much more so than their male peers. Even those who reported they felt ignored and overlooked were known in their immediate divisions and spotted when they did something unusual. But the ones who felt ignored also seemed to be those in jobs not enmeshed in the interpersonal structure of the company: for example, a woman in public relations who had only a clerical assistant reporting to her and whose job did not occupy a space in the competitive race to the top.

In the sales force, where peer culture and informal relations were most strongly entrenched, everyone knew about the women. They were the subject of conversation, questioning, gossip, and careful scrutiny. Their placements were known and observed through the division, whereas those of most men typically were not. Their names came up at meetings, and they would easily be used as examples. Travelers to locations with women in it would bring back news of the latest about the women, along with other gossip. In other functions, too, the women developed well-known names, and their characteristics would often be broadcast through the system in anticipation of their arrival in another office to do a piece of work. A woman swore in an elevator in an Atlanta hotel while going to have drinks with colleagues, and it was known all over Chicago a few days later that she was a "radical." And some women were even told by their managers that they were watched more closely than the men. Sometimes the manager was intending to be helpful, to let the woman know that he would be right there behind her. But the net effect was the same as all of the visibility phenomena. Tokens typically performed their jobs under public and symbolic conditions different from those of dominants.

The Two-Edged Sword of Publicity

The upper-level women became public creatures. It was difficult for them to do anything in training programs, on their jobs, or even at informal social affairs that would not attract public notice. This provided the advantage of an attention-getting edge at the same time that it made privacy and anonymity impossible A saleswoman reported: "I've been at sales meetings where all the trainees were going up to the managers—'Hi, Mr. So-and-So'—trying to make that impression, wearing a strawberry tie, whatever, something that they could be remembered by. Whereas there were three of us [women] in a group of fifty, and all we had to do was walk in and everyone recognized us."

But their mistakes or their intimate relationships were known as readily as other information. Many felt their freedom of action was restricted, and they would have preferred to be less noticeable, as these typical comments indicated: "If it seems good to be noticed, wait until you make your first major mistake." "It's a burden for the manager who gets asked about a woman and has to answer behind-the-back stuff about her. It doesn't reach the woman unless he tells her. The manager gets it and has to deal with it." "I don't have as much freedom of behavior as men do; I can't be as independent."

On some occasions, tokens were deliberately thrust into the limelight and displayed as showpieces, paraded before the corporation's public, but in ways that sometimes violated the women's sense of personal dignity. One of Indsco's most senior women, a staff manager finally given two assistants (and thus managerial responsibilities) after 26 years with the company, was among the five women celebrated at the civic lunch for outstanding women in business. A series of calls from high-level officers indicated that the chairman of the board of the corporation wanted her to attend a lunch at a large hotel that day, although she was given no information about the nature of the event. When she threatened not to go unless she was given more information, she was reminded that the invitation had come down from the chairman himself, and of course she would go. On the day of the luncheon, a corsage arrived and, later, a vice-president to escort her. So she went, and found she was there to represent the corporation's "prize women," symbolizing the strides made by women in business. The program for the affair listed the women executives from participating companies, except in the case of Indsco, where the male vice-presidential escorts were listed instead. Pictures were taken for the employee newsletter and, a few days later, she received an inscribed paperweight as a memento. She told the story a few weeks after the event with visible embarrassment about being "taken on a date. It was more like a senior prom than a business event." And she expressed resentment at being singled out in such a fashion, "just for being a woman at Indsco, not for any real achievement." Similar sentiments were expressed by a woman personnel manager who wanted a pay increase as a sign of the company's appreciation, not her picture in a newspaper, which "gave the company brownie points but cost nothing."

Yet the senior woman had to go, the personnel manager had to have her picture taken, and they had to be gracious and grateful. The reaction of tokens to their notice was also noticed. Many of the tokens seemed to have developed a capacity often observed among marginal or subordinate peoples: to project a public persona that hid inner feelings. Although some junior management men at Indsco, including several fast trackers, were quite open about their lack of commitment to the company and dissatisfaction with aspects of its style, the women felt they could not afford to voice any negative sentiments. They played by a different set of rules, one that maintained the split between public persona and private self. One woman commented, "I know the company's a rumor factory. You must be careful how you conduct yourself and what you say to whom. I saw how one woman in the office was discussed endlessly, and I decided it would be better to keep my personal life and personal affairs separate." She refused to bring dates to office parties when she was single, and she did not tell anyone at work that she got married until several months later—this was an office where the involvement of wives was routine. Because the glare of publicity meant that no private information could be kept circumscribed or routine, tokens were forced into the position of keeping secrets and carefully contriving a public performance. They could not afford to stumble.

Symbolic Consequences

The women were visible as category members, because of their social type. This loaded all of their acts with extra symbolic consequences and gave them the burden of representing their category, not just themselves. Some women were told outright that their performances could affect the prospects of other women in the company. In the men's informal conversations, women were often measured by two yardsticks: how *as women* they carried out the sales or management role; and how *as managers* they lived up to images of womanhood. In short, every act tended to be evaluated beyond its meaning for the organization and taken as a sign of "how women perform." This meant that there was a tendency for problematic situations to be blamed on the woman—on her category membership—rather than on the situation, a phenomenon noted in other reports of few women among many men in high-ranking corporate jobs. In one case of victim-blaming, a woman in sales went to her manager to discuss the handling of a customer who was behaving seductively. The manager jumped to the assumption that the woman had led him on. The result was an angry confrontation between woman and manager in which she thought he was incapable of seeing her apart from his stereotypes, and he said later he felt misunderstood.

Women were treated as symbols or representatives on those occasions when, regardless of their expertise or interest, they would be asked to provide the meeting with "the woman's point of view" or to explain to a manager why he was having certain problems with his women. They were often expected to be speaking for women, not just for themselves, and felt, even in my interviews, that they must preface personal statements with a disclaimer that they were speaking for themselves rather than for women generally. Such individuality was difficult to find when among dominants. But this was not always generated by dominants. Some women seized this chance to be a symbol as an opportunity to get included in particular gatherings or task forces, where they could come to represent all women at Indsco. "Even if you don't want *me* personally," they seemed to be saying to dominants, "you can want me as a symbol." Yet, if they did this, they would always be left with uncertainty about the grounds for their inclusion; they were failing to distinguish themselves as individuals.

Women also added symbolic consequences to each other's affairs. Upper-level women were scrutinized by those on a lower level, who discussed the merits of things done by the higher-ranking women and considered them to have implications for their own careers. One woman manager who was passed over for a promotion in her department was the subject of considerable discussion by other women, who felt she should have pushed to get the opening and complained when she did not.

The extension of consequences for those in token statuses may increase their self-consciousness about their self-presentation and about their decisions, and can change the nature of the decisions that get made. Decisions about what to wear and who to sit with at lunch are not casual. One executive woman knew that her clothing and leisure choices would have impact. She deliberately wore pants one day as she walked through an office—not her own—of female clerks supervised by a man who wanted them to wear dresses, and she noted that a few women cautiously began to wear pants occasionally. She decided to let it be known that she was leaving at 4:00 P.M. for ballet lessons once a week, arguing that the men at her level did the same thing to play golf, but also knowing that ballet was going to have a very different meaning from golf. Her act was a gesture performed with an audience in mind as much as an expression of preference. The meaning of "natural" in such situations is problematic, for in doing what they might find natural as private beings, tokens as public personae are also sending messages to the organization.

Business as well as personal decisions were handled by tokens with an awareness of their extended symbolic consequences. One woman manager was faced with the dilemma of deciding what to do about a woman assistant who wanted to go back to the secretarial ranks from which she had recently been promoted. The manager felt she jeopardized her own claims for mobility and the need to open the system to more women if she let her assistant return and had to admit that a woman who was given opportunity had failed. She spent much more time on the issue than a mere change of assistants would have warranted, going privately to a few men she trusted at the officer level to discuss the situation. She also kept the assistant on much longer than she felt was wise, but she thought herself trapped.

Sometimes the thought of the symbolic as well as personal consequences of acts led token women to outright distortions. One was an active feminist in a training staff job who, according to her own reports, "separated what I say for the cause from what I want for myself." Her secret ambition was to leave the corporation within a year or two to increase her own professional skills and become an external consultant. But when discussing her aspirations with her own manager in career reviews or with peers or informal occasions, she always smiled and said, "chairman of the board of Industrial Supply Corporation." Every time a job at the grade level above her became vacant, she would inquire about it and appear to be very interested, making sure that there was some reason at the last minute she could not take it. "They are watching me," she explained, "to see if women are really motivated or if they will be content to stay in low-level jobs. They are expecting me to prove something one way or the other."

The Tokenism Eclipse

The token's visibility stemmed from characteristics—attributes of a master status— that threatened to blot out other aspects of a token's performance. Although the token captured attention, it was often for her discrepant characteristics, for the auxiliary traits that gave her token status. The token does not have to work hard to have her presence noticed, but she does have to work hard to have her achievements noticed. In the sales force, the women found that their technical abilities were likely to be eclipsed by their physical appearances, and thus an additional performance pressure was created. The women had to put in extra effort to make their technical skills known, and said they worked twice as hard to prove their competence.

Both male peers and customers could tend to forget information women provided about their experiences and credentials while noticing and remembering such secondary attributes as style of dress. For example, there was this report from a salesman: "Some of our competition, like ourselves, have women salespeople in the field. It's interesting that when you go in to see a purchasing agent, what he has to say about the woman salesperson. It is always what kind of a body she had or how good-looking she is or "Boy, are you in trouble on this account now." They don't tell you how good-looking your competitors are if they're males, but I've never heard about a woman's technical competence or what kind of a salesperson she was—only what her body was like." And a saleswoman complained in an angry outburst, "There are times when I would rather say to a man, 'Hey, listen, you can have our bodies and look like a female and have the advantage of walking in the room and being noticed.' But the noticeability also has attached to it that surprise on the part of men that you can talk and talk intelligently. Recognition works against you as well as for you." And another: "Some of the attention is nice, but some of it is demeaning to a professional. When a man gets a job, they don't tell him he's better-looking than the man who was here before—but they say that to me." The focus on appearance and other nonability traits was an almost direct consequence of the presence of very few women.

Fear of Retaliation

The women were also aware of another performance pressure: not to make the dominants look bad. Tokenism sets up a dynamic that can make tokens afraid of being too outstanding in performance on group events and tasks. When a token does well enough to "show up" a dominant, it cannot be kept a secret, since all eyes are upon the token, and therefore, it is more difficult to avoid the public humiliation of a dominant. Thus, paradoxically, while the token women felt they had to do better than anyone else in order to be seen as competent and allowed to continue, they also felt, in some cases, that their successes would not be rewarded and should be kept to themselves. They needed to toe the fine line between doing just well enough and too well. One woman had trouble understanding this and complained of her treatment by managers. They had fired another woman for not being aggressive enough, she reported; yet she, who succeeded in doing all they asked and brought in the largest amount of new business during the past year, was criticized for being "too aggressive, too much of a hustler."

The fears had some grounding in reality. In a corporate bureaucracy like Indsco, where "peer acceptance" held part of the key to success in securing promotions and prized jobs, it was known how people were received by colleagues as well as by higher management. Indeed, men down the ranks resented the tendency for some top executives to make snap judgments about people after five minutes' worth of conversation and then try to influence their career reviews and create instant stars. So the emphasis on peer acceptance in performance evaluations, a concept known to junior managers, was one way people lower down the managerial hierarchy retained some control over the climbing process, ensured themselves a voice, and maintained a system they felt was equitable, in which people of whom they approved had a greater chance for success. Getting along well with peers was thus not just something that could make daily life in the company more pleasant; it was also fed into the formal review system.

At a meeting of ten middle managers, two women who differed in peer acceptance were contrasted. One was well liked by her peers even though she had an outstanding record because she did not flaunt her successes and modestly waited her turn to be promoted. She did not trade on her visibility. Her long previous experience in technical work served to certify her and elicit colleague respect, and her pleasant but plain appearance and quiet dress minimized disruptive sexual attributes. The other was seen very differently. The mention of her name as a "star performer" was accompanied by laughter and these comments: "She's infamous all over the country. Many dislike her who have never met her. Everyone's heard of her whether or not they know her, and they already have opinions. There seems to be no problem with direct peer acceptance from people who see her day-to-day, but the publicity she has received for her successes has created a negative climate around her." Some thought she was in need of a lesson for her cockiness and presumption. She was said to be aspiring too high, too soon, and refusing to play the promotion game by the same rules the men had to use: waiting for one's turn, the requisite years' experience and training. Some men at her level found her overrated and were concerned that their opinions be heard before she was automatically pushed ahead. A common prediction was that she would fail in her next assignment and be cut down to size. The managers, in general, agreed that there was backlash if women seemed to advance too fast.

And a number of men were concerned that women would jump ahead of them. They made their resentments known. One unwittingly revealed a central principle for the success of tokens in competition with dominants: to always stay one step behind, never exceed or excel. "It's okay for women to have these jobs," he said, "as long as they don't go zooming by *me.*"

One form peer retaliation against success took was to abandon a successful woman the first time she encountered problems. A dramatic instance involved a confrontation between a very dignified woman manager, the only woman in a management position in her unit, who supervised a large group of both male and female workers, and an aggressive but objectively low-performing woman subordinate, who had been hired by one of the other managers and was unofficially "sponsored" by him. The woman manager had given low ratings to the subordinate on her last performance appraisal, and another review was coming up; the manager had already indicated that the rating would still be low, despite strong protests of unfairness from the worker. One day after work, the manager walked through a public lounge area where several workers were standing around, and the subordinate began to hurl invectives at her, accusing her of being a "bitch, a stuck-up snob," and other unpleasant labels. The manager stood quietly, maintaining her dignity, then left the room, fearing physical violence. Her feelings ranged from hurt to embarrassment at the public character of the scene and the talk it would cause. The response over the next few days from her male peers ranged from silence to comments like, "The catharsis was good for X. She needed to get that off her chest. You know, you never *were* responsive to her." A male friend told the manager that he heard two young men who were passed over for the job she was eventually given commenting on the event: "So Miss High-and-Mighty finally got hers!" The humiliation and the thought that colleagues supported the worker rather than her was enough to make this otherwise successful woman consider leaving the corporation.

Tokens' Responses to Performance Pressures

A manager posed the issue for scarce women this way: "Can they survive the organizational scrutiny?" The choices for those in the token position were to over-achieve and carefully construct a public performance that minimized organizational and peer concerns, to try to turn the notoriety of publicity to advantage, or to find ways to become socially invisible. The first course means that the tokens involved are already outstanding and exceptional, able to perform well under close observation where others are ready to notice first and to attribute any problems to the characteristics that set them apart—but also able to develop skills in impressions management that permit them to retain control over the extra consequences loaded onto their acts. This choice involved creating a delicate balance between always doing well and not generating peer resentment. Such dexterity requires both job-related competence and political sensitivity that could take years to acquire. For this reason, young women just out of college had the greatest difficulty in entering male domains like the Indsco sales force and were responsible for much of the high turnover among women in sales. Women were successful, on the other hand, who were slightly older than their male peers, had strong technical backgrounds, and had already had previous experiences as token women among male peers. The success of such women was most likely to increase the prospects for hiring more women in the future; they worked for themselves and as symbols.

The second strategy, accepting notoriety and trading on it, seemed least likely to succeed in a corporate environment because of the power of peers. A few women at Indsco flaunted themselves in the public arena in which they operated and made a point out of demonstrating their "difference," as in refusing to go to certain programs, parading their high-level connections, or bypassing the routine authority structure. Such boldness was usually accompanied by top management sponsorship. But this strategy was made risky by shifting power alliances at the top; the need to secure peer cooperation in certain jobs where negotiation, bargaining, and the power of others to generate advantage or disadvantage through their use of the rules were important; and the likelihood that some current peers would eventually reach the top. Furthermore, those women who sought publicity and were getting it in part for their rarity developed a stake in not sharing the spotlight. They enjoyed their only-women status, since it gave them an advantage, and they seemed less consciously aware than the other women of the attendant dangers, pressures, psychic costs, and disadvantages. In a few instances, they operated so as to keep other women out by excessive criticism of possible new-hires or by subtly undercutting a possible woman peer (who eventually left the company), something that was also pushed for by the male dominants. Thus, this second strategy eventually kept the numbers of women down both because the token herself was in danger of not succeeding and because she might keep other women out. This second strategy, then, serves to reinforce the dynamics of tokenism by ensuring that, in the absence of external pressures like affirmative action, the group remains skewed.

The third choice was more often accepted by the older generation of corporate women, who predated the women's movement and had years ago accommodated to token status. It involved attempts to limit visibility, to become "socially invisible." This strategy characterizes women who try to minimize their sexual attributes so as to blend unnoticeably into the predominant male culture, perhaps by adopting "mannish dress," as in reports by other investigators. Or it can include avoidance of public events and occasions for performance—staying away from meetings, working at home rather than in the office, keeping silent at meetings. Several of the saleswomen deliberately took such a "low profile," unlike male peers who tended to seize every opportunity to make themselves noticed. They avoided conflict, risks, or controversial situations. They were relieved or happy to step into assistant or technical staff jobs such as personnel administration or advertising, where they could quietly play background roles that kept men in the visible forefront—or they at least did not object when the corporation put them into low-visibility jobs, since for many years the company had a stake in keeping its "unusual" people hidden.

Those women preferring or accepting social invisibility also made little attempt to make their achievements publicly known or to get credit for their own contributions to problem-solving or other organizational tasks, just like other women reported in the research literature who have let men assume visible leadership or take credit for accomplishments that the women really produced—the upper corporate equivalent of the achieving secretary. In one remarkable laboratory experiment, women with high needs for dominance, paired with a man in a situation where they had to choose a leader, exercised their dominance by *appointing him* the leader.[1] Women making this choice, then, did blend into the background and control their performance pressures, but at the cost of limited recognition of their competence. This choice, too, involved a psychic splitting, for rewards for such people often came with secret knowledge—knowing what they had contributed almost anonymously to an effort that made someone else look good. In general, this strategy, like the last, also reinforces the existence of tokenism and keeps the numbers of women down, because it leads the organization to conclude that women are not very effective: low risk-takers who cannot stand on their own.

The performance pressures on people in token positions generate a set of attitudes and behaviors that appear sex-linked, in the case of women, but can be understood better as situational responses, true of any person in a token role. Perhaps what has been called in the popular literature "fear of success in women," for example, is really the token woman's *fear of visibility*. The original research that identified the fear of success concept created a hypothetical situation in which a woman was at the top of her class in medical school—a token woman in a male peer group. Such a situation is the kind that exacts extra psychic costs and creates pressures for some women to make themselves and their achievements invisible—to deny success. Replication of this research using examples of settings in which women were not so clearly proportionately scarce produced very different results and failed to confirm the sex-linked nature of this construct. Seymour Sarason also pointed out that minorities of any kind, trying to succeed in a culturally alien environment, may fear visibility because of retaliation costs and, for this reason, may try to play down any recognition of their presence, as did Jews at Yale for many years.[2] Fear of visibility, then, is one response to performance pressures in a token's situation. The token must often choose between trying to limit visibility—and being overlooked—or taking advantage of the publicity—and being labeled a "troublemaker."

The examination of numerical effects leads to the additional question of tipping points: How many of a category are enough to change a person's status from token to full group member? When does a group move from skewed to tipped to balanced? What is the impact for a woman of the presence of another?

In the exempt ranks of Indsco, there were a number of instances of situations in which two rather than one woman were found among male peers, but still constituted less than 20 percent of the group. Despite Solomon Asch's classic laboratory finding that one potential ally can be enough to reduce the power of the majority to secure conformity,[3] in the two-token situation in organizations, dominants several times behaved in ways that defeated an alliance between the two women. This was done through setting up invidious comparisons. One woman was characteristically set up as superior, and the other as inferior—exaggerating traits in both cases. One was identified as the success, the other as the failure. The one given the success label felt relieved to be included and praised, recognizing that alliance with the identified failure would jeopardize her acceptance. The consequence, in one office, was that the identified success stayed away from the other woman and did not give her any help with her performance, withholding criticism she had heard that might have been useful, and the second woman soon left. In another case, a layer of the hierarchy was inserted between two women who were at the same level: one was made the boss of the other, causing great strain between them. Dominants also could defeat alliances, paradoxically, by trying to promote them. Two women in a training group of twelve were treated as though they were an automatic pair, and other group members felt that they were relieved of responsibility for interacting with or supporting the women. The women reacted to this forced pairing by trying to create difference and distance between them and becoming extremely competitive. Thus, structural circumstances and pressures from the majority could further produce what appeared to be intrinsically prejudicial responses of women to each other. There were also instances in which two women developed a close alliance and refused to be turned against each other. Strong identification with the feminist cause or with other women was behind such alliances. Allied, two tokens could reduce some of the pressures and avoid some of the traps in their position. They could share the burden of representing womankind, and they could each be active on some pieces of "the woman's slot" while leaving time free to demonstrate other abilities and interests. Two women personnel trainers, for example, on a six-person staff, could share responsibility for programs on women without either of them becoming overidentified with it.

A mere shift in *absolute* numbers, then, as from one to two tokens, could potentially reduce stresses in a token's situation even while *relative* numbers of women remained low. But two were also few enough to be rather easily divided and kept apart. It would appear that larger numbers are necessary for supportive alliances to develop in the token context.

NOTES

1. Margaret Hennig, *Career Development for Women Executives*, Ph.D. diss., Harvard Business School, 1970, vi–21. The experimental study of high-dominance women was [by] Edwin Megaree, "Influence of Sex Roles on the Manifestation of Leadership," *Journal of Applied Psychology*, 53 (1969): 377–382. See also Cynthia Epstein, *Woman's Place* (Berkeley: University of California Press, 1970); Edith M. Lynch, *The Executive Suite: Feminine Style* (New York: AMACOM, 1973); Margaret Cussler, *The Woman Executive* (New York: Harcourt, Brace, 1958).

2. See Adeline Levine and Janice Crumrine, "Women and the Fear of Success: A Problem in Replication," *American Journal of Sociology*, 80 (January 1975): 967–974. Seymour Saranson's argument is in his "Jewishness, Blackness, and the Nature-Nurture Controversy," *American Psychologist*, 28 (November 1973): 962–971.

3. Solomon E. Asch, "Effects of Group Pressure on the Modification and Distortion of Judgment," in *Group Dynamics*, second edition, D. Cartwright and A. Zander, eds. (Evanston, Ill.: Row Peterson, 1960), 189–200.

One Young Woman in Publishing

DEBRA A. MATSUMOTO

Competition has always been a dirty word to me. As long ago as I can remember, I have never felt comfortable competing with others. Even relay races in grammar school seemed unnatural and cruel exercises, which manipulated individual will and ambition. Why was it necessary to be pitted against others in order to discover one's potential? Why were we trained to seek and rely on external stimuli to spur us to do our best?

I like to think that I am no longer as naive as I was in grammar school, and after being in the work force for four years, I've come to view competition less simplistically. I see now that competition is only a framework in which one has a choice of how and whether to compete. A relay race and applying for a job are two of many forms competition can take. It is a structure, essentially neutral, and it is its players or competitors that define its parameters and rules. As a friend pointed out, one can be either competitive or not competitive within the structure of a competition.

Competitiveness, on the other hand, is a state of mind. Although potentially constructive, competitiveness often includes those less ethical but very human characteristics such as spite, envy, egoism, and duplicity. We can never thoroughly transcend the petty components of competitiveness, but by better understanding them, we can direct them, thereby utilizing competitive stimuli constructively and ethically.

When the editors of this anthology approached me about writing an essay on competition among women in the workplace, I was thrilled for the opportunity to be published. But I felt competitive with the other contributors when I learned of their credentials. I have since tried to harness my insecurities and to use this competitive stimulus more constructively. The experience has been insightful and has given me some new thoughts, which have helped to shape this essay. I must therefore thank the editors and other writers for helping me decide to focus my essay on my personal experiences as a young Asian-American woman entering the competition of the publishing industry. I include discussion of competitive situations I encountered as a college intern at a trade publishing company in San Francisco; as a recent college graduate in a publishing course at a private university; as a novice member of the 9-to-5 work force; and, finally, as a self-employed editor and proofreader.

During my senior year at the University of California at Berkeley in 1982, I took a field studies seminar with an emphasis on writing that offered internship placements at various bookstores and publishing offices. In a class of exceptionally intelligent, talented, and creative students, I felt ill at ease. I remember a hush that fell over the class when one of the students, a former editor of the campus newspaper, was introduced. Others had had some editorial experience, or had had poems or other works published. I had done no previous writing except that required by my English classes. The only endorsement I had for being in the class was my interest in learning about a trade that could support both me and my enthusiasm for books. I possessed almost no concept of either the process or the industry of publishing. More than once I had to ask myself whether I belonged in that class, and my insecurities awakened my competitive instincts.

In spite of the instructor's encouragement of solidarity, a classroom structure naturally engenders competition. The number of available internships was limited, and we were asked to write essays in support of our desired placements. We were told that our first choices would be accommodated if possible, but that the quality of our essays and our compatibility with the internship would also be considered. Thus, at the time that we were all students with a common interest in publishing, striving to establish solidarity as peers, we were also applicants in competition for limited employment that could possibly lead to full-time work.

In this early stage of the quarter, we had yet to feel any solidarity. On the contrary, in being placed in the competition of writing the essays, we were actually being solicited to establish individual distinction. Once we were assigned our respective internships, however, and had accepted the fact that there was little we could do to change them, we began to view one another with less suspicion. We all felt anxious and apprehensive in our new surroundings, and empathy and common fears intermittently replaced our feelings of competitiveness with a sense of solidarity.

I was assigned with two other students to intern at a San Francisco publishing house. In sharing the feeling of embarking on something challenging and new, Ed, Ann, and I forgot that our backgrounds were dissimilar and that we had met for the first time just the previous day.[1] Our sense of camaraderie overrode our competitiveness, and we left the office after our first day of work feeling like the Three Musketeers.

As the school quarter progressed and we gained individual confidence, however, our camaraderie diminished. It didn't completely dissipate, but it decreased to the point of being vulnerable to challenge. One day Ed was still at the office doing work for Sue, the publicity director, when my shift started. I felt a tinge of possessive jealousy. I was especially fond of Sue and, quite irrationally, felt that our rapport entitled me to a monopoly of her projects and attention. And because it was such a friendly office, it was difficult to distinguish between objective praise and personal interest. How could Sue be as complimentary and friendly with Ed as she was with me? Wasn't there a special bond between us as women?

My reaction was very disconcerting to me. I realized that I was being excessively defensive as well as presumptuous. Our shared gender did not automatically prescribe sisterhood, entitling me to Sue's exclusive admiration. My feelings were doubly upsetting because I also felt guilty and disloyal to Ed. He and I were both interns about to graduate with the hope of breaking into publishing. Shouldn't he be my ally instead of Sue? What had happened to the camaraderie I had shared with him?

My competitive instincts have always been aroused whenever my sense of self-esteem is threatened, and it is most often threatened by those I consider my peers. My peers are typically my strongest competitors because, in sharing similar qualities, I feel I have no justification for not doing as well as they. They represent obvious standards by which I judge myself. Similarly, if a competitor excels without having superior professional qualifications, the realm of the personal then becomes an obvious target for examination. It is in this arena that individual self-esteem is especially vulnerable, more likely to engender that type of competitiveness accompanied by invidious and petty feelings. Thus, although Ed undermined my confidence as a worker, he presented a greater threat to my personal self-esteem, since I viewed him as a rival for Sue's friendship. And because I thought Sue's compliments to Ed revealed a personal preference, my feelings of competitiveness were compounded by my defensiveness, and I reacted with chagrin and petty jealousy.

Soon after, another conflict arose, questioning my responsibilities as a Musketeer. Curious about a certain publishing course, I asked our internship supervisor for some general information. In response, he called the New York office to sign me up as a candidate for the company's fellowship program. I felt confused, guilty, and embarrassed. I recorded the incident in my class journal, mentioning my "betrayal and feeling like a shrewd go-getter." That was how I felt and how I thought Ed and Ann would also view me. Psychologically, I was not prepared for such personal endorsement, and the individual distinction made me uncomfortable. I craved the comfort provided by the uncomplicated and noncompetitive motto of "All for one, and one for all."

Recalling our instructor's advocacy of solidarity, I thought it an unethical transgression to take a step forward unless it was a step we three took together. And what would I do if I actually won? Nobly defer it, or silently rejoice?

In all honesty I wanted the advancement, but without the possibility of raising invidious feelings. I had wanted Sue to favor me over Ed, and I did want to win the scholarship—I just didn't want anyone else to know that I had won. Must success be in opposition to solidarity? Or could camaraderie encompass personal success as well as mutual failure?

Being affiliated with a group gives one the constant urge to feel accepted as an equal member as well as distinguished as an individual, or perhaps a superior. According to psychiatrist Harvey Ruben, there exists in practically every area of competition "a tension between belonging and esteem" that "is a central factor in the way competition is organized."[2]

The nature of solidarity, then, is like a two-edged sword. The camaraderie I felt most with Ed and Ann, and somewhat with the other members of the class, provided the security of a surrogate family against threats in the larger sphere of publishing. At the same time, pledging allegiance to a group often entails certain ethics and responsibilities, with the potential to cause inner conflict if opposing interests arise. Thus, tension can be both alleviated and generated by group allegiance, and I was soon to learn the relative value of various trade-offs.

Nearing the end of the quarter, it was time to begin work on our final projects. During the weekly seminar which accompanied the internship we were all students again, competing for superiority in another game of competition. In keeping with the seminar's emphasis on writing, the final project was to write either a short story or a book review, to be shared with and critiqued by class members. Naturally, we were uneasy about having our creativity made vulnerable to criticism by our peers, and the insecurity once more stimulated competitiveness. I found the ambivalence of our solidarity confusing. Why was allegiance here so elusive?

Most of us were graduating seniors. For those of us who would pursue careers in publishing, we were soon to be competitors in the job market. Two students had already been offered full-time employment at their places of internship, the rest of us applauded their success. Solidarity is most easily maintained when confronted with threats from the outside.

Initially, I doubted that we would ever achieve the solidarity the instructor had earnestly advocated. But, after we embarked on our careers, we discovered collective empathy and found comfort in the thought that we were not alone with our fears and doubts. On occasion, I run in to former members of the seminar. We inquire, we catch up, and we network. The competitive situations I encountered while I was simultaneously an employed intern and a college student were enlightening experiences. During that last quarter of my senior year, I found that I had to reassess my view of competition.

Within any educational institution, competition is an inherent structure. And at a university such as Berkeley, students are typically encouraged to feel not empathetic but competitive with one another. The university has a reputation to maintain, classes are large and filled with students from all over the world, and many professors grade "on the curve" so as not to give out "too many" A's. Our competitors are our peers, those with whom we should feel most empathic.

It was a new and confusing experience for me to establish camaraderie with my competitors in the seminar. I did not realize that an individual had a choice of *how* to compete in spite of what the structure of a competition might impose. Up to that time, I had viewed competition as something taboo and did not think it could encompass solidarity. I had not known that there was such a thing as healthy, not hurtful, competitiveness. The field studies seminar proved to be a microcosm of the publishing world, introducing me to situations and issues that I continue to encounter.

After the seminar I enrolled in a publishing course at a private university, which presented a significantly different environment from that at Berkeley. At first, I was just as apprehensive and insecure, but my competitive instincts were not aroused. I cowered.

The program lasted for two weeks. It was expensive, and it was geared toward people already working in publishing. Out of 150 participants, the average age was 36. I was 21. I formed a private nucleus with four other young women who were also recent college graduates.

I was instinctively deferential and noncompetitive with the majority of the participants because I felt subordinate. They were mostly upper-middle-class whites with an average of six years' experience in publishing. Because I automatically conceded, my self-esteem was never given the chance to be threatened and therefore challenged. And, as I suggested earlier, I find it psychologically easier to lose to those least like myself.

Also opposing competitiveness was the convivial atmosphere in the class. To appear aggressively competitive would have been out of place. The majority of the participants were not there to steal jobs from one another. They were there to commingle, to share war stories, and to learn of publishing trends. The five recent graduates were the most serious and intense of the group, although we instinctively kept this fact hidden. We had no jobs or war stories; our ambition there was to steal jobs.

Having completed my internship, I thought myself well-armed to storm the fortress of the publishing industry. I thought I had gotten used to being the youngest, the least experienced, and the only minority in a group of more socially and politically privileged people. I had felt misplaced in my college seminar because the talent and intelligence of the class intimidated me. Those were disparities, however, that were combatable, and within the classroom I had an equal opportunity to compete. This two-week program, however, represented to me the elitist world of publishing, and I became more aware of my ethnicity, appearance, and social status, facts of my life that I could not change.

The women in my private nucleus were not my superiors, as I felt the majority of the participants were, yet I felt subordinate even to them. The competition did not challenge my skills but my ability to acculturate, and I did not know how to compete to compensate for my inferiority.

Although the five of us became friends, we were never comrades. We grouped together because of our common gender, age group, and desire to have someone to eat lunch with. Such commonality, however, does not naturally engender solidarity. When we chatted together, we did not share our hopes, fears, and strategies of job hunting. We complained about men, gossiping as friends do, and I suspect we all knew that our friendships would last only for the duration of the course.

We did not feel empathetic because we did not have common experiences to draw upon, and we were not going to have them after the course. A similar background is not always necessary for empathy—as I had learned with my fellow interns—but empathy must spring from some stimulus. Fear is a common one, but at this two-week program it seemed to be lacking. And, unlike in my undergraduate seminar, we had no guiding light to encourage solidarity, to steer us from unconstructive competitiveness. The course did emphasize making contacts, but this is not necessarily the same as networking. Perhaps the distinction I make is purely rhetorical, but for me networking implies a mutual exchange of information. The accumulation of contacts is primarily a self-serving means to an end.

I do not mean to suggest that empathy is a necessary criterion for solidarity, but merely that it is usually an ingredient. I found it difficult to feel empathetic with my nucleus of friends for the same reasons that I found it difficult to compete constructively with them. They had more options and advantages than I which made them fit better in both the course and the elitist publishing world. I was a third-generation Japanese-American from a working-class family. Although not necessarily more intelligent or qualified, they were traditionally more acceptable visually and socially.

Unlike many of them, I do not have family on the East Coast, the mecca for publishing in this country, or relatives who own and operate their own magazine. I was not pursuing publishing to carry on a family tradition, and I lacked the contacts and mobility afforded by those who were. Also unlike some of my friends, I did not grow up having wine with dinner or being accustomed to other such social graces. I felt this disadvantage most at the receptions given for us by local publishing companies, which were our opportunities to mingle and make contacts over wine and Brie. I also credit my family and ethnicity with indoctrinating me with patient determination rather than over-confident assertiveness. As a result, I do not hustle. I was an unassertive and poor mingler who did not drink wine. How was I ever to find a job in publishing? Would I always feel misplaced?

Up to this time, I had assumed that the most qualified person in a competition would win. That was why I had felt guilty toward Ed and Ann over the scholarship. I knew that I was not necessarily more qualified than they, but that I had simply been the intern who happened to inquire. In this publishing course, I felt that my friends were not superior to me in the way of experience or any other objective endorsement—yet they won this game of competition without even trying.

I also felt that the parameters of the competition were much broader and more ambiguous than any I had previously encountered. My competitors were not just the participants of the course but members of the upper echelons of society as a whole. Even within my nucleus of friends, I felt that I was not competing with a peer group, for they too represented to me a sector of privileged society. I could not change the competition, but I could control how I would compete.

Because I lacked the resources and tools to compete on their terms, I was left to develop my own assets and, by the end of the course, had cultivated greater confidence and self-reliance. I decided I had other avenues in which to compete constructively without being forced to acculturate to social mandates. I rebelliously stopped trying to acquire a taste for wine and saw that perhaps diligence and perseverance would get me far. I learned to lose my naïveté and to accept the fact that the most objectively deserving person is not always the victor in a competition. The lesson I learned was one of self-acceptance and inner maturity.

After graduating from college, I discovered that those relay races I had dreaded in grammar school continued in the working world, taking on new dimensions. Jockeying for position, I found myself unwillingly competing with fellow graduates for entry into the publishing industry. Jobs were scarce, and a breakthrough for a young woman with little working experience into what is known as a "gentleman's profession" would be tough. I was an Asian-American female trying to succeed in a traditionally elitist profession dominated by men—strike one—and WASPS—strike two. I had to contend not only with other young women who had resumés similar to mine but also with people who had far more impressive publishing histories.

California, especially the Bay Area with its high concentration of publishing companies, attracts discontented people from East Coast houses, who have formidable resumes and are often willing to take positions for which they are overqualified. And since California boasts a multitude of colleges and universities, many editorial assignments can be freelanced to semi-retired professors or to mothers with graduate degrees who are qualified and eager to edit and proofread manuscripts at home. I was in competition with them all.

During the two-week publishing course, I was essentially still a student and used that fact as an excuse for my inexperience. Now that I was entering the work force, those more experienced were no longer my superiors. They were potential colleagues and competitors, and I felt I had no time to lose in acquiring comparable marketability. For two months, I made phone calls and sent out resumés. My former internship supervisor wrote a letter of recommendation and referred me to friends of his in the industry. Everyone was quite nice, but no one offered me a job.

One interview in particular stands out. It was for the position of a field representative with a textbook publisher. As part of their interviewing process, I visited a professor at a university and presented him with a proposal for a book adoption for a course. His reply was that I was a beautiful girl and he was awfully sorry, but he already had all the books he needed. Had I proposed a book adoption or dinner for two? The professor made no comment on my presentation or my professional manner, which I had worked so hard to perfect. I had encountered yet another factor in the competitive arena.

Previously, it had been my ethnicity that made me aware of my appearance. Now I became aware that my sex was a factor as well. The professor felt compelled to cushion his refusal with a compliment on my appearance. Was he trying to appease me by appealing to "womanly" vanity? Perhaps he did not see me as a professional at all, but solely and sexually as a woman.

After this incident, it occurred to me why women in the workplace sometimes use their looks as a competitive tool. In all competitive arenas, a woman's attractiveness is a factor, inseparable from the rest of the package. Especially in positions that involve a lot of public interaction, those of receptionists and sales representatives for example, women are frequently preferred over men because they are considered the more decorative and congenial of the sexes. In Japan, it is a new trend for young women seeking employment to undergo cosmetic surgery before they interview. And a friend of mine recently complained that she feels extremely competitive with a new employee in her department, "probably because she is young and good-looking."

In our society, women are assigned many roles. Thus it is difficult for our superiors, who are often men, to isolate these roles and make proper judgment using appropriate standards. Competition among women becomes even more complex when we, too, begin to experience this confusion of identity. The parameters of our competitive arenas become blurred if we simultaneously view ourselves as career woman, supportive wife, nurturing mother, and sympathetic sister. In trying to be so many people at once, our self-esteem becomes extremely vulnerable to threats, which, in turn, stimulates competitiveness.

The professor was judging me by a standard he chose. If I had been wearing a wedding ring, perhaps he would have presumed to compliment me on being a good wife. My friend is competitive with her new co-worker not because of her skills, but because her sexuality as a woman is threatened. In a work environment that is patriarchal, we must insist on self-definition and dictate ourselves the standards by which we are to be judged.

I got my first full-time job in publishing without any ferocious competition or inner turmoil. In fact, I am almost embarrassed to relate how easy it was: I answered an ad in the newspaper and went to work the following Monday. It was a very large corporation, and I anticipated ugly office politics and petty games of competitiveness among co-workers and among departments. I was surprised to learn that, in comparison, a small office is not necessarily warmer and cozier. Invidious feelings can be more discernible and advancement often more competitive in a small office, since there are fewer available positions. With one exception, the environment at this company remained for me comfortable and extremely uncompetitive during my two years there.

Being one of 270 employees, I felt very secure in my anonymity as a permanent member of a staff. Each editorial group tended to be small, which countered feelings of isolation. My group consisted of only five people. Generally, competitiveness did not surface within the group because promotions were based on objective tests. We also had to work closely with one another, which encouraged cooperation and positive interdependence.

It would be inaccurate for me to imply that the company was completely void of competition and competitiveness. Those who aspired to climb the corporate ladder and who were at levels of upper management encountered it. Overall it simply did not exist for me. First, I had no intentions of building a career there. Consequently, I was unconcerned about the supervisory positions that became available. Second, the structure of the company was very corporate and uncreative.

Corporate policy provided firm guidelines, and thus one's position and responsibilities were never ambiguous. The lack of creativity decreased competitiveness because it provided distance between self and work. And because the company was a producer of law books, the nature of our editorial tasks was technical, based on standard procedures rather than personal input, thus diminishing the possibility of threats to self-esteem.

I include this account primarily to dispel a myth regarding competition in the workplace. I found that an individual is not necessarily more isolated or competitive in a large corporate arena. On the contrary, such an environment can provide security. The one exception to my overall noncompetitive experience was a co-worker named Jill. Although corporate policy clearly defined one's position, Jill felt insecure and threatened. She appeared to be particularly distrustful of other women, preferring and getting along better with the men in the office. I can only hypothesize that, in suffering from low self-esteem, she felt ferociously defensive and competitive toward her peers. Thus, she instinctively saw other women as competitors and treated them with guarded hostility.

Jill made it clear from the start that she viewed me as her primary competitor, and thus I became unwillingly engaged in a very ambiguous and unconstructive game. Although we were in the same editorial group, Jill did not feel competitive with me as a co-worker, but experienced me as a personal threat and competitor. We were not competing for a promotion or for greater editorial responsibility. In fact, the goal seemed to remain unfixed except for the times I suspected that we were competing for the attention of our supervisor. I eventually began to see that Jill was envious of me as a person and that I threatened her self esteem simply by being who and what I was. I learned from others that she thought of me as a privileged person and was jealous because my life, in comparison to hers, had been much easier. I have never thought myself intimidating, and it was a new experience for me to be viewed as a threat as well as a member of the elite.

I thought of how I had felt trying to compete with my privileged friends at the two-week publishing course and remembered my own hostility toward Ed during my internship. I learned to empathize with some of Jill's feelings and discovered that we were actually a lot alike. We were both insecure; we both suffered from low self-esteem; and we both felt somewhat threatened by the sexuality of other women. I believe Jill illustrates that chain of emotions I described earlier: an individual's self esteem is especially vulnerable to threats viewed as personal, and, in a personal arena, invidious and petty feelings are far more likely to accompany the ensuing competitiveness.

Such petty feelings can be controlled and competitive stimuli constructively utilized. If a person possesses a good sense of self-esteem and a secure ego, then healthy competition or competitiveness can follow. A musician friend of mine once remarked how much she enjoys playing with other musicians who are better than she. Her self-confidence allows her to meet the challenge of the competition, and she utilizes the motivation constructively so that she ultimately benefits by performing better. Another friend explained that her self-esteem is not threatened if a peer gets a job instead of her. She is glad to know that she was at least close to being what the employers were looking for, and that she herself had come close to winning. These examples illustrate forms of positive competitiveness, possible because of the secure sense of self-esteem of the competitors.

After two years with the law publisher, I decided to become a freelance proofreader and editor. I realized that I would, in a sense, be reentering the job market. The security provided by my former staff job is now gone. I have to hustle to obtain assignments and must prove myself anew with each one. The competition is continual, and the competitiveness within the competition can be destructive.

It has been my experience that solidarity and networking are common among freelancers in the Bay Area. I have a friend named Meg, whom I met in a publishing class, who has sent me job listings and articles pertinent to publishing for the past two years. We see each other only half a dozen times a year, but we work to keep up our correspondence. Even though our networking has been rather one-sided since I quit my permanent job, Meg, who has a full-time job in publishing and access to trade journals, continues to keep her eyes open for job leads for me.

I doubt that Meg feels our networking has been one-sided. If she did, she would stop. And I think the fact that she continues makes a statement regarding her faith in me. Meg's conscientiousness in networking impresses me, and thus she now has an equally faithful sister in solidarity. Should she quit her job in the future and need some names to get started as a freelancer, I would provide them. One day we will come full circle.

I don't mean to suggest that all freelancers possess such a crystal-clear vision of their responsibilities to one another. Competitiveness does creep in. Freelancers can have petty feelings toward their competitors. But we are lucky that the nature of the business strongly requires ethical networking and cooperative competition in order for a freelancer to function and to continue to work successfully. Because networking plays such a central role in a freelancer's procurement of jobs and because of the interdependent nature of networking itself, it is far more advantageous for one to compete ethically and cooperatively.

Although the competitiveness I feel as a freelancer is minimal, it is not nonexistent. I notice that I am discriminating in my networking, and this is a form of competing. I am more guarded with information about companies that produce books I especially enjoy working on. These publishers—of fiction, biographies, and English translations of foreign works—tend to put out only a small number of books per year, and thus the competition among freelancers is high. Whenever a fellow freelancer who is not a personal friend inquires about such a company, my initial reaction is to reveal as little as possible. Although I know that my seniority would be respected over newcomers, I feel possessive of certain companies. I try to reserve them as special contacts, comfortably sharing them with only my closest sisters in solidarity. Thus, the presence or absence of solidarity is what prescribes how selective, or competitive, I am in my networking and sharing of contacts.

Most newcomers to freelancing are women. As much as one-third of an editorial workshop may be composed of women in their thirties through fifties who are re-entering the work force or wishing to make a career change. Freelancing attracts them because the flexibility of the work allows them to honor other commitments, or because they want to operate their own businesses.

Generally, I am not intimidated by such women. And although I hesitate to share my more prized contacts with newcomers, I do applaud the efforts and ambition of these women. In past situations, my competitive feelings have always been augmented when my opponent was another woman. But as a freelancer, I have become accustomed to working with women as equals and sisters, and they no longer threaten my self-esteem. I now crave the company of other women, enjoying the sisterhood and empathy we share. I suspect that when I was working in patriarchal environments, I felt uncomfortable with the underlying emphasis on women's sexuality. In feeling that I was being categorized according to my sex, I subconsciously felt obligated to compare myself to, and thus compete with, other women. They were my peers and thus my competitors.

Publishing is a relatively small industry. The community of editorial freelancers is a part of it that also tends to be closely knit. News travels fast, and recommendations are often made by word of mouth. The benefits of networking and solidarity far outweigh those gained by going it alone, and I am especially grateful for having learned their value early on. As a freelancer, I have more control over my work and how I choose to compete than I did as part of a permanent staff. The responsibilities are greater and there are more choices to be made. But thus far the trade-offs have been worth it.

I am no longer as resentful of having been pitted against my friends in grammar school relay races. Competition itself is a neutral framework and is largely what we choose to make it. Within each competition, the stimuli will differ and our advantages and disadvantages will differ. What might remain constant is an individual's competitive inclinations and ethical makeup—that is, how he or she chooses to meet the challenge. As I stated earlier, the structure of competition does not dictate competitiveness; conversely, a highly competitive person could turn any situation into a competition. The workplace needn't be more competitive than any other arena.

NOTES

1. All personal names used in this essay are fictitious.
2. Harvey L. Ruben, *Competing* (New York: Pinnacle Books, 1980), 160.

"I Don't Do No Windows": Competition Between the Domestic Worker and the Housewife

ELAINE BELL KAPLAN

INTRODUCTION

This essay is based on interviews I conducted with black domestic workers and the middle-class women who employ them. Although my focus is primarily on these two groups of women, I also interviewed some employers' husbands and daughters and some domestics' daughters.[1] In many instances, I found that the housewife-employer and her domestic were caught up in a conflictive, potentially competitive relationship, a struggle centered on women's traditional role as housewife.

Most often, housewives turn over to their domestics only the heavy housecleaning chores, retaining for themselves those tasks that fulfill the traditional housewife role without distracting from their image as the "lady" of the house.[2] In other words, in establishing clear boundaries between herself and the domestic, the housewife emphasizes the class and race differences between them. Domestics are thus perceived as "conceptual unequals" and a potentially competitive environment—in which definitions of femininity would be at stake—is kept under control. The issue of class is important here because the definition of *femininity* in this country is class-

Earlier versions of this essay were presented at the Bay Area Marxist-Feminist Group, January 1983, the American Sociological Conference, August 1984, and the conference of the National Women's Studies Association, June 1985. In revised form, this essay also appeared in the August 1985 issue of *Sojourner*. I want to thank Lewis Kaplan and Rivka Polotnick for their valuable comments and suggestions. This essay also benefited from many exciting conversations with Lucy DePertuis about her experiences as a domestic worker and from the use of her unpublished materials, which she generously shared with me. Also I am deeply indebted to Arlie Russell Hochschild for her thoughtful reading of and suggestions on an earlier draft.

bound. Because the "feminine" attributes of helplessness and delicacy can apply only to a comparatively small number of females of the dominant class, the mass of women are compelled to undertake many forms of strenuous and "unladylike" activity.[3] And when one thinks about the image of black women as strong workers performing chores usually reserved for men, the issue of race becomes important as well:

> As slaves and as freedwomen, black wives and mothers labored for white masters and mistresses even as they sought to provide for the everyday needs of their own families. Most slave women toiled in the fields for a portion of their lives. . . . Some toiled as servants . . . or laundresses. . . . With slavery abolished and the last cannon silenced, an enduring image of black womanhood remained in the mind of the white South— that of a servant who responded to the daily demands of white people of all ages.[4]

Despite the fact that black women have been domestic workers in this country since the days of slavery, they have received little attention from feminists.[5] Their work experience, however, provides important insights into the intersection of race, class, and gender, and into the dynamics of relationships between black and white women. Tensions, conflicts, and competition between white employers and black workers—the haves and the have-nots—suffuse these relationships. For both kinds of women, paid and family work blend together, creating an unending day of caring for and waiting on others. When a maid cannot work, the housewife who employs her must. Given this situation, the domestic worker and the housewife could strive for solidarity: The domestic worker needs a job; the housewife needs help and can afford to pay for it. The domestic worker should be treated as a professional who has had years of hard-won experience. After all, both worker and employer are women who are largely confined to servicing and maintaining men and children. In fact, some men even think of their wives and maids as nearly interchangeable. In response to the question, "Who does the housework in your home?" a married man said to me, "When the maid doesn't come or doesn't finish her work, I tell her to just leave it, my wife will finish it." In earlier times, the stereotype was that black women who were capable of doing backbreaking or "dirty" work, like my mother did, were masculinized characters, certainly not women. "Feminine" women did not work at all.[6] Today the swelling ranks of white, middle-class women in the labor force challenge that notion, but the idea that black women are tough, strong, and "macho" lingers on, having evolved from the earlier image of them.

I will discuss five power strategies that emerged from the interviews I conducted and from patterns I have observed in my mother's work relationship with women employers. These strategies suggest that housewives who are insecure, who have incorporated on a deep level a sense of their "interchangeability with their domestics," tend to divide domestic from housewife space and to divide household chores into ladylike and unladylike tasks. They reinforce their differences from their domestics by the way they dress, by giving gifts to the domestics, and by demanding that their family's needs come first. These are all ways of controlling hostility and expressing class differences. In addition, these strategies work to emphasize the housewife's claim to femininity at the same time that they deemphasize the domestic's femininity.

The domestic workers I interviewed, however, are able to counter the housewives' strategies with a few of their own. They can develop the maid's gossip mill, exchanging information about their employers. They can circumvent the housewife's power by aligning themselves with her husband. Ironically, these strategies do nothing to ameliorate the domestic situation and reinforce the social order and structure of patriarchy that oppresses them in the first place. Before I elaborate on these strategies, I will present a brief discussion of how the slavery experience led to the present-day relationship between these two groups of women.

THE HAVES AND THE HAVE-NOTS

The history of black domestic workers is rooted in the slave legacy of U.S. blacks. Female house slaves performed a variety of work roles, serving as personal maid, cook, babysitter, and companion. After emancipation, domestic work was one of the few occupations open to black women in the South. In the North, white immigrants dominated domestic work until black women moved into northern urban areas and began to compete for jobs by accepting lower wages.[7] Most immigrant women were able to find jobs in the new industrial factories. Black women, on the other hand, were generally restricted to domestic work.[8]

By the 1980s, 172,000 black women were giving personal service as domestics in private households.[9] Unlike the slave women of yesterday, black domestics today, like Ella Mae Robinson (one of the women I interviewed),[10] receive some pay. Most of the maids I interviewed earn a yearly income of $3,000 for part-time and $6,000 for full-time work.

Ella Mae Robinson, a woman who has raised five children, works five hours a day, five days a week, in a middle-class home. She receives no paid vacations, health care, or sick days, and, as she puts it, "definitely no holidays off, unless Mrs. Coleman is going away or it's a big one like Thanksgiving or Christmas." When she started working twenty years ago, she "had to scrub floors with brushes because most of the people didn't have carpets. I remember scrubbing walls and ceilings." Today, she cleans rugs with vacuum cleaners and puts dishes into the dishwasher while clothes tumble dry. Now, she cleans two houses a day:

> "I work as quickly as I can. I dust all the rooms, vacuum, mop the kitchen, den, clean the bathrooms, cabinets, put dishes in the dishwasher, and do some ironing. Many times I have to take the clothes to the cleaners, feed the cat, wash the woodwork, and pick up the clothes off the floor and off the chairs. Most women like me, and this Christmas I got a blouse."

Because she works for two employers, she may be subjected to two totally different

94   DAILY REALITIES

sets of whims and moods. In addition, like the slave woman, she must serve "in a civilized manner, respecting the social ways of [her] owners."[11]

The white employers I interviewed said they hired domestics to do, as one woman put it,

> "the cleaning and other things I don't want to do. We have what we used to call maids. . . . I don't want to give you the impression that we were that wealthy. . . . My mother would just contract these women . . . for a long time we had women who lived in the house, live-in maids, who helped take care of the house and helped take care of the kids."

Some housewives hire domestics to free them from housework drudgery so that they can pursue a leisure life-style. A lawyer I interviewed admitted that she would rather hire than do the work herself: "I have an awful lot of help, the housekeeper who does the other things I don't want to do. If you want to have children and have a career, I can't think of any other way to do it. Except maybe living in a foreign country and hav[ing] tons of people taking care of your kids."[12]

One woman, a doctor, talked to me about her childhood when the black women did all the chores. She was "shocked" to find, when she married, that she was expected to do the cleaning. Immediately, she hired a housekeeper:

> My dear, I never made a bed in my life until I got married. I had a full-time housekeeper. Now I would like someone to take over my housekeeping responsibilities. I was really indulged in housework terms. I was almost incompetent in a lot of ways, never cooked, never washed, never picked up my clothes because they were gone when I got up. So marriage was, physically speaking, a harsh blow. When I woke up the next morning, the same things were there that were there the night before. It was most puzzling to me.

She compliments her housekeeper: "My housekeeper is excellent. She does everything. She does the cleaning, the meal planning, marketing, and knows what's going on in the house. She keeps this place very clean which is a big thing because I am very fussy."

These women's statements touch the heart of my argument. Naturally, only the housewife or a lower-class woman is expected to cook and clean, not the housewife's husband. The housewife who can employ a domestic has the privilege of satisfying her personal needs or of becoming a "lady." She can transform herself into a "species of commodity. . . . For the lady's freedom to engage in community and voluntary activities, to take up recreation or self-improvement, depend[s] on the availability of another woman to do her housework."[13] Hiring another woman to work in the home emphasizes the fact that all women are expected to do this kind of work. Note, however, that the housewife-employer manages to retain a primary role by making all the decisions about the housework, although another woman does the dirty work. And race clearly separates the two groups of women. The housewife's power strategies enhance her race and class privileges which further define her as different from the domestic—another woman.

THE HOUSEWIVES' POWER STRATEGIES

The Space Strategy

The strategies I discuss are effective in an environment that emphasizes the cultural and physical differences between the domestic and the housewife. Of all the elements governing the black domestic's interaction with the white world, "space, with its implications both physical and cultural," is perhaps the foremost. Trudier Harris writes:

> The black woman is presumably at home in her own environment: but when she enters the white woman's kitchen, she moves into a culture which is at least apart from her own, if not alien or openly hostile. Black town and white town have metaphorical connotations as well as physical dimensions. . . . When she immerses herself in the white culture, she loses the psychological security derived from familiar surroundings and must make adjustments accordingly.[14]

When Ella Mae Robinson opens the door to her employer's middle-class home, she has to conform to a script written by her mother's mother and her mistress's mother and grandmother. She knows that the housewife believes that however "motherly" her maid, she can never be "like one of the family." Most of the women I interviewed wondered how any employer "gets away with saying we are part of the family."[15]

If the maid is young, her employer may think she is a "hot momma;" the maid has to be "reassuringly invisible and self-effacing."[16] And so both women take their places in the one terrain where they share their powerlessness: the family home. The housewife sits at her desk in the den writing her list of instructions, ready to confront this black woman with whom she shares so much, yet who is so different from her.

Domestic service in a white mistress's home exposes many black women to the frustration of a daily experience of difference between their own standard of living and that of their employers; such a situation that does not exist in any other line of work. To see what other people have, and what she herself does not have, can almost be called the essential job experience of the domestic servant. Toni Morrison's novel *The Bluest Eye* explores the deep psychological toll of these differences. One of the main characters, a black domestic worker named Mrs. Breedlove, finds a permanent job in the home of a wealthy white family whose members are generous to her:

> Here she found beauty, order, cleanliness. She reigned over cupboards stacked high with food that would not be eaten for weeks, even months; she was queen of canned vegetables bought by the case, special fondants and ribbon candy curled up in tiny silver dishes.[17]

It takes only a superficial understanding of psychology to imagine what Mrs. Breedlove had to endure. Each day she was subjected to living in an environment that made her own home seem shabby.

In some employers' homes, however, maids are not allowed full entry. Harris writes about employers who establish the kitchen—or, as she calls it, "the Nigger's room," a room associated with cleaning supplies, food, and dirt—as the space in which the domestic must stay most of the day when she is not cleaning the other rooms. The black woman cleans the living room or the dining room or the bedroom or the bathroom, and retires to the kitchen. She sits in the kitchen when she has time for sitting, and waits there for requests that she go to other parts of the house.[18] One woman I interviewed wondered why, when she was at a relative's home for dinner, her cousin's maid did not join them in the living room after the meal. "I thought that she couldn't possibly be working in the kitchen all the five or six hours I was there."

The women I interviewed do not feel that they have the right to decide what to do, or when and how to do it. Ella Mae's work is confined to what she has described as "washing and cleaning." She does what the housewife sees as the "most physically demanding, dirtiest, and most dangerous work." In addition to lifting furniture and clearing away large amounts of trash, she is exposed to all kinds of household germs and she breathes in chemical cleaners. Actually, the division of tasks is very important when one considers that many of these women still regard housework as their primary task. When they can afford to hire women to do some of the more unpleasant chores, they need to make sure that their housewife's role is not usurped by the domestic.

The housewife, if she helps at all, establishes her race and class differences by ordering the maid to handle the more dangerous chemical bottles like oven cleaners, wax removers, and painting materials, while she does work such as rearranging closets and shelves.[19] She tells the maid which cloth to use in cleaning the silverware and how many different types of polishes she must use to clean the bathroom, the kitchen floor, and the sinks. She will give the maid a written list of chores. She is able to show the maid that she is in charge and at the same time deny the maid's work experience. Against this assertion of rights, the maid has to respond even when she cannot win. Ella Mae said that over the years she has had to learn to "tell 'em, don't give me no list. I know what to do. But they keep right on doin' it. It makes me feel like I don't know how to work, I have to keep askin' her for the next thing to do. It slows me down and then I have to work real hard to get done by the end of the day."

The Dress Code Strategy

Another strategy the housewife uses to separate herself from the maid is to rob the maid of her individuality. The housewife chooses whatever she herself wants to wear but expects the domestic worker to wear "some depersonalized dress":

Just as cleaning and cooking are expected, so too is a certain physical appearance.

The maid is expected, for example, to wear a uniform, which aside from its practical functions, symbolically negates individuality. When the black woman takes off the clothes in which she has ridden the train or bus to her job and puts on that uniform she becomes THE MAID, not somebody's mother or sister or wife. Her primary function is to serve the needs of the family which has thus defined her.[20]

Domestic workers usually wear old housedresses that add years to their age. I recall meeting my mother at work and being surprised when she came to the door. It was hard for me to believe that this woman wearing an old, faded housedress was my mother. Ella Mae Robinson discussed the way her employer reminds her of the dress code: "Honey, you could hear Mrs. C gettin' all excited and makin' a big deal over my clothes. I hate to have to answer her questions about why I'm looking 'extra pretty today.' She makes sure I get them clothes off before she moves one step."

The dress code enhances the separation of the housewife from the domestic; it works to eliminate the symbols of the maid's personhood or her status as a sexual being. This strategy also alleviates the housewife's insecurity about her own position. After all, as the husband said earlier, the housewife and her domestic are really "interchangeable," so they must be made at least to look as different as possible. The construction of appearance, like the division of space and tasks (and the gift-giving strategy I will discuss next), work to make the maid experience her inequality. At the same time, on a much deeper level, these strategies also serve to emphasize the housewife's claim to femininity. In this sense race becomes important in that the black woman has always been seen in white culture as something less than a woman.

The Gift Strategy
A domestic servant's real wages are usually meager, and supplemental wages in the form of food and cast-off clothing can be a blessing—or a curse. Harris is right to say that "the incongruity of living in a tiny walk-up apartment, barely able to pay rent or installments on refrigerators, and eating [expensive meat] is grossly absurd."[21] The useless items, like decorative bowls, that my mother used to bring home illustrated the point to me. Our very small apartment was filled with expensive sheets, blankets, dresses, and shoes. Each item cost more than the $50-a-month rent. Such handouts, or "service pans," as they were called during slavery days, are considered by the housewife as a domestic's fringe benefits. Yet they seem to be designed partly to discourage petitions for wage increases.

One housewife who used such gifts seemed to need to overcome her feelings of guilt: "I certainly feel that I have more than enough food and clothing here, and she must need some of these things. I don't mind sharing them. We are so fortunate, you know, and these things are still good. I think it cheers her up." On some level, the housewife must suspect the maid of envying her status and wealth. After all, paid domestic work in other people's homes involves an exposure to a particular set of frustrations and resentments generated by the extreme asymmetry of power

DAILY REALITIES

and wealth. Domestic workers certainly experience the difference between their own standard of living and that of their employers. As Jacklyn Cock suggests, the situation can become "psychologically mined."[22] It must lead to a tremendous amount of pent-up resentment which cannot help but create a desire for aggressive compensation. Given the class and race position of the two women, it is safe to say that the housewife is quite satisfied with the status quo and wants nothing more than to maintain it. The have-not, the maid, is apt to be less satisfied.

According to George Foster, who writes of the "growing fear" of the middle class, because an inferior can take from a superior only through an aggressive act, the superior suspects that her servant is envious and thus "fears the evil eye." She worries about being seen eating an expensive dinner or wearing expensive clothes. She may fear "outright attack."[23] If Foster is right, Ella Mae's gift may be seen as the housewife's attempt to soothe the domestic's feelings, to alleviate her possible hostility and envy. The gifts also give the housewife an edge, since Ella Mae is not in a position to reciprocate. Finally, the unreciprocated gifts reinforce the woman's role as the "lady" of the house, by underlining the class differences.

Certainly cleaning women like Ella Mae Robinson recognize this injustice. She realizes that the hand-me-down dresses and leftover food she receives as "gifts" cannot possibly compensate for the physical deterioration of the body—especially the bad backs, the sore feet, and the varicose veins—that will inevitably result from a maid's hard work. My mother did not quit domestic work until she was 72 years old and then only because she lost the use of her legs.

The Invisible Family Strategy

The prevailing concept of the black domestic is that of a woman whose primary responsibility is to the family of her employer. Like slave families, the families of domestic workers lose out. The domestic worker's "ultra-exploitation is evidenced by deprivation of their family life."[24] When I talked to daughters of domestics, I was surprised at how much they resented their mothers' work. Some of them felt that they had had to forsake their childhood because they were required to take over the family chores of babysitting, housecleaning, and cooking. In fact, the domestic worker and her daughter may find themselves involved in a competitive relationship too, stemming from the fact that the domestic is responsible for the upkeep of her own family as well as her employer's family.

Some of these women are so tired at the end of the day that they cannot face another load of laundry and dishes. "You don't feel like washin' your own windows when you come home from out there, scrubbin'," Maggie Holmes told her interviewer.[25] The eldest daughter may have to take on many of her mother's domestic tasks and parental responsibilities.

For example, in Ella Mae Robinson's family and in my own, the eldest daughter (generally not the son) was assigned the care and feeding of her sisters and brothers until the mother returned. This kind of arrangement sets the daughter up in direct competition with her mother over who decides what has to be done when. The mother tries to regain power by criticizing and withholding praise. Many daughters of domestics talked about the resulting conflict. One daughter said, "I could boss my sisters and brothers around during the day, but when my mother came home, she never would say that I did a good job. She would immediately find something I did wrong. By the time I was fifteen years old, I was sick of taking care of kids. And I never could play with the other kids."

Her story touched me. As the oldest daughter, I acted as the substitute mother. At the age of 12 I was scolding and bossing my brothers and sisters. My assumption of authority led to several major arguments with my mother over who should establish rules for the children. At the time, we did not understand why we had these problems.

This situation is not unusual. Historically, working class girls have been required to take over the chores for their working mothers. In fact, my role as a substitute mother matched that of girls in nineteenth-century Britain, who were expected to contribute indirectly to the economic maintenance of their households by acting as "little mothers" to the younger children. Jacklyn Cock has observed this pattern:

> The mother's two economic roles as wage-earner and as housewife frequently con-flicted, and when the demands of outside work had to be put first, her female children automatically took over the household duties, which involved not only the housework and cooking but also the tending and care of the younger members, as well as nursing the sick members of the family. Thus, to allow the mother to go to work, the elder female children frequently had to relinquish the opportunity of going to school and stay home.[26]

Yet, unlike the factory or office worker, the domestic must give preference to the needs and the desires of the employer's family. Often my mother had to forego dinner with her own family in order to serve dinner at late-night dinner parties. Of all the strategies the housewife employs, this is certainly the most exploitive, and its impact is cross-generational.

There may be an added dimension to the mother-daughter relationship. Toni Morrison depicts the subtleties of class and race dynamics by showing how the domestic and her daughter may become entangled in the world of the housewife. Morrison's character, Mrs. Breedlove, fantasizes that she is in charge of her em-ployer's elegant house. She cleans the house, orders expensive food, and grooms the children as if she was their mother. Her own daughter, Pecola, a latchkey child, takes care of herself. Unfortunately, during a visit to her mother's place of employ-ment, Pecola has a chance to see herself in relation to the white employer's daughter. Pecola is awed by the luxurious home and by the little girl in fancy clothes. She also learns that this little girl has the right to call her mother by her first name, Polly. Pecola has always called her Mrs. Breedlove.[27]

The housewives' daughters I interviewed, by contrast, often stereotyped the do-mestic as a matriarch or a tower of strength—tender, kind, tough, and supportive (in some cases, more supportive of them than their own mothers). Generally, they did not know much about their maids' families. One daughter said that she felt her mother did not want her to know about the domestic's family: "If I asked our housekeeper any questions about her family, my mother would frown." Most of the daughters claimed to "love the maid like a second mother," as one daughter put it. And they believed that the maids loved them—so much that they would happily offer free psychological counseling to both daughter and mother. Some daughters of housewives said that they could talk to the maid when they could not talk to anyone else.

THE DOMESTICS' STRATEGIES

Domestics also have strategies. They can undermine the housewife by passing word around about her. Alice Childress wrote *Like One of the Family*, a novel about her experiences as a domestic. Authors like Toni Morrison and Alice Walker, among others, have used the domestic worker in their novels to verify the black woman's work experience and her relationship with white women.[28] Other women, less inclined to write their stories, have used other strategies. For instance, although they generally work alone, some domestics (usually those who work in apartment buildings) go out of their way to meet other domestics in laundry rooms or in elevators. According to my mother and other domestics I interviewed, they pass the time advising each other about bad and good employers and how to handle them. Some domestics demand to be addressed by their last names even though they call their employer by her first name. Although this is not a common occurrence, several employers I interviewed mentioned that they were expected to address their maids this way.

When I asked my mother to explain what domestic work is all about, she hesitated. In all those years of rising early in the morning to catch the bus and coming home late in the evening after serving food at numerous cocktail parties, she had never been asked about her job. "How do you get along with them?" I finally asked. "Do they talk to you about their family and do you talk about your family to them?" My mother answered, "I have to listen to them, but I don't talk. It's none of their business. When they ask me how I'm doing, I say just fine. That's all I say. They want to know my business so that they can tell their friends."

My mother's experience is not that different from other domestic workers'—all of whom see their work as alienating. For example, when I described my mother's feelings about her work to several domestics I interviewed, they nodded their heads in agreement. One said, "Yes, I can believe it. Most likely she spends her whole day responding to her employer with head nods, or one-liners like, 'Yes, I understand,' or, 'No, I don't,' or, 'how nice.' If it's a personal issue, she says, 'it's too bad.' She makes all the appropriate responses—like a robot who is not expected to have feelings or ideas." Actually, I saw my mother's response as a strategy of her own, in which she had the power to keep her personal life away from the housewife.

It is well known that white men used black slave women as sexual partners, and accounts of domestic workers having to "give it up" to their employers' husbands are common. The women I interviewed did not talk about sexual relationships with their employers' husbands. Perhaps it is not a problem for them, or they may just not be willing to talk about it. Some did mention sexual harassment, however. When my mother was younger, she was harassed quite often in full view of party guests and the housewife. The husband, everyone suggested, was "joking around" or "too drunk" to be held responsible for his actions. And, according to my mother, the housewife "pretended not to notice." Actually, I suspect she took one look at her cleaning woman in her matronly dress and decided that she did not count as a woman. Then again, perhaps the housewife cannot afford to notice that the cleaning woman is a woman too.

The employer's husband may also figure in the maid's strategies to keep the housewife in her place. Ella Mae Robinson credited herself with knowing "who the real boss is." She took it upon herself to tell me that domestics know that the housewife's husband, not the housewife herself, has the ultimate power. One domestic worker said: "Whenever Mrs. Jones tells me to wash the windows, I wait until Mr. Jones is home, I tell him that I didn't want to bother Mrs. Jones, 'but I can't wash no windows.' He understands and takes care of it."

A housewife I interviewed told me:

> "I found out that even maids don't expect to be treated nice. Even when I was uncomfortable about having maids, because I got out of the university with this very Socialist Marxist idea. We were not supposed to hire maids. But we needed one, so I hired a black woman to live in. I didn't want her to dress in dirty clothes—condescending—but I gave her clothes so that she'd look nice in the house. My husband opposed my dishing out food for this lady. He said that she had to take food out of the pot herself. He said we were treating her as an equal. She started to take advantage of me. And I suppose she saw that he was in control, and she totally disregarded me. I couldn't get her to do anything. They [she] didn't expect to be treated right and so we couldn't treat them [her] well. I told my husband that I think part of the problem is that they [she] can see that you are obviously controlling me and that I have no power. I said to him, 'please don't relate to the maid. Let me do it.' But he wouldn't keep out of it."

This statement suggests that the housewife may have the power to hire the domestic but it is the husband who has the final say. The domestics' interviews indicate that most of them realize the importance of this strategy; they need to know who is really the boss and to use that knowledge whenever necessary.

CONCLUSION

The five strategies I have described create a push-pull dynamic that has deep impact, yet is so subtle that the women involved may not grasp the nature of their struggle. It is a relationship replete with tension and competition. The housewife is winning the competition because she has the money and power to distance herself, to reinforce her felt superiority to this other woman. The housewife has to maintain her primary role as homemaker without doing the dirty work. The demands she makes on the domestic worker take their physical and emotional toll, often victimizing the domestic's daughter, who often has to do her mother's work for their family.

Some people argue that the tension between domestics and housewives would be lessened by a domestics' union. Angela Davis has suggested that business firms hire out domestics, thus eliminating the personal aspects of the housewife-maid relationship. The business firms' cut might mean lower wages for the domestics,[29] however. And organizing and unionizing will not change class differences.

The points I want to stress the most have to do with the way housework is defined as "women's work" and the way in which housewives adopt strategies to maintain the kind of world in which black women can be seen as conceptual unequals. As long as some women rely on the oppression of other women to augment their limited power, they will be acting in concert with the patriarchal superstructure. Their strategies also obscure the fact that the black domestic stands between the housewife and her acknowledgement that housework is demeaning and demoralizing, that only women do it, and that women do it as a service to men. Housewives, "ladies," are deflected from thinking about their own oppressive situation, since they do not see the women they hire as *women.*

This essay may also suggest one response to a question I am often asked: "Why have many black women stayed away from the feminist movement?" Some people assume that black women's issues are different from those of the movement as a whole, and to some degree this is true. But one of the major ways black women have come to know white women has been through domestic service. It should not be surprising that black women would not want to join white women in supporting feminist causes, even when they really believe in women's rights. This point is painfully clear in an incident that Audre Lorde has recounted: "I wheel my two-year-old daughter in a shopping cart through a supermarket in Eastchester in 1967, and a little white girl riding past in her mother's cart calls out excitedly, "Oh look, Mommy, a baby maid.' " The mother did not correct her child, Lorde notes.[30] What is needed is further exploration of the interaction between black and white women in order to understand why we have never had a sisterhood. I present this essay as only a beginning.

NOTES

1. These interviews are taken from a major research project on the dual-work family, "The Second Shift: Inner Tensions in Two-Income Families," directed by Arlie Russell Hochschild and funded by a National Institute of Mental Health grant. One hundred and eleven interviews were conducted with couples with preschool children who work 35 or more hours a week. Many of the black women in the couples I interviewed talked about their mothers' domestic jobs and about the impact of that kind of job on the family. I then interviewed five of the mothers who had worked as domestics. I do not mean to suggest that the patterns I discuss in this essay occur between all housewives and domestics.

2. The role of "housewife" is a family role. Yet it is also a work role. As Ann Oakley defines her, a housewife is "the person, other than a domestic servant, who is responsible for most of the household duties (or for supervising a domestic servant who carries out these

duties)." Housewifery as the dominant "mature feminine role" emerged out of industrialization's impact on the family. Oakley adds, "Our window on the world is looked through with our hands in the sink. The metaphor of the hands in the sink expresses the captivity of women within the home, that is, the dominance of the housewife role in the lives of women, and its separation from other roles and other worlds beyond the home." In *Woman's Work, The Housewife, Past and Present* (New York: Random House, 1974), 1, 32.

3. Jacklyn Cock, *Maids & Madams* (Johannesburg: Raven Press, 1980), 263.

4. Jacqueline Jones, *Labor of Love, Labor of Sorrow* (New York: Basic Books, 1985), 115.

5. Carl N. Degler, *At Odds* (New York: Oxford University Press, 1980), states that when Elizabeth Cady Stanton urged women to pursue work outside the family, she was really referring to "those women who had domestic servants, grown children, or no children" (p. 391). Julie A. Matthaei, in *An Economic History of Women in America* (New York: Schocken Books, 1982), reports that slave women were engaged in the "double day" since in the earliest days of slavery, "they often combined personal service with skilled production—caring for children, cooking, minding the dairy, and sewing clothes" (p. 92).

6. Gerda Lerner, in *The Majority Finds Its Past* (New York: Oxford University Press, 1979), p. 26, reports that during the 1830s the "cult of true womanhood" developed the ideals of femininity toward which middle-class white women strived.

7. See Gerda Lerner, *Black Women in White America* (New York: Random House, 1973), 226. Degler found that during the years 1900 to 1940, more black working women than immigrant working women tended to be married and raising families. Degler, *At Odds*, 391.

8. Matthaei, *An Economic History of Women in America*, 224. Around 1935, black journalists in New York City saw a scene they later described as the "Bronx Slave Market." They witnessed dozens of black women gathering early every morning at the corner of Simpson and Jerome avenues in the Bronx to parade in front of wealthy housewives who had come to "buy their strength and energy for an hour, two hours, or even a day at the rate of fifteen, twenty or if luck would be with them, thirty cents an hour." These women, under the rigid watch of the housewives, would be hired to scrub floors on their bended knees, to hang precariously while cleaning the windows of mansions, luxurious apartments, and modest middle-class homes, and to strain and sweat over steaming tubs of heavy blankets, spreads, and furniture covers. See Bettina Aptheker, *Woman's Legacy* (Amherst: University of Massachusetts Press, 1982), 121.

9. See *Statistics on Black Women*, 1984, compiled by U.S. Department of Commerce Bureau of the Census.

10. To respect the confidentiality of the women interviewed, all names have been changed.

11. Matthaei, *An Economic History of Women in America*, 92.

12. I am using the term "housewife" to refer both to women who work outside the home and to women who stay at home full time because all the women I interviewed (whether professionals or not) viewed the responsibility of housework as belonging to them primarily.

13. Cock, *Maids & Madams*, 133.

14. Trudier Harris, *From Mammies to Militants: Domestic Service in Industrializing America* (Chicago: University of Illinois Press, 1981), 14.

15. See Alice Childress, *Like One of the Family . . . Conversations from a Domestic's Life* (New York: Independence, 1956). She handles the interaction between the domestic and housewife with humor and much sadness.

16. Harris, *From Mammies to Militants*, 20.

17. Toni Morrison, *The Bluest Eye* (New York: Holt, Rinehart & Winston, 1970), 101.

18. Harris, *From Mammies to Militants*, 15.

19. Lucy DePertuis of the Sociology Department at the University of Guam makes this point in an unpublished paper on domestic workers.

20. Harris, *From Mammies to Militants*, 12.

21. Ibid., 25.

22. Cock, *Maids & Madams*, 68.

23. George M. Foster, "The Anatomy of Envy: A Study of Symbolic Behavior," *Current Anthropology* 13 (1972): 165–184.

24. Cock, *Maids & Madams*, 315.

25. Studs Terkel, *Working* (New York: Avon Books, 1974), 164.

26. Cock, *Maids & Madams*, 275.

27. Morrison, *The Bluest Eye*, 86.

28. See Alice Walker, *The Color Purple* (New York: Harcourt Brace Jovanovich, 1982).

29. Angela Davis, *Women, Race and Class* (New York: Random House, 1981), 224–244. The women I interviewed did not belong to a union and, like most of the domestic workers I knew, did not feel they had the energy or the time to participate in one. Moreover, they did not think that a union would resolve all of their problems with their employers.

30. Audre Lorde, *Sister Outsider* (New York: Crossing Press, 1984), 126.

"Women in Development" Ideology and the Marketplace

MARJORIE MBILINYI

Tanzanian women's struggles for self-advancement, survival, and power have involved two forms of competition. One is market competition, the product of capitalist market relations which developed during the international slave trade from the sixteenth to the seventeenth centuries. Market relations deepened after the establishment of the colonial state by the Germans in the 1880s. As all areas of life were commercialized, women and men—and women and women—competed with one another for access to scarce resources, including land, labor, and money. This competition occurred within classes, as well as between them. The struggle for power between dominant and dominated groups underlay market competition, however, and is the second form of competition to be examined. A brief history of the colonization of Tanzania, and the development of market relations, is presented in the following section.

Two major, conflicting perspectives about the nature of women's oppression and women's liberation in the Third World developed during the 1970s. The dominant perspective, argued by "Women in Development" (WID) practitioners, holds that

This article is based on the Mbeya Regional Integrated Development and Economic Planning (RIDEP) Report by Marjorie Mbilinyi and Mary Kabelele, "Women in the Rural Development of Mbeya Region" (Dar es Salaam: United Nations Food and Agriculture Organization [FAO], 1982) and on research carried out in 1983 in neighboring Rungwe region, funded by the United Nations International Labor Organisation (ILO) and the Denmark International Development Agency (DANIDA). It has benefited from criticisms of earlier work at the Institute of Development Studies (IDS) 1983 staff seminar at the University of Dar es Salaam, at the 1983 annual meeting of the Tanzanian Home Economics Association, and in discussion in the Women's Research and Documentation Project (WRDP).

women have not progressed because they have not been fully integrated into development. According to WID, the solution is to increase women's participation in the economy as it is now structured. The alternative point of view argues that most women are producers in African society, and have been oppressed and exploited as a result of the way they have been integrated into development and of the exploitive structure of development. The goal in this alternative view is women's liberation—that is, a complete transformation of gender, race, class, and nation relations—not women's advancement, improvement, or development in the system as it currently exists. The second part of this chapter examines the development of WID ideology in the Third World and in Tanzania specifically, in the context of struggles between these two conflicting perspectives. This struggle is concretized by examining the case in Mbeya region, in southwestern Tanzania.

THE COLONIZATION PROCESS

Tanzania's history of colonization began early. Swahili city-states had developed by the eleventh century along the coast of present-day Kenya, Tanzania, and Mozambique, as a result of Arab and Persian colonization in earlier centuries. Portuguese invaders conquered the city-states in the sixteenth century, but were driven out by the seventeenth century. The city-states, including Zanzibar, grew on the basis of slavery and control over trade. Financiers and merchants from India, western Europe, and the United States competed with Arab and Swahili interests for control of the lucrative trade in slaves and ivory. The East African peoples themselves were devastated by the ravages of the internationalized slave trade during the period extending from the seventeenth through the nineteenth centuries.

The sultan of Omani conquered the city-states during the nineteenth century and created the Zanzibar Commercial Empire. Slave plantations owned by Africans, Swahilis, and Arabs were established on the islands of Zanzibar and Pemba as well as along the coast and inland. Indigenous forms of slavery were intensified during this period. More than half of all slaves in Africa were women.[1]

The Zanzibar rulers were conquered by Western powers at the end of the nineteenth century. The Zanzibar islands became an English protectorate, and Germany took Tanganyika during the infamous Berlin Conference of 1885. After the German defeat in World War I, Britain was awarded Tanganyika as a League of Nations mandated territory. British rule persisted from 1919 until 1961, when self-government was proclaimed. Tanganyika and the Zanzibar islands, including Pemba, merged to create the United Republic of Tanzania in 1964.

Self-government did not entail the creation of an independent nation-state with full economic, political, and cultural sovereignty. Like all of the other "independent" African nations, Tanzania has remained economically bound by developed capitalist nations. Its dependence on foreign sources of capital investment and loans has dramatically increased in order to enable it to finance government administration as well as development expenditures. The rubric of "aid" disguises the reality of "financial conquest." Foreign institutions provide credit schemes to import goods and services from developed countries. Agribusinesses owned by transnational corporations (TNCs) are the primary beneficiaries of World Bank financing of large-scale agriculture and small peasant crop schemes, such as the tea scheme in Rungwe (discussed below). Loans by the World Bank and other financial institutions are used to create joint ventures which benefit both foreign and national entrepreneurs, but not the laboring classes of peasants, workers, poor traders, poor artisans, and other petty commodity producers. The size of the debt owed to foreign governments and institutions has short-circuited whatever freedom Tanzania once exercised in foreign and domestic policies.[2]

Public and private large-scale commercial and capitalist producers are locked into the production of agricultural and other commodities for the world market. Exports are supposed to provide foreign exchange, which is necessary to repay the growing national debt and to pay for the imports needed in all industrial branches, including agriculture, and in social services and government administration. World prices for agricultural exports have been declining, while the prices for oil and manufactured imports have been rising. These poor terms of trade create ever-growing pressure on the government to extract as much labor as possible from the laboring classes in the production of export crops. At the same time, a growing portion of subsistence needs in the families of laboring classes is obtainable only from the market, with money earned from producing goods and services for the market.

The large-scale public and private sector produces most of the sisal, tea, sugar, wattle, and seedbeans (the beans produced by small commercial producers as well) for export. Peasants produce most of the cotton, coffee, pyrethrum, cashews, and tobacco. National food markets rely on the large-scale public sector for the production of wheat, sugar, and half of the rice that is marketed. More than half of all peasant cultivators, agricultural workers, and animal caretakers are women. Women represent up to 70 percent of cultivators in the younger, most productive age groups in rural areas. Large-scale enterprises and small commercial and rich peasant farmers compete for labor with the peasant sector and with primary commodity producers in general. This has led to what the companies call a "labor crisis," despite extremely high rates of unemployment and underemployment among women and men. The labor shortage they refer to is partly the result of the low wages and poor working conditions on the plantations and estates which workers and peasant workers reject.[3]

According to the 1978 population census, one-fourth of the townswomen in Tanzania were working in wage employment, compared to nearly three-fourths of the townsmen. Half of the townswomen were working in some form of off-the-books, or informal, enterprise, in self-employment, or as casual laborers. The census figures indicate very low percentages of rural women and men in wage employment (2 percent and 12 percent, respectively, in 1978). Women were categorized as family workers or in self-employment (including casual laborers who are misclassified). These statistics are not reliable, however, due to the kinds of categorizations used and the fact that most women are engaged in multiple economic activities. Employers in the state-regulated formal sector, and in the off-the-books sector, rely increas-

DAILY REALITIES

ingly on the system of casual seasonal labor in agriculture and nonagriculture activities. They are also hiring a larger percentage of women on regular and casual terms.[4]

Women are forced to take casual day labor work or to produce for the market, due to the impoverishment they and their families have experienced during the 1970s and early 1980s. Real wages and real producer prices have declined, while the costs of living have risen. Women end up providing an increasing portion of family requirements that are purchased from the market, in addition to the food and other goods and services they have historically provided.[5]

There are very few wage employment opportunities in the formal sector of state-regulated enterprises, and thus intense competition for those jobs among women and men. Women have had to create employment opportunities for themselves in off-the-books activities, which have mushroomed in villages and towns. Women represent more than half of those so engaged, even in the underestimates of the 1978 census. A fortunate few become entrepreneurs on the basis of the exploitation of the labor of other women and men. They have set up cottage industries and sweatshops in the garment industry and in home-brew beer manufacture, food preparation, farming, crop marketing, hotel and restaurant services, and prostitution.[6]

Women entrepreneurs compete with each other, and with laboring women, for access to credit, machinery, raw materials, markets, labor, and land. Entrepreneurs, peasants, workers, and poor traders are increasingly integrated into international and national market relations. Competition is an organic attribute of these market relations. Poor peasant workers and full-time workers also compete for jobs. Rising unemployment and underemployment increase the competition for jobs, and for access to the means of survival as a self-employed producer or trader. Market relations have affected the world of academia and intellectual endeavor as well. Nearly all funding of research and publications originates outside Tanzania. Nationals compete with foreign women on an unequal basis, having less access to education and literature resources and being the victims of racist ideology. This has changed only recently, as a result of demands by African women researchers for a greater share in WID and other research programs, and of the donors' need to "window-dress" their WID programs with "native" spokespersons (see below).

The movement of Tanzanian women into commodity production has contributed to heightened consciousness of their oppression as women within each class.[7] The nature of that oppression varies, however, depending upon class and race. It is impossible to generalize about their gender relations.[8]

THE DEVELOPMENT OF WID

The concept of Women in Development began to be promoted by Western development agencies in the mid-1970s as a response to the growing political unrest in the Third World and the inability of laboring women to maintain their families, especially in Africa. Women peasants resisted forced crop cultivation, forced labor in government projects, forced marketing of crops. Women petty commodity pro-

ducers and workers resisted the efforts of governments to outlaw off-the-books activities like beer brewing, food processing, and prostitution, and entrepreneurs evaded
taxation laws and zonal regulations.[9] These resistances contributed to the drop in
crop sales to official marketing agencies, which affected food supplies and foreign-
exchange earnings. Women's insistence on their right to migrate and to settle in
towns, and to maintain themselves in legal and illegal activities, has apparently
threatened ruling classes in several African countries. Periodic roundups of "unat-
tached" townswomen and attempts to expel them have occurred in Kenya, Tanzania, and Zimbabwe.

I believe that the combination of women's resistance and the inability of laboring
women to maintain their families has threatened the reproduction of the labor force
and the social reproduction of neocolonial power relations. These factors have provoked the development of WID programs and projects in order to intervene on
their behalf. The World Bank policy paper entitled "Recognizing the 'Invisible'—
Women in Development" is representative. In its preface, the then president of the
World Bank noted that the bank intended

> to improve opportunities for women to participate in development and to help them
> overcome some of the economic and social factors that limit their participation in this
> process. . . . Expanding the social, political, and economic opportunities of women
> beyond their traditional roles of motherhood and housekeeping enables them to chan-
> nel their creative abilities over a much broader spectrum of activities.[10]

The mythical imagery about women is obvious in this statement, especially when
applied to Africa—and the policy paper devotes much of its attention to African
women. Women already participate in development. Indeed, laboring women have
resisted further subjugation to unjust economic and political relations. African wom-
en had never been confined to motherhood and housekeeping roles until European
colonialists tried to domesticate middle-class women in this way.

WID programs try to find out about the patterns of self-organization in women's
groups and networks "that have traditionally been important sources of support for
women . . . so that projects can work through them and enhance, rather than
destroy, their potential."[11] The use of feminist jargon about "making the invisible
visible" thereby legitimates an infiltration program to find out more about women's
activities in off-the-books activities and in self-organized groups.

WID denies the reality of class differences among women, and the way these
differences intersect with national and racial differences. Intrahousehold and intra-
class differences between women and men are emphasized, rather than their shared
interests vis-à-vis the women and men in the ruling classes. Completely neglected
are the relationships that have historically developed between men of the dominant
classes and women in the dominated classes, the most oppressive and exploitive
relations of all. One outcome of this neglect is a proliferation of peasant household
studies which examine the sexual division of labor in household activities and the
distribution of whatever small incomes the household members acquire. Totally

absent are studies of, for example, sexual harassment in the workplace and in the villages or towns, and the benefits and profits that large-scale enterprises reap from female labor.

Nearly all bilateral and international agencies now have a WID policy which guides their development policy. Special WID staff are posted to Third World "recipient" countries as liaison to (and to infiltrate?) local women's groups and organizations. The most common outcome is the financing of separate women's projects, which are characteristically low in funding and prestige and ghettoized from overall development plans and programs. The greatest priority has been given to the promotion of "income-earning" projects. The amount of income earned is usually negligible or nonexistent, and at great cost to the participants in terms of labor input.[12] The leaders of these projects often benefit by using their assets for private accumulation and by outright embezzlement.

WID projects are commonly known as Band-Aid efforts in the context of extreme deprivation and need. WID policy has nevertheless been adopted by governmental and nongovernmental (NGO) organizations and departments in the Third World. It fits government efforts to intensify women's labor in production for the market and production to maintain the family. To use Janet Bujra's apt phraseology, WID policy is "urging women to redouble their efforts" without challenging global or national relations of class, nation, and sex. This deepens the oppression and exploitation of laboring women, instead of liberating them. It also enriches a few women who control the money and assets that are funneled through foreign and national agencies.

An example of these outcomes was observed in a sewing group in Tukuyu, the district headquarters of Rungwe District in Mbeya, Tanzania. The group was originally organized by townswomen under the leadership of a local entrepreneur-politician. Several groups had been formed to engage in training, production, and trade. They had succeeded in setting up a shop to sell their goods. The leadership sought to get a Peace Corps volunteer assigned to their groups, ostensibly to promote women's activities and to teach sewing. They were sent a very young, white volunteer who edged out the local tailor who had been the former instructor in all the groups. The tailor had taught the women how to cut designs from cloth without using patterns, which are unavailable in Tanzania. The volunteer relied on patterns she had brought with her. She also provided needles, thread, scissors, and sometimes cloth, all of which were unavailable in local shops. The sewing group in town consisted mainly of lower-middle-class women, by virtue of their husband's positions, and primary school teachers.

The social relations that began to develop in the group were the epitome of neocolonialism. The volunteer talked baby talk to the women, all of whom were much older than she. Some pretended to go along with her maternal condescension, doing a giggling act in return. Others remained silent, presenting her with a stony exterior and making outraged expressions with their eyes. She was trying to teach them how to sew on buttons. Her class included domestic-science teachers who had been teaching women how to sew on buttons for decades. It is doubtful that anyone did not know how. She seemed eventually to get the message that people were dissatisfied with her, because she announced to me in a voice loud enough for group members to hear that

> This is the worst group. I don't like it as much. I like the villagers. They really need help. These women, they're primary school teachers and stuff. Their husbands have good jobs, they've got plenty of clothes . . . the village women don't know how to do anything. They wear dresses torn at the armpits [she gestures under her arm]. I've been teaching women how to sew on buttons for the first time.

The volunteer did not know how to relate on a peer basis with African women, including the tailor who could have taught her a thing or two. At the same time, the group and the leadership were dishonest about their intention, which was to get access to otherwise unobtainable producer goods like needles and thread. The situation had unfair consequences for all concerned.

When women's groups in Tanzania seek assistance from government and NGO agencies, they are urged to focus on income-earning activities. This has been true of the local Community Development Trust Fund, USAID, and the Women to Women group which was initiated by the then Peace Corps director in Tanzania.[13] Researchers are guided, by research proposals prepared by outside donors, to study obstacles to greater intensification of women's labor in production activities and to the commercialization of their work. The United Nations conceptualization of WID imposed itself on the deliberations that resulted from the Copenhagen Conference on Women in 1980 and that preceded the Nairobi Conference in 1985. In Tanzania the planning of a national plan of action for women enabled middle-class and ruling-class women to articulate their own needs to themselves and others, and to coordinate efforts to secure resources from government and foreign agencies. They had to win support for their own priorities, in competition with those of laboring women. The Chang'ombe Seminar of December 1981, which was organized by the government to prepare the national plan of action, was a venue for the struggles that arose between the two perspectives.[14]

The participants in the meeting were sent guidelines that had been set up by the recommendations of the Copenhagen Conference in 1980 and by the UN themes of education, health, and work. The parameters of discussion were meant to cover the development, not the liberation, of women. Representatives of donor agencies attended, but women belonging to the laboring classes were excluded. The main government paper presented by the office of the prime minister of Tanzania concentrated on the kinds of projects that were believed to be attractive to foreign donors.

The two lines were clearly discernible at the meeting, and their spokespersons ended up in intense debate. The WID group focused on discrimination against women in high-level education and employment and on women's "careers." The national press immediately picked up their intentions with a front-page headline that "Women Want Promotions." This kind of issue refers, by definition, to a tiny minority of women. It may be a just demand, but it does not reflect the priorities of the majority of Tanzanian women. It could lead only to a reformist demand for a separate Ministry of Women to "promote the interests of women." Such a ministry would not threaten the status quo that oppresses and exploits laboring women, however. Instead, it would strengthen the status quo by coopting more women into the bureaucracy and technocracy.

Other participants argued that these issues and demands were irrelevant to laboring women, that the plan of action should center on the right to work and the right to a real subsistence wage or income for all women and men. Measures should be adopted to ensure that peasant women benefit from the proceeds of their labor at village and household levels. Women's labor load should be eased by promoting the production and distribution of new kinds of technologies for production and for domestic work. The need for democratic institutions at all levels which recognize and promote the rights of laboring women was also expressed.

The debate between these two different perspectives was not reflected in the final set of recommendations for the plan of action. Spokespersons of the dominant ideology controlled the secretariat and pushed through the WID proposals. Similar confrontations occurred during the preparation for the Nairobi Conference in 1985.

WID in Mbeya Villages and Towns

According to its decentralization policy, each region of Tanzania has been allocated to a different foreign donor to fund regional integrated development plans and to coordinate their implementation. The sole exception is Rukwa region, which was allocated to the Institute of Resource Assessment at the University of Dar es Salaam. FAO took charge of Mbeya region, with DANIDA (Denmark) funding. Mbeya is one of the southern Cinderella regions that were opened up recently by the building of the railroad and road to Zambia. Major export and food crops are produced in Mbeya in large-scale plantations and farms as well as in peasant farms. Women's labor has been intensified in the production of all crops, in the provision of firewood and water, and in head transport of crops, wood, and other goods. During the 1950s, women began to leave the farms in Rungwe, a district within Mbeya region, for the towns or the copper belt in search of a better life. Women traders in bananas, other foodstuffs, secondhand clothes, and other goods are a dynamic force in towns and villages today. Women peasants in Rungwe, for example, are also highly politicized, partly as a result of struggles they have fought over crop choice and trade.[15]

A special women's consultancy in which I served was set up by the co-director of the Mbeya RIDEP (Regional Integrated Development and Economic Planning) program in 1981.[16] It was one among several short-term consultancies set up to carry out research and to provide plans for particular topics. Both foreign and national experts were hired. The women's consultancy was the only one whose membership was restricted to national citizens, and, initially, to native researchers. The concept of "native" corresponds with colonial ideological categories of race. The rationale for this exclusiveness was that the women's issue was too sensitive to be dealt with any other way.[17]

The search for native women to carry out WID work illustrates a policy that has now been adopted by most foreign donors. They have correctly perceived that WID is not widely accepted in Africa, and they need to have national spokespersons to win support and to window-dress their activities. The donors prefer to associate themselves with women who epitomize their view of the African Woman. They are thoroughly confused when confronted by citizens of Swahili, Arab, Asian, mixed-race, or European origin, some of whose ancestors date back hundreds of centuries in eastern Africa. Believing their own racist ideology, the representatives of such agencies do not comprehend that ideological notions of race have no biological reality, and that political outlooks and ideological perspectives are defined neither by biology nor by origins.[18] At issue are competing and opposite views about the nature of women's oppression and women's liberation.

The impact of all the carrots of aid that WID programs were dangling before regional, district, and village leaders was clear during a RIDEP tour of six rural district headquarters and ten villages. The district and regional authorities originally planned that the women's team would visit three villages in each district. This would have given us a total of about 20 minutes per village, which was totally inadequate for the kind of women's assemblies we intended to organize. In order for us to spend more time in the villages we did visit, the number was reduced to one per district. The authorities were necessarily upset with our reaction, because they had been under extreme pressure from local entrepreneurs and leaders to "spread it around," that is, our visit and the hope of foreign assistance later. Village leaders competed with one another to get on the regional list for our itinerary.

Leaders and rank-and-file villagers expected the usual form of a dignitary's visit. Typically, the official delegations sweep into a village and are taken directly to a shop or an office for consultations with local leaders, having no contact whatsoever with the rank-and-file except that they consume a feast provided by village women and sometimes watch a "traditional dance" if time allows. The actual consultations center on the presentation of a shopping list by village leaders—which nearly always includes sewing machines—and matching promises from the dignitaries.

We used an *uchokozi*—a provocative set of statements—to redefine the purpose of the women's assemblies. Women were invited to talk about any subject that interested them: women's work, their lives, their position in the village government, women's groups; land, credit, and other inputs in farming; labor proceeds and their distribution, problems of "villagization" and the solutions they had adopted; or changes in women's lives, beginning in the colonial period. In every case, leaders (women and men) tried to answer on behalf of the rank-and-file women. Usually this was not a deliberate attempt to hide anything, but simply that the leaders were accustomed to dominating such gatherings. Women villagers pointed out later that this was the first time such an assembly of women had been held, where leaders and experts came to listen to the people. In our system, once women seized control of the meetings, men were allowed to raise questions or respond to challenges, and very heated exchanges ensued.[19]

The following list shows the main issues about which women villagers talked at length. The numbers in parentheses indicate at how many villages (from a total of 10) each issue was considered at length.

- Control over cash proceeds in the family (7 villages)
- Supplies of commodities like soap and sugar, and inputs for women's shops and other activities (7)
- Too much work in farming and domestic labor, especially in pounding and water collection (6)
- Women have to pay for food and children's clothes (3)
- Women are afraid to enter official politics, because they will be beaten by husbands and scorned by fellow women (3)
- Male discrimination against women in elections and in village assembly meetings (3)
- Poor leadership among women (3)
- Withdrawal of male labor from farming and into migrant labor or nonfarm activities (2)
- Polygamy (2)
- Wife beating, loss of labor proceeds, and oppressive work force women to leave their families in protest and go to towns (2)

Below are examples of some of the statements made by women villagers in public meetings which numbered 250 people in one village (150 women included), 175 in another (125 women), and never less than 10 or 15 people. The dignitaries included high-level regional and district authorities of government, the party, and UWT (*Jumuiya ya Umoja wa Wanawake Tanzania*, the national women's organization). The courage with which the women spoke contradicted the assertions made by leaders before each meeting that rank-and-file women were too shy or backward to speak. The name of the village is given in parentheses.

"The husband is the boss— he decides how much cash from coffee to give the wife." (Mbalizi)

"Isongole! Trouble! The children have no clothes. Laborers make 600 per month, but it doesn't enter the house." (Isongole)

"We only tolerate things. Who will you leave your children with? There is trouble in all of Tanzania. We advise the men. But at the end of the month, he has no news about what the children eat for two weeks. When the money is finished, he comes back to quarrel." (Isongole)

"Will they eat gold? There is no food. What will you eat?" (Kiwanja)

"Our husbands marry other women with money." (Uyole)

"We work from morning till night." (Uyole)

"We have received no help. To build a house we need help. We asked, the men refused. But we help to build the school and the party building. If it's our farm, refusal." (Isongole)

"We have no soap. . . . We smell . . . just imagine, once a year to bathe with soap, is that nice?" (Halungu, by a very old and beautiful woman who danced as she sang this out)

"We are afraid to talk, afraid to be beaten by husbands who say, 'You should be home cooking!' Also fellow women attack you." (Uyole)

"We haven't been educated enough by UWT [on how to speak in public and to hold office]." (Mbalizi)

"They throw out the one with voice, and choose the one who is quiet" [talking about nominees for village leadership from among the women]. (Isongole)

"Some say, 'Down with men.' " (Isongole)

"Some women cannot tolerate things, but you remember the children. You return. In the end you go crazy." (Isongole)

These individual statements reflect the processes of pauperization and proletarianization discussed earlier. They reveal growing tensions in family and village and competition among women for attachments to men in order to get some kind of payment for their services. The way women have been disenfranchised in official politics by fellow women, as well as by male leadership, is also shown.[20] Open confrontations over conflicting perspectives such as the one described below illustrate powerfully the impact of market relations on all aspects of people's lives, and the heightened consciousness that is developing among women of different classes.

In village X, where 175 people met, 125 of whom were women, a debate arose over whether women's groups received adequate assistance from the village government. This led to a general criticism about the village leadership and the organization of production. At the beginning, a spokesperson for the village power bloc told us that women had organized group activities that included growing maize and running a shop and a beer club. They reported that the income was being saved. At that, a critical voice rose, saying, "We tried to establish groups, but we don't have a teacher." Someone else said that women had no time to weed their women's group farm, because they had to work on the village farm, "otherwise—a fine! We are oppressed at the village farm and at home." Another pointed out that "the men refuse [women's groups], they object, they say we are looking for men, maybe we don't learn anything there, we should not come."

One of the very vocal women was able to move the assembly to cheer. Her words were not meant to be taken literally, and contained a message that was critical of the neglect peasants and other villagers have experienced from the ruling classes, and probably of the way they accumulate wealth on the basis of women's labor.

> "Fellow women, our mourning has been heard, we have had ideas about development from a long time ago, but we didn't know where to start and what direction to take. Now our leaders have remembered us. Let us push ourselves to keep up with them, let us not be behind them, so that they leave us behind and we lose our way. Let development be today, not tomorrow, that of yesterday has passed us by."

The villagers use irony, as revealed, for example, when asked how many women are on the village council. Their reply was, "We can't answer. The chairman knows. He doesn't call us." The village branch secretary of UWT tried to protect the village leadership by disagreeing with this, and said, "If we need help, we go to the village secretary. With regard to production, we are not oppressed. We work for the village two days and one day for UWT." Her statement was soundly hissed by the rank-and-file women.

Another rank-and-file critic said that it was difficult to get access to the village tractor from the leaders. We found out that the village farm was one hundred acres, compared to the women's joint farm which was one and one-half acres. The ward secretary (a "ward" is a cluster of villages) said, "That's not bad. The village farm is theirs [the women's], it's for everybody together. It is not for distribution of proceeds, but rather to produce more wealth." The reactions of the women were mixed. It was a highly controversial statement. First of all, the leaders control the proceeds of the village farm, despite official policy, so it clearly does not belong to the women. Second, rank-and-file members of village cooperative activities and of other kinds of cooperatives often favor distribution of some proceeds because of their desperate need for cash and their suspicion of corruption among the leaders.[21] The leaders favor reinvestment, partly because this is official policy. In the case of this particular village, it was later learned that the capital that had been initially set aside by the women for the women's shop was stolen in 1978.

The critical perspective that was presented in this assembly linked together women's oppression in the family and their exploitation in the village and wider society. The competition between women's groups and village cooperative activities for control of women's labor and the proceeds of their labor is a major issue. This point was also raised in the other villages where some form of village cooperative activities had developed.[22] Although rank-and-file women villagers perceived the way they were oppressed by men in their families and class, they concentrated on class issues, on the way laboring women and men were exploited by others. Once we recognize the way that patriarchal forms of family relations are relied upon by international and national rulers to control women and youth and to organize the labor process in peasant economies, then the link between intra-household oppression and class exploitation becomes understandable. This link permeates the perspectives of laboring women, who become very impatient with WID ideas that try to make them focus on intra-household relations. Intra-household relations alone do not explain why these women lack soap, tractors, food, and a subsistence wage.

Our final report on women and development in Mbeya presented the different perspectives and quoted extensively from the village assemblies. The recommendations reflected the needs and interests of laboring women as we perceived them. We rejected the idea that the first priority was to promote new income-earning activities, which had been an assumption made by the RIDEP directors. The problem laboring women faced was their lack of control over labor proceeds at village and household levels and the poor returns for their work. We recommended some form of proceed sharing at village and household levels, and the promotion of self-organized village groups led by rank-and-file village women. These positions were also adopted in the draft RIDEP plan (1982), which integrated all of the separate consultancy reports. However, the FAO preparatory mission that produced the final RIDEP plan was highly critical of the draft plan's "emphasis" on women (sic). It especially opposed the proposal of payment to the producer, and gave the following reasons:

> As regards the proposals for initiating change in the present pattern of income distribution between members of a single family, the Mission considered that such measures would be difficult to implement. In addition, *the effects of income redistribution on social welfare within a community has yet to be determined,* e.g. the effects on the aged and children. [My emphasis]

The mission was also alarmed about the growing resistance by women to oppression and exploitation:

> The effects of the national education system [*sic*] on the long-term future of the social and economic condition of rural women need also to be analyzed, particularly in relation to their attitudes towards performing traditional activities (such as weeding, etc.) and the effects of education as presently designed on production and family welfare.[23]

These are damaging statements. They reveal the donor agency's intention to keep laboring women in their place as oppressed unpaid family labor and/or cheap casual labor, and to rely on male-dominant patterns of family relations to "discipline" them. Women's resistance against oppressive family social relations is perceived to be potentially revolutionary, not only by foreign consultants but also by top national leaders. When our recommendation of "payment to the tiller" was presented at a regional meeting, top bureaucrats rejected it. One expressed their views as follows, "Whatever happens, we don't want revolution. If women have their own money, why will they marry?"

NOTES

1. Claire C. Robertson and Martin A. Klein, eds., *Women and Slavery in Africa* (Madison: University of Wisconsin Press, 1983).

2. See Barbara Dinham and Colin Hines, *Agribusiness in Africa* (London: Earth Resources Institute, 1983); Marjorie Mbilinyi, "The Impact of the Economic Crisis on Women's Employment, Wages and Incomes," Professorial Lecture presented at the University of Dar es Salaam, 1985; and Ruth Meena, "Foreign Aid and the Question of Women's Liberation," *The African Review* 11, no. 1 (1984): 1–13.

3. Mbilinyi, "The Impact of the Economic Crisis on Women's Employment, Wages and Incomes."

4. Ibid.

5. D. Bryceson and M. Kirimbai, eds., *Subsistence or Beyond? Money-earning Activities of Women in Rural Tanzania* (Dar es Salaam: BRALUP and the Union of Women of Tanzania, 1980). See also Bertha Koda, "The Kighare and Ntenga Women's Projects"; Marjorie Mbilinyi, "The Politics of Cooperation Organization in Isonge Village"; Asseny Muro, "The Mawella Women's Project"; Anna Nkebukwa, "The Performance of UWT-Tuke Consumer's Cooperative Society, Morogoro"; Alice G. Nkhoma, "Beer-brewing as an Income-Generating Activity in Utengule Village, Mbeya Region"; Zubeia Tumbo-Masabo, "Palm-Oil Production and Fish Trade at Ujiji"; Ulla Vuorela, "Economic Projects for Women in Manyoni Town, Singida," all in *Cooperation or Exploitation? Experiences of Women's Initiatives in Tanzania*, ed. Marjorie Mbilinyi: (Geneva: International Labor Organisation, in preparation).

6. The following papers examine the activities of women entrepreneurs and businesswomen: Freda U. Chale and Generose H. Ngonyani, "Report on a Survey of Cooperative Income-Generation Projects for Women and Its Impact on the Welfare of Children and the Family," paper presented to the BRALUP Workshop on Women and Development, 1979; Muro, "The Mawella Women's Project," Nkebukwa, "The Performance of UWT-Tuke Consumer's Cooperative Society, Morogoro," Nkhoma, "Beer-brewing as an Income-Generating Activity in Utengule Village, Mbeya Region"; Vuorela, "Economic Projects for Women in Manyoni Town, Singida."

7. Janet M. Bujra, " 'Urging Women to Redouble their Efforts . . .': Gender and Capitalist Transformation in Africa," in *Women and Class in Africa*, ed. Clair Robertson and Iris Berger (New York: Holmes and Meier, 1984).

8. I thank Barbara Fields for helping me to clarify and strengthen my position on this and other questions presented in this essay. See Part One in Ophelia Mascarenhas and Marjorie Mbilinyi, *Women in Tanzania* (Uppsala: Scandinavian Institute of African Studies, 1983).

9. See the case studies in Mbilinyi, ed., *Cooperation or Exploitation?* and Part One of Mascarenhas and Mbilinyi, *Women in Tanzania*.

10. World Bank, "Recognizing the 'Invisible'—Women in Development" (Washington, D.C.: 1979).

11. Ibid.

12. For examples, see Bryceson and Kirimbai, eds., *Subsistence or Beyond?* and Mbilinyi, ed., *Cooperation or Exploitation?*

13. See Mbilinyi, ed., *Cooperation or Exploitation?*

14. Personal observation as one of the seminar participants. For more details, see Marjorie Mbilinyi, " 'Women in Development' Ideology: The Promotion of Competition and Exploitation," *The African Review* 11, no. 1 (1984): 14–33.

15. Mwaiseje Polisya, *Banana Trade and the Position of Women in Rungwe District*, M.A. diss. University of Dar es Salaam, 1984.

16. Mbilinyi and Kabelele, "Women in the Rural Development of Mbeya Region."

17. Personal communication from the FAO co-director of Mbeya RIDEP.

18. For further analysis of the ideology of race, see Barbara J. Fields, "Ideology and Race in American History," in *Region, Race, and Reconstruction: Essays in Honor of C. Vann Woodward*, ed. J. Morgan Kousser and James M. McPherson (New York: Oxford University Press, 1982).

19. See Mbilinyi and Kabelele, "Women in the Rural Development of Mbeya Region."

20. Marie Antoinette Oomen-Myin, *Involvement of Rural Women in Village Development in Tanzania: A Case Study in Morogoro District* (Morogoro: Sokoine Agriculture University, Department of Agricultural Education and Extension, 1981).

21. Mbilinyi, "The Politics of Cooperative Organization in Isonge Village"; Nkebukwa, "The Performance of UWT-Tuke Consumer's Cooperative Society, Morogoro"; Nkhoma, "Beer-brewing as an Income-Generating Activity in Utengule Village, Mbeya Region"; Vuorela, "Economic Projects for Women in Manyoni Town, Singida."

22. Mbilinyi and Kabelele, "Women in the Rural Development of Mbeya Region."

23. Cited in a report shared with me by the former FAO co-director of Mbeya RIDEP.

Little Women and "Cinderella": Sisters and Competition

TONI A. H. McNARON

Little Women and "Cinderella" are powerful and contradictory stories, known to most women by their teenage years. In each, sisters are the focus; one tells of a group of girls working together to support one another's dreams, never doing worse than engaging in playful fun at a sister's expense; the other depicts two blood sisters fighting each other like proverbial cats and dogs, able to act concertedly only against their poor stepsister. I believe these two mythic tales jostle each other uncomfortably in many a girl's heart as she attempts to relate to her sister as a member of her family.

In this essay, I want to discuss some of the patterns that seem to obtain in such relationships, patterns found both in historical cases and in present sister pairs. I will emphasize three specific patterns: (1) sisters deciding, albeit unconsciously, not to develop all of their potential, letting one sister have the field in certain respects, minimizing competition; (2) sisters bonding strongly at an early age in order to resist family or outside pressures toward competition; (3) sisters simply competing, openly or indirectly, for parental affection, peer approval, and worldly recognition. Needless to say, many sisters will not fit into any of these groups: some sisters I have spoken with recount ignoring a younger sister as much as possible, thereby not competing, but also losing opportunities for closeness; some sisters grow up in families that support harmonious, warm relationships and so escape most competitive pressures. But the usual picture does conform to one or another of the patterns suggested here. While the examples of sisters drawn from history are all white and middle class, the group of contemporary sisters surveyed includes black women, women of widely varying ages and class backgrounds, and, in at least one instance, twins.

I recently put together a series of essays focusing on sisters' relationships *(The*

Sister Bond: A Feminist View of a Timeless Connection). Some of the theoretical material in this piece comes from my prior work on that collection. My interest in sisters is based in two realities of my own life. First, I have a sister for whom I feel a complex web of emotions, and I thought studying other pairs of sisters might help me clarify my own relationship. And second, I am a lesbian feminist, intensely drawn to any woman-to-woman relationship, and particularly to the sister bond because of its special intimacies.

Girls growing up in the same house are presented with ample opportunities to compete. Sometimes these are quite overt: one sister is called the apple of her father's eye or her mother's little darling or princess; one sister is told repeatedly about how wonderful her (usually) older sibling is and asked why she cannot be more like her. More often, the lures toward competition rather than cooperation are covert, even invisible. Such situations are hard to work free from since their webs elude everyone.

Covert competition comes in many disguises, one or more of which is surely familiar to most of us who have sisters.[1] One sister is very pretty hence popular with boys, while the other makes good grades in school and is seen as brainy. Each sister will envy the other. The pretty one will at times feel like a flyweight, knowing as she grows into adolescence and early adulthood the terror that accompanies female beauty—beauty is fleeting and once gone, where will her power reside? The smart one will at times feel plain, socially dull, inadequate as a female—knowing, as she matures, a chill that comes from realizing that most eligible males are intimidated by bright women. The two sisters may never tell each other how they feel, or may do so only after both are away from home, living personally rewarding lives. But their relationship is poisoned by doubt and jealousy. More than likely, neither girl will take her pain to a parent, since at some level each wants the approval of those central figures.

As for the alternative pattern—mutual support and cooperation—it often grows out of the sisters' realization that by working together they stand a better chance of surviving. Signs of such a substructure include such phenomena as private languages used by sisters, incomprehensible to anyone else in the household; clothing, jewelry, or toys shared by voluntary agreement rather than parental enforcement; secret games, stories, or other framed activities that effectually shut out the grown-ups, and even the male siblings. When such an alliance is formed in childhood, it tends to persist throughout a lifetime, unshaken by adult choices which, under a competitive model, can erase whatever tenuous attachment may have existed earlier between sisters.

My own case can serve as a beginning to understanding this deep and complex bond. My sister was almost seventeen when I was born, so at first I lumped her with other adults. When I realized that she was not exactly like my parents and that we were sisters, I liked her better. But I seldom confided in her. My early feelings can best be defined as a combination of awe and fear. An event that occurred when I was about nine strongly influenced my silence. It was late at night and my mother was lecturing me about something that I thought trivial. When she went on longer than I could bear it, I decided to walk away. I'd never exercised so much power in relation to my mother. In order to win and keep her love, it seemed necessary to stand still and take her talk. But walk away I did, right into the breakfast room off to one side of our kitchen. The refrigerator was there and I needed something soft and comforting. I didn't bother to turn on the kitchen light, figuring the refrigerator bulb would do. As I opened the door, my fury at my mother spilled out into what I thought was the empty night air. I said, under my breath so she couldn't possibly hear me, "Go to hell." Scared from so heady a declaration of personal independence, I went straight for the vanilla ice cream. As I carried the container toward the sink to get a bowl, I saw my sister standing near the back porch where it seems she had been all the time. She had heard me and was shocked. "How can you say such a thing about Mamie when she gives you everything and asks nothing?" By siding with my mother, my sister dampened any hopes I might have had of taking her into my confidence about what it sometimes felt like to be in our family.

As I matured, my sister came to like me for my quick mind and ready vocabulary which she spent time making even larger. While I received encouragement from her, I seldom felt at ease. I remember conversations at the Sunday dinner table when I was a teenager. My mother invariably got around to my seeming lack of interest in dating. When she would say, "You have to find some nice young man to take care of you when I'm gone," my sister would counter with, "Oh, but she doesn't have to depend on a man—she can equip herself to take care of herself by becoming a professional and being very smart." At such times, I felt grateful for her belief in me, though I later suffered by comparison: She was very smart and yet also had been able to attract boys by the droves.

If I envied her that chameleon quality, she envied me my physical energy and drive. As signs of this changed from playing outside as long as possible to becoming a first-rate athlete in high school, I began to hear tinges of sarcasm when my sister praised me. "You really are developing a bicep, while little me remains a weakling, you see," or "How can you stand to get so dirty and full of perspiration just before dinner—but then I forget, you are the athlete in the family."

All other arenas for competition paled before the central one: our mother. My sister had had my mother's full attention for over sixteen years, so I felt it was hopeless for me to try to catch up. She knew the same words as my mother so they could talk all the time, fast and happily, or so it seemed to me as a small child. They left the house together while I had to stay behind in diapers and later in rompers or seersucker playsuits. Shut out from so many of their adventures, I assumed my mother had less energy for me.

For my sister's part, she says she never felt anything but happy about my coming onto the scene, but that is belied by a story my mother told often and with great humor. It seems that when my sister heard of my imminent arrival, she said, "I will not speak to the brat if I cannot name it." My mother let her do precisely that, and so I am called "Toni" by my sister's choice. It interests me now to consider both the source and nature of my name. To the extent that names help determine our personalities, I am deeply bound to my sister rather than my parents. And by choosing a name that would suit equally well regardless of my sex, she inadvertently allowed me a less militant history around role expectations.

Assuming my sister is not categorically different from most other human beings, she must have felt angry and scared at my mother's unexpected announcement. After all, at 40 a woman is not likely to bear children. My sister was enmeshed with her mother, and the presence of a third party could not fail to strike fear in her heart. When I ask my sister whether she helped take care of me, I get no answers. The closest I've come is her admission to liking me more once I could carry on a conversation. While it may be true that my sister is unsure how to behave around small children, I believe that she shied away from me those first few years out of an unwillingness to acknowledge my presence as a wedge in her relationship with her mother.

As I have argued elsewhere, one sister often allows the other to carry certain qualities or behaviors, thereby freeing her to cultivate more fully other qualities or behaviors.[2] This partial development of the self may also be seen as a coping mechanism, a way of managing competition. One way for two or more persons not to compete is for them to agree, albeit unconsciously, that no one of them will try to do or be everything. By facilitating such a complementarity, sisters often sustain very close bonds. Each becomes terribly important to the other, since without their tacit agreement, various life decisions would be made more difficult if not impossible. Again I can best illustrate by citing the case of my own sister and me. As I've said, she was able both to succeed in school and to attract boys. While at the conscious level I envied her this feat, at a much deeper level I could let her be the one in our family who did that. Then I could be at liberty to develop other parts of my self, including physical coordination and an intellectual focus. Similarly, while my sister has often spoken of how much she would love to travel and to be independent, she has almost never acted on those wishes. Choosing to live with our mother, even after marrying, my sister has seldom left home. When she has, she has returned at the earliest possible moment, having experienced acute homesickness. I, on the other hand, began traveling at the end of my junior year in college and do so often. I have achieved a high degree of independence, thereby relieving my sister from having to do so. And her need to stay close relieved me of the guilt I might have felt for leaving home, especially once my mother was widowed.

We have each constructed lives that, if not exactly what we might have dreamed, have been less stressful than they would have been if we had felt it necessary to push through our ambivalences. We have also avoided direct competition by stepping aside to "let sister do it." I find much evidence, from both historical study and current data, to suggest that many sister pairs or groups function similarly. Perhaps if we all grew up in a culture whose fundamental values were less aggressive, competition would recede or fade away altogether. But we do not, and if we wish to form genuine bonds with other human beings, we must find alternative modes of interaction. This unspoken bargain between sisters seems to me to be one of the more effective modes, even taking into account that it may in some cases inhibit realization of one's fullest self.

I believe the bond between sisters constitutes one of the deepest connections in a woman's life. Because it is exclusively female, it remains relatively unexamined in the literature. A cursory look through the library catalogue shows that existing studies on competition within families focus on so-called sibling rivalry where it involves brothers or a brother and sister. Furthermore, the theories concerning such competition will probably not serve when we think about two or more sisters, since any woman-to-woman dynamic has to be taken out of the prevailing context if we hope to develop new ideas.

We all need to be reflected by others, and a sister offers one the closest image of oneself that life is apt to give. Hence having a sister tantalizes us to think we can actually achieve that level of oneness which we all desire and which the culture promises us if we follow its heterosexist rules. Yet one's sister is clearly entirely separate and different from anyone else, even if she is a twin. This tangle causes many sisters to feel charged emotions, since being so close to realizing an illusion only to have it denied causes acute confusion, even anger.

I want to look at the bonds between some famous sister pairs and then look at what sisters today say about themselves, their sisters, and competition. If we think back in time, we can list sisters who had close bonds or were central to each other.[3] The stories in *The Sister Bond* can further our understanding of the complex ways in which sisters handle the problem of competition.

The Nightingale girls, Florence and Parthenope, offer a clear case of sisters unable to resist the competitive model in their relationship with each other or their parents. Each girl was favored by one of her parents, but Florence had the advantage of being her father's darling. Consequently her mind was developed and her independence encouraged in ways not possible for Parthenope, given her mother's conventional attitude toward female maturation. As Florence struck out in ever wider directions, Parthenope clung more closely to her mother for protection and solace. Simultaneously Parthenope became obsessed with needing Florence's presence in order to be healthy and happy. When Florence decided to leave home to study and practice her nursing, Parthenope fell into a decline that progressed to an outburst which did indeed affect her health. Florence's mother begged her to delay her departure just until Parthe was better. Florence had watched her sister closely enough to know that if she relented in this instance, the illness could well drag out indefinitely. With her father's blessing, Florence kept to her plans, departing her home amid efforts literally to pull her back.

Hurt and angry at her adored sister, Parthenope joined her mother in casting aspersions on Florence's efforts to heal the sick and wounded, calling her "no proper woman" and similar culturally loaded terms. Needless to say, by this time Florence had little tenderness for Parthenope, and even wrote and published a short, ostensibly fictional, work about a devouring sister. In their old age, however, when Parthenope was genuinely ill and after each had made some efforts to reconcile, Florence of her own volition came and nursed her sister until her death.

The point of this sad story may well be that parental influence plays a crucial role in whether sisters grow up feeling rivalries or a sense of cooperation. Parents can so easily encourage the former, even without intending to. The Nightingales were not evil or even bad parents. They simply could not see the rift building between their two young girls as the (valued) father smiled more on one while the (devalued) mother leaned more toward the other. So we see a sisterly bond of great intensity turned sour and made into an unhealthy dependency from which the stronger sister had little choice but to flee. Only years later could they know anything like affection or compassion, and then it may have been only on Florence's part.

The Dickinson sisters, Emily and Lavinia, and the Stephen sisters, Virginia (Woolf) and Vanessa (Bell), offer fascinating studies of sisters coping with potential competition by working out a system in which each has a distinctive and accepted role. In each case, the sisters remained close only by fulfilling their function, by not stepping over an invisible but well-understood line separating each from the other.

Emily loved her sister deeply, but also felt that her parents' disapproval came down more heavily on herself than on Vinnie, who more docilely learned to sew and clean and cook. Determined not to let anything come between them, Emily established a kind of household myth in which she was the writer while Vinnie was the domestic creature. We have no record of Vinnie's feelings about this arrangement, but she acquiesced, seemingly out of a deep love for Emily. We know from Dickinson's letters that in daily life, the two women did not always play their parts. Emily loved to bake bread, surely something better placed within Vinnie's purview; Vinnie was the first person to whom Emily showed many of her poems because she so valued her sister's critical acumen and honesty. It was as though, once the myth was safely in place, behavior could veer outside its boundaries. If asked, either would have fallen back into the prearranged plan, telling the outside and indeed the inside world that Emily was the reclusive writer, Vinnie the more social and domestic of the two.

Since Emily constructed the story and since her role was the more dignified and serious in society's eyes, Vinnie may have resented her assignment to second-class status. Certainly Emily depended upon conventional notions of roles, casting herself as the "male" and Vinnie as the "female." But their love and devotion seems to have been stronger than the conventions within which they placed themselves. In letter after letter, Emily makes it abundantly clear that without her sister she would wither emotionally and artistically. I find it significant that by taking matters into their own hands, the sisters were able to steer clear of the kinds of poisonous competition offered them by their temperaments and their surroundings.[4]

Similarly, Virginia Stephen worshipped her older sister, Vanessa, but also painfully felt their differences. In Virginia's eyes, Nessa was the beauty (like their mother) while she was scrawny, awkward, and plain. From Vanessa's point of view, Virginia was quicker-witted, deeper, a genius. These girls had then the perfect invitation to compete. While unable to escape it totally, they managed to reduce the tension greatly by developing their artistic talents in two different media—words for Virginia; line, shape, and color for Vanessa. Though Woolf's writings belie her often-stated ignorance about painting, she insisted that Nessa was the one with the eye and she with the ear. Complementarily, Vanessa loved literature, read enthusiastically, and gave Woolf excellent literary criticism of her prose, but always put herself down as not really knowing how to judge the written word—that was Virginia's forte.

As artists, then, these sisters stayed clear of competitive traps. As women, however, they did less well. Virginia's sense of inferiority persisted throughout her life, made worse by her husband Leonard's decision that she was not "fit" to be a mother. Wanting children very much, Virginia saw herself as even less of a whole woman than she had when her primary criterion was only physical beauty and attractiveness. When Vanessa had three lovely children, Virginia found herself lacking by comparison. Quite often Vanessa left her sons with Virginia (and Leonard) while she vacationed in sunny Italy with her lover, Duncan Grant. The boys adored their Aunt Virginia, who seems to have taken wonderful care of them, materially and spiritually. Ironically, this reality did nothing to dent her inferior picture of herself as an incomplete woman, being without the children she very much wanted.

Virginia never felt equal to her sister. She seems to have cared more for Vanessa than Vanessa did for her. Her letters, frequent and full of self-effacing references, testify to this. She often lived within walking or biking distance of Vanessa, and would have liked to see her daily. But she wrote tortured notes in which she would say she could come for lunch or tea or dinner, only to retreat in embarrassment, saying Nessa would probably be busy with other guests or her work or her children. When Vanessa traveled, she wrote infrequently, a fact that hurt Virginia deeply. But whatever anger she felt was kept carefully under control. Virginia clearly cared more about keeping her sister's affection, even if it was less than she wanted, than about standing up for her rightful consideration—and this from a woman reputed to have had one of the sharpest tongues in London.

Lest we conclude that too many sister pairs have actively competed or formed contorted alliances which caused one or both considerable discomfort, I want to talk about two early-twentieth-century American sisters who seem to have been truly cooperative. Edith and Grace Abbott grew up in a supportive, loving household with parents who were intellectually and politically progressive. They may even have been less invested than was typical for their time in cultural norms for gender behavior. In any event, both parents seemed to have encouraged both children. The results were a close family and an even closer sisterhood.

Grace and Edith not only developed professional lives, but were active in the same profession: social work. One was slightly more effective in public, so she made the speeches and dealt with officials. The slightly more retiring one wrote policies, administered programs, and handled other delicate matters. But neither saw herself as more or less central to the success of their overall scheme, which became no less than making social work a true profession rather than something women with random training did out of the goodness of their hearts. Neither sister married, and they were devoted to each other throughout their lives. When Grace died, Edith never quite recovered. Though she carried through certain of their joint projects, she lacked the heart and drive that had clearly come from her partnership with her sister.[5]

If we look at what present-day sisters say about their relationships with each other, we often find very similar data. In questionnaires administered by several researchers,[6] women say that, though they have difficulties with their sisters and have competed from childhood, the connection between them is worth struggling to preserve except in rare cases. Perhaps the most significant response to inquiries about the sister bond concerns the influence of parents on it.[7] In cases where children have felt encouraged by one or both parents to be close, the sister relationship has progressed easily and has endured all sorts of pressures in adult life. Conversely, where sisters have felt parental apathy or fear about bonding, or where parents have actively worked against close ties, sisters have most often failed each other emotionally. At best, in such circumstances, the women have achieved surface relationships, but have missed the intimacy that lies behind statements like this one:

> I have loved some women more passionately [than I have my sisters] because of their differences from me and probably because of the incest taboo, but my sisters have remained beloved longest. They allowed me to trust and love women as my parents did. But the sisters helped me to learn how to treat friends, how to be disinterested, to love who friends become, to work in groups with women, to support women. Theirs is a steadiness which mirrors what I think I have in my marriage—it grows and is lifelong. We are connected. They are the river which supports me and my other women friends as we float and swim along.[8]

What these stories from the past and present teach us about how sisters deal with competition is the crucial role parents can have in the eventual path taken by the girls. If one or both adults encourage bonding between sisters, then the sisters are much more likely to find ways around or through the temptations to rival each other. But if these same adults discourage, however subtly, real connection between their children, then the girls succumb all too easily to the readily available invitations to compete. An obvious extension of this pattern occurs when parents themselves model competitive behavior in their own interactions within the home or in the outside world.

Even when sisters do compete with one another, consciously or unconsciously, they express sadness and pain about the resulting rifts and distance between them. And, as in several of the cases cited here, they often go to unhealthy lengths to circumvent possible competition, even if that means only partial self-development. Willingness to stunt the self bespeaks a compelling need to bond. For many women, their connection with their sisters stands in importance just below their connection with their mothers. Relationships involving only women threaten the patriarchy for sound reasons. They represent the only situations in our culture that exclude men, and since history has taught men the power of gender exclusion, many males fear such bonds. As for the women involved, they experience a degree of intimacy not possible elsewhere.

In our quest to know ourselves, we seek mirrors in others. The romantic line about seeing oneself in the beloved's eyes does not persist out of mere convention. When a girl or young woman looks at her blood sister, she comes very close to seeing herself. Yet her sister is also inescapably other. I believe this paradox lies at the heart of the intensity that usually accompanies relations between sisters. The bond carries the illusion of total connection at the same time that it painfully reinforces the truth that each of us is finally separate from everyone else. If we cannot achieve union with a sister, with whom, then?

This intensity also explains the bitterness that does not fade with age or time if sisters have not and cannot make peace with one another. Recently, I talked with my sister over the phone on her sixty-fifth birthday. In the course of our conversation, I told her about Susan's and my putting up our 40-odd storm windows for winter. Her response was, "Oh, I will never understand why you do that, I find such activity essentially futile and redundant." Later, I told her I had sent flowers to our mother's grave to mark her birthday. After a cursory acknowledgment that my gesture was nice, my sister launched into a recital of all the times she had called the florist or cemetery to have work done around the plot. At the time, I felt cut down; upon reflection and talk with friends, I realized that both her responses were competitive—in the case of the windows, getting across to me that she is more advanced in her thinking, and in the case of the cemetery, that she is more attentive, hence more loving of our mother.

So the lures do not vanish, nor does the sting that accompanies giving way to them. When other people react to me in competitive ways, I slough it off with a sentence or two about feminist process. I go away from such exchanges sure that my way is best for me. With my sister, there is no such clarity or calm. I just feel cut down, hurt, and angry. Such feelings do not accompany distant relationships; they are the stuff of our oldest, most tangled, and probably most precious bonds.

NOTES

1. I do not believe that brothers and sisters experience such relatively subtle pulls, since historical gender distinctions ensure bald-face competition more often than not. I remember a friend telling me about a fight her son and daughter, separated by four years, had. They fought fiercely over a scrap of scratch paper so small no one could have used it for much of anything.

2. For a fuller discussion of this idea, see my introduction to *The Sister Bond: A Feminist View of a Timeless Connection* (Elmsford, N.Y.: Pergamon Press, 1985.)

3. For a fascinating discussion of these sisters, see Sylvia Strauss's chapter, ibid., 69–81.

4. For a fuller exploration of this construction of roles, see Adalaide Morris's chapter, ibid., 81–91.

5. For a lengthy discussion of the Abbott sisters' partnership, see Lela B. Costin's chapter, ibid., 11–23.

6. The existing literature on sisters contains only two full-length studies of the subject:

Dale V. Atkins's *Sisters: A Practical, Helpful Exploration of the Intimate and Complex Bond between Female Siblings* (New York: Arbor House, 1984), and Elizabeth Fishel's *Sisters: Love and Rivalry Inside the Family and Beyond* (New York: Quill Trade Paperbacks, 1979).

7. I am endebted to Susan Cygnet for making this linkage between parental atmosphere and sisterly connection clear to me. She argues this quite forcefully in an unpublished paper, "Sisters: Their Relationships with Each Other and with Their Families," 1985.

8. *The Sister Bond*, 127.

Mothers and Daughters

ERIKA DUNCAN

There is a figure who is strangely missing from our literature and myth. It is the evil, murderous usurper daughter. Although there are treacherous women galore, who lead men of all ages to their doom, there are no female Raskolnikovs who, in irrational rage, kill or undo an older woman. Although there are evil sisters galore (usually older), obsessed with undoing "good" sisters, and galleries of shriveled witches, jealous of the life-filled young, there are no female murderers of queens in Shakespeare, who pursue their ruthless goals in order to themselves rise to the top. Alas, even Lady Macbeth takes up a sword only to kill a king. She stains her snow-white hands only to make another king; no woman dies to make her queen! There are no women waiting in line to cut the golden bough by murdering the aging matriarch, to take in turn their own ritually designated positions. Why should this be?

Looking for images of competition in the mother/daughter relationship, I recently reread *The Lost Tradition*, a study of mothers and daughters in literature spanning 40 centuries.[1] The collection had come out in 1981, announcing by its very presence, an absence. Indeed, despite my attraction to this massive act of reclamation, boasting chapter titles like "Reentering Paradise: Cather, Colette, Woolf and Their Mothers," "How to Light a Lighthouse for Today's Women," and "'Don't forget the bridge that you crossed over on,'" I was struck most forcibly

---

This piece is dedicated to my daughters, and to Linda Hogan, whose poems in *Daughters I love you* will live forever in my mind. And it is dedicated to my mother, Florence Volkman Pincus, who has struggled through to the other side of this with me, who—even as this goes to press—has reentered my life, changing again the ever-growing and unfinished tale this tells.

by the headings denoting absence: "Jane Austen and the Tradition of the Absent Mother," "Unmothered Daughter and Radical Reformer: Harriet Martineau's Career," and "The Great Unwritten Story: Mothers and Daughters in Shakespeare."

"The absence of mothers," wrote Susan Peck MacDonald in her study of Victorian women writers,

> seems to me to derive not from the impotence or unimportance of mothers, but from the almost excessive power of motherhood; the good supportive mother is potentially so powerful a figure as to prevent her daughter's trials from occurring, to shield her from the process of maturation, and to disrupt the focus and equilibrium of the novel. But if she is dead or absent, the good mother can remain an ideal.[2]

MacDonald went on to observe that "if the mother is to be present during her daughter's maturation, the mother must be flawed in some way, so that instead of preventing her daughter's trials, she contributes to them."[3] But even this becomes a drama more dependent on the mother's influence than on the daughter's independent activity. And even this becomes a story rarely told, a drama rarely worked through in the larger-than-life medium of art.

I reread an article by Myra Glazer Sholtz that mourned the absence of the great mother-daughter cathexis in Shakespearean drama.[4] I had spent the summer of 1985 rereading Shakespeare, and I too felt that absence, bridged only so briefly in the ending of *The Winter's Tale*, and then so quickly lost. I felt the sadness of that absence, not only in Shakespeare—who, after all, missed much that could have been in Cleopatra's character as well—but in almost all art by men and women throughout the centuries.

It is not that the mother-daughter theme has not been touched. Increasingly women today are trying to explore it. However, I believe that there is a level of taboo about it that accounts for its previous absence, and that the deepest area of that taboo emerges not around the mother's jealousy, or even her devouring rage, but around the daughter's own competitive feelings. In trying to understand the depth of our own fears of wishing to outdistance our mothers, I think it is useful to look for a moment at the nearly total absence of competitive daughters in our literature.

While the image of the destroyer prince, out to usurp his father's power, has grown up side by side with images of evil giants—the mythic forms becoming humanized as our drama, poetry, and fiction become more rooted in echoing temporal life—no image of the destroyer princess has come into being, in either myth or literature. While hungry witches did and do continue to proliferate, daughters don't tend to seek what their mothers have; they don't seek to build kingdoms of their own out of their mothers' flesh. Although fairy-tale daughters can and do kill mothers, they do so only in self-defense, when their own lives are threatened and they are *forced* to choose. Unlike the male heroes who provoke the giants, deliberately designing to usurp the giants' property, female heroes come to witches only when they are hungry or lost without housing. It is hardly coincidental that Gretel is caught in the act of eating the candy shingles that constitute the roof of the witch's counterfeit shelter; it is hardly coincidental that, in order to save their own lives, she and her brother must put the witch into her own wrongly used cooking oven, smothering her in her own rejecting womb.

Finally, in the fairy tales, the females who kill evil female power figures are always children. Grown women—women who have reached the age of sexual desire—do not kill bad queens and jealous witches by themselves. Rather, they are rescued by sexually potent princes whose love automatically undoes the power of the older, evil queen.

How does this pattern translate into the more self-conscious literary forms? It doesn't. Because poetry, fiction, and drama depend so heavily upon the "adult" voice, the figure of the killer daughter cannot be directly drawn; if ever it appears at all, it is only a ghostly shadow from a realm of rarely penetrated, distant memory. While centuries of elaboration have honed and refined the depiction of the usurper son, the daughter's battle to live beyond the life her mother lived is rarely played out with a real and living mother. Indeed, that very vulnerability that makes us so afraid to let our fictional daughters overpower their mothers directly on stage turns in upon itself, and causes us, the writers, to pre-kill the mothers long before our fictional daughters can wreak their fury on them, long before they and their fictional daughters can interact. Even the Electra story, frequently presented as the paler parallel of the Oedipal myth, deals with revenge for the death of the father and not with any autonomous desire to possess what the mother possesses. And even in a context where her own mother can kill (a man), Electra does not directly shed the maternal blood. As in the case of princesses in the fairy tales, here too the male must effect the grown woman's matricide. While the child Gretel can join Hansel in killing the witch, in the adult context Orestes must take over the matricide for both siblings.

What is it that differentiates the mother-daughter drama from that of the father-son? It is my belief that the difference is complicated and deep-rooted; while the father-son drama takes place around temporal gain, the mother-daughter drama is a struggle over essence far more fraught with danger and taboo.

On one level, as the dictator of essence, as the one whose giant presence gives the child of the same sex its form, the mother is so powerful that as long as she stays on the scene, the daughter may not act separately. On another level, however, as a being separated from the act of mothering, she is completely insignificant. Thus she simultaneously provides far too much and far too little to usurp. The child, who is the product of her mother's mothering, cannot outstrip that mothering without in some way invalidating what the mother has created: her own self. Whatever the daughter's choices in the realm of mothering will be, whether she will choose to have ten children or none, whether she will be an excellent mother according to popular imagination, or a terrible one, she will be unable to outdistance her mother without also outdistancing herself. Thus, while the son outdoes the father openly, the daughter turns all of her equally powerful competitive feelings inward, upon herself.

* * *

"O that this too, too solid flesh would melt," says Hamlet, who must bear his father's flesh mixed with his mother's in his own. As he hesitates to take on the expected male role of avenging his father's death, it is the flesh itself he turns on, in his hatred of action, his hatred of the living breath.

I remember once sitting in the lamplight, looking at my feet. I had never looked at them carefully before, but my toes were stiff, and I needed to unlock them. I was suddenly seized with the horrifying realization that they were my mother's feet. Then I looked at my hands. They were much thinner than my mother's, but they *were* my mother's hands. I changed their position. They were still my mother's hands. Perhaps there was something about the particular quality of the lamplight on that winter afternoon that rendered them so familiar. Perhaps I had once looked at my mother's hands and feet in such a light. I went into the bedroom to look at myself in the mirror. I did not look at all like my mother. But inadvertently, as I drew a breath, my shoulders widened until they looked increasingly like hers. No wonder that I had refused to take the art of breathing seriously. (Indeed, even when my lack of ability to draw a deep breath was declared medically dangerous, it was many months before I could learn how to let air pass unobstructed, in and out of my lungs.)

It was right after I betrayed my mother by deciding that I hated her that I embarked on having daughters of my own. I was 19 years old. I would experience the perfect love she could not have. I chose a man whose energy came from a pure and passional place, unmarred by the intellectual distraction that I had, in my youth, blamed for the deadening of passion in my parents.

What did I take from my mother when I left her? Why did I have to leave her so early and so completely? Long hours I spent wandering through art galleries and the dim chambers of dark churches, looking at images of madonnas and children, beatific and serene. I was trying to be a visual artist then, so I drew many mothers and children, in playgrounds and on subway trains. Then suddenly I found myself longing for a baby. Although I was scarcely more than a child myself, I became obsessed with the wish to have a child to take care of, to nurture and to love. Out of my newfound sexual love, I'd do the thing my mother could not do: I'd make the perfect mother-child relationship.

I remember vividly the winter of my first pregnancy. I reached my twentieth year when I was in my seventh month. As I grew big with the new being turning and turning inside me, I felt a wholeness and a beauty I had never felt before. No more could the old women in my daytime painting class hurt me by judging me, by thinking me awkward and strange. I carried a man's seed; I was a maker of life. I carried the fruits of sexuality and passion in my body, visibly. I was a woman, more fully a woman than the shriveled older ones who taunted me and claimed my marriage wouldn't last, because, they said, marriages between people so young rarely survive. All loneliness left me as I took my husband's wonderfully solid head to my naked belly, so he could listen to our baby's heartbeat and its hiccoughing. I had surpassed my mother and I hated her for having tortured me so long, reminding me of my own weakness.

When Rachel was first born, she was the perfect baby of my fantasies. But she had not yet come awake. My husband took many beautiful pictures of her nursing at my breast, pictures that had that familiar contented aura of the madonnas that I loved so. I held my breath, feeling that at last I had conquered the downward rush of my destiny. I would not inherit my mother's anxiety or pain. Though I was very young and inexperienced, a spirit of love dwelled in me that would save me. Although I had always been an atheist, I was quite sure that I was blessed.

I remember one time when I was nursing Rachel and my mother came to visit me. She started to cry, at the beauty of it, she said. She had wanted so badly to nurse me, I knew, but she had had no milk. In an era in which bottle feeding had been the vogue, she had bravely defied the decrees against breast feeding, choosing the warmer, more vulnerable human form. I remembered vividly her tales of the other women in the hospital, whose bound breasts dripped with the milk they would not give, while her proffered breast remained empty, and I, unable to appreciate the largeness of the offering, cried with starvation.

Now Rachel is going away to M.I.T. For days she has been washing her clothing, packing it into boxes and taping them shut. The boxes are piled high next to the exit door, blocking the comings and goings of the family that will be left behind. It seems that she is taking everything she owns, as if she will never come back. She is going to be a scientist; she will never do what I did, subjecting herself and others to the starving artist's life. She will never get married to a man she cannot love forever. She does not believe in divorce. She will not have children until she has money and wisdom enough to care for them. She is a staunch believer in taking responsibility for one's own actions. "You blame your mother too much for the way that you turned out," she often says to me. She is going to take full responsibility for herself. Quietly she has worked toward this moment. She earned the grades and scholarships that made it possible, shutting her door, mentally blocking the sounds of the mice running through their squeaky homemade ferris wheels that came from her middle sister's balcony built in tier fashion just above her own, those animal sounds that were all too soon replaced by the thumping of raucous rock-and-roll, blocking out her younger sister's quarrels with me. "It's much too late to change our family," she'd say to me from time to time. "You had already messed it up, and anyway I will be leaving soon. I'll never do the things that you have done."

I was her age when I married her father. My parents had not found real love with each other, but I would. I was a year older than Rachel, feeling confused, empty, and lonely. I began to wander through playgrounds looking at mothers, wanting her, wanting the happiness my mother had once dreamed with me, that then we could not keep.

* * *

Soon after my mother came to watch me feeding Rachel, crying at the beauty of it all, Rachel began to cry at feeding time. Something had happened to my body. Every muscle in it was tense and drawn. Every time that Rachel's big blue eyes would wander up toward mine, I felt an anxiousness that must have frightened her. I imagined myself as a demon very terrible, to scare a baby so. Gone was the beauty I had worn in pregnancy, and the illusion that I could defy my mother's destiny. And yet I continued to have daughters, looking, looking for something that was lost.

As I watch Rachel pack for college, a strange envy creeps up in me for all that she will know, and that I lost long ago by marrying so young. Is she eager to enter the new life that I look at with such longing? It is hard to tell. She talks only about wanting to get away from all of us, for in a deep way we all have disappointed her. Day after day, envelopes come in the mail for Rachel. She gets her voter's registration card and notification of the date for her driving test. She takes care of all of her packing and all of her business by herself. She never once admits vulnerability or fear. Then one day she mentions that she wants a teddy bear to take to college. She is very businesslike even about this. She doesn't want it to be a gift, she says. She goes to the bank with her card to take out money to buy it. She goes with her best friend to pick it out.

After the first disappointment about perfect breast feeding, I stopped trying to replicate the closeness with my children that my mother claimed to have had with me. I held them facing outward so that they could see the world instead of me. Gently, half hiding myself, I tried to help them make their way into the world. I never dared try to be too close to them yet, strangely, over the years a closeness grew.

I remember once, long ago, reading Bettelheim's *Children of the Dream*. It must have been when the children were quite young. The details of the book are hazy to me now, but I still see clearly in my mind a chapter heading that read: "They were too big and we are too little." I must have stared at that chapter heading for a long, long time, taking it in. I remember that the mothers in Bettelheim's study had relinquished their roles because they felt smothered by the grandeur of their own mothers. They preferred to have their children reared by the community, rather than subject them to the intensive imprints of individual and monolithic mothering.

But now I am reading Virginia Woolf, exalted images of the everyday. Into my head come rather simple pictures: my mother's kitchen, a certain ambience of comfort that I knew in her house. How fully I fled from that comfort out of fear of her. I am tired suddenly of the ladders that my artist husband built, the money worries and awkwardly reached sleeping balconies that he left to me. I want to talk to my mother about kitchens and coffee tables, serving things. I want to watch her cook a thousand dinners till I learn to prepare food easily and gracefully. "I left too soon," I want to say. But years of mutual meanness swell like swords.

Shyly, timidly, I explain to my three daughters that I am writing an essay on competition. May I write about them? May I use their stories? I know that they are not completely comfortable with the tale-telling part of my writer's personality, the lack of privacy about my writer's life. To my amazement, Rachel and Gwynne give an immediate yes. Jane, who has a bit of a legal bent, tells me that there is a small chance she might agree to allow me to include material about her if I decide it is worthwhile to do the hard work of writing those sections on speculation. I am moved and surprised at their willingness, at the trust that has been so long in coming and so difficult to finally let in.

"Don't forget to tell the kitchen story in the essay," Gwynne says. Aptly, one day, she points out to me that I will never work in the kitchen unless one of the children keeps me company. "You must have had happy memories of working in the kitchen with your mother," she suggests. "They must have been your only happy memories. But if I help you, I prefer to work alone." She is the child who gave her father her own quilt when I asked him to move away. Coming from a broken home, and seeing so many broken homes all around her, she is very worried about her own future happiness. She is a year and a half younger than Rachel, and has never learned to shut out the unhappiness of others, even though, more and more lately, she shuts her door. She is the artist of the children, and wants to have children of her own. She is quite sure of that. But she wants to escape the suffering. She has a tendency to take too much responsibility for others, draining herself, leaving too little for herself. Unlike Rachel, she is very concerned that the family "heal" before she leaves it. The other day she handed me my wedding ring. She had been saving it for years, she said, because she was worried that I would lose it. Now she thinks I am ready to take good care of it. She tells me that she also has our marriage license, which she found pressed in a book of *Gauguin* prints. Over and over, she asks me to talk about the good things about the marriage, the good things about her father. In love, at last, with another man, I am finally ready to do so. As a child, I was told too many tales. Perhaps, I worry, I have told too few.

I remember the time that Gwynne came to me, explaining that she no longer wanted to share her secrets with me. She must have been about 11. "I always felt I had to share my secrets with my mother," I said to her. "I think it is probably healthier that you move away." When she was very small, she was extremely close to me. But then for years she idolized her father, hardly allowing me to touch her, keeping me away. Now as her image of her father's absolute perfection shatters, she comes to me to share her pain. She complains to me that she worships me almost too much. And I cry: Don't! From time to time she talks to me about my wisdom, about my courage. And suddenly I am afraid—afraid of this late-found affection, afraid of surpassing my own mother in my mothering. What if I find a way to keep my daughters, when my mother could not find a way of keeping me?

My mind is wandering. Piled high upon my desk are the loose pages of Phyllis Chesler's forthcoming book: *Mothers on Trial: The Battle for Children and Custody.*[5] are more than a thousand pages filled with passionate case histories of women who lose children through being judged "not good enough." "This book is about what it means to be a 'good enough' mother," the preface begins. It is a massive study of the ways in which the expectation of maternal perfection sabotages women in the battle to maintain child custody. "Mothers have always been custodially endangered," the opening chapter reads. "Black slave mothers; impoverished, racially despised, 'immoral' or unwed mothers; white married 'ladies'; Princesses and Queens; women of independent means; and women of creative genius; were all custodially challenged and victimized by their husbands or the state." Did the daughters grieve for their lost, maligned mothers? Or did they collaborate in attacking their mothers, demanding of them a perfection that no human being could meet, denying their sense of loss while taking into their own beings the attacks? And when in turn the daughters became mothers, inevitably flawed, did they allow the world to flagellate them, as once it had flagellated their mothers, now that they realized that they too were participants in that inexorable maternal legacy of falling short?

I return to Virginia Woolf, to Mrs. Ramsey who is looking for a picture of something sharp with jagged edges for her son to cut out from his catalogue. She knows the son feels furious at his father, and she is looking for something with complicated blades to distract him. Later, after Mrs. Ramsey has died, her son will imagine piercing his father through the heart. But the mother has been killed by natural forces, not by her daughters. In that famous passage in which time itself becomes a whirlwind, obliterating its own traces, she is killed invisibly, offstage. It is not coincidental that later one of her daughters also dies, in childbirth.

I remember that day looking at my hands and feet, hearing a quality in my voice that reminded me of my mother, and realizing that I would always bear her deep within me. It was then that the suicidal sense completely went away, as a knowledge of its origin suddenly came upon me—a knowledge of the depth of my desire to kill the thing that was my mother in me, to melt, in melting my own flesh, all that was left of her in me. It was a violence that had had no place, so it turned inward, daggerlike, on me.

They say that at about the age of 40 a strange letting-go occurs. I have another year or two to go, but already I can begin to feel a softening, a muting of the harsh demands I used to place upon myself. I remember my mother at forty. She still had my father then. She still had me. "Do not be afraid," I want to say to Gwynne, "to do what I can't do." I am doing fairly well now, but for many years after her father left, I was not a very good mother. Beginning to read Phyllis Chesler's manuscript, I realize belatedly that it is not actual custody I have been fighting for, but custody of my children's affection. I was so afraid that I would lose them to their father as my mother once lost me. For years I wore myself to a frazzle, trying to be perfect against every odd and feeling always that I was failing, failing miserably.

As I try to collect my thoughts, Jane comes into the room. So often, it seems, she is in mortal competition with me for the possession of my own mental space. So often, it seems, we war about who lives in whom, and who dictates the movements of the other in and out. And yet there is a richness in that war, a compassion and closeness.

A staunch sense of proximity to her own truth has kept her from developing that "tollkeeper" that so often protects us and others around us from our most primal and frightening thoughts. "I wish you would commit suicide," she has cried out from time to time, when she has felt my presence most threatening to her own essence. More violent and graphic than the standard "I wish you were dead," her cry becomes a terrifying and yet moving plea, asking me to obliterate that larger-than-life essence of myself that roots inside her very flesh, that *me* in her that smothers her own sense of separateness.

Though my daughters are leaving me physically, I feel them coming closer with the passing years. Even with Jane, my youngest, as she enters adolescence, there is a breaking of a certain warfare wherein lay a certain kind of bond. Though still, occasionally, I feel that she is in competition with me for my time, demanding that we both be there for her, doing whatever *she* must do, demanding that I look at her and listen to her totally, leaving my own thoughts, my own work and dreams, more and more often now she runs away, into her own room toward the telephone and her own friends. She looks so lithe and lovely now. She is not quite as tall as I am, but I know that in another year she will be taller, as her sisters are. Already she is starting to outgrow my shoes. She used to wear my curvature upon her spine, but it has been surgically corrected. For a while she was furiously angry at me, for the inherited deformity. But hers is fixed now. Mine, a milder form, remains, a visible reminder. Sometimes she turns on it—on me—with hate. But gradually even that anger fades. She cares well for her beautiful body, her beautiful face. Will I be big enough to rejoice in all my daughters have that I was unable to have, that I may never have? Will I be big enough to let them grow bigger than I can ever be?

And yet, as I look at the literature, as I look at my own feelings—playing over and over again my own earliest memories, through teaching and through mothering and making art—as my own mother at last shrinks to become only another uncertain human, making all too human errors in her attempts to give and receive nurture, I wonder whether most of the competitive feelings do come from the demonized, larger-than-life-sized mothers, or whether this image is merely a manifestation of the daughter's great, somewhat inexplicable, discomfort with her own competitive feelings, with her own desire to be the unmentionable usurper princess of our darkest dreams. I wonder what might happen in a world where all people shared equally the joys and burdens of the competitive feelings now relegated to men, the important mandates of compassion and nonviolence which are now only women's legacy. I wonder what new loves might be unleashed, if only we might dare to touch the other images of our own violent fantasies against our makers in ways destined to unleash movement and gentleness, new hope.

For a long time after I rejected my husband, I didn't dare to love another man. My mother didn't have a man. I left my mother early, right after my father left her. Long years it took before I felt the punishment for that early betrayal come down on me full force. Now, as I reach toward loves that will be possible again, I feel the loss of many, many years. "And yet," my lover says, "you made three books during those years; you made three babies. Your time wasn't really lost."

My babies are becoming women now. I worry about how I might have hurt them, how I might have damaged them. The books, out in the world in ways I never can take back, are full of evil mothers and hurt daughters looking for a rescuer, disappointed daughters turning on themselves.

I see my three daughters standing together. Gradually, after long years of rivalry, they are starting to grow fond of one another. I am quite glad of this, though I feel a bit wistful for the time when I was their center. And yet, I do not want to be the center of their wheel, as my mother once was for me. "Hate me, when you want to; run from me, when you have to. Do not try to make me perfect. Do not worship me," I want to cry out, so they take in instantly all that I struggled for so long to know.

"Hate me from time to time, when you have to. Don't be afraid to outdistance me. Disparage what you don't want to inherit. Be brave. Be beautiful. Don't worry if it will be hard for me.

"I love you."

NOTES

1. Cathy N. Davidson and E. M. Broner, eds., *The Lost Tradition: Mothers and Daughters in Literature* (New York: Frederick Ungar Publishing, 1980).

2. Susan Peck MacDonald, "Jane Austen and the Tradition of the Absent Mother," in *The Lost Tradition*, ed. Davidson and Broner, 58.

3. Ibid., 59.

4. Myra Glazer Sholtz, "The Great Unwritten Story: Mothers and Daughters in Shakespeare," in *The Lost Tradition*, ed. Davidson and Broner.

5. Phyllis Chesler, *Mothers on Trial: The Battle for Children and Custody* (New York: McGraw-Hill, 1986).

DAILY REALITIES

Measuring Maternity

MICHÈLE FARRELL

How do mothers, and mothers and daughters, relate to one another? A great deal has been written in recent years of the idyllic sharing that takes place between and among women in these relationships. Within the patriarchal social economy of relationships, however, it is just so often evident that mothers are pitted against one another, and against their daughters as well.

Obvious paradigms of such agonistic relationships are served up regularly in sublimated form in television commercials. Serene mothers with happily diapered infants are contrasted with aggravated women dealing with leaky, sagging diapers on whiny children. Beautifully shampooed and coiffed caring mothers and matching daughters romp gracefully through poppy fields, setting examples for viewer—mothers, seeking respite from household chores and children during empty afternoon hours, impossible to emulate. Which are the better mothers? The competition is on.

In the same vein, the viewer is asked to guess, in the course of an ad for dishwashing detergent, whose hands look younger, the mother's or the daughter's; and, in an ad for hair rinses, which woman is, in fact, the mother, which the daughter. Maternal competence, youth and beauty, not to mention identity, are issues that divide and alienate women. Mothers compete with their daughters in teamlike fashion against other mother-daughter couples, and compete against their daughters as well for social value and esteem.

In the example of Mme de Sévigné and her daughter, we find the opportunity to examine this phenomenon of maternal competition dispassionately. In this case, we are able to examine a distant model of two women who lived hundreds of years ago, and to appreciate the historical dimension of a social disposition that persists in troubling relationships between and among women.

Mme de Sévigné, a seventeenth-century French aristocrat and Parisian salon figure during the reign of Louis XIV, is one of the few recognized female contributors to the Classical French literary canon. Her letters, written primarily to her daughter, Françoise-Marguerite, Countess of Grignan, are acclaimed as models of original and pleasing prose style, and as a rich resource for details on daily and official life in France under Louis XIV.[1] Traditionally, her *Correspondance* has also been viewed as an outstanding expression of maternal sentiment. Whatever discord or tension evident in the epistolary exchange between Sévigné and her daughter has been dismissed as idiosyncratic[2] or as the consequence of fundamental temperamental incompatibility.[3] Contemporary feminist investigations into the nature of motherhood and its articulation in mother-daughter relationships provide a new cultural context within which to reread these tensions.[4] Examination of their dynamic both prompts revisions of the traditional Sévigné portrait[5] and offers a historical touchstone for current considerations of mother-daughter relationships.

This essay examines, in particular, the salient theme of competition as it informs Sévigné's expression of maternal feelings.[6] Her tendency to compare herself, her daughter, their relationship, with her contemporaries and their mother-daughter relationships suggests perhaps a search for behavior models and guidance in an uncharted domain, but her drive to excel in her performance of motherhood and to surpass even her own daughter in professing affection suggests a need to valorize herself publicly in that role. Why need a mother compete for a reputation of affective excellence with other mothers, and why need a mother and her daughter compete with each other affectively? I argue in this essay that such striving indicates a will to lay claim to a limited resource: the only resource evident under such circumstances being that of attention, of public acclaim, the acclaim of the father.

In aristocratic seventeenth-century France, the art of letter writing flourished. It served as a worthy and improving way of occupying leisure time. It also served the purpose of keeping up-to-date those friends and relatives who were in the provinces or abroad, absent from the intimate, elitist salon circles of Paris and Louis XIV's court. Mme de Sévigné (1626–96), a distinguished widow of adequate means, found herself in an ideal situation to explore and to extend the possibilities afforded by the epistolary genre. Upon her daughter's marriage and departure from Paris to take up residence with her husband in the south of France, Mme de Sévigné initiated a voluminous exchange of letters which was to last 23 years. The correspondence was interrupted only here and there when mother and daughter visited each other. Sévigné wrote faithfully to Mme de Grignan twice a week, starting, adding to, and completing letters as she awaited the arrival and departure of the king's couriers. Thus the letters represent a continuous flow of energy and attention to cultivating and sustaining her relationship with her daughter. They also attest to a great love of writing.

It was common in seventeenth-century salon circles to share letters with one's friends, to circulate them, and to join in collective appreciation of their merits not only as conveyors of news, but as works of art in themselves. Sévigné's letters became famous in her own time, finding publics both at their point of inception and at their point of reception. She frequently penned her letters in salons among friends who participated in her writing activity, adding postscripts and messages to her text not only for the addressee's pleasure, but also for their own immediate amusement. Upon their reception, the letters would be shared by the daughter-addressee with her entourage in turn.

The letters were savored not only for the abundance of information, gossip, and court politics they offered from the capital, but for the easy and entertaining style Sévigné affected as she wrote on anything that struck her fancy. Her letters emulated the art of conversation and seemed to extend her salon and those she frequented to embrace and include absent friends, and her daughter in particular, within a privileged circle of communication and understanding. Her letters were copied, circulated, even offered to the king. Upon her death, interest in her correspondence was sustained. Various spurious versions began to appear, and pirated editions of her letters were even published abroad. To put an end to this, her granddaughter organized an official edition, hired an editor, and instated herself as censor of these family documents.

Sévigné's letters passed easily into the canon of French literature. To the feminist reader today, however, a question occurs, the answer to which opens the text for a revision of the traditional Sévigné profile: Since this was indeed an epistolary exchange, where are the daughter's letters? Sévigné's good literary fortune and her place as maternal paragon become suspect as the answer is considered. The daughter's letters, so vital to sustaining the exchange, and, as evidenced within the test of the mother's letters, so faithfully penned, were destroyed.[7] Mme de Simiane, granddaughter and editor of Mme de Sévigné, and daughter of Mme de Grignan, destroyed them. As she completed the direction of the publication of her grandmother's letters, she destroyed her own mother's half of the exchange. The mother-daughter antagonism discernible in the Sévigné letters was repeated in the next generation. Mme de Simiane silenced her mother, creating thereby a void in her grandmother's text. Only recently have readers ventured to peer into that seeming emptiness.

My reading of the *Correspondance* is based upon an attempt to restore the daughter's voice, to hypothesize her role in the epistolary exchange, and to understand the relationship from her point of view. Sévigné's letters offer ample material from which to reconstruct, through telling reverberations, the addressee. In the light of such an approach, the conventional Sévigné profile as maternal paragon recedes, and in its place emerges a picture more familiar to the contemporary reader: one of mother-daughter struggle. What sets this example apart from most recent variations on the same tale is that here the daughter's voice has been stifled and must be reconstructed. Women who write in France today of relationships between mothers and daughters from their own experience tend to be the daughters. Marie Cardinal, Luce Irigaray, and Violette Leduc are just some of the writers that come to mind.[8] These women tend to access their pasts in the process of attempting to restructure their present. In some more notable cases, a tone of vindication informs daughters' works as they unburden themselves of sufferings experienced and damage done. In the United States we have the example of Barbara Davis Hyman, daughter of Bette Davis, who in *My Mother's Keeper* reveals her anger at her unsatisfactory relationship with her famous mother, an anger that seems to be based on a dynamic of rivalry and will to control between the two women as they focus on the same male as object of desire.[9] Another example of filial scriptoral revenge can be seen in Angelica Garnett's *Deceived with Kindness: A Bloomsbury Childhood,* in which Garnett, niece of Virginia Woolf, bemoans her victimization by her free-spirited mother, Vanessa Bell.[10] In the Sévigné *Correspondance,* we have the opportunity to examine a mother's discourse and to shed light on some 'maternal' behavior with which daughters might well have difficulty coping.

Social recognition and approbation as meted out within the confines of patriarchal society appear to answer a paramount need in Sévigné's inscribed experience of motherhood. She regularly alludes in her letters to the maternal behavior of her contemporaries and to other mother-daughter ties, returning in each case to a consideration of her own. This tendency to compare generates a dynamic of competition both within and around the mother-daughter couple, and situates the maternal in a social and performatic context. It can be seen to inform Sévigné's entire epistolary project, which serves as her mode of entry into the male world of writing.

The existential fact of maternity suggested to Sévigné the cultivation of a public role. Such an ambition was motivated by her need to assign distinctive meaning to her otherwise unfocused life, and was legitimized by her claims of instinctual attachment to her daughter. The performance of maternity was also a novel enterprise, for, in Sévigné's day, motherhood had not yet been idealized and eulogized as it would be by Rousseau in the next century. In Sévigné's epistolary relationship with her daughter, a penchant for comparing other mother-daughter relationships with their own indicates her drive to compete, to excel in her role of mother, and to encourage complementary rivalrous behavior in her daughter. There appears to be a deliberate attempt to pass from the private sphere of domestic relations into the public domain of social performance, the success of which will be crowned finally by the publication of this personal correspondence.[11]

As Domna Stanton, contemporary scholar and feminist theorist, has pointed out, Sévigné inscribes her drive to distinction within a politically conservative framework; she affirms "her friends, her daughter and her self as exceptional women, since their coding as exceptions does not undermine the prevailing system of sex roles."[12] Sévigné does not content herself, however, with functioning as merely another member of an exceptional female community; she seeks, through her relationship with her daughter, to distinguish herself even within that group:

> Only you, my darling, and myself, I dare say, place such a dear and precious friendship foremost, and are more moved by it than by all the other things of this world. These feelings are rare; every day we see arrangements quite the contrary, but let us rejoice in the pleasure of not being at all like the others.[13]

Sévigné revels in her achievement in the maternal sphere, not necessarily because of any specific gratification to be had there, but, at least as she expresses it in the passage just cited, because it represents for her a mark of difference and, therefore, of superiority over others. She derives pleasure from the self-favoring act of comparison, and includes her daughter as she exults in a spirit of self-congratulation.

It does not suffice that Sévigné should enjoy an intense and intimate relationship with her daughter; she seeks, through her epistolary performance of maternity, visibility and acclaim in the social arena. Maternal affection, commonly viewed as pertaining to the sacred realm of the unconditional, the instinctual, regulated only by its own private momentum, appears paradoxically measurable here as it enters the world of display. In transforming maternity through her writing into a public role, Sévigné shapes her experience according to values borrowed from the patriarchal social sphere in which she seeks distinction. She invents and savors a dynamic of competition in her newly established domain of affective competence, and can be seen thereby to "masculinize" maternity.

The projection of the maternal persona depends crucially on the cooperation of her daughter, cast in a supporting role. As Sévigné measures maternity by scrutinizing other mother-daughter relationships, she seeks to shape supportive behavior in her daughter, Françoise-Marguerite. To that end, she dwells particularly on the behavior of other daughters. In an early letter to her daughter in Provence, Sévigné introduces the first filial comparison, and she does not at all assure Françoise-Marguerite of her primacy as model daughter. She confronts her with the example of another daughter, Mme de Soubise, who writes superb letters because she is inspired by the subject matter, her own mother, Mme de Rohan, and who inscribes herself socially and textually in her mother's domain via the letter: "My darling, you are not the only one who loves her mother. Here, Mme de Soubise writes letters that surpass her usual abilities. . . . Mme de Rohan reminded me of a measure of my own sufferings in her separation from her daughter."[14] Sévigné devotes more admiring attention to the filial devotion exemplified in Mme de Soubise's letters than to the maternal model afforded in Mme de Rohan. This mother's grief is equal to only part of her own, whereas Mme de Soubise, the daughter, outdoes not only herself but, by implication, Françoise-Marguerite as well. The subliminal message proposes a relationship of rivalry; it instructs the daughter to do the same and to surpass Mme de Soubise, just as Sévigné surpasses the mother, Mme de Rohan, in the plenitude of her suffering.

Such comparisons suggest an invitation to compete for mother-daughter epistolary excellence and renown. Françoise-Marguerite resisted her mother's urgings, and preferred to protect the privacy of their exchange, as evidenced by her mother's reproaches: "You hide the tender thoughts I send you, rascal; whereas I show sometimes, and to certain people, those that you write to me. . . . I want people to see that you love me."[15] The daughter's reluctance, in the interest of forging a less dependent identity for herself, to circulate her mother's outpourings in her salon was a source of continued frustration to Sévigné. Nevertheless, by keeping up her end of the exchange, the daughter participated, in passive-aggressive fashion, in enabling and sustaining her mother's project.

Sévigné actually expresses territoriality regarding the domain of maternity as she scans the horizon for other mother-daughter pairs. She needs such other figures in order for there to exist such a domain within which to establish the grounds of her own excellence. She has staked out her claim as maternal paragon, and all pretenders to the title are subject to her scrutiny. Again, she focuses on a daughter's active part in the relationship rather than on the mother's: "There is a young girl here who wants to get involved in loving her mother, but she is a hundred steps behind you, although she speaks and acts very nicely; it's Mme de Nangis."[16] Here Françoise-Marguerite receives an actual compliment, but she receives with it forceful reminders that she is engaged in a competition of filial devotion, even though it is of her mother's devising rather than of her own choosing. The daughter's performance is measured, weighed, and compared; it could conceivably some day be found lacking. Such comparative vignettes function parabolically in the Sévigné rhetoric of maternity. They are not subtle; the immediate references—Sévigné and her daughter—always dominate in the comparison, and the lessons so often seem to be designed for the specific edification of the daughter.

Sévigné privileges the Rohan-Soubise mother-daughter couple as a convenient standard. In the following passage, she locates herself as judge of the compared daughters' epistolary prowess, and thus devises and occupies a position of authority on proper filial address. In her evaluation, she distinguishes between content and form, and Françoise-Marguerite receives a compliment, via the comparison, on her writing:

> I saw a miraculous letter from a daughter to a mother. This daughter doesn't write as you do, she doesn't have your wit, but she does have tenderness and affection like you; it's Mme de Soubise to Mme de Rohan. I was surprised yesterday to see the depth of her feeling for Mme de Rohan, and also what natural tenderness Mme de Rohan feels for her.

This comparison is distinguished from the preceding citation concerned with filial devotion by Sévigné's attention to the reciprocity of affection between the mother and daughter. One wonders what kind of "tenderness" other than "natural" Sévigné might have in mind that requires her to use the qualifier, or is it simply her urge to prolixity, as she satisfies her need to write, that insists on such expansion? On another occasion, Sévigné generously admires a daughter's self-sacrificial attentions to her ill mother, Mme de Montlouet, and comprehends the mother's consequent concern for the daughter's health:

> Mme de Montlouet has small pox. Her daughter's worries are infinite; the mother is in despair as well since her daughter refuses to leave her side to take some fresh air as she has been told to do. As for wit, I don't think they have the sharpest, but for feelings, my dear, it is just as with us, just as tender and just as natural.[17]

In discussing what appears to be a private sickroom drama, Sévigné indicates the potentially public dimension of all situations in her society, and the performative aspect of all relational activity. The world at large is privy to the mother-daughter dynamic as it is played out around the sickbed, and sits in constant judgment; the "natural" then always has a concern for effect, and must be understood as a contradiction in terms within the Sévigné discourse.

Sévigné reads a visual and behavioral text in her observation of the sickbed drama here. As she evaluates the relational manifestation, she reiterates the textual distinction of form and content, and amplifies it once again as she opposes "wit" and "feelings." The intellectualizing of experience corresponds with "wit" and aligns thus with form, and the emotional apprehension of life underlies the equation of "feeling" and content. It is not surprising that in her repeated dichotomizing, Sévigné should be prepared to concede comparability with this other couple in those affective areas (feeling and content, in the sense of materiality) traditionally allotted to women, while she expresses more competitive concern for excellence in the traditionally male domains of writing, wit, and form. It is telling to note that Sévigné's privileging of the rational eventually backfired. Her daughter-disciple carried it to the extreme, and became a fervent practitioner of Cartesianism, leaving her mother-model behind in a muddle of puzzled emotional bewilderment and resentment toward her daughter's passion for reason.[18]

Occasionally Sévigné congratulates herself and her daughter on their epistolary fidelity; not only the relationship but the exchange of letters itself seems to have stabilized into an unusual routine: "I don't think there has ever been seen an exchange such as ours; it's not strange that I should take pleasure in that. And, it is something that is hardly ever seen, and that is what I savor thoroughly." What seems to please Sévigné particularly about the correspondence, just as with the relationship, is not the exchange itself, but the fact that it is unparalleled, that it defies comparison. As exceptional, it has succeeded in transcending the vicious circle of comparability and has established itself as unique, that is, so excellent as to surpass all similar others. She reiterates the same pleasure at its singularity in the following passage, written a few weeks later: "The liveliness of our exchange is a great consolation for me; I don't believe there exists an example of a similar one."[19]

While the concern to conform to prescribed etiquettes characterized the general tenor of social exchange under Louis XIV, ancillary to that movement of submission was the corollary drive for distinction, the need to establish an independent identity and to stand out from the crowd—ultimately, to attract the monarch's attention and favor. Such a competitive environment influenced even the most discreet of activities. Not only did Sévigné find pleasure and consolation in writing to her daughter; she also took obvious pride in the novelty of her maternal and epistolary enterprise. Pleasure and consolation are feelings that might result from the most private of exchanges, but the feeling of pride can derive only from a scanning of the social horizon, from finding and classing as inferior other similar arrangements, thus establishing as outstanding and therefore meritorious her own.[20]

Such competitiveness characterizes Sévigné's attitude toward other mother-daughter pairs. It motivates her to invent incentives for securing demonstrations of filial devotion from her daughter. These appear, in the course of the correspondence, to be ever greater, and never sufficient. This drive reaches even into the relationship between the two women, where it stimulates comparison, protest, and controversy. When the two women exchange compliments on style, they vie at insisting on the greater talent of the other. This is in keeping with the greater value assigned, as seen earlier, to form and wit. But each insists on claiming for herself the greater love for the other. Sévigné fuels the contest of the greater affection by insisting on the naturalness of maternal love, maternal instinct, as opposed to a lack of tradition of filial devotion. This insistence on the primacy of maternal instinct functions as a pretext for self-absorption in the letters of the mother, and generates appropriate cooperative protest on the part of the daughter.

Sévigné generalizes about maternal and filial capacities for affection. Having established that her caring is merely in keeping with the nature of the maternal, while her daughter's is not at all typical of the filial response and is therefore the more "extraordinary" of the two, she then claims to surpass her daughter's remarkable "affection" by virtue of that same unique and inspiring daughter:

> I am convinced that no one knows how to love as you do, that is, if not me, but maternal affection is so natural, and that of children so extraordinary, that whereas I do simply as I must, you are a prodigy. I believe however that there is a measure of affection in my heart that is inspired by you personally and that other mothers don't experience, which is what made me say, a while ago, that I loved you with an affection tailored specifically for you.[21]

Her position on maternal love stands in contradiction to the one recently posited by the social historian Elisabeth Badinter, who, on the basis of research done on maternal behavior in France from the seventeenth century to the present, finds grounds to refute the notion of any primordial maternal instinct: "Maternal love is a human feeling. And, like any feeling, it is uncertain, fragile, and imperfect. Contrary to many assumptions, it is not a deeply rooted given in women's natures."[22] The assumption of maternal instinct, traditionally expressed in mythological, religious, literary, and folkloric modes, reflects perhaps not so much a truth as a profound human desire shaped by the history of social organization. It provides, in Sévigné's rhetoric, the context essential to her aspiration to exceptionality, while the emphasis on the superiority of her daughter as love object offers even further justification.

In order to sustain the epistolary and affective dialogue that constitutes her exceptionality, Sévigné is obliged to share some of the glory with her correspondent-daughter. She weaves a discourse of seductive flattery regularly into later letters, as she acknowledges expressions of affection received from her daughter and sustains the epistolary exchange: "The affection of mothers does not usually set the rule for that of the daughters, but then you are not at all like the others."[23] The pact of mutual admiration, instigated by the mother, implicating and isolating the daughter,

DAILY REALITIES

serves to posit the mother in the authoritative, "ruling" role within the couple, and ensures her uncontestable title to her self-designed but publicly recognized maternal crown. Her affection, her daughter, their relationship, their correspondence—all of these are different from and superior to all other comparable arrangements, so she claims. Paradoxically, this epistolary celebration of maternal love suggests a will to social alienation just as persuasively as it points to an example of intimate harmony. At the heart of the project is self-apprehension, which appears to require constant sustenance from the testimony of the other—of the daughter, of society, and ultimately of the father. That testimony is predicated upon an activity of establishing a common ground, seeking and emphasizing difference, measuring it and coming out ahead, inventing and surpassing the necessary other.

The theme of comparison, as traced through the examples above, points to currents of competition and rivalry, to instances of performatic behavior, and to ambitions for excellence. Such traits lead me to construe the process of measuring maternity as endemic to its introduction into the public domain and to the elaboration of maternity as a social role in seventeenth-century aristocratic France. Sévigné privileged and cultivated her maternal persona in order to establish a visible identity, to feel a sense of purpose in her life, and to secure an outlet for her creative, assertive, and otherwise frustrated drives. She concentrated these understandable desires in her epistolary relationship with her daughter because this was at once a novel and an acceptable activity for a woman in a man's world, that is, an appropriately marginal genre in the male domain of writing.

La Bruyère, as arbiter of seventeenth-century mores, speaks for the classical world of letters in France when he pronounces that it is in the epistolary art that women deserve recognition: "This sex goes further than ours in this sort of writing."[24] Such praise at once situates and subordinates women writers within the hierarchy of genres, where the epistolary art enjoyed less status than others such as tragedy or epic poetry. The desire of women to pen letters, an activity bridging domestic assignment and writerly aspirations, was more easily tolerated and assimilated than, say, a will to write novels, history, treatises. Theirs was not to analyze, define, describe, or prescribe, but to maintain through relational writing the traditional social network that constitutes the base of male power. La Bruyère's pronouncement tellingly situates women in relationship to his intended readership ("ours" = male), that is, outside of it, excluded. Nor does he actually name a single woman letter writer in this passage. Female scriptoral authority is thus at once confirmed and effaced. Ultimately, then, and even in comparison with other women writers of her own time, such as Mlle de Scudéry and Mme de La Fayette who ventured into the world of fiction, Sévigné's writing represents a conservative and therefore pragmatically successful solution.

Sévigné's performance of maternity might be read as a microcosmic illustration of reverberations of the patriarchal dynamic played out in French society under Louis XIV. Through the epistolary codifying of her motherhood into a publicly recognizable and operative role, Sévigné realized the "maternal" in a "masculine" mode along the lines prescribed for women's public behavior in patriarchal society.

By persuading her daughter, through the invention and deployment of a rhetoric of competitive maternity, to cooperate "filially" (i.e., "dutifully")[25] in the elaboration of the *Correspondance*, she devised and performed a monumental role, and succeeded in inscribing herself in the male domain of writing.[26]

Here, in Sévigné and her daughter, can be seen the ancestors of those beautiful mother-and-daughter TV couples as well as the mothers with cleaner and shinier floors than their daughters, and the daughters with more efficient and economic vacuum cleaners than their mothers. Patterns of desire, imitation, and rivalry among women are traced and retraced through history as long as patriarchal order prevails, and "success" for women within that system is determined by the extent to which they subscribe to that order and accept to compete against one another within it.

NOTES

1. Madame de Sévigné, *Correspondance*, I, II, III, texte établi, présenté et annoté par Roger Duchêne (Paris: Bibliothèque de la Pléiade, Gallimard, 1978); I follow Duchêne's edition throughout and most references will be included in the text. All translations are my own.

2. Proponents of these views are, respectively: Eva Avigdor, *Mme de Sévigné; un portrait intellectual et moral* (Paris: Nizet, 1974); and Jean Cordelier, *Madame de Sévigné par elle-même* (Paris: Editions du Seuil, 1973).

3. Roger Duchêne's earlier work *Réalité vécue et art épistolaire: Madame de Sévigné et la lettre d'amour* (Paris: Bordas, 1970), falls into this category.

4. Elisabeth Badinter, *Mother Love: Myth and Reality—Motherhood in Modern History* (New York: Macmillan, 1981); Simone de Beauvoir, *Le deuxième sexe* (Paris: Gallimard, 1949); Nancy Chodorow, *The Reproduction of Mothering: Psychoanalysis and the Sociology of Gender* (Berkeley: University of California Press, 1978); Adrienne Rich, *Of Woman Born: Motherhood as Experience and Institution (New York: Norton, 1976).*

5. *Some critics have begun revisions of the Sévigné mother-daughter profile in their work:* Harriet Ray Allentuch, "My Daughter/Myself: Emotional Roots of Madame de Sévigné's Art," *Modern Language Quarterly* 43, no. 2 (1982); 121–137; Jacqueline Duchêne, *Françoise de Grignan, ou le mal d'amour* (Paris: Arthème Fayard, 1985); Roger Duchêne, *Madame de Sévigné ou la chance d'être femme* (Paris: Arthème Fayard, 1982); Solange, Guénoun, "La Correspondance de Madame de Sévigné et de Madame de Grignan: une séparation littéraire," Ph.D. diss., Princeton University, 1980; Louise K. Horowitz, *Love and Language: A Study of the Classical French Moralist Writers* (Columbus: Ohio State University Press, 1977); idem, "The Correspondence of Madame de Sévigné: Lettres ou belles-lettres?" *French Forum* 6 (1981): 13–27; Frances Mossiker, *Madame de Sévigné: A Life and Letters* (New York: Alfred A. Knopf, 1983).

6. Michèle Farrell, "Sévigné's *Correspondance:* The Rhetoric of the Letter and the Performance of Maternity," Ph.D. diss., University of Michigan, 1984; the theme developed here has its roots and amplification in my dissertation.

7. *Correspondance* I, p. 765.

8. Marie Cardinal, *Les mots pour le dire* (Paris: Bernard Grasset, 1975); Luce Irigaray, *Et l'une ne bouge pas sans l'autre* (Paris: Editions de minuit, 1979); Violette Leduc, *L'Asphyxie* (Paris: Gallimard, 1946).

9. Barbara Davis Hyman, *My Mother's Keeper* (New York: William Morrow, 1985).

10. Angelica Garnett, *Deceived with Kindness: A Bloomsbury Childhood* (New York: Harcourt Brace Jovanovich, 1985).

11. Bernard Bray touches on the theme of the dynamic of rivalry generated in Sévigné's correspondence, but does not extend his analysis to a consideration of the implications for the relationship between the correspondents, in "L'Epistolière au miroir: Réciprocité, réponse et rivalité dans les lettres de Mme de Sévigné à sa fille," *Marseille 95*, 4e trimestre (1973): 23–29.

12. Domna Stanton, "On Female Portraiture in Sévigné's Letters," *Papers on French Seventeenth-Century Literature* 8, no. 15, 2 (1981): 92.

13. *Correspondance* III, letter 1203, pp. 854–855.

14. *Correspondance* I, letter 162, p. 246.

15. Ibid., letter 143, p. 182.

16. *Correspondance* III, letter 981, p. 322.

17. *Correspondance* I, letter 197, p. 336; *Correspondance* II, letter 404, p. 19.

18. Jane Flax offers an interesting subtext to this discussion in her article "The Conflict between Nurturance and Autonomy in Mother-Daughter Relationships and Within Feminism," *Feminist Studies* 4 (1978): 171–189.

19. *Correspondance* I, letter 359, p. 657; letter 364, p. 677.

20. In *Le Détachement* (Paris: Flammarion, 1983), Michel Serres theorizes on the practice of comparison and competition endemic to Western culture and based on the scarcity model; he points to its self-inflicted nature:

> Le grand pourquoi le nommer grand, le grand ne connaît pas de petits, la grandeur n'a pas besoin de petitesse. Le coq seul a besoin de la basse-cour. . . . La force résiste à la concurrence, elle se distingue de l'aggression, la puissance est de résister à la comparaison, la grandeur est de résister à l'échelle des tailles, qu'il soit bienheureux celui qui vit dans l'espace neuf que ne ravage pas la relation d'ordre [p. 166]. . . . A demeurer au théâtre, il faut se battre pour les places, les places sont rares, le cirque n'est bâti, n'est formé que pour produire cette rareté [p. 175].

21. *Correspondance* III, letter 1196, p. 837.

22. Badinter, *Mother Love*, xxiii.

23. *Correspondance* III, letter 1206, p. 868.

24. Jean de La Bruyère, *Les Caractères, ou les moeurs de ce siècle* (Paris: Editions Garnier Frères, 1960), 76.

25. Simone de Beauvoir, *Mémoires d'une jeune fille rangée* (Paris: Gallimard, 1958); the title as translated, *Memoirs of a Dutiful Daughter* (New York: Harper Torchbooks, 1958) comes to mind. Other connotations of the term *rangée*, such as "classed," "arranged," "measured," converge with "dutiful" in this discussion.

26. To his credit, the renowned nineteenth-century critic Charles-Augustin Sainte-Beuve does not fail to note the relationship between the mother's love for her daughter and her exploitation of this passion as she transforms it into a public role. He points succinctly to its function as pretext and posture: "Elle idolâtrait sa fille et s'était de bonne heure établie dans le monde sur ce pied-là." In "XVIIe siècle: Mémorialistes, épistoliers, romanciers," *Les Grands écrivains français*, Etudes des lundis et des portraits classés selon un ordre nouveau par Maurice Allem (Paris: Garnier Frères, 1930), 53.

High Stakes, Meager Yields: Competition Among Black Girls

DAPHNE MUSE

I think competition promotes the piece of the pie mentality. Whereas cooperative participation teaches you how to make the whole pie and at the same time learn its essential ingredients. We certainly weren't competing to get on them slave ships. And now it truly baffles me to see how much we compete to lose our identity and remove ourselves from the very grounding that was such an integral part of our being, our visions, our future.

—Junetta Juness Junebunny Jones
Community Activist/Civil Rights Organizer,
great great granddaughter of grassroots philosophers
Junebug Jabbo Jones and Juness Junebetta Jones

Circumstances, history and capitalism have forced us to become a highly competitive people. After all, we live in a society that thrives off of competition. In order to survive within the context of who we are in 1986 and where we live, black people must compete or fall prey to the perils of extinction. And black girls are on a path where competition has become the marrow of their survival. Whether it is culturally appropriate or not is not the real issue. The real issue is will it allow us to survive long enough to finally gain control of the conditions and circumstances that are shaping the lives of our grandchildren, and will shape the lives of our great grandchildren and their great grandchildren's children?

—Dr. Juness Junebunny Jones
Anthropologist/Scholar/Activist,
granddaughter of Junetta Juness Junebunny Jones[1]

As a 1960s activist with a 13-year-old 1980s daughter, I often think about the kind of world my daughter is journeying through as she grows further into womanhood. I wonder if she will choose to be part of maximizing the best in the human potential. Will she have a community of friends who are encouraging and supportive of what she does? Will she work to strengthen that community or will she function only in her own self-interest?

I fear that she, as an emerging young woman in a society that encourages competition and discourages cooperative participation, will become intricately caught up in the web of a kind of competition that will be detrimental to solid relationships and to the trustworthiness that serves as the framework for so many long-term personal and professional relationships.

Integration, the civil rights movement, the women's movement, the conservatism of the 1980s, and culture as a capitalist commodity certainly have all played a major role in the degree to which black girls and female adolescents compete with and against one another. Integration has raised the stakes, broadened the arena, and made for a sometimes volatile but more often smoldering tension between black girls and their Asian, Native American, Chicana, and white peers.

The competition factor exists in every arena of their lives and, whether for attention in general, boys, grades, status in the community, economic viability, or recognition, it is a reality that is shaping and determining the lives of the majority of our girls and female adolescents. Having spent time in a socialist country, I'm often dismayed at how the combination of capitalism, conspicuous consumption, and societal pressures forces us not to cooperate in the trusting spirit that could lead to maximizing our potential as women and purveyors of the best in the human potential.

As members of a twice oppressed group, black girls are often placed in the position of calling attention to themselves in ways that other girls don't have to. The incredibly high pregnancy rate among black girls and female adolescents points to the fact that competition for affection is keen. Babies are often viewed as a victory or status symbol in the affection arena. They up the ante and serve as concrete proof that a round was won in the competition-for-affection-and-attention war. A recent study by the National Research Council estimates that a whopping 40% of black girls will have been pregnant at least once by age 18.[2]

Though I have my own thoughts about how black girls and adolescent females are coping with the stresses and complexities that often accompany competition, I feel that it is imperative for me to hear their voices directly. While preparing to write about this topic, I availed myself of every opportunity to discover how black girls and young women feel about the competition in their lives. I interviewed them in between meetings in Washington, D.C., riding public transportation in the San Francisco Bay Area, in movie houses, on the streets, and through educational opportunity programs. Their names and identifying details have been changed throughout to protect their confidentiality. I also spoke with parents and adult professionals who work with girls and female adolescents .

I found a real consensus among the girls and adolescents I spoke with: Competition is a reality in their lives and they're doing all in their power to prepare themselves to deal with that reality. The fact that there is a particular kind of emotional turmoil that accompanies the competition seems to be of little or no concern to the majority of the girls and adolescents I spoke with. Even those who were reticent on other issues were often very vocal on issues connected to competition. They especially made their feelings clear when it came to men and money. For twelve-year-old Tina from South Carolina, for example, both men and money were priorities in her life and she planned not be be without either. "I want it all, got to have it all, and will get it all," she stated with adamant confidence. When queried about what the "all" was, most spoke in terms of material trappings and felt that spiritual development was not a real issue in their lives. Many equated a notion of spirituality with material abundance much in the same way that contemporary evangelists of the Reverend Ike ilk do.

That view crossed class and geographical boundaries and it was just as intense in girls eight to ten as in young adults fifteen to eighteen. I was often amazed by what appeared to be a callousness about the nature of competition and what it does to relationships. While some felt it was necessary, others felt it was an incentive that kept them wanting more in their lives. The "more" generally has a high price tag and does little to spirtually or intellectually nourish them. The equation in which material abundance equals happiness seems to balance for them. Spiritual satisfaction and intellectual stimulation count for little in most of their lives. Competition produces tangible commodities. That which is abstract seems to be less relevant and certainly not nearly as important.

Laurie is 14 and soon to become a mother for the second time. "Having Robert's baby was one way of saying to all my friends that I had Robert. He was mine and that was that. He had been going with my friend L'Tanya, but I knew he really liked me and that I was better for him than she was. I got what I wanted. L'Tanya got mad and threatened to kick my butt. We were friends, but friends come and go. It's really no big deal. Robert comes around from time to time. The other day, he took Billy to the park. I mean he ain't never going to shop, cook, or do that kinda thing. He don't work that way," noted Laurie with a kind of benign acceptance in her voice.

What they lose out on when competing for men—men who are often transient in their lives, playing the most momentary role and then escaping to find pleasure elsewhere—seems not to even dawn on them. Attitudes held by adolescents like Laurie are prevalent and speak to the fact that the caring/nurturing quotient is very low in our society. The constant focus on material trappings, as a measure of who and what you are, produce this kind of attitude.

While seven-year-old Monique was visiting the San Francisco Bay Area from New Orleans, I met her at a cultural event. She was visiting an aunt and recovering from the devastation of not being selected to perform in an upcoming spring production by a New Orleans ballet company. She told her mother she wanted the part more than anything she could think of. Her confidence bordered on arrogance and there were many times I couldn't believe I was talking with a seven-year-old. "My best friend Andrea got the part. I'm really angry with her because she hasn't even studied as long as I have and she's just really mediocre," said Monique. I got the sense that she was mimicking the language and possibly the desires of the adults surrounding her. When I asked her if she would go to see Andrea in the performance, an intense haughtiness arose in her voice and the words "not on your life" rolled off her tongue with the sharpness of a shark's teeth.

Many psychologists agree that rejection is difficult for all of us. But becoming embittered to the point of dismissing your best friend for winning is not a healthy sign. If uncorrected, such behavior sets a weak standard for the support and development of relationships at all levels. To a great extent parents seem to play a significant role in promoting the kind of competition that often ruins relationships between their children and their children's friends. One mother I spoke to went so far as to state, "I know my child is not only brilliant and beautiful, but I'm depending on her talent to support me in my later years. I've got to push her to make sure she uses it all to give herself the best and hopefully make me comfortable too. My own parents didn't push me far enough or hard enough, and I don't have nearly enough. She can have it all and I'm simply doing my part to see to it that she gets it."

"Healthy competition is vital to the empowerment of black girls and empowerment is essential to their ultimate survival," a professional in the field of child development told me.

"But what we must keep uppermost in mind is the fact that competition is not for every child. Some will thrive as a result of competing and others will be destroyed. We can't afford to lose any more of our children to any kind of destruction. We really have to develop systems that support the growth of the best in each of our children. Our girls are being forced to compete for so much: fathers, husbands, jobs. And with the primary responsibility for family falling on their shoulders, the competition ante is upped one more notch."

With entry into the world being competitive, race and class are certainly conditions for competing for spaces in those hospital nurseries. The travesties that accompany the competitive mentality are apparent in situations involving even very young children. With parents drilling three-year-olds so that they can be accepted in the best preschools, or eight-year-olds discussing their resumés and showing their portfolios, less and less time is being devoted to childhood. The frequency with which I see children climbing trees, jumping rope, or playing jacks is quickly diminishing. These are activities that involve healthy, fun, and noncompetitive interaction. With the focus on heavily competitive activities, jumping rope, climbing trees, and playing jacks will become fodder for sociological study and not the fun and nurturing activities that make for great childhood memories and community comraderie.

"The world has become so much smaller," commented a fourth-grade private school teacher.

"These kids are having to compete at the international level. It's a worldwide job market and not merely a state or national market. I keep telling my students it's not just about other black or white people you'll be dealing with in the world. You'd better learn to speak Japanese, Chinese, Arabic, Russian, and Spanish. You'd better be prepared to accept customs and traditions totally new to you, and most of all you must learn to come to terms with the fact that all the smart children in the world don't live in America."

Blacks see regular evidence of competition with other blacks, especially in the entertainment and sports worlds. But they don't see themselves competing as often in the business or academic arenas and when they do it's with a vengeance to hold on to or get a position. In business and academia, they often dismiss principles in order to hold on to scarce jobs.

In many ways, the women's movement has urged girls to come together to share their skills and knowledge to make things better for those who will lead in the future. But that movement has never quite gotten around to examining and working through its own racism. Black women have never really felt a part of the women's movement and consequently many black girls don't have a real understanding of the roles they can play in such a movement. Ten-year-old Johnnetta lives in Mississippi. She told me:

"I like going to the meetings with my mom and watching her take charge of stuff. She looks important when she does that, and other people treat her that way. She tells me she does these things so that my sisters and I can have opportunities she didn't have. I want to have them too. But I want them so life in Mississippi can be better for the people I know. I wrote an essay about my mom taking charge in our community meetings and it won second place in the whole county. It made me feel happy to be able to write about my mother and win a prize."

As the movement has waned, however, so has the cooperative spirit that many tried to imbue it with. But to a certain extent, the spirit has been imbued in some people to such a degree that it will live on in spite of circumstances, history, and the conservative 1980s. "I'm seeing some incredibly wonderful things happen with the young women in my program," Philip Lawson, an academic career advisor with Upward Bound at Mills College in Oakland, California, told me.

"The kids live for the Upward Bound Games. Every summer we have a competition where everyone gets to try their hand at something. You can emerge as the Upward Bound checkers champion, swimming champ, or math whiz. My job is to help them discover that good, and assist them in putting their lives on course in such a way that they can grow. Some of the kids have the opportunity to compete on teams and as individuals. We certainly want them to win, but not at the cost of a friendship, hostility towards another program or the provocation of violence towards one another. Many of these kids would be involved in gang activities if they were not in programs like these. And we know what kind of competition gangs promote.

"I've actually seen the bonding between our girls grow. You know boys and men have had a brotherhood for a long time. But the brotherhood is not held together with the same kind of bonding element that the sisterhood is. Even though the sisterhood is newer in some ways, it's stronger. I also think that our young men can learn a great deal from the sisterhood. Girls and women value their friendships and support them in ways that we men don't. I don't think women take their friendships for granted the way we often do. I've seen these girls come together to help one another win and I really like that. They want to be able to say they were a part of the victory and share in the feelings that come with it. With all the cutthroat rivalries that go on in most of their environments, it's tough to promote that as a value. But then, we're looking to give them more than academic matter. We want them to 'gift' the world with something and leave a meaningful legacy.

"They don't use the victories to beat up on their friends. We try to point them to the fact that each one of them has something to offer and we want them to give it. It's easier to do this with the girls. They're simply more receptive to new ideas and feelings. We're working on our boys.

"It's the same kind of spirit I want to see in my own children. I want them to achieve, but not at the cost of friendships or their own personal integrity. When you lose those kinds of things, all else is irrelevant. They become the grounding wires of your life."

"I've been very competitive all my life—sports, academics, and relationships," noted 17-year-old Columbia University sophomore Debbie. "I think I'll transfer to Stanford next year. I need to be where the best of everything is. I can get more mileage out of being there. Yale, Stanford, and Bryn Mawr wrote me letters of acceptance. Basically, I knew that I would be accepted by all the schools to which I applied. There was never any doubt in my mind. But you really have to push for these things. They don't just come to you. I'm real pushy and plan to stay that way to get what I want. But sometimes, I must admit I do feel sorry for some of my friends who just don't push." Debbie admits that money is a real goal and makes her more determined. "But there is a side of me that wants to be this famous surgeon because I'm smart and can do it a lot better than many people I know who want to become surgeons. This guy I used to go with wants to be a surgeon, but he barely has the brains to cut bread. But I really don't think I'd like cutting on people. Just dissecting little animals makes me feel weird. I know I'm smart enough and aggressive enough to be anything I want to be." Debbie has excellent graphics skills but won't even consider becoming a surgical illustrator. She smirks at the thought of that occupation, because it doesn't carry the weight, economic clout, or status that being a surgeon does.

For Debbie, as well as for scores of other young black women, personal fulfillment comes on someone else's terms and not her own. It's the yuppie I-want-to-be-better-than-anyone-else syndrome which promotes further competition and takes away from many of the spontaneous and creative moments life has to offer. It's also the kind of competition that puts your life in a box; one that in later years many struggle to release themselves from.

For many black girls and adolescents it's part of a larger struggle. Being black still means you have to prove yourself and therefore you're forced to compete just in order to have your existence acknowledged. You have to compete to prove that you have a brain, while it's assumed that others already have theirs. The double discrimination against black girls and adolescents is further compounded by the fact that now they are competing with black males for positions and driving a serious wedge into intraracial male-female relationships. "It was enough that I had to compete with girls in school. But when I found girls who thought they could shoot hoop and dunk better than I could, I was too through," noted William, a second-year student at the University of California at Los Angeles.

Single-minded decisions that serve the interest of the individual over the interest of a larger group are almost epidemic in the 1980s, the continuation of the me generation/yuppie syndrome. It doesn't appear as though the syndrome will play out any time in the near future, either. Though the cooperative and collective driving force of the 1960s has not totally dissipated, it is definitely not a priority in the minds of most young people. Fourteen-year-old Natasha notes flippantly:

"I mean, who can really afford to do that kind of stuff? My parents talk about how people pulled together in the sixties and made it possible for those in my generation to have access to the things we take for granted. We don't really take it for granted; it just is. You know I can't live the past. I keep telling them that was then, this is now, and I have to live in the now. The now says to get it however you can and that's what I'm going to do. This is America and my mom keeps telling me about the sixties and Afro-American dreams. I told her to put them dreams onto the mirror of reality and wake up and smell the money, honey."

Much of the music, movies, and scores of videos for young people certainly encourage that kind of thinking. In many of the current popular videos, the "get it however you can" theme runs prominently through the songs of contemporary performers like Vanity, Aretha Franklin, and Prince. More often than not it relates to women getting their men however they can. If it means you have to shake your best friend to do it, you just have to do it. The cooperative spirit also emerges, though not as often. The recent anti-apartheid hit, "Ain't Gonna Play Sun City," stresses political and personal comraderie in a very substantive way. The fact that so many well known musicians are in the same video is a statement in and of itself. It also clearly points out what can happen when people who share similar talents decide to share similar vision as well.

There is an interesting arena in which, for the most part, the players function in the interest of and with concern for one another. Virginia Hamilton, Eloise Greenfield, Tom Feelings, Sharon Bell Mathis, and Candy Dawson Boyd are creators of black young adult fiction. In their works they often take great care to create characters who work to accomplish goals collectively and cooperatively. These writers have made a concerted effort to maintain some of the finer vestiges of African traditions. In fact, it is my impression that the vast majority of the young adult novels written by black authors point to that kind of cooperative spirit.

Candy Dawson Boyd's *Circle of Gold*, Eloise Greenfield's *Aliesha* and Virginia Hamilton's *Zeely* are young adult novels that are prime examples of the cooperative ethic and spirit that remains so dear to many. All of them focus on noncompetitive avenues for achieving self-acceptance as well as for developing inner strength. Boyd's *Circle of Gold* focuses on the importance of mutually supportive friendships among adolescents. Greenfield's *Aliesha* illustrates how a disabled girl can function well with her peers and not be pressured into competing for their attention through devious behavior or contrived participation in relationships. Written in 1968, Hamilton's *Zeely* was the first juvenile novel in which black physical features are revered, accepted, and sought after. In this classically rendered novel, a healthy kind of competition takes place when a black girl seeks the beauty and wisdom of a Zulu princess. In some ways *Zeely* set a standard and established a tradition that writers like Greenfield, Feelings, and Boyd would follow. One reader of these books, 16-year-old Jasmine, reflects these values, saying that:

"[Competition is] just not a part of my spirit. Until I was fourteen, I grew up in a collective household. There were four families that lived together and we shared everything. It was real neat and I miss the fact that we now live like an ordinary family. There was always someone who had time for you. We played together, including the adults, learned how to cook and sew together and everyone took turns reading stories to one another. It was always so much fun. It gets boring and now that my brothers are out of the house, there's no one at home to hang with.

"I don't like seeing people get hurt, and competition seems to hurt more than it helps. I know this girl name Cindy who is driven beyond the brink to compete for everything, including the most popcorn at the movie. She gets all her jollies from competing. She wears the best clothes, dates the best boys, eats the best food, and refuses to associate with anything or anyone who does not meet her 'best standards.' She wants to be an actress and can't imagine life without going up against something or someone. She tells me it's the nature of the beast. But I try to tell her that it will make her the beast. I once saw her make this girl cry in front of all these people. This girl had gone out and gotten all 'trensied' up in an effort to become more like the others. Cindy talked about her like a dog. Told her she looked like the leftovers from a flea-market. Folks thought it was funny. You could see the pain swell in her cheeks. I told Cindy inflicting that kind of pain on people was unnecessary and that she needed to check out her own mind. She told me I was a simple-minded wimp and to go back to my daisy-wearing, bead-brained tribe.

"I get all A's in school and probably will get scholarships. But I don't want to go to college right away. And Harvard, Yale, and Stanford are definitely out. Right now, going to college feels real overwhelming. The stories I hear about how you have to compete for everything make me a bit nervous. I want to travel and experience other things about the world. I might go to college when I'm twenty-five. My parents aren't terribly crazy about the idea, but I think I want to be a chef, and cook my way around the world."

While competition has served as a real inspiration for some of us, it has driven others to the brink and beyond. There are ways in which competition can turn your morals, principles, and values completely around. The need to feel part of the group, and as accomplished as the rest, remains great. A few years back, a young black woman reporter for the *Washington Post* wrote a story about a child who was a drug addict. The story won a Pulitzer Prize and, in the process, it was discovered not only that the story was untrue but that the young woman did not possess the credentials indicated on her resumé.

Rosa competes for food stamps, a better social worker, and the guts to tell the bureaucrats she must deal with on an almost weekly basis what to do with their food stamps. She's been receiving public assistance for two years now. Her mother died and left her with the responsibility of raising three younger siblings. At 17, she's constantly exhausted, but mainly from having to fight to get every penny she can to help out her family.

> "I feel as though I've become some kind of vicious animal. I'm always arguing with social workers, teachers, or somebody just to get what I know is rightfully ours. For me it's not even about competing for anything; this is basic survival. If I just sat back and didn't do anything, me and my brothers and sister would starve. I'm not letting them put them in a home, so I have to do all kinds of maneuvering to stay on top of things. I don't have time to compete with my friends for nothing. Like I said, I'm doing basic survival."

If those who are fortunate enough to fulfill their visions and dreams can remember to reach back and bring others along, the competition may be worth it. But if others are not brought into the fold to learn how to make the pie, as well as to control the apportionment of the pie, then all the individual accolades, accomplishments, and kudos will mean nothing. We will have only put one foot in front of the other and gone nowhere.

NOTES

1. Dr. Juness Junebunny Jones and Junetta Juness Junebunny Jones are direct descendants of Mr. Junebug Jabbo Jones. Mr. Jones, who is alleged to have come over on the Mayflower, is an activist and grassroots philosopher created in the late sixties by members of the Student Non-Violent Coordinating Committee

2. National Research Council, *Risking the Future: Adolescent Sexuality, Pregnancy, and Child-rearing* (Washington, D.C.: National Academy Press, 1987), 51.

A.M.D.G. Revisited

YVONNE

We were Roman Catholic boys and girls. We were citizens of the United States of America after World War II. In school until the 1960s we sat at wooden desks. Probably oak. Single desks or double desks, attached to wooden runners like railroad tracks. We sat in nailed down rows before the plain, heavy, huge, but movable, desk of our female instructor who was swathed in a graceful, time-honored, dark, heavy dress and veil. We called her Sister. Behind her was a black chalkboard with a crucifix nailed neatly above it. In the center. A small U.S. flag hovered above the classroom door like a limp sleeve on a thin, stiff, wooden arm. Daily we stood to pray to our crucified Saviour. Daily we stood to pledge allegiance to our nation's flag. Then we all sat down facing the same direction.

A.M.D.G. is an abbreviation of the Latin phrase, "All for the Greater Honor and Glory of God." In the parochial schools I attended during the Eisenhower and Kennedy years, students were asked to write these letters on their work, particularly their tests. This small form of dedication acknowledged that our tasks were ultimately in praise of God who, in Catholic doctrine, is Three Persons: the omniscient Creator/Judge, the forgiving Saviour/Teacher, and the inspiring Holy Ghost. All for the Greater Honor and Glory of God. This rubric transformed all our strivings for excellence and all our errors and failures. It took our endeavors out of the realm of mere schooling and thrust them into the greater arena of good versus evil, where the Truth defeated the Father of Lies. We children were ignorant of the full import of this dedication. We were simply doing our ABCs.

We all sat down facing the same direction: to hear and listen, to see and believe, to question and answer, to memorize. The boys sat in the front half of each vertical row of desks, the girls in the back. We had all been taught the New Testament lesson that if one had five talents, one should give back ten, and if one had ten talents, one should give back twenty. Even if one were born with only one talent like the slow-witted or the poor (or the pagan babies in Asia and the colored people down South?), well, even then, one dared not bury that one talent, "lest thou be cast out into utter darkness." So we all hoped to be correct, to be asked what we knew, to please, to be suitable. And were some students more suitable than others? Were there places of honor along these orderly nailed-down rows of desks? Yes. In the last desk in each row sat the really smart girls. Indeed, the last shall be first.

The contemporary dictionary definition of *competition* stresses rivalry. A *rival* is defined as existing when two or more people strive to reach or obtain a goal only one of them can possess. Only one person can be the winner. The theological context of the Catholic schools of my childhood did not fully endorse this definition of competition. Although the nuns acknowledged achievement and encouraged it by giving prizes, theoretically the ultimate goal was never something only one person could attain. The ultimate goal was to please God, and He was never inaccessible. Even the lowliest failure was guaranteed God's attention if one's intentions were sincere. Of course, one's motivations were often hidden from the world and could be truly known only by God who is omniscient. So the ultimate goal of pleasing God is somewhat invisible and cannot be humanly judged. How then could the Catholic Church through its teachers justly encourage and reward the achievements of its students? Was competition gratuitous?

In the New Testament, Jesus Christ taught that we should render to Caesar the things that are Caesar's, and to God the things that are God's. The Catholic Church has usually interpreted Caesar as the practical demands of life, and as long as they are not immoral according to the Church's teachings, we are permitted, if not obliged, to satisfy these responsibilities. Consequently, Catholic children are obliged to take their studies seriously, and the ultimate goal of working to please God absorbs, rather than contradicts, the intermediate goal of academic success.

The nuns in my school were formidable taskmasters who monitored and tallied our daily scholastic progress with jesuitical precision. A frenetic comparing of scores among the students was more likely in elementary school than at higher levels of education, but the spirit of competitiveness never seemed to reach a delirious pitch. On the contrary, if one were too eager to reveal one's grades when they were commendable, one was considered a show-off. Pride was a cardinal sin, and the nuns, through their vocation of wordly renunciation, were visible signs of one of the most praiseworthy virtues, humility. No student could ever be as humble as a nun, but one could try.

Still, what about jealousy and envy? Was this quasi-religious environment exempt from such normal human dynamics? Somewhere in my education I had learned a distinction between jealousy and envy. Jealousy is the coveting of what rightfully belongs to oneself. Thus, God in the Old Testament calls Himself a jealous God. But envy is the desire to take what rightfully belongs to someone else. In Catholic schools we were taught that all our work must be dedicated to God. Our intention was as important as our actual accomplishment. To covet someone else's accomplishments might mean coveting someone's prayer to God. This was the first sin of Cain, who murdered his brother Abel because God had found Abel's sacrifice (read intention) more sincere. Yes, envy can be a murderous emotion. And it can destroy the one who envies as much as the one envied. Through envy one's goal becomes the duplication of another's skills, rather than the fulfillment of one's own inherent talents. One becomes someone else's clone. Why, then, should one strive? To be better than a rival? Or to be better than one's previous achievements? Again, the moral key rests not so much in one's behavior as in one's motivation.

The last could be first. But we could not choose to be overlooked, ignored, hidden by the student in the desk in front of us. All of us were obliged to strive. Work was a biblically sanctioned debt. No one was exempt. Neither the boys in the front of the room (because they could not be trusted), nor the girls behind them (in the footsteps of Eve). And the really smart girls sat in the places of honor, the last desk in every row. Smart girls were helpful: they wrote assignments on the chalkboard, graded test papers, were left in charge whenever the nun left the room. And they were encouraged to strive and to double their talents to win the "best smart girl" award. At the end of each year in every class there was one smartest girl and one smartest boy. There were almost never any ties for these titles. Yes, we were all children of God, but there was only one coat of many colors. So, boys competed with boys; girls competed with girls. Once in a while they competed as coed rows of students; row two brought in the most money for the pagan babies; row six swept under their desks most efficiently. But only in spelling bees did all openly strive as individual adversaries for the same goal. Often a girl would win. Appropriate. Didn't girls like to write on the chalkboard for the nuns? Spelling was a feminine task, like clapping the erasers.

Clapping the erasers free of chalk dust, washing the chalkboards, handing out paper, crayons, scissors, any girl could be the most indispensable student. Yet performing such menial tasks, whether assigned or chosen, conveyed an ambiguous status. While beneficial to the nun (and thus pleasing to God), they did not bestow power over one's peers. Besides, the boys had their menial tasks also, such as waxing the floors. Only the really smart girls had the status jobs in the classroom. And they were required to be as good as they were smart. It may not have been intolerable for a boy with a 95 academic average to get a C in self-control. But a smart bad girl was a freak. In fact, she did not exist. If a girl was bad, she had to be dumb, also.

Otherwise, how could she be helpful? How could she grade papers without gossiping about them? How could she be trusted to be in charge when the nun left the classroom?

Curiously, there always seemed to be a larger pool of smart girls than smart boys in those Catholic elementary schools. Was it because smart girls were given extra tasks which made them distinct? Perhaps. But smart boys had their own dutiful rewards. Within the prestigious liturgical conventions they could serve as altar boys and choir boys. In church the men dominated. Smart girls had to satisfy themselves with classroom politics where the nuns reigned. By giving smart girls all the extra clerical and supervisory responsibilities, were the nuns subliminally assuaging their own subordination and liturgical insignificance? Or were they teaching humility— "to whom much has been given much is required"?

Smartest boy. Smartest girl. Never smartest student.

Competition and its rewards were segregated by sex in parochial schools. Since seating arrangements discouraged communication, both boys and girls were made ignorant of the kind of dynamics that might occur when people of the opposite sex work together on a particular intellectual project. Whenever there was a choice, boys preferred to work among themselves, the girls likewise. The students really formed two separate and distinct social and intellectual groups within the classroom, which seemed equal and natural. Girls were never told they were not as smart as boys, nor were they treated as subordinates. And, as mentioned earlier, they were often left in charge. Had it not been for the signals she received from the larger secular communities of family, neighborhood, ethnic group, and finally nation, a really smart Catholic girl might have assumed that she could grow up to be president (if not priest). Were the nuns inadvertently encouraging subversion? Hardly. For the separation of boys and girls in academic competition reflected and supported what was going on outside the classroom. A boy never had to face the humiliation of being "beaten" by a girl. Not only was this segregation favorable to males in the adult secular spheres, but within the Catholic Church it fostered an orderly supervision of the laity. Everyone had his or her assigned place. It was like the great medieval Chain of Being. Staying in one's place was identified with peace, harmony, and self-fulfillment. Staying in one's place was a function of character.

In Catholic schools students were assessed by character grades in addition to academic ones. One earned strictly objective numerical grades like 98 in geography, and more subjective ones like B in obedience. These character grades guided students along their predetermined paths as males and females. As mentioned, it was common belief that discrepancies between academic and character grades were more tolerable in boys than in girls. It was believed that boys were not assessed in the same way as girls in areas like obedience, self-control, or cooperation. For example, in the grading of health habits—which evaluated neatness and cleanliness, not one's medical condition—a girl's neatness was a kind of precondition of her intelligence. The nuns were believed to be more indulgent with a boy's sloppy penmanship than with a girl's wrinkled blouse. But lest I be accused of finding bias for the sake of wit, I must confess that I never compared my report card with that of an equally smart boy. It simply was not done. Nor was there any practical reason for such comparisons. Women did not compete with men in the real world, so why should girls compete with boys?

Hormonal tension, sexual rivalry, unnatural competition.

After elementary school, Catholic boys and girls were assigned to separate schools. It was a clean surgical procedure. Now the girls could compete to their hearts' content—among themselves. They could vie for the chemistry prize as cooly as if it were for French, for never would they find a cancer cure in the pantry (Madame Curie, pardonnez-moi). They could ruminate upon Aquinas till the cows came home, for never would they be priests. Yes. Competition among the girls could be ruthless (down to the 1/100th of a grade point), and even blessed as long as it remained within the all-female institution. There it was a harmless virginal diversion, not unlike the segregated rivalry of beauty contests. Ultimately this academic dueling among the girls would be beneficial to men—all that rigorous preparation to become the helpmates of doctors, lawyers, bankers. All that cultivation for a brief reign as Queen for a Day, then off to the scullery. (What man ever majored in physics to prepare for modern fatherhood?)

Although it was axiomatic before the 1970s that girls did not grow up to be president of the United States, academic achievement was not minimized in all-female Catholic high schools. In fact, intellectual acumen among women is a long-standing Catholic tradition. Witness the numerous teaching and contemplative orders of nuns. Ironically, the first strictly intellectual role models for Catholic boys and girls were most likely women, the nuns. The nuns we had might not have been smarter than mothers, but they were doing something that had professional status in the secular world. To a child a nun may have seemed smarter, and more than one really smart Catholic girl has feared the convent as her legitimate fate. But if she were not asked to be married or "called" to the convent, a really smart girl had two other worthy alternatives: She could be a lay teacher in the parochial schools or a professional nurse in a Catholic hospital.

So, we girls could compete—but not with the boys. We could compete—but only if we were good and helpful. We could compete—but only with our own kind.

Our own kind? But, Lord, who is my neighbor? Tribe. Sex. Nation. Race. Species. A convergence of tributaries. Community. Lord, who is my neighbor?

In Latin the word *competere* means to come together, to agree, to be suitable. In Late Latin it means to seek together. Even in its etymology, competition implies a group. Either a group of individual competitors, or two or more groups against one another. To compete against someone is to acknowledge him or her as a person, albeit an adversary. Someone against whom to excel. Someone to beat, to outrun, to outsmart. Competition implies a certain solidarity. Opponents recognize each other's traits and skills. To compete means to be in the game. To compete means to be recognized, to be considered for evaluation, to be respected. But in many competitions one must first qualify to participate. Games are not open to anyone who simply steps up to the starting line.

The game of Catholic schooling was no exception. Until the financial crises of the 1960s, Catholic schools were for Catholics only, most of whom supported the schools at the parish level. It was a separated education, like yeshivas freely chosen by the students or, more accurately, by their parents. This separation, however, was founded on an equal opportunity policy, namely, a missionary prerogative: "Go forth, teach ye all nations." My black American family was the beneficiary (for better and for worse) of that prerogative. Through baptism my family received an indelible but invisible mark as token of our lifetime, and possibly eternal, membership in the communion of saints. This membership could be lost only by our own willful and knowledgeable choice through grievous sin. Through baptism we became qualified for a particular communion and, in certain circumstances, competition. This baptism of water (more social than baptism of desire, less painful than baptism of blood) was the great equalizer. Or was it?

Until the riots in Philadelphia in the late 1960s, a black Catholic girl had never been chosen May Queen in the predominantly white parish school where I was educated. This was typical of similar parishes.

Born black and Catholic,* I had received the religion prize (read the second-place smart girl prize) for five consecutive years in this academically progressive school. I competed against every other really smart girl—there were nine of them, all white. Each year I was defeated for first place by minuscule margins. In the eighth grade three of these girls tied for first place, but I was never part of such an unusual coincidence. Interestingly, none of these winners surpassed me at the girls' parochial high school in which we all—except one—then enrolled. This lone exception won a scholarship to a small Catholic girls' academy. But she and I encountered each other again as scholarship students at a Catholic women's college on the main line. There I surpassed her in overall academic achievement and student leadership. I can only surmise that competition at the higher levels of education may have been more objective because it was not a neighborhood affair. Perhaps there was less pressure on a nun to favor her own tribal roots when conferring prizes.

I do not want to indict the Catholic school system as a bastion of racism comparable to de jure Jim Crowism in the postbellum South. In fact, in the 1950s one overriding reason prompted many black conversions to Catholicism: the reputed superiority of parochial elementary schools. Twenty years after the death of Rev-

---

*Theologically speaking, no one is "born Catholic," but in everyday parlance Catholics often say this. It means that one was baptized close to the time of birth and has never been a member of another religion. Unlike some Protestants, Catholics believe in infant baptism, and not baptizing a newborn is considered a serious negligence on the part of a Catholic parent.

erend Martin Luther King, Jr., significant percentages of black Protestant children attend Catholic schools, particularly in black neighborhoods. The Catholic schools must be doing something right.

Undeniably, the Catholic school is a product of the American dream. It was a major instrument in the Americanization of European immigrants, as was its secular counterpart, the public school. Its rituals and dogmas served as familiar and comforting guideposts to these strangers in the Promised Land. They could remain tribal (read ethnic) as they cast off the garments of illiteracy, peasantry, disenfranchisement, and poverty. They learned to relish competition within a new context, the Catholic U.S. neighborhood, a context they may have perceived to be more permanent than it actually proved to be. My own family lived in a series of white neighborhoods. We always managed to be among the first arrivals on a changing block. As a result, I was always one of the only blacks in the parish school. As an "only," I functioned as a test case for U.S. Catholic magnanimity in these schools. I was often told how good it was for the students (read whites) that I was there. As a "good" girl, I was a specimen of Catholic missionary zeal. As a really smart black, I was a harbinger of trouble: Now the white Catholic children would have to compete with the Negroes just as they had begun to make gains on the WASPS and Jews. It was not fair.

When a Catholic school tipped, that is, when it became more than 20 percent black, the adjustment was often less violent than were comparable changes in public schools. This was because the neighborhood surrounding the church school had also been racially changed. The new students had not been simply bused in. Also, most of the blacks in the Catholic schools would have been Catholic (at least, in the early stages of this change). So, they had the minimum qualifications for this particular communion.

Communion: a body of Christians having a common faith and discipline.

Now competition is inevitable in any social situation where more than one person has a particular skill that is appreciated by the group. Competition is part of the dynamic of gathering together for a particular purpose. The wealthier in talents the group members, the more competition. However, when a group has built into its structure a means by which all talented participants have an equal chance and obligation to contribute, envy as defined earlier in this essay is somewhat mitigated. When a member perceives that he or she has no chance to fulfill abilities within the group, that member becomes an adversary and may either leave the group or work within it to gain acceptance and fulfillment. Working from within may produce behavior interpreted as unorthodox or hostile. Conflicts fester and may erupt. Dissension may lead to the total dissolution of the group, to reformation, or to schism. To maintain harmony and preserve itself, a group should develop a structure and a philosophy that affords each member a sense of necessary participation. The Church, while segregating its female members, has nonetheless made them feel necessary, which may account for their long-standing loyalty. However, in the United

States it may be questioned whether blacks feel needed in the Catholic communion. Black U.S. culture is predominantly Protestant. So, black Catholics keep a low profile in the more outspoken professions of publishing and education. Black Catholics are not encouraged by the media, black or white, to share our particular journey toward the American dream. As a result, there is scanty documented material on the effect of Catholic moral and educational discipline on blacks' competitive skills. Was conversion an asset or a deprivation? This is critical since the pope has traveled through Africa proclaiming that the continent is ripe for the Catholic harvest. No religion is pure morality or theology. Every religion has its hidden agenda of maintaining the tribe and the nation. Render to Caesar the things that are Caesar's.

The Catholic Church in the United States is famous for its managerial acumen. Much of this skill was acquired through the fund-raising efforts of the bishops and priests during the great school- and church-building decades. Their goal: Every Catholic child in a Catholic school from first grade to graduate school. The Catholic Church was determined to save itself in Protestant North America by mainstreaming its members. To an amazing degree it has been successful. But have all its members profited equally from this mainstreaming? What about the students who are at the bottom rung of this quasi-corporate religious ladder? What might they have learned from this parochial school experience? And more specifically, what did the competitive, really smart girls learn?

The corporate-managerial structure developed by the bishops and priests during the church- and school-building era had its counterpart within the various orders of nuns. At the highest levels of the schools and hospitals that the nuns founded, staffed, and supervised were women, with up-to-date college and university degrees despite their quaint medieval garb. These administrators and scholars came from their own ranks. It was not impossible for a girl to enter the convent at 18 years of age, complete her higher education as she was taking her final vows, and after years of work and accomplishment, rise to the position of Mother General. Yes, Mother General: a common title for the head of a religious order of women. No sobriquet, it was a sign of real power. Although every religious order, male or female, is to some extent under the jurisdiction of the bishop, archbishop, or cardinal of a particular region, these religious groups have much autonomy, which may manifest itself in something as real as property.

This autonomy has led a few to reorganize themselves radically since Vatican II and, at times, to challenge the bishops. Post-Vatican organizational changes, at times shocking to the rest of the laity (of which nuns are members since they are not priests), were in keeping with the tradition of religious orders, many of which were founded by energetic, educated, wealthy, and, not least of all, holy women. Women who saw the need for a particular way of life or a particular job to be done and simply did it. But how much of that legacy of power, innovation, autonomy, as well as dedication to a spiritual ideal was made visible and thus available to the hundreds of thousands of girls these religious women educated? How many really smart Catholic girls knew enough about the lives of the religious foundresses to emulate them? Were only the spiritual aspects of convent life raised before us and not the practical, professional work? Nuns were viewed as asexual, meek followers, not assertive policy makers.

Seven girls in seven desks. At the ends of seven rows. Smart girls. Good girls. Helpful girls. Miniature nuns. Tradition. Part of the unwritten code. Indelible as the Baltimore Catechism which tested us in the law. The law. The convoluted Roman Catholic law in neat question-and-answer doses. Who is God? What is a Supreme Being? Why did God make us? Neat questions and answers to show us how to behave, how to do God's will. According to our talents. According to our gender. According to our place.

The Baltimore Catechism of my childhood was authorized by the U.S. bishops, and introduced us students to Catholic faith and morals in a simplified, orderly style. Not only did it offer clear behavioral guidelines to students, but it also channeled and subtly discouraged students' questions. After all, all possible questions had been given in the book. All one had to do was learn them. The best learners were rewarded modestly with a good grade and perhaps something extra like a holy card or religious medal. An effective instructional method, the catechism was nevertheless challenged in the 1960s and has given way to other teaching styles, which recognize the value of student initiative in this highly competitive national culture. The Church seems to be addressing the old mainstreaming problem again. It is altering its style, not its dogma.

The rise of Catholic coeducational schools at the secondary and college levels is another example of ecclesiastical facelifting. Primarily a response to financial troubles, coeducation will undoubtedly alter student relationships, as it has in nonsectarian schools. The gender segregation of childhood competition has all but passed away at the college and university levels. Those Catholic colleges that remain women's institutions often have cooperative programs with coed and men's schools, where faculty and facilities are shared. Also, the profile of the student body at these women's colleges is changing. With the advent of the women's movement, many older and usually married or divorced women attend college to start or to continue their higher education. With their particular problems in the job market, these older female students have probably had an influence on the courses, the career counseling, and the overall intellectual atmosphere of these all-female colleges. Younger women, too, now have more conscious career goals. Whether these academic changes will increase Catholic lay women's power within the U.S. Catholic Church remains to be seen.

The Catholic woman's competitive legacy would seem to be akin to that of all women in similar single-sex circumstances. Since traditional Catholic schools have always given capable girls extra responsibilities, such girls will undoubtedly measure up in professional situations. From a purely secular academic perspective, a Catholic education is not a disadvantageous one. However, Catholicism is a highly visible religion. Despite the sophistication of its hierarchy in this country, its official stance on artificial contraception, abortion, and divorce is not shared by the more progressive social institutions in U.S. culture. Is the Catholic Church perceived in the popular mind as medieval and foreign? If it is, there may be a greater burden on the Catholic professional, particularly a woman, to prove how secular she is. It is commonly perceived that a Catholic woman will always have more qualms about modern U.S. morals than will other women. She may be perceived as someone who must always answer to the pope rather than to her conscience. She may be perceived as someone whose life is under the scrutiny of a conservative religious government and not a personal and intimate God. Such attitudes in the minds of many non-Catholics may prove a significant factor, although subliminal, in the Catholic woman's competitive stance, particularly in highly visible public policy professions. Can a woman be the vice president of the country and remain Catholic? This question will continue to reverberate long after Geraldine Ferraro's candidacy.

Daily we stood to pray to our crucified Saviour. Daily we stood to pledge allegiance to our nation's flag. A small U.S. flag hovering like a limp sleeve above the classroom door. Through every open door stood another closed door. Every unobstructed corridor led to a dead end. All detour signs were written in archaisms. If you have been given five talents, you must give back ten. To whom much has been given, much is required. Every Catholic child in a Catholic school, college, university. Catholic nurses in Catholic hospitals. Catholic ethics in Catholic business, Catholic welfare agencies. And government? What about government? What profit to lose your soul? Your self? All for the Greater Honor and Glory of God. On the top of every test paper. Like an imprimatur. Like an indelible sign. It hovered somewhere above our sexualized brains. Then. Now. Like a miraculous cloud of manna preceding us into mainstream America.

Dialogue, Dialectic, and Dissent

BARBARA ROSENBLUM and SANDRA BUTLER

Eschewing class privilege and a corned beef sandwich and some chili, our two heroines sat at the local feminist café to plan their paper. The corned beef was rather standard but well complemented by posters of Amelia Earhart, Angela Davis, and Sacajawea.

"OK, OK. Let's start by making a list." Barbara wrote at the top of a yellow pad, as she always did, "To Do." Sandy flinched but kept silent.

Define terms. Clarify focus. Identify issues. Assign tasks. Alternate drafts. She hunched over the paper, earnestly making boxes with headings.

"Come on. You don't need to make this a monumental task. It looks like naval maneuvers. Let's just start by talking about the ideas here."

Barbara lifted her head from the yellow pad and said with her customary asperity, "My process is different from yours and I need to make a shape first——"

"Oy. We start with the process now. Let me just give you some of my suggestions for topics. Sexuality is always interesting. I mean competition around sexuality."

"That's a good one. Do you think we should focus on heterosexual women competing for men or competition around sexuality in general?"

"I meant in general. We all participate in that behavior, I think," said Sandy.

Barbara looked puzzled. "I don't think lesbians compete for women in the same way that straight women compete for men."

"Baloney. Of course we do. Do you think we are immune from sexually competitive feelings? That we don't ever try to move on each other? Seduce each other? Or at the very least try to be 'interesting,' 'compelling,' and——"

"You do?" Barbara questioned sharply.

"Well, before I met you I did," Sandy responded soothingly.

"Funny, we never talked about that before," persisted Barbara.

"Well, let's not talk about it now." Sandy stuffed the remaining half of the sandwich into her mouth and began to chew rapidly.

"Well, since you seem to be the expert, perhaps you ought to write the first draft of that argument," Barbara said stiffly. "It appears that we are indeed dealing with some previously unacknowledged competition between us. I didn't think we could be competitive. We're too different. Why, we're not even good at the same things!"

"But now we're on the right track. Let's start with some good old feminist process that begins with C-R. Let's examine our relationship and see if we can uncover, decode, and deconstruct it," said Sandy in a self-congratulatory way.

"Is this a Derridean diversion?"

"No, it's a thermal inversion, silly. Let's begin."

"OK," said Barbara, poised to think, "Who's smarter? Who's funnier? Who is innately more intelligent? Who is more creative? Who is more well liked? Who has the capacity to earn more money in a lifetime?"

Sandy continued. "Who is the better dresser? Who is cleaner? Who does her fair share of the housework? You mean stuff like that?"

"Yes," Barbara replied eagerly.

"OK. Let's take one of the above and work with it. I have more of a sense of humor than you do. You might be more playful than I am, but I am definitely more witty than you," Sandy said.

"Hold it right there. Am I to understand that you no longer find me sexy but not funny either?"

"Certainly you're funny, but I was simply trying to make some distinctions that would clarify differences between us and help us generate open-hearted appreciation for the other rather than a feeling of trying to be better in the same area."

"So," Barbara interrupted, "under all that verbiage is the bald truth that you think you're funnier than I am!"

"Well, let's just say that my sense of humor is more subtle and sophisticated, and you are given to pratfalls and punchlines."

"Well," Barbara hissed, "I'll have you know that just last night when I was having dinner with A and W, I had the entire table in stitches, all laughing at my subtle and sophisticated humor."

Sandy narrowed her lips and muttered, "Go ahead. I can see we won't get on with this until you tell it."

Barbara relaxed and smiled widely. Leaning forward across the cracked vinyl oilcloth, she asked, "What is *theodicy?*"

"What is it? What is it?" Sandy asked impatiently.

"A book by Homer. Get it? A book by Homer!" Barbara began to chortle enthusiastically as she always did at her own jokes, often beginning the chortle even before getting to the punchline.

Sandy studiously arranged herself on the hard chair. The women fell silent as the room filled with the loud strains of a scratched version of "We Are Family." The women at the adjoining table tapped and bounced over their coffee.

Our heroines sat drinking their shared pot of red zinger tea, uncertain about how to proceed. Barbara broke the awkwardness by saying, "Let's apply Gilligan's argument that men are raised to be autonomous and independent and not very relationally inclined, and that women's world is centered on relationships and being nurturant. Then wouldn't the quality and character of competition vary in those two spheres?"

Sandy reached for her ballpoint pen. "Nice. Very nice. You mean like who is the most nourishing?"

"Or who is the most autonomous," interjected Barbara. "See, in heterosexual relationships, these attributes and characteristics are divided on the basis of gender, and it therefore defuses competition between men and women. But competition in same-sex relationships could be more invidious and insidious."

"Well, I'm not sure," argued Sandy. "Even within the relational sphere, there are different styles within the same sex. Like, I'm less schmaltzy in my close relationships, but the depth and intensity is there for decades. But I don't think this is moving us along. It's trite and not useful."

"Really, not useful is one thing—but *trite*? What's trite about it?"

"It's Gender Roles 101."

"Or the war between the sexes, Graduate Seminar 404," recovered Barbara.

The two began to laugh, remembering their own lives as students and teachers, and the earnest humorlessness of both roles.

"I think we are brought up to believe we must choose between love and power and, in making that choice, for those of us who even do, we must understand that power is stunningly male-defined. Power *over*, I mean, rather than power to affect and make changes," Sandy began again.

"*Stunningly? Stunningly?* What kind of purple prose is that? Are you making a speech or writing a draft? We have to process our different writing styles. I write much tighter than you——"

"Can't we just stay with the ideas, please?" pleaded Sandy. "The writing process hasn't even begun."

"Well, where are you going with this? What's your point?"

"It's not a point. It's a discussion." Sandy took a deep breath. "I am trying to say that the issue of power is central to the issue of competition, and as feminists we really have to reexamine our relationship to power and reshape its meanings and function so it can encompass our vision."

"But rather than engage with power directly, we avoid it, diminish its importance, and deny the central function it serves as we reevaluate issues of power? Is that where you are going?"

"Yes, I guess so."

"Well, that's good, but we can't do that until we determine whether the focus of our piece is going to be externally, structurally imposed, scarcity pitting us against each other for limited resources, or a psychological perspective that emphasizes unlearning and relearning and working out the feelings that have been socialized into us. Feelings we ward off because they generate anxiety and abandonment."

Dialogue, Dialectic, and Dissent   173

Sandy cut in. "Already I lost you. And if I lost you, what do you think the reader is going to do with this piece? And besides, your either/or construction is too simpleminded for thinking about these issues."

"So. How should I think about it? The way you do? Is this our moment of lesbian fusion?" Barbara slammed her spoon into the lukewarm bowl of chili.

Sandy took a sip of tea and said reassuringly, "Never mind applying theory. Let's start with empirical cases, and how about looking at some of our personal experiences in the real world? How about your struggle with the tenure system? Tell me how you felt, what it was like for you and so on."

"Well," Barbara said, leaning back, "I remember that there were four of us competing silently for that one slot. Each of us had different areas of specialization and we were all good. "But the one who finally got tenure was the one whose work was most similar to that of the boys who awarded it. Her area of specialization was mathematical methodology. It was pretty bland and contentless—there were no people in it, just lots of numbers, and, Lord knows, no politics. So the nature of competition was loaded from the start. She was destined to 'win' and the three others were destined to 'lose.' "

"But what's psychological about having limited options in the job market? Why is it necessary to apply words like *fear, abandonment, anxiety?*" challenged Sandy.

"Everything is psychological. We have psychological responses to structural oppressions. Both have to be analyzed," Barbara snapped.

"Well, you have to feel that everything is psychological. Look at all the years, the money, and the psychological investment you have in psychotherapy."

"It certainly keeps me from displacing and projecting my feelings all over the place," replied Barbara defensively. "Good therapy helps us find the balance between the internal and external forces and avoid the need for endless reenactments and repetitions. And if you weren't so damn stubborn . . . ," her voice drifted off, the rest of the sentence unnecessary since they had had this conversation many times before.

Barbara began again, after reaching for Sandy's shoulder and draping her arm across it. "I think the main point I would want to make is that a model of scarcity is one primary context for a discussion of competition. Men as scarce resources. Career success. Tenure positions. Love objects. Because there is an imagined scarcity, we become pitted against one another. Our individual responses are societally induced. And it has difficult implications depending on class background and expectations and how much therapeutic work a person has done."

Sandy exhaled noisily. "Yup. I knew that would come up sooner or later. You always bring up your class background when you want to get an edge over me."

"Edge? What is now with the edge?"

"Don't pretend you don't know what I mean. You are the poorest. The one who had to pull yourself up by the bootstraps—only in your family, it was poorly made sandals from a pushcart. Talk about competition. You pit yourself against everybody."

"Oh, now we're talking in the language of bulldogs?" Barbara muttered, removing her hands from Sandy's shoulder and jamming it into her coat pocket.

"Your sense of humor is about as strained as the quality of mercy," Sandy murmured placatingly, reaching for the hand now hidden under the tabletop. "Let's try again," she urged. "Let's begin with the statement that competition is not necessarily bad for feminists. It can push us to our fullest selves and be a source of discipline that can be in our best interests."

"Ridiculous," Barbara responded. "Competition is a way of measuring accomplishment that is utterly patriarchal in its conception. And speaking of that, the techniques of measurement are utterly male-defined. Who else but a man would take a picture of the horses' noses to see which one finished first? Nosology, epistemology, typology, and taxonomy. They are all male-generated systems of classification. Should we say that nosology is the theory and typology the practice?"

"Isn't part of our work to take language and redefine it in ways that represent a feminist vision? Just because the boys use words in a particular way doesn't mean those words are forever unusable for us. We just need to reclaim them. I think it's crucial that feminists can be excellent, can achieve in the world, can reach our best selves without submitting to the boys' methodologies," Sandy said, her voice rising, a speech only moments away.

"That's the most naive and romantic statement I ever heard," said Barbara. "Let's be honest here. When I pick up a journal and see the dreck that passes for analytic thinking, I am motivated to write a piece of my own. My envy of their getting into print motivates me. But can I really challenge the system of selection of the boys at the top, the ones who decide who's the winner?"

Sandy crossed her long legs and asked, "Who's writing the other pieces for this book? If we could get a sense of what other women are going to say, maybe we could find a way to make ours the best. We have already generated too many ideas."

"That isn't the point," Barbara replied in an overly righteous way, relieved that the subject had been changed. "It isn't about the best. It's about a variety of perspectives, diversity of viewpoints, a representational cross-section. But ours will be the best anyway," she whispered in her partner's ear. "So, what do you really think will be in this anthology?"

"A representative sampling of the disciplines, the classes, the races, and the perspectives," said Sandy assuredly. "Some psychology about autonomy and individuation. Some sociology, probably about the way boys and girls are socialized. A look at competition in capitalism. Don't forget one editor is a writer and the other a philosopher, so I expect the pieces to be rigorously argued and well written. No problem, Toots. No problem."

"There is one final organizational issue to deal with."

"What's that?" Sandy asked.

"Well, issues like how long it should be, how much time we have until deadline, and, uh, whose name should go first."

"Ah," Sandy cut in. "I get it. How about alphabetically?"

"Well, I think it should be the one who has published more. And furthermore, don't forget that this is essentially within my field of expertise. The methodology and analytic training are second nature to me by now. It would be inappropriate for you to have senior authorship. After all, I essentially contributed all the important ideas here."

"All right already. But I think we should hold off decisions about authorship until the piece is finished." Sandy looked up at the wall, noticing that the clock indicated that they had only another hour before they would be leaving for a book party a mutual friend was having. Barbara followed Sandy's eyes and snapped, "Are we timing this now? Is the meter running? What did I tell you about male-defined methods of measurement?"

"No. It's just that Angela's book party starts in an hour, and I don't want to show up when it's busy and crowded. I thought we could show up early, stay for a few minutes, and then slip away when it gets too noisy."

"You're not planning to go to a book party dressed like that, are you?" inquired Barbara.

"Certainly I am. What's wrong with the way I look?"

"Well, it seems a bit on the garish side. You look like a Day-Glo star-spangled banner."

"What a way you have with images," Sandy replied caustically. "Most of my friends find me a very colorful dresser. Not everybody dresses in well-matched tones of beige as a sign of tastefulness."

"Well, I can assure you that most of the women will not be dressed that way. Do you really want to stand out that much?"

"I don't mind at all. Is this conversation finished now?"

Barbara hesitated and said, "I guess what I mean is that I feel so drab today. What I, uh, dammit, what I really mean is that you look so much better than I do. Can you dress a little differently so that I won't feel so drab?"

"What does one thing have to do with the other? Why should how I look have anything to do with you?"

"It shouldn't but it does," Barbara responded sheepishly.

"Well," Sandy said, "This can become part of the piece too. Let's look at this."

"I don't want to look at it. I'm looking at you, and I feel like a field mouse next to a peacock."

Imitating Ed McMahon's voice, Sandy sang out, "——and *here's* . . . competition!"

The two women laughed, then signaled for the bill.

As they were rising to leave, Barbara said, "Let's do it this way. You do a draft. I'll do a draft. Either we'll merge them or publish them separately."

Arms around each other, they left for the party.

Transition

HELEN E. LONGINO and VALERIE MINER

The final section of this forum explores some of the themes from Part II and reaches toward alternative visions. In the previous section we considered the role of competition in undermining women's solidarity through the essays by Myrna Kostash, Toni A. H. McNaron, Erika Duncan, Michèle Farrell, Daphne Muse and Barbara Rosenblum and Sandra Butler. We observed the role of competition in dividing and controlling the work force through the eyes of Evelyn Fox Keller and Helene Moglen, Rosabeth Moss Kanter, Debra Matsumoto, and Marjorie Mbilinyi. We considered the value of competition in self-empowerment through the articles by Grace Lichtenstein and Jennifer Ring. And we confronted competition between groups with different privileges in the essays by Elaine Bell Kaplan and Yvonne. Now, in Part III, other authors ask further leading questions. Who gets to compete? What role does competition play in differentiation and individuation? How can we obliterate competition—or find ways to make it benign and useful—or replace it with other ideologies and behaviors? Why do may women initially resist the contention that competition might have constructive forms?

While the wave of feminist activism demonstrated by these writers has not succeeded in abolishing competition, it has revealed the self-defeat of competing in a fixed game. In the early and mid-1970s Matina Horner's thesis that women fear success held much currency. Rosabeth Moss Kanter offers one alternative interpretation in her discussion of the unbearable pressure on visible tokens. Psychologist Georgia Sassen has argued recently that a more fine-grained analysis of the data for the Horner thesis shows that women avoid not success but competition. In particular, Sassen suggests, women shy away from situations in which their success means another's failure. This anthology shows that competition among women takes many forms—conscious and unconscious, chosen and unchosen. It also suggests that competition may not be the unmitigated evil it appears to be at first sight.

The editors believe that as long as competition maintains its current material and symbolic role in our social and economic organization, the idea of appropriate competition will be problematic. As more and more human life is made vulnerable to market forces, as access to power and resources and, increasingly, to the very means of life is mediated by competition, no arena, no defense of competition will be immune to the taint of social Darwinism.

Developing appropriate competition requires thinking about the context in which competition occurs. We call for a change in our models of human nature and society: the replacement of our current model of self-interested and antagonistic individualism with a model of community, "cooperative sociality," or "imaginative collectivity." These models recognize what the individualist models conceal—the interdependence of human beings—and transcend the borders of race or nationality. The activity of any human being is dependent upon and conditioned by the activity of others, directly and indirectly. Feminist scholars such as Carol Gilligan, Sheila Rowbotham, Nancy Chodorow, and Paula Gunn Allen have elsewhere examined the ways in which this dimension of human life is ignored or denied by our male-centered Western cultural traditions. By its emphasis on human relationships this volume continues in that tradition of scholarship.

Just as antagonism emerges from the exclusive acceptance of individualism, so cooperation emerges as an imperative of sociality, of the recognition of human interdependence and the power of each to touch the lives of others. As the essay by María Cristina Lugones and Elizabeth V. Spelman shows, interdependence isn't necessarily beneficial. The power to condition the lives of others is not always exercised to the benefit of those others, nor even exercised consciously. Cooperation is not a spontaneous expression of interdependence, but must be deliberately chosen as a consequence of recognizing that the possibilities and opportunities for all are enhanced by ensuring the well-being of each.

In communities that were committed to mutual assistance, reciprocity, and the general welfare, competition would be contained and directed. In contrast, competition within our current economic system takes on a meaning far beyond its inherent significance. The girl who wins the race or who shines at basketball may be earning not only a ticket out of stifling poverty but ultimately excessive power over the lives of others. The girl who performs poorly in a competitive classroom may be permanently stigmatized by teachers and subsequently incapacitated for a fulfilling and productive life. Some people may feel that competition would disappear from a genuinely cooperative society. We suspect instead that the members of that society would find healthy competition useful in challenging one another toward individual and collective self-development.

One major theme in Part III is the possibility of an "enabling competition." After discussing the treacheries of envy, jealousy, and resentment in the literary marketplace, Valerie Miner calls for "an imaginative collectivity of readers and writers." She also suggests that honest competition among writers *could* in some circumstances help them to develop their work. If this is true for writers, it might also apply to other artists. Psychotherapist Joyce Lindenbaum suggests that the deliberate cultivation of (limited) competition in lesbian couples may help prevent the merging identities that often plague and even destroy women's partnerships. Both writers assign some positive functions to competition within limited and ritualized scopes. As long as such competition does not have boundaries imposed by an external cooperative context, it will retain its double-edged potential and the capacity to become disabling rather than enabling.

The work of imagining some other social forms for that context is begun in the next four essays. Paula Ross discusses ways to avoid competing for oppression. Martha A. Ackelsberg and Kathryn Pyne Addelson offer us inspiration from the anarchist activists in the Lawrence, Massachusetts, Textile Strike and the Vancouver Women's Health Collective. María Cristina Lugones and Elizabeth V. Spelman outline a fundamental revision of the virtues of public life toward the development of mutual understanding, community, and collective progress. Significantly, these two essays are examples of what they call for—cross-cultural, collaborative, feminist projects. Finally, Helen E. Longino examines the moral discourse of competition, sorts out different concepts of competition, and argues that both the individualist's embrace and the feminist's or socialist's rejection of competition depends on conflating these concepts. She suggests a rethinking of the different forms of competition as the grounds for feminist evaluation. Each essay navigates us in the direction in which we must move to create an environment in which individual good and collective good have the same value.

Part III

FEMINIST TRANSFORMATIONS

Rumors from the Cauldron: Competition among Feminist Writers

VALERIE MINER

Why do I sometimes feel a twinge when another woman succeeds? Why do I occasionally become livid? Shouldn't I feel gratified when any of my sisters does well? Isn't feminism antithetical to competition?

The impetus for this essay[1] and, indeed, for this book came from the 1980 National Women's Studies Conference in Bloomington, Indiana. The variety of panels about crucial issues, presented with feminist perspective as a given, filled me with exhilaration. Since I am a novelist and not a scholar, I've always experienced more pleasure than anxiety at academic conferences. Since this one was about women's issues, I knew I had landed in particularly exciting territory. The euphoria dissipated when I visited the book display. There I was gripped by an old, humiliating jealousy of other writers. I tried to be grateful that women's voices were available. Still, I wondered, why has *she* been published more? I tried to revel in the emergence of a new feminist literary tradition. Yet, I wondered, why did that editor like *her* work better than mine? Because I write about lesbian and other "marginal" characters? Because I come from a working-class family and thus don't have the proper demeanor or degrees or contacts? Because I'm a Westerner, living too far from the center of U.S. literary power? Because I have brown hair? With the same intensity that I experienced excitement at the panels, I now felt competitive with other feminist writers. Then I was drenched in guilt. How could I begrudge a sister her success? Instead, shouldn't I be raging at the men who manipulated the gentlemanly hypocrisy of publishing? Somehow I found myself more and more aggravated with other women.

An abridged version of this essay appeared in *Women's Studies International Forum* 8, no. 1 (1985): 45–50. Copyright © 1985 by Pergamon Journals Limited.

I wrote to a friend about these feelings. Oh, yes, she commiserated, she felt the same way. Then I talked with women from other fields. Oh, yes, it was horrible; they had never admitted it before, but they, too, felt especially competitive with women. Soon I began to wonder whether it was harder to talk about competition in the women's movement than about sexuality. Competition is a moral problem and an emotional tangle and a political conundrum. In this essay I am more interested in opening a forum for discussion than in posing specific remedies. I resist the kind of holy authorship through which the author becomes a rigid authority, so identified with her ideas that when someone disagrees, she uses all her spirit to defend (rather than confer about) the right answer. I am conscious of asking many questions here. I look forward to a variety of answers in the future—in conversation, on panels, in other essays and books.

I must begin by acknowledging all the momentum and support I've received from the women's movement.[2] I do not think that competition is the final step in an inevitable downward spiral of sisterhood. I do think we have to face the existence of competition if we are to preserve feminism and our sanity.

During the last few years, I have learned how we often confuse competitive feelings with competition, suffering with virtue, and criticism with conflict. I have found a need to distinguish between competition for ego gratification within the androcentric system—that is, for fame and status—and competition in meeting our own standards of aesthetic excellence. Ultimately, I want to consider the possibilities of a cooperative framework in which we "compete" with one another's ideas and with our own ideas toward collective wisdom. Is it possible to return to the Latin root of the word *compete* ("to meet," "to be fitting," "to strive together toward") and develop a "feminist competition" which allows for both individual and collective progress?

First, some stories I've gathered from a variety of women. We've all told such tales—on the telephone, over supper; we've told them with anger and confusion and a sense of betrayal. We all know rumors from the cauldron.

"I had a mentor. Well, we didn't call it that then. But she read everything I wrote. Gave me criticism. Advice. And when my book was honored, she turned away. It was almost as if she were jealous."

"I had a student. I gave her all I had. Time, concern, contacts. But always she seemed to be measuring herself against me, needing to prove her worth by diminishing me."

"I had a friend. We worked in a writing group together. Without her, I would have stopped writing poetry. But when my work was published, she ignored it. Didn't come to the book party. Wouldn't talk to me."

"I had a play produced in New York and another in California. My New York friends said, 'Oh, it must be easier to produce in California, with all those funky artistic people.' And my California friends said, "Oh, New York, of course there are so many theaters there. Of course it must be easier in New York."

Competition among women, especially among women writers, is a highly charged topic. Literature is a peculiarly public product of a particularly private endeavor. Writing is dismally paid labor, putting extra pressure on us to make our work visible because only the most renowned writers even earn a living by it. The average American author makes $4,775 a year from writing, and of course the story is sadder in many other countries.[3] Our avenues to achievement are frighteningly ephemeral and therefore escalate the anxiety over success. What *is* achievement in feminist literature? Writing well? Finishing a good book? Being in the vanguard? Making money? How much money? Gaining recognition? Recognition from whom? Readers? Feminist critics? The *New York Review of Books*? Too many writers are caught in the contradiction that it is a privilege to publish and a personal failure not to be published.

The dilemma descends in part from a broad social denial of the labor involved in the making of art. Contradictions compound each other. While society celebrates some artistic competition with televised award ceremonies, critics demand that "serious" writers eschew any notion of contest. Readers often require a special purity of motive from authors who they expect will place personal vision above base material considerations. The pressures are exacerbated for many women authors, who have more ambivalence than men authors about conflict, achievement, and success. Feminist writers bear additional, valid qualms about hierarchy.

Street sense says that decisions about who gets published, granted money, well-reviewed, and honored with awards have as much to do with connections as with merit. Even when outsiders are acknowledged it can be a political maneuver. Black critic Barbara Christian tells me: "The establishment seems to have room for one of us a year. It's easier to accept a black novel if you perceive it as *one* point of view, as the culture of an isolated individual." So what should feminist writers do? Some women prescribe ignoring the patriarchal literary scene altogether. Yet if one tried to be completely separatist, could one create a feminist publishing world sanitized of petty politics? Perhaps I've skipped a step. It's worth considering how we already *do* behave before speculating about how we *might* behave.[4]

In studying the market, it becomes clear that this is a men's emporium. It's useful to distinguish between short-term friction generated by limited resources and the long-term development of feminist literature. Immediately, we do seem to compete for advances, publication, review space, and acknowledgment. Everyone knows of cases where *her* poem was published instead of ours, where *she* got a grant and we didn't. Arts money is tight and there are still unofficial quotas working against women. While admitting the constraints of the current market, I believe that most competitive behavior among women is pointless shadowboxing. In the long run, reading one feminist novel leads to reading another feminist novel. Publishing one feminist journal leads to publishing another feminist journal. While we may compete today, what we do with our competitive feelings can shape our mutual creativity in the future. We need to make more room for ourselves.

For a clearer view of competition, we have to find our way through a cave hung with veils. The webs of envy, jealousy, and resentment. The net of manipulative criticism that keeps us from taking each other's work seriously. The mystique of creative magic that hides the fact that art is work. Finally, beyond these veils, we may escape androcentric competition and even discover ways for competition to serve feminism.

Only by acknowledging competition, then reclaiming and redefining it, can we endure in and surface beyond the misogynist literary establishment. To most of us competition is a hot word, associated with rabid capitalism and the self-serving impulse to elevate oneself while diminishing others. So I am tempted to replace the word *competition* with *cooperation* or *collaboration* or another currently politically correct term. But I'd like to entertain the possibility of a *feminist competition* because I think it may afford us a special edge from which we can stretch for personal and collective excellence. The Latin root for compete does not pose an exclusive winner. It suggest that we "meet, be fitting, be capable, strive together." In this sense feminist writers may *need* competition for survival. Our work depends on and flourishes within an "imaginative collectivity of writers and readers."[5]

THE STEPSISTERS: ENVY, JEALOUSY, AND RESENTMENT

One reason this topic causes so much emotional distress and political wariness is that often it is easy to confuse the *feelings* of envy, jealousy, and resentment with the *process* of competition.

The "competitive syndrome" for women writers proceeds something like this: First a woman internalizes her fears about writing and her frustrations about getting published. Then she sees that another woman has been published or honored. She feels jealous. She may begin with self-denigration: "I'm not good enough." Often she swivels to resentment: "But is *she* good enough? Why her?" Then she feels remorse. She talks with someone else, someone equally marginal, about their relative lack of success. She scapegoats the "successful" woman writer. She trashes. She allows her impotence in male literary terms to paralyze her power to communicate with other women.

Personally, I also feel envy of male writers, but never with the same intensity I feel of women writers. One reason is that I know that in the current system, women have a smaller portion of the publishing pie. Beyond this, I am more likely to compare myself with other women writers, particularly other white, U.S. women from working-class homes.[6] This is, I believe, a natural searching for context. It is when the context becomes confinement, when we assume the unfairness of family patterns, that sibling rivalry ensues and becomes destructive.

Envy, jealousy, and resentment are emotions. Competition is a behavior, about which we might feel many different ways. Given the current squeeze on publishing, many of us are bound to lose and consequently to feel badly. Because the modes of judgment seem arbitrary, at best, and usually quite biased, it seems naive to ask advice about how to improve our lot. Because those in power are often invisible or inaccessible, we often direct our fury and bitterness at sister writers. Some people get ruthless, undermining the work of others to serve their own careers. After someone wins an award, her next book may be reviewed with special harshness. The anger about our "failure" is misdirected at her "success." In this sense, perhaps, envy, jealousy, and resentment become blocks to a feminist competition. The problem arises when we take the male literary arena too seriously, when we buy the rules of their fixed game, when we look outward for our core of artistic validation.

If one woman writes a good story, does that mean I can't? Of course not. If she publishes, does that mean I can't? Of course not, in the long run. One journalist I know suggests that "if we worked together, we could change the blockbuster system of conglomerate publishing. But jealousy doesn't wait for collective action, except where we turn and scapegoat other writers."

THE SHROUD OF AMBITION

Discussing competition also induces anxiety because many women are squeamish about owning their ambitions, and because ambition itself is difficult to contain or to quantify. Earlier I asked what achievement is. Novelist Betty Roszak says, "What is success anyway? Once you have one thing, you want another." Women are conditioned to avoid external conflict. We perceive a contradiction between personal achievement and collective success. Critic and novelist Diane Johnson tells me, "There is a taboo on success. People move away from you when you're successful."

Personally, I have always been more afraid of succeeding than of failing. The latter would be expected, comfortable. We are so thoroughly trained that we often can't even recognize our own accomplishments. If we sat back and absorbed our own success, enjoyed it for a moment, we might feel less contentious about other writers.

Women's psychological resistances to success are legend. Some women identify public awards with their fathers and think them unnatural for themselves. Others associate power with evil. Some fear they must choose between love and work. As Phyllis Chesler observed fifteen years ago in *Women and Madness:*

> Women mistrust and men destroy those women who are not interested in sacrificing at least something for someone for some reason. Rather than achieve at least half or all of Caesar's power, many women, including some feminists, would prefer to leave it in Caesar's hands altogether and, in a misguidedly "novel" gesture, sacrifice their individual advancement for the sake of less fortunate women.[7]

It often feels easier to recognize someone else's success than to admit our own. Perhaps because as Toronto feminist organizer Leah Erna says, "Women have breasts and guilt." *It seems more sisterly to struggle than to be successful.* And "being successful" is different from "succeeding." People may celebrate with you the night your novel turns into a movie, but what happens the morning after? Or the morning after that?

Better to suffer together than to achieve in isolation. Barbara Christian tells me, "Our criteria as feminists seem to be different from the establishments.' They have art and success. We have art and suffering. Then there's the question of what we do to people who are successful in the establishment. Once the establishment acknowledges you, the readers drop you. If you're successful, then you're not suffering and you're not with us."

WHO WINS FROM OUR COMPETITION?

Not everyone suffers when feminists evade success or when we fight unnecessarily among ourselves, and it's crucial to consider who benefits from our fuzzy competitiveness. Louise Bernikow observes in *Among Women:* "Tradition tells me that we compete for men, that our conflict takes the form of envy, jealousy and pettiness. We are brought up to think of other women as enemies, to be in a state of conflict with them, but not to express it directly."[8]

Friendships like that between Virginia Woolf and Katherine Mansfield can get so caught up in sisterly rivalry that the women fall mute. They resist each other where they might shout back at the father. Why do we continue to sulk and snipe and spit when we could be confronting patriarchal publishing together?

As Christian points out, we compete for suffering. Perhaps this is because we have become too cynical about the possibility of success for feminists in this world. Perhaps it is also because we confuse suffering with virtue.

A lot of the envy between women that crosses the DMZ of race, class, sexuality, and culture is actually misdirected fury at privileged white men. Clearly feminists need to confront racism, classism, heterosexism, and imperialism inside *and* outside the women's movement. The point of this knowledge is not to create a grading system, but to develop an understanding of the obstacles and a solidarity in overcoming them. It is important, for instance, for white women to acknowledge and to fight against the double jeopardy experienced by women of color. It is important for heterosexual women to understand that lesbians experience both sexism and homophobia from publishers. But why do we waste time bickering about who is more oppressed by conventional publishing? This is a successful divide-and-conquer routine if there ever was one. When we claim "more oppressed than thou," we are often really asking who is more oppressed by men. How is this different from other ways of competing for men? We spend our spirits fighting our sisters rather than helping each other pull away from the roots of our common oppression and moving together to more fertile ground.

Literary standards get lost in all this—whether we compete for suffering or for grudging approbation from the male academy. Wouldn't it be more productive to concentrate on developing our multi-ethnic, cross-class, international literary criticism?

COMPETITION IS NOT DEADLY

Good critics stimulate feminist literature, yet reviewing is an arena in which envy, jealousy, and resentment can fester. The greatest respect we can give each other's work is attentive, constructive criticism. But sometimes criticism is abused as a distorted expression of power. Timid critics are afraid to knock a sister's right to write. Fair feminist criticism is not unqualified applause. It is fully informed, honest response.[9]

Joanna Russ complains in *Sinister Wisdom*:

The Feminine Imperative is forced on all of us. . . . The women's community as a mystically loving band of emotional weaklings who make up to each other by our own kindness and sweetness for the harshness we have to endure in the outside world is a description that exactly characterizes the female middle-class subculture as it's existed in patriarchy for centuries—without changing a thing. . . . So honesty goes by the board, hurt feelings are put at a premium, general fear and paralysis set in, and one by one any woman who oversteps the increasingly circumscribed area of what's permissible is trashed.[10]

While we shouldn't tiptoe as critics, it's also worthwhile to remember not to tromp into a review without trying to enter the writer's vision of her book. I cringe at the memory of the first review I wrote. It was a self-important, overly critical piece about someone's first book. Now I see that I, like a lot of new reviewers, was expressing jealousy that this book—and not mine—was being published. (At the time I hadn't even written a book.) During the next few years I grew more tolerant and generous in my reviewing. But in the period just before my first novel was published, I compared everything that crossed my desk to my own "brilliant" manuscript. I decided to stop reviewing novels for a while, which was good for both me and my potential victims. I was happy reviewing nonfiction. In due time, my first novel did appear. Then, lo and behold, I became a very sympathetic critic of fiction.

Some feminist critics, in their fervor to make a political point, rampage against one author on false assumptions. Being intelligently critical is an intricate balance. Fiction writer Sandy Boucher says, "It's OK to dislike a piece of work, but it's important to distinguish between that work and the person and the person's next piece of work."

Equally, as readers of reviews, if we understand criticism as perspective rather than mandate, we can use reviews as assessment and not censorship. When competitiveness causes us to ignore or to dismiss our sisters' writing, whether from our own envy or from secondhand bias, it is having its most insidious effect.

WORK NOT MAGIC

Writers are workers. Books are products; sometimes services. Often we seem to forget this. We romanticize art as solitary genesis. We confuse the writing with the writer herself. Readers are often envious of the imagined status of writers. They sometimes hold onto conflicting mythologies by venerating an artist's victimhood while investing her with special powers and privileges. Jane Rule argues forcefully against making writers into heroes:

I am not . . . as a writer, setting myself up as a leader or role model for anyone. If my community, egged on by the media, tries to turn me into one, I will fail just as others have failed before me, not simply because I am a writer but because leaders of that sort are damaging to the sense of self-worth and self-direction all women's consciousness raising is about.[11]

One reason many North Americans don't understand writing as work is that we live in classist societies where we rate professions above trades and art above professions. How can art be labor? In addition to cherishing our status, writers are often reluctant to remember all the time and sweat and retyping that went into a good piece. We would far rather imagine sitting in the morning sunlight, drinking French Roast coffee (or in the moonlight, sipping brandy) and "catharting" onto the page.

If we recognized writing as labor, we would be less hurt by rejections. We might see that what is being rejected is our manuscripts, not our personal characters. As Margarita Donnelly, an editor for *Calyx,* said at the American Writers' Congress in October 1981: "We get so many manuscripts, we can't possibly use them all. So we return some. Don't think of it as being rejected. Think of it as having your manuscript returned." In addition to struggles for recognition and for income, writers have notoriously treacherous working conditions as we battle restrictive libel laws and increasing censorship. In many cases we are no better off than the employees of corporations, like Gulf and Western or ITT, which own our publishing houses.

Too often, however, when we finally *do* budge from our grandiose self-images as singular geniuses, we fall into competitiveness with other writers. We assume we are fighting other geniuses for survival. In the short run, it may be a choice between her work and ours. But literary fashions change over time. And, if we looked more closely, we would notice how everyone slogs and struggles. We might lose glamour, but gain solidarity. If we actually talked about drowning in empty white pages and typing until our fingers grew numb and chasing through book after book for a necessary reference, we would perceive the universal drudge. If we considered another writer on the eighth draft of her novel that is just not working, sitting in a cold flat worried about how to rewrite the first sentence, buy clothes for her daughter, and find enough money to heat the place before winter sets in, I'm confident that we would feel less combative. However, even after years in the field, many writers still believe in the romance, the romance that *other* writers must be experiencing. Most publishers pay so poorly and give us so few design consulting rights because by the time we've won our imaginary battles with other writers, we're so grateful to be printed that we accept their "protective" advice.

Writers have a lot to learn from coal miners and steel workers whose unionism erases any false notion of privilege about the right to be paid or to be treated decently for work done. We might come to realize that the scarcity model of artistic ability is not so different from the conservative faith in the necessity of unemployment to balance the economy. The real "artistic scarcity" is the amount of resources made available by wealthy institutions to hardworking artists. Some progress has been made by writers' unions in various countries. But until we recognize ourselves as part of a larger scheme of workers, we will be organizing in a vacuum. Ultimately, I think, we need to go beyond alliances with other writers to form connections with all book people. Without feminist editors, agents, publishers, printers, reviewers, booksellers, librarians, teachers, students, our words would be invisible. This "imaginative collectivity" is the heart of feminist writing.

CONCLUSION: COMPETITION FOR COLLECTIVE SUCCESS?

So far I have considered competitiveness within the androcentric system and have asked who is served by it. I have acknowledged how feelings of envy and inadequacy enshroud us. I have shown that writers struggle against each other rather than confront publishers about change. Now, is there any way to get competition to serve us, to work for individual satisfaction and collective progress? What would a feminist competition be? The question is addressed by other writers in this book, who will no doubt spark yet more answers from provoked readers. Meanwhile let me offer a few ideas. First, I'd like to return to the Latin root, "to meet, be fitting, be capable, strive together." Paula Gunn Allen tells me, "Traditional Indians— particularly Pueblo Indians—by and large view competition within a group frame-work, and by and large see it as a socially useful trait."

For me the feminist writing circle has been a microcosm of cooperative competi-tion. What makes such a group feminist is its process as well as its content. Every-one has a chance to speak and to be heard. In Toronto during the early 1970s, I met with other feminists to discuss how our work was being treated by editors and how badly we were getting paid. At first we were very guarded, each of us protec-tive of her reputation as a "successful young writer." We called ourselves feminists although individually we did not believe we had experienced discrimination. (We had yet to learn a whole new way of seeing.) Gradually, we came to trust one another, to share our worries, and to investigate the experiences of other writers. We discovered two things· All writers were being mistreated, and women writers were being especially mistreated. Our collective was one of the seeds of a national writers' union (now called The Periodical Writers' Association of Canada).

We continued to meet for several years to write a book together, *Her Own Woman* (by Myrna Kostash, Melinda McCracken, Valerie Miner, Erna Paris, and Heather Robertson). Several years later in London, I began working with four British women on *Tales I Tell My Mother* (by Zoë Fairbairns, Sara Maitland, Valerie Miner, Michele Roberts, and Michelene Wandor), a fictional documentary of the British women's move-ment. The *Tales* group was a springboard for all of us in different parts of the world. Six years after the book was published, we presented a panel at the Institute of Con-temporary Art in London, discussing the impetus we had received from each other. Between 1978 and 1984, the members of the group published 27 books. In 1986, we published a collection of our new work, *More Tales*. Since I moved back to California, I have written and published five novels—*Blood Sisters, Movement, Murder in the En-glish Department, Winter's Edge,* and *All Good Women*—within the stimulus of writers' groups.[12]

None of these collectives has exhibited flawless sisterhood. In each of them, we have bickered, felt jealous, arrived late, gossiped too much. Yet, because we moved together through some of the same veils, because we discussed the labor of writing, we were better able to surface above petty obstacles and to invigorate each other's work. Here we witnessed other women stretching their imagination and skills and were encouraged to stretch (compete with?) *our own abilities* toward literary excellence.

I am now involved in two writers' groups. Recently one of the groups sat around talking about jealousy. First, of course, we began talking about outside people of whom we were jealous. Then Sandy admitted that she was jealous of Judy's fame, of the fact that she is invited to give so many talks, even though Sandy herself isn't particularly interested in being a public speaker. Paula said she was also jealous of the public appearances—until she started to get invitations and to feel oppressed by them. Judy said that she was jealous of Sandy's royalty advances from a major publisher. I said I was jealous of the grants the other three had received.[13] Sandy said she was jealous of the fact that I had published four novels when she hadn't yet published one. And so on. As we talked, the air got easier to breathe. I found myself stretching comfortably on the floor of Paula's studio. It was a relief, simply, to speak the forbidden. One conclusion was that some of us use jealousy to remind us that we haven't "won" yet or to give us permission to own what we have achieved. We agreed that we rarely felt jealous when we were happy with our work, that often jealousy was a channel for other painful feelings about ourselves. Finally, we articulated areas where we wanted to learn from each other—about structure, about poetic language, and so on—and made plans to discuss these areas at future meetings.

Madelon Sprengnether, a poet and essayist, says her writing group in Minnesota has "provided a stimulus and a permission. The success of others provides an opening for my work. Success seems possible and not too distant. Friends hold you to your best work." I agree. In my other current group, for instance, Mary has a genius for pace in her novels. When I see how well her new book is moving, I think, I can do that too. Sue and I are both working on books about World War II. She knows more about poetry of the period than I. This knowledge not only helps me but spurs me to read more, to broaden my own expertise. Mimi has a gift for physical detail. I read her work and try harder with my descriptions next time. In some sense the writing group is like the family in which I want to be the best child. On a primal level, I want my details to be *sharper* than Mimi's. Intellectually, I understand that they will only be different. What I hope for is *the best book I can produce.* Their achievement opens the possibility of my own. The group provides the necessary provocation and support for self-competition. Unlike my birth family, I entered this dynamic voluntarily and as an adult. The group provides a measuring stick for the craft of writing and the craftiness of getting published. I "compete" with the others by stretching toward my own literary excellence and professional achievement.

The worldly success of my collective sisters has also spurred me to compete for similar gains. Three of the five *Tales* members published novels before I did. For months I felt jealous and depressed. But I was also stimulated to try harder to get my work published. Later one of the women had her second novel rejected by a press that was publishing two of my books. Now the two of us have published four novels each. The competition between us wasn't always conscious, but the very presence of the other writer made us try harder—gave us both a permission and a further incentive—to get our work published. We gave each other a mutual momentum. In contrast, I personally would find it hard to work in isolation, without news of other writers' successes and failures. Current publishing procedures are so arbitrary that this kind of competitive comparison not only challenges my work; it keeps me sane.

We're not going to end masculinist competition, not for a while. But we do have some choices about how we respond to patriarchal publishing. The real danger is ignoring or censoring a sister's writing because in doing so, we are drawing down a blind on all our work.

In the larger feminist forum, meanwhile, we can stir art in each other. Cooperative competition (I still lean toward reclaiming the old word rather than creating a new one) can provoke us to go deeper emotionally, to play more boldly with form. It can offer comradeship in an all-too-lonely job. It can lend a sense of reality to labor whose ephemeral acknowledgment is crazy-making. It can help us to create new standards of criticism. It can give us the spirit to continue writing.

Cooperative competition creates a better feminist literature. We use each others' work as models for achievement. We see each others' success as a promise of our own. We keep the long-term vision of the enormous bookshelf (with room for everyone's books) while being provoked by daily accomplishments that may preclude our own in the short term. Unlike a race which is won/lost in an instant, a book and a career are built over time. Indeed, they are never finished as long as readers go on reading. Cooperative competitors eschew the veils and acknowledge the vicissitudes of publishing—by fighting for our rights as workers; by challenging the sexism and racism of publishing; by providing a critical forum in which all our work is taken seriously. Now we don't have control over our books, but we do have control over our attitudes about our books and each other's books. And we can "strive together toward" by inciting each other to be better writers and readers.

NOTES

1. Some of the material in this essay was presented at a panel about competition among women at the National Women's Studies Conference, June 1982, at California State University, Humboldt, California; at the Bay Area Marxist Feminist Group, January 1983, Oakland, California; and at the Society for Women in Philosophy (Eastern Division), April 1986, Hamilton College, Clinton, New York. I am grateful for the feedback I received on each of these occasions.

2. Thanks go to a number of writers who have helped me with the thinking behind this essay during the last few years. Some were formally interviewed. Others talked with me informally. They include Paula Gunn Allen, Sandy Boucher, Maureen Brady, Dorothy Bryant, Charlotte Bunch, Barbara Christian, Renate Duelli-Klein, Erika Duncan, Zoe Fairbairns, Kathleen Fraser, Sally Miller Gearhart, Judy Grahn, Susan Griffin, Jana Harris, Carolyn Heilbrun, Diane Johnson, Ke Yan, Myrna Kostash, Denise Levertov, Helen E. Longino,

Mary Mackey, Karen Malpede, Tillie Olsen, Norma Rice, Wendy Rose, Ruth Rosen, Betty Roszak, Susan Schweik, Eleanor Scully, Madelon Sprengnether, Charlene Spretnak, Hannemieke Stamperius, Mary Helen Washington, and Yvonne.

3. Suzanne Gordon, "Too Long at the Mercy of Publishers—Time for a Writers' Union," *The Boston Globe* (November 28, 1981).

4. For more information about feminist publishing, readers might consider *Quest* 3, no. 2 (Fall 1976), a theme issue entitled, "Communication and Control."

5. I developed some of these ideas more fully in a previous essay, "Writing Feminist Fiction," *Frontiers* 6, no. 1 (1981). I discuss "the imaginative collectivity of writers and readers" more fully in a previous essay, "Reader Is Writer Is Reader," *Hurricane Alice* (Winter/Spring 1984): 11–12.

6. I also feel twinges when male writers of my background or age or politics win something I don't. But my primary comparison is always with other women writers. Perhaps this is because I see my feminism as the core of my politics. Perhaps it is because I was the only girl in my family, and I learned early it was senseless to waste my time expecting equal treatment with my brothers.

7. Phyllis Chesler, *Women and Madness* (New York: Avon Books, 1972), 279.

8. Louise Bernikow, *Among Women* (New York: Harmony Books, 1980), 195.

9. Some of these ideas are developed more fully in my previous essay "The Feminist Reviewer," in *Words in Our Pockets*, ed. Celeste West (Paradise, Cal.: Dustbooks/Booklegger, 1985).

10. Joanna Russ, "Power and Helplessness in the Women's Movement," *Sinister Wisdom* 18 (Fall 1981): 51–52.

11. Jane Rule, "Lesbian Leadership," *Resources for Feminist Research* (Canada: Summer 1983), 56.

12. Myrna Kostash, Melinda McCracken, Valerie Miner, Erna Paris, and Heather Robertson, *Her Own Woman* (Canada: Macmillan, 1975); Zoë Fairbairns, Sara Maitland, Valerie Miner, Michele Roberts, and Michelene Wandor, *Tales I Tell My Mother* (London: Journeyman Press, 1978, and Boston: South End Press, 1980); idem, *More Tales* (London: Journeyman Press, 1986); Valerie Miner, *Blood Sisters* (New York: St. Martin's Press, 1982 and London: The Women's Press, 1981), *Movement* (Trumansburg, N.Y.: Crossing Press, and London: Methuen, 1985), *Murder in the English Department* (New York: St. Martin's Press, 1983 and London: The Women's Press, 1982), *Winter's Edge* (Trumansburg, N.Y.: Crossing Press, 1985, and London: Methuen Press, 1984). *All Good Women* (London: Methuen, 1987).

13. As I was writing the final draft of this essay, I received my fifth rejection from the National Endowment for the Arts. This was compounded by recent rejections from The Guggenheim Foundation, The Rockefeller Foundation, The Bunting Institute, and other institutions which help some writers earn a living wage from their work. On the day of the NEA rejection, the only thing that kept me from exploding was going downstairs and doing more thinking and rethinking of this essay.

The Shattering of an Illusion: The Problem of Competition in Lesbian Relationships

JOYCE P. LINDENBAUM

During the past ten years, the progressive psychiatric establishment has attempted to depathologize homosexual relationships. Once defined as a "perversion," homosexual object choice is now viewed as an "alternative life-style." The difficulties that homosexual couples encounter in relationships are beginning to be seen as no more unusual than the marital problems of their heterosexual counterparts. A rising divorce rate and increasing acknowledgment of child and spousal abuse has stimulated much political and social concern about the "crisis in the [heterosexual] family"—a crisis which has been attributed to everything from the women's and gay liberation movements to a troubled economy. Interestingly, there has been little psychodynamic explanation for the escalating tensions and frequent divorces within heterosexual relationships. Homosexual relationships, however, have long had a reputation for being short-lived. Psychological explanations for this phenomenon abound, viewing it as yet another indication of the inherent pathology and immaturity of homosexual object choice. More recently, various social factors, including discrimination, homophobia, lack of adequate role models, and, in most cases, the absence of shared child rearing have been recognized as significant contributors to the frequent dissolutions of gay and lesbian relationships.

As a psychotherapist, over the past decade I have frequently observed a particular

I want to thank the following friends and colleagues for their intellectual and emotional encouragement: Alice Abarbanel, Sara Hartley, Sue Elkind, Adria Blum, and Valerie Miner. Kim Chernin deserves special thanks for challenging me to clarify my thinking and nurturing my capacity to write. Finally, I am deeply grateful to my patients for helping me to understand. This essay is reprinted, with changes, from *Feminist Studies* 11, no. 1 (Spring 1985): 85–103. Copyright by Joyce P. Lindenbaum.

interpersonal phenomenon in the lesbian couples whom I have treated. It is a behavioral pattern that generates a crisis, and commonly results in the dissolution of the relationship. Although it is not restricted to lesbian couples, I shall discuss why relationships between women are more predisposed to this experience and shall argue that competition is a useful way of managing this crisis.

The crisis occurs when one of the women begins to feel that she has become lost in her partner. She no longer has a sense of who she is. She feels invisible, unacknowledged, "less than." Some might call this an "identity crisis," but the feeling runs even deeper. It is not simply that changing jobs or becoming more secure in one's career would solve the problem. The affect here is one of panic and despair. There is a confrontation with separateness or emptiness, a frantic search to retrieve something that seems to have disappeared. There is the shattering of an illusion, accompanied by a feeling of disappointment and abandonment which is so profound it seems it can only be resolved by ending the relationship.

At this stage of crisis, one or both partners frequently thinks of herself as attempting to become independent and autonomous. But in fact the lesbian couple is often engaged in a more primitive struggle. In my work with these women, I have come to believe that I am seeing, with all its distortions, the re-creation of a primary experience: an effort to develop a separate self.

Yet the question remains: Why does this struggle require that the relationship end? Why can't these women be separate in the context of a relationship? Can these women only experience themselves as "whole" in the absence of a relationship? To answer this, it is necessary to look more closely at the kind of intimacy two women can typically create.

There is agreement in the psychiatric literature that the experience of primal intimacy is a prototype for adult intimate relationships. "This primary tendency, I shall be loved always, everywhere, in every way, my whole body, my whole being—without any criticism, without the slightest effort on my part—is the final aim of all erotic striving."[1] Adult relationships are, in part, unconscious re-creations, distortions, and attempted reparations of primary intimacy and merging, as well as other early familial experiences. Of course, the attempted reproduction of primary intimacy involves some degree of ambivalence. Along with the blissful experience of mother-infant oneness comes the terror of possible identity loss, object loss, and absolute dependence.

Given that women are the major caretakers in this culture, a love relationship between two women has a particular potential to evoke certain aspects of mother-infant intimacy. As Nancy Chodorow, following Michael Balint, suggests, "a sexual relationship with a woman reproduces the early situation more completely and is more completely a return to the mother"[2] than is a sexual relationship with a man. What emerges so powerfully, albeit often unconsciously, in the lesbian relationship is a profound desire for and concomitant fear of the primal experience of psychic and bodily oneness. Ultimately, the lesbian couple's re-creation of primal intimacy gives rise to the excruciating terror of primal loss. Thus, the couple finds itself in a tremendous dilemma: How can the women fulfill their original desire to merge, and simultaneously subdue the terror it arouses? This dilemma is at the root of the difficulty that many lesbian couples have in sustaining their relationships.

Primary pre-oedipal preoccupation, of course, is not the only constellation for female homosexual object choice. However, the fact that, for both partners, the relationship can closely recapitulate primal intimacy leaves the couple vulnerable to experiencing this as a regressive threat, although not all such regression is pathological. Mature intimacy requires that the partners move comfortably between more merged and more differentiated relational positions. That is, the capacity for adult intimacy depends on each partner's ability to appropriately lose and establish psychological boundaries in relation to the other. Furthermore, the longevity of the relationship is enhanced by the recognition of and capacity to tolerate the partner as separate and different from the self.

Among the lesbian couples I have seen, the inability to resolve the conflict between a wish to re-create primal merging and the fear of loss of self that accompanies this prevents these couples from making comfortable relational transitions. The phenomenon that I am about to describe is the couple's unconscious endeavor to reconcile this apparent contradiction.

Having stirred the memory of primal intimacy and passionately dissolved the boundaries between them, the lesbian couple arrives at the first step in their behavior pattern: *the sacrifice of sex*. Though it may take weeks or months, sometimes even years, these women gradually stop making love. This sacrifice of sex has usually occurred by the time the couple seeks psychotherapy. Interestingly, not all couples enter treatment with much distress at having given up sexual intimacy. Those who do will often agree that they cannot seem to find the time. One partner will claim that she does not feel sexual, or both will assert that they have different rhythms. Others insist that sex is not important. What is important is "the relationship," "the communication" between them. In any case, these couples are no longer experiencing sexual intimacy, and it is essential to understand that both women are participating in this sacrifice—even when it appears that only one is responsible.

A question naturally arises about heterosexual women. Certainly they, too, experience difficulties with merging and differentiation. I have seen many heterosexual couples who have sacrificed sex. How are the women in these couples different from their lesbian counterparts? Often, they are not. However, even in instances where the behavior appears to be the same, the underlying motivation may be different. Heterosexual women may, for example, sacrifice sex out of a sense of anger or disappointment or failure at re-creating an experience of primal intimacy, for which they, too, have yearned. Homosexual women, on the other hand, frequently sacrifice sex because they have succeeded all too well at re-creating primal intimacy and are terrified of its consequences. In short, lesbians sacrifice sex out of having successfully re-created primal merging, while heterosexual women sacrifice sex out of having failed.

The sacrifice of sex, then, is the lesbian couple's first effort at quieting the terror of the merging that has occurred. It is, however, only a provisional solution that soon gives rise to another problem, and then again to another solution which also fails. Thus, the lesbian couple unconsciously begins to move through a sequence of patterned behaviors, which ultimately lead to the dissolution of their relationship.

Another question now arises. If these women sacrifice sex as a means of managing their terror, how do they simultaneously satisfy their need to merge? At the same time they are giving up sexual intimacy, the women are creating the sought-after merger in the nonsexual aspects of their relationship. This occurs, in part, because women have the capacity to develop a nonsexual intimacy that is "less differentiated," an intimacy of familiarity, comfort, and reciprocity. There is a sense of shared identification, of knowing what the other feels (or assuming one knows). It is an empathic intimacy that has its origins in various aspects of the mother-infant relationship, one of which is that women are mothered by women.

Both Nancy Chodorow and Carol Gilligan have described how a daughter's identification with her mother contributes to a gender identity based on nondifferentiation and intimacy rather than differentiation and separation.[3] That female gender identity is based on a sense of connectedness and reciprocity, rather than separateness and hierarchy, explains in part the capacity women have for re-creating primal intimacy in another, nonsexual form, when the anxiety of sexual merging becomes too overwhelming. This *nonsexual merging* the lesbian couple now brings about is in fact the next step in the pattern I am describing, and seems to occur simultaneously with the sacrifice of sex. But it requires a closer look. For there is an aspect of this nonsexual merging that is not simply gender-based but is particular to lesbian couples. Its source is an unconscious fantasy that has as its prototype a faulty experience of mother-infant oneness.

Concealed within this nonsexual merging is a hidden attempt on the part of each woman to sense and provide what the other needs. Because each views herself as so much "like-the-other," she often presumes that their needs are the same. In time, each one comes to believe that she can fill an unconscious emptiness and longing that exists in her partner. A certain complementarity develops: an effort to complete the other, to make the other "whole." Thus, the one who is always the life of the party teaches her awkward partner to dance. And the one who loves sports buys her timid partner a racquet. Each gives the other a part of her self. This happens intuitively. They sense what is missing in the other. And they are brought together because both women are searching for lost parts of themselves. Soon each is convinced, when she speaks to the other, that she has never met anyone who knows her so well. Throughout this unconscious, nonsexual merging, the other gradually begins to be seen as the self. All this is done out of love and devotion. It seems the most natural thing in the world. There is little, if any, sense of pain or loss. Both partners feel, in the most profound way imaginable, that each can be the person the other has longed for.

I am suggesting, then, that an original experience of faulty merging promotes each woman's attempt to provide "good-enough-mothering" for the other.[4] In the couple's unconscious re-creation of primary intimacy, the other becomes the idealized mother; and each woman becomes what she was for her own mother as child.

Both partners engage in this subtle seduction. It is a symbiotic fantasy in which each comes to believe that she keeps the other alive.

The lesbian couple's conscious experience is quite compelling. Each woman has a palpable sense of being held and made to feel alive by the exchange of exciting ideas, the intimacy of similarity, identification, and empathic responses. Who but two women would be better prepared to engage in this nonsexual merging, this "less-differentiated" mode of relating? It is familiar, comfortable, and socially reinforced.

When two people are involved in an undifferentiated merging, the emergence of "difference" is experienced as a sign of differentiation. Merging gives the illusion that two people are one. If I am merged with someone who has a particular quality, then by virtue of the "fact" that we are merged, I come to imagine that I have that quality as well. Because we are merged, I expect the other person to handle situations in the same way that I would handle them. The other should feel what I feel. But if a "difference" emerges, if the other appears to feel differently, it indicates the difficult truth that we are not merged, that we are two separate people.

"Difference" now takes on an affectively laden significance. One has the experience of "felt difference." The difference has some emotion attached to it. It is not simply that one has blue eyes and the other has brown eyes, or that one is a parent and the other is not. These are differences which will not evoke intense affect unless there is some personal, historical, or social meaning attached to them. Imagine, for instance, that Ellen is a woman who does not experience herself as particularly sexually "attractive," and that Sheila, her partner, is someone who has the experience of attracting many people, someone who "exudes" sexuality. Because Sheila is attractive and attracted to Ellen, Ellen feels attractive as well. But then they go to a party and someone flirts and Sheila responds by flirting back and does not acknowledge the primary nature of her relationship with Ellen. Suddenly, Ellen no longer feels attractive. All she feels is an incredible anguish that she cannot flirt, she is not sexy, and she cannot hold Sheila's attention. Thus, Ellen loses the sense she has had of being attractive. At this point, she feels enraged, betrayed, abandoned. She feels as if part of her is missing, that Sheila has something she wants and cannot have, that she must take back the quality she believes she has lost. Sheila, on the other hand, is afraid of Ellen's rage; is worried that she has taken something away; and feels guilty, angry, self-deprecating, confused.

This is what I mean by "felt difference." It is a subjective experience that occurs when something that has been experienced as part of the self is now experienced as being part of the object. In the context of an undifferentiated merger, "felt difference" is accompanied by a particular affective reaction. This reaction occurs on a conscious level when one person believes that she is not capable of having or being or doing the same as her partner. The conscious experience of this feeling is "she has it [or is it, or does it] and I don't." The unconscious feeling is that "something which [in more extreme cases, 'someone who . . .'] I experienced as part of me is being withheld from me, has been taken away from me."

The affect that arises in the couple's moment of "felt difference" when the soothing merger has been disrupted is known as "envy." Envy is important in this discussion because it is the affect that lies at the root of competitive behavior. Ultimately, I will suggest that competition can be a constructive way of managing this painful and potentially destructive feeling.[5] For now, I want to focus on envy as the affect that emerges at the point of differentiation in the lesbian couple. And I want to describe exactly what occurs when couples have difficulty managing this feeling.

Envy is a primitive affect that is aroused by an early experience: wanting what the other person has and hating, feeling rageful, that one cannot have it. It is common to find people who have entered into relationships with the unspoken hope that One could acquire what the Other has, simply by being involved with that person. Frequently, in my clinical work, I have seen couples who have been drawn to each other because One perceives in the Other a quality that she (or he) finds lacking in her (or him) self. Perhaps One is the writer that the Other longs to be, or One is more serious or extroverted or nurturant. I mentioned earlier that lesbian couples experience a time of disappointment in each other. An illusion is shattered, and the disappointment is so profound that it seems it can only be healed by ending the relationship. The illusion, of course, is that Two have become One. And the disappointment occurs because this relationship, like most, began with a secret hope—that each woman would come to possess the very qualities that drew her to her partner from the start. But by now it has appeared that this exchange of qualities has not taken place. And each is shocked to discover that One's ability to be nurturant has not enabled the Other to comfort herself, or One's skill as a writer has not made the Other more facile with words.

When the internal representation of one's self is merged with the partner (an object), the experience of "felt difference" evokes a deep sense of abandonment and, depending on the pathological extent of the merger, a perceived loss of self. In other words, "Something that is mine, that is part of me, is gone. It has been taken away from me, and she has it. Therefore, I am incomplete." And in more extreme cases, "I no longer exist." Envy, a destructive affect, emerges to defend against this loss. It is a desperate attempt to eradicate the separateness, the experience of "felt difference," by spoiling what the other has, or by taking it back for one's self. Aspects of this experience can be so toxic that they often remain unconscious. Envy, at its most raw, contains a wish to harm the other, who seems to have taken the quality away, perhaps even to destroy her—as if destroying the "container" will provide access to its contents. At this moment, the problem inherent in the couple's effort at nonsexual merging arises. It, too, is part of the pattern that I am describing, and it requires further examination.

Aspects of this dynamic are apparent in the relationship of Betsy and Sue, who have been together for three years. Throughout their relationship, Betsy has criticized Sue for being "passive," "forgetful," "spacey." She complains of repeated incidents of stoves left on, doors unlocked, and other "irresponsible behavior." Sue responds to Betsy's criticisms by being apologetic and self-effacing. She is fairly accepting of Betsy's constructions of reality and has difficulty demanding that she be treated as an adult. In this way, one partner appears young and accommodating, while the other is anxious, overinvolved, and controlling. There is a certain complementarity here. Sue secretly wishes she could organize her life in the adultlike manner that Betsy has. Betsy harbors a wish to give up her exaggerated sense of responsibility. Betsy, who is about to complete a professional degree, has encouraged Sue to enter a similar profession. Sue, who has always been interested in this field, has been saving money to go back to school, and will enter the same program that Betsy is finishing. Unlike Betsy, who argued and worried her way through school, Sue is approaching it with great excitement and very little anxiety. In fact, Sue appears unconcerned about the potential difficulties of this program. This is a "felt difference." Betsy envies Sue's joy and enthusiasm. She manages her envy by trying to get rid of the difference. Betsy repeatedly insists that Sue will find it impossible to survive at school unless she becomes more conscientious and aggressive. As their therapist, I suggest to Betsy that she is envious of Sue. Sue, in turn, has difficulty with Betsy's envy, fears its destructive nature, and manages her discomfort by trying to convince Betsy that she has nothing to envy.

The experience of "felt difference" occurs, to some extent, in the context of any intimate relationship, heterosexual or homosexual, where the partners have difficulty establishing psychological boundaries. However, this experience is particularly difficult for women, because female gender identity is based on a sense of continuity, connectedness, of being "in-relationship." "Felt difference" confronts women with a knowledge of their individuality and separateness. There is more potential for intense envy to accompany this experience when two people are identified with each other. And there is a tendency toward overidentification in lesbian relationships. The same-sex nature of the relationship, women's comfort with "less-differentiated" relational modes, the recapitulation of primary intimacy and merging, and the social oppression that locks the lesbian couple in the closet, contribute to this overidentification. In this context, being separate, the discovery that "I" am "not you," the sense of "felt difference" is a shock, a threat, and the emergent envy has the capacity to destroy the relationship.

It is no wonder, then, that two women who have unconsciously set out to re-create primary intimacy and merging would want to avoid the experience of "felt difference" and its accompanying envy. What better way to squelch this murderous rage, to kill the experience that threatens to rupture the much-needed merger, than to deny differences? What better way for these women to avoid the anguish of "felt difference" than to pretend that they are alike?

I want to call the process by which a couple pretends that they are alike *pseudomutuality*. And I want to point out that, once again, we are at a crucial step in the couple's spiral of problems and attempted solutions. Pseudomutuality is an effort to solve the inevitable problems of separateness and envy. It is an avoidance of "felt difference," and an establishment of a unified front. A kind of exaggerated accommodation develops; one that goes beyond the sort of compromise that is essential in order for any two people to maintain a relationship. The one who used to be the life of the party claims the couple is content just being at home. She rarely eats Chinese food because her partner is much more fond of Italian. But she does not insist; "it's not worth the fight." The two take similar stands on political issues. And they never eat meat, because it's bad for their health. To most people it would appear that these women were made for each other.

It is necessary, here, to distinguish pseudomutuality from nonsexual merging. Nonsexual merging is, itself the (nonsexual) re-creation of primal intimacy. It is, in essence, the longed-for merger in an emotional form. Although it involves behavioral changes, these transitions are frequently unconscious. The partners do not focus on the accommodations they have made. Nonsexual merging is felt to be benevolent, altruistic, and deeply pleasurable. Each partner has a conscious and unconscious experience of *giving* (her self) *to* the other, and dissolving all boundaries between them. On the other hand, pseudomutuality is a tactic that is used to protect the couple from the threatening experience of "felt difference." In pseudomutuality, each partner is aware of the accommodations she makes. The one who has stopped going to parties begins to feel trapped when her partner is home. She eats Italian food, but she misses Chinese food. Though she gave up on meat, she craves corned beef on rye. Politically speaking, she is not really sure what she believes. The couple, in its efforts to manage envy by killing off difference, has forced each person to *give up* too much of her self.

Now, to handle the resentment each feels because of this loss of self, and to reinstate a sense of separate self, the couple enters the next step in the pattern. They create the appearance of difference, as a reaction to not feeling separate enough. This *pseudodifference* can take many forms, and its content will seem of major significance. More often than not, it contains the resentment that has been building between the partners since the inevitable envy emerged.

The following conversation took place in my office, between two women who had been together for many years. This couple discusses what they, and countless others, did to avoid the experience of "felt difference," of envy, in their relationship. They also reveal the solution that they chose in order to feel like two separate selves. Note that this is not a conversation about sex. This couple gave up sex over a year ago.

Joan: We were young when we came into the relationship, but we were people with our own ways of doing stuff.

Lisa: Yeah, but I feel like I don't know that anymore. I've just been reacting off you for so long. I don't know who *I* am!! You don't seem to understand that. . . .

Joan: I don't know who I am either! I've just been reacting off you.

Lisa: Well, doesn't that bother you?! Doesn't it *bother* you? (Lisa is crying now.) It really bothers me! I just feel like I'm defined by you. It's so automatic. I don't even know what I want sometimes. When you get mad or you don't like something, then I just give in. I just go along with you, even if I don't agree. But deep down I guess I get resentful. And I guess that's why I've been doing things that I've been doing; you know, like having an affair and not telling you. I feel insecure. It's like we're this one person. We're this unit against the world or something. Like with one opinion and one set of values. It's easier to give in than to fight. I just wanted everything to be nice. I didn't want to jeopardize our relationship.

Joan and Lisa, for a while, pretended to be more alike. Then Lisa decided to have an affair. She did this, I believe, in order to feel more separate from Joan. In this way, the couple created a pseudodifference about monogamy and nonmonogamy. After months of arguing about monogamy and nonmonogamy, Joan and Lisa came to see me, stating that their six-year relationship had come to an end. This pseudodifference might just as easily have appeared as an issue of alcohol or drug abuse, sexual dysfunction, child-rearing practices, or the expression or withholding of feelings in the relationship. All these are desperate attempts to establish a sense of separate self in a relationship where separateness has been a threat to the longed-for merger. It does not matter which person drinks or has the affair. Both women suffer from not feeling separate enough. The one who is drinking has had her drink poured by the one who claims she never touches the stuff. And the one who is looking for an affair has been invited to do so by the one who is always waiting at home.

Is it any wonder, then, that I rarely see competition within the lesbian couples who come to me for help? Competition requires two people, each of whom has a sufficiently separate identity to risk measuring her self against the separate identity of the other.

Given that the issue of "sameness" is central in lesbian relationships, I was, at first, perplexed by the absence of competitive behavior. In fact, I was so perplexed I began to doubt my perceptions. I wondered if I was really looking at what was being presented to me. A few of my colleagues seemed to be seeing differently than I. They claimed that there was quite a bit of competition, but that the behavior was focused around such typically "female" issues as "who was better at the relationship," that is, who was more communicative, nurturant, other-directed. I still disagree. I see envy, and I think that gets confused with competition.

Carol and Debbie illustrate a common transactional pattern. Their interaction looks like competition, but it is really an experience that remains at the level of envy. Carol and Debbie have created an undifferentiated merger, and the following pattern occurs at a moment of "felt difference."

If Carol is upset, for any reason, Debbie "automatically" becomes upset as well. They argue about each other's lack of emotional availability, about who takes care of whom more often. Finally, Carol stops being upset and takes care of Debbie. This cycle repeats itself each time that Carol expresses any distress. Eventually, Carol, claiming that she is protecting Debbie, stops telling her partner when she is upset. Debbie experiences this as withholding, or she comes to believe that she is the only one in the relationship who ever "talks about [her] feelings." This, of course, is frustrating and humiliating to Debbie, so she decides to stop telling Carol when she is upset too. This upsets Carol which upsets Debbie, and the pattern begins again.

The clue to the undifferentiated nature of Carol and Debbie's intimacy is that one's distress consistently activates the other's distress. This time, Carol's activates Debbie's. The initial brief instant of "felt difference," when Carol is upset and Debbie isn't, is intolerable to this couple. Both women unconsciously fear, in this moment of difference, that something is being withheld or taken away. Debbie unconsciously fears that she has caused Carol's distress, and that Carol, in the end, will deprive her of nurturance. Carol believes that Debbie withholds nurturance, that "Debbie automatically takes my feelings away." It would appear, as the interaction continues, that Carol and Debbie "compete" to see who is the most upset, or who has been the most emotionally available. They keep score. The "winner" is supposed to receive nurturance from her partner. Of course this implies that there is only enough nurturance for one person and, moreover, that nurturance comes from the other and not from the self. There is never the assumption that each woman could remain upset, nurture herself, and in this way, nurture the other as well.

Clearly, this is not true competition. Sit with this couple for a little while and be swept into the painful, churning, repetitive undercurrent of something being withheld, something being taken away. Sense the powerful pull of this unconscious undertow of deprivation, of loss, of not-enough-to-go-around, which this couple experiences in their moment of "felt difference." These women are drowning in envy. Each is frantically clutching the other in hopes of saving herself. This is not a competition between two women who are confident in their own and each other's ability to survive.

I believe that, more often than not, my colleagues who claim to see competition are really watching the struggle of two envious women trying to wrest particular qualities from a partner. These women are trying to get hold of the other's nurturance, expressiveness, creativity, rather than each assuming that she can develop that quality for herself.

A distinction between competition and envy may seem purely semantic, but I believe it is extremely important, because the confusion of these two processes can lead to a misguided interpretation of what is actually occurring within the relationship. For instance, returning to an earlier example, had Ellen's envy of Sheila's "attractiveness" arisen within a relationship to two "whole" selves, it might have been transformed into a competition. Each might then have expressed her own sexiness, rather than assume there was only enough for one person and that Sheila had it. Competition is a constructive process that can evolve when an experience of "felt difference" occurs between two separate selves in relationship. If, however, this experience of "felt difference" emerges between two women who are not separate, the couple's interaction will remain at the more destructive, difficult, painful level of envy.

Competition has acquired a bad reputation among women, and certainly within the feminist community. I want to discuss some of the reasons for this. Then I will argue that it is essential for women to become comfortable with competition.

Lesbian couples, in particular, must begin to see it as a way to manage envy and to encourage the development of "whole," separate selves in relationship.

The following comment was overheard at a party: "There's no competition in our relationship. We have different careers. But Donna and Kate. They're both writers. I don't think they compete either." "No," her friend stated quite proudly, "I don't think lesbian couples are very competitive." Lesbian couples, and women in general, dread competition because they think of it as a process whereby someone gains something at the expense of another person. In other words, there is an assumption that one's coming to possess a certain quality means that one has taken something away from someone else. By now this has become familiar to us as a paradigm for envy, which evokes conscious or unconscious feelings of rage; a wish to harm the other; and a concomitant terror that thinking or feeling this way will, in fact, contaminate or destroy the Other, the Self, and/or the Relationship. Rather than experiencing competition as a particular kind of relatedness, these couples experience it as a lethal separateness that they imagine will destroy the relationship. In truth, envy—not competition—is the potentially destructive element here.

It is this fear of loss—loss of Other, of Self, of Relationship—that ostensibly lies at the core of women's psychological difficulty with competition. I am suggesting, however, that competition is not the cause of this type of loss. In many of the relationships that I have seen, true loss occurs precisely because the partners have been afraid to compete. True loss occurs when repeated experiences of envy have not been afforded any constructive outlet. Competition, on the other hand, can be a functional means of sublimating envy and generating a sense of separate self in relationship. For, in essence, competition detoxifies envy. It encompasses the intense affects that envy evokes and encourages their benign expression.

In competition, the envious wish to harm the Other is modified by displacing this aggression onto the task of developing the desired quality in the Self. In order to compete, one must call up the quality in the Self that has previously been attributed to the Other. To recall our earlier example: Ellen cannot continue to allow Sheila to embody *her* sexiness, or *her* flirtatiousness, or *her* femininity, if the relationship is to last over time. Initially, albeit unconsciously, Ellen may have been attracted to and dependent upon Sheila's ease with sexiness. Sheila became an incubator, a container, providing a protective environment in which Ellen could safely experience being sexy. Eventually, however, Ellen must give up the illusion that the only way she can be sexy is by being connected to Sheila. This is a reciprocal process: Sheila must give up the illusion as well. For she, too, has had an unconscious investment in being the container of the sexiness in this relationship. Instead, Ellen must come to understand that, for whatever reason, the envied quality lies dormant in herself. What she has acquired from Sheila is not the desired quality itself, but the permission to express that quality. A quality that Ellen feared in herself has now acquired value in her own eyes, precisely because she valued it in Sheila. Thus, Ellen must risk having and exhibiting the quality of which she felt herself to be deprived. And she must commit herself to the slow, complicated, often arduous task of developing it.

This, of course, is what happens in a true competition. One is provided with the opportunity to become competent. It is not an easy task, nor is it one that can always be accomplished. There is still the possibility of deep disappointment. But it is hardly the toxic, damaging, irreparable self or object loss that repeated episodes of unresolved envy can produce. In undertaking the challenge to compete, to become competent, one has, at the very least, the experience of developing a particular aspect of the Self and observing that the Other is not destroyed by this success. When One gets better, the Other does not have to get worse.

The following story, told to be my a colleague, offers a sense of the way competition can develop from envy and can provide a couple with a productive experience of two separate selves in relationship. This woman told me of her fervent wish to become a skilled public speaker. As it happened, her partner of many years was quite an accomplished public spokeswoman. My colleague would eagerly attend her partner's public appearances, secretly harboring this belief: "She is a part of me. Therefore, her performance is mine as well." Repeated experiences of what I have termed "felt difference" forced these women to begin to relinquish their illusion of oneness. Still, my colleague would sit in the audience with great pleasure, now consciously hoping to acquire the skill herself. "In the beginning, I loved to go when she spoke. I loved to sit in the audience and beam. But pretty soon, I wanted it myself. But I kept thinking, 'If I have more of it, she'll have less. If I compete, she'll be damaged.' "

This, of course, implies my colleague's belief that her capacity for public speaking rested in the person of her partner. Her feelings imply that there was only enough "public-speaking ability" for one person, and that her partner had it. In considering that she might develop her own capacity to speak in public, my colleague feared that her partner would become envious. This, too, seemed a reason to avoid competition. Initially, then, this couple's interactions stayed at the painfully difficult level of envy. My colleague found herself becoming increasingly critical of her partner's work and would often provoke hurtful arguments prior to a performance. Eventually this woman was able to acknowledge her envy. She and her partner spoke of the "felt difference" between them, and began to develop genuine competition. "Now in our relationship, she and I compete to see who is the better public speaker. . . . We are benignly competitive and we keep goading each other on. It's like someone sets the bar higher and the other springs over it." I do not mean to imply that each woman must strive to express a particular quality or ability in the same way that her partner expresses it. That one woman envies her partner's passion for public speaking does not mean that she must work to become a skilled public speaker herself. It is the *passion* that is envied. The capacity to be passionate about something is what must be examined and developed.

Competition solidifies an experience of two separate selves. It is a process that depends on separate selves in relationship. The illusion of oneness may be shattered, but it is important to remember that in competition "the relationship" remains.

Yes, there is a net which separates two tennis partners. Of course there are differences in each person's playing styles and skills. But it is impossible to play the game without a partner. And during the game, one's sense of one's self as separate and different comes from being in relation to one's partner. Competition, then, in a process that promotes competence, and emphasizes separateness and difference in the context of relatedness.

I admit that I am simplifying a very complex set of behaviors and circumstances. Women are socialized not to compete, especially with men. These cultural expectations have economic and social/historical roots, and leave women with little or no constructive outlet for their experiences of envy. In fact, the social system discourages competition and encourages envy by training women to devalue themselves and each other. But I oversimplify in order to make a crucial point. Women, in general, and lesbian couples, more specifically, have a psychological propensity to subordinate their individuation to the perceived continuation of the relationship. This propensity has been created and reinforced by a culture in which women are the primary caretakers. It is a propensity that is based on the female development of the Self, a resultant comfort with "less-differentiated" relational modes, and women's socially instilled sense of caretaking responsibility. Thus, women come to perceive that separation-individuation is a threat to relatedness. But why not view differentiation as a particular way of being connected? Why not see competition as a particular way of expressing a separate self in relationship?

I would like to view competition as a kind of relatedness in which two women who are separate selves motivate each other toward some heightened capacity without fearing damage to one's self, the other, or the relationship. The partners are separate *and* connected in a competitive process. The process itself can encourage a separateness that is relational rather than reactive, a sense both of the ongoing presence of an other and of a self that is separate and whole.

NOTES

1. Michael Balint, *Primary Love and Psycho-Analytic Technique* (New York: Liveright Publishing, 1965), 50.

2. Nancy Chodorow, *The Reproduction of Mothering: Psychoanalysis and the Sociology of Gender* (Berkeley: University of California Press), 194.

3. Ibid., 109, 167; Carol Gilligan, *In a Different Voice: Psychological Theory and Women's Development* (Cambridge: Harvard University Press, 1982), 8.

4. It is beyond the scope of this essay to discuss fully what I call "faulty merging." It can best be summarized as a "failure of fit" between mother and infant, according to D. W. Winnicott, *The Maturational Process and the Facilitating Environment* (New York: International Universities Press, 1965). The development of object relations and the self are usefully discussed in Winnicott's work, in Balint, *Primary Love and Psycho-Analytic Technique* and in Balint, *The Basic Fault: Therapeutic Aspects of Regression* (New York: Bruner Mazel, 1979). Equally relevant, but impossible to present here, is a discussion of the unconscious elements involved in female homosexual object choice. For an excellent psychoanalytic interpretation, see Joyce McDougall, "The Homosexual Dilemma: A Study

of Female Homosexuality," in *Plea for a Measure of Abnormality* (New York: International Universities Press, 1980).

5. For an excellent, more complete discussion of envy, see Melanie Klein, *Envy and Gratitude and Other Works, 1946–63* (New York: Dell Publishing Co. 1977).

Women, Oppression, Privilege, and Competition

PAULA ROSS

The air is bright blue over the redwood trees in the hills above California's Monterey Bay. Immersed in the intense atmosphere of a residential writing community, I spend two weeks each summer here as co-director of Women's Voices: A Creative Writing Workshop.

This community is all female. Our common goal is the nurturing, encouragement, and expression of the female literary imagination. As individual women, we represent a diverse collection of experiences, cultures, ages, physical abilities, occupations, classes, races, sexual preferences, and social and political beliefs.

The potential for misunderstandings arising from any single pair of these elements is immense. In combination, it is almost incomprehensible. And so, despite the commitment we share to discover and develop the voice of the woman inside each of us, this assembly of so many different kinds of women is often an uneasy one. Yet it is within the context of the unease, the discomfort that comes from confronting *difference*, that I have learned critical lessons about women, oppression, privilege, and competition.

The process of learning these lessons occurred in the course of my own growth as a writer. To illustrate them I will use my experiences with the Women's Voices workshop because that is the context with which I am most familiar. I think, however, that the lessons themselves have applications far beyond Monterey Bay and my own work.

Women's Voices was born in Santa Cruz, California in 1977. It is very much a product of the time of its birth—the height of the second wave of feminism in this country. And as far as I know, it is one of only two such programs in the United States. Women come to Women's Voices to write in retreat. For two weeks, they live a life free of the family and other obligations that make it so difficult for artists in general, and women artists in particular, to create.

I attended Women's Voices in 1980 as a participant. At the time, I had just resumed my career as a news reporter after spending three years as an administrator for a federal grant program. My experience in Santa Cruz was the beginning of a new phase in my writing life.

The structure of Women's Voices is simple. Women who attend are strongly enncouraged to live in workshop housing, to claim for themselves "a room of one's own—and more." They are required to attend and actively participate in one two-hour class a day. The rest of their time is free. There are scheduled readings by instructors, guest speakers, and each class. Spontaneous readings, discussions, and support groups spring up in response to the particular needs and interests of the women attending any particular session.

In 1982 when I joined founder and co-director Marcy Alancraig in administering Women's Voices, my primary personal and professional goal, as a black woman, as a writer, was to increase the number of women of color who attended. A scholarship program was already in place. Its main purpose was (and continues to be) to provide financial help for women who historically do not have access to life in an artistic community. These include women of color, single mothers, and low-income women. Consequently, the creation and maintenance of a diverse community was as much of a deliberate and conscious choice as was the provision of "a room of one's own."

That decision, to recruit *actively*, not just passively to *accept* a broad spectrum of women, means that Women's Voices can be a prickly, uncomfortable experience. But in the last five years, I have watched the kind of growth that can occur when, as women and as artists, we confront and learn to support one another in *all* our differences.

At the same time, I believe that "difference" is at the heart of a strange kind of competition between and among women, between and among the disenfranchised in general. Based on my years with Women's Voices and my experiences as a black feminist who came of age in the late 1960s and early 1970s, I see this brand of competition falling into three categories. Competition to represent: (1) "The Most Oppressed," also known as "The Oppression Derby"; (2) The Feminist Ideal; (3) The "All-American" Ideal.

THE OPPRESSION DERBY

I

However the image enters
its force remains within
my eyes
rockstrewn caves where dragonfish evolve
learning to survive
where there is no food
my eyes are always hungry

and remembering
however the image enters
its force remains.
A white woman stands bereft and empty
a black boy hacked into a murderous lesson
recalled in me forever
like a lurch of earth on the edge of sleep
etched into my visions
food for dragonfish that learn
to live upon whatever they must eat
fused images beneath my pain.

IV

Emmett Till rides the crest of the Pearl whistling
24 years his ghost lay like the shade of a raped woman
and a white girl has grown older in costly honor
(what did she pay to never know its price?)
now the Pearl River speaks its muddy judgment
and I can withhold my pity and my bread.

. . .

   Within my eyes
the flickering afterimages of a nightmare rain
a woman wrings her hands
beneath the weight of agonies remembered
I wade through summer ghosts
betrayed by vision
hers and my own
becoming dragonfish to survive
the horrors we are living
with tortured lungs
adapting to breathe blood.
A woman measures her life's damage
my eyes are caves, chunks of etched rock
tied to the ghost of a black boy
whistling

—from Audre Lorde, "Afterimages"

Audre Lorde reads many poems that hot summer night. Heat continues to radiate
in the cooler air of morning. A young boy dies for whistling at a white woman.
The poet has touched a collective nerve. And the room quivers with the swaying
of antennae searching for the source of the shock. Worlds are about to collide.

A woman speaks. She is young, white, and brave. "I'm gonna put myself out here," she says. It is this poem that impels her. This poem and the pain she is feeling because of it. "Sometimes," she says, "I feel like there gets to be this elitism of oppression among women. Like in the poem, I just feel like just to *breathe* on this planet it's like really hard. It's hard for everybody."

Another woman, also white, responds. It's not that the poet did not feel compassion for the white woman in "Afterimages," she says. "I was struck by that image and also the image of Emmett Till. But I felt that the image of Emmett Till overshadowed the white woman's pain. I didn't feel it was equal."

Every black woman in the room (and some who are not black), feels these words slice through her gut. "We are all women here but our pain is *not* equal!" reverberates through the room.

"But," the white woman cries out, "I am who I am and it's as hard for me in a sense as it is for you! I try and stress the *sameness* about us."

The room erupts. From out of the chaos, the voice of the poet thunders,

"We must recognize the sameness of our struggle and that recognition will *nevah* happen until we recognize our differences. Once we recognize the ways in which we are different and recognize that this is not a reason for jugular-vein psychology, is not a reason for instant attack, once we learn to recognize difference and use that difference creatively, then we can begin to plant our feet in something similar and work together. It doesn't mean becoming the same, it means recognizing who we are.

"You see, traditionally, oppressed people have always had to recognize the images of the dominant group because it meant survival for us. I *have* to know what you are seeing 'cause I mean, your daddies wrote the books, they drew pictures of you. I've been living with the sense, since I was born, that I occupy your space. So *I* know what your images are but you *don't* know what mine are. If you do not know what mine are, you are, to begin with, always at the mercy of my knowledge of *you*."

After watching this and similar scenes being played out, year after year in the bright blue light above Monterey Bay, I am beginning to understand what it is I am seeing.

Native American women rage against a legacy of devastation that has reduced this country's native population to half a million people. Black women explore the scars of the heritage of slavery and its aftermath. Chincanas and Latinas recall the shame and humiliation to which they were subjected, often by their own parents, who were anxious for their children to be "accepted" for speaking the tongue of their birth. Asian women call out against the constrictions and myths that bind them as members of the so-called model minority. Jewish women try to come to terms with the Holocaust. Lesbians shine uncompromising lights into the closets where they have been forced and onto the terror they feel when breaking out, even if only for a little while. Disabled women challenge *everyone's* assumptions and lack of awareness about the issues of disability.

And the white women, the straight women, the able-bodied women, any women who feel they can't "compete" in this Oppression Derby, begin to feel outnumbered, isolated, and invisible. They feel rootless, without a culture, pale, colorless, and incredibly guilty. Their perceptions become distorted. Their ability to take in and process information is eroded.

When I first observed this process, I was confused. It was clear that these women were honestly perplexed, that they genuinely experienced the voices of these *different* women as assaults, as personal attacks.

• A young Jewish lesbian reads a story about a summer she spent working in Alaska with two gay male friends. Another Jewish woman, old enough to be the younger's mother, married, with a lesbian daughter of her own, becomes agitated and upset, convinced that the younger woman is passing judgment on marriage in general and her marriage in particular. The older woman is sure that the younger thinks that *all* women should be lesbians and that no self-respecting feminist could possibly be married. I reread the story and can find no references, implied or otherwise, to the subject of marriage.

• Women's Voices has maintained a constant level of 70 percent heterosexual women and 30 percent lesbians (all self-identified). There has never been any attempt to manipulate those figures one way or the other. (One year the percentages were reversed, a phenomenon that remains a mystery and has never been repeated.) Up until 1986, admission was strictly on a first-come, first-served, basis. The current policy combines first-come, first-served with evaluations of writing samples and the match between what Women's Voices will provide and what the applicant wants to accomplish.

Despite the *actual* numbers of lesbians who attend a given workshop, straight women continue to perceive the numbers as being much, much higher. The issues and concerns voiced by the lesbians are seen as "taking over," monopolizing the floor.

That this happens, year after year, is at least in part a phenomenon we have inherited. At one point in its early history, there was a rumor afloat that the women's movement was "overrun" with lesbians. We were everywhere. By the early 1980s, this widely reported phenomenon had died down. Instead of screaming headlines in various mainstream and feminist publications, there were just genteel rumblings. The fears, the anxieties, the suspicions, however, simply went underground.

• This third example of the They're-Taking-Over syndrome occurred when I was part of a group of women soliciting and selecting material for an anthology of women's writing. The project was totally unrelated to Women's Voices, but the dynamics were very similar. There were six of us. One woman periodically rejected a piece because of its lesbian content. We didn't pay too much attention to this. Then she began voicing doubts about the biographical statements that included lesbian self-identification. When this didn't produce much response either, she finally told us very directly that she was afraid the book wouldn't be acceptable to a lot of women because it was "over half lesbian." That got our attention, particularly those of us who *were* lesbian. Over half?! How had we missed that? As the editor, I'd been over and over the manuscripts countless times. I did not have the sense that the book was anywhere near half lesbian. I suggested doing a count. Afterward, we could talk about what if anything we wanted to do about the results. I did two tallies: one of the number of women who I knew from my personal knowledge to be lesbian or who so identified themselves—there were 26 out of 75, or 34 percent; the second of all the pieces that contained any clearly lesbian content—there were 7 pieces out of 86, or 8 percent. When I presented these figures to the group, there was little discussion. The numbers spoke eloquently for themselves, and we continued with the planning of the book's production.

When our perceptions become distorted because of racism, anti-Semitism, homophobia, or other "isms," we need to stop and look to see if what we are afraid of does in fact exist. If it does not, the next step should be to ask ourselves what it is we are really afraid of. And sometimes, when we find ourselves arguing, "But don't you feel there's a little *too* much representation by *fill in the blank* in this group?" the absurdity of that question can often be quickly demonstrated by substituting the words "white men" in place of the alleged interlopers.

Until and unless this kind of honest, often painful analysis occurs, personal and interpersonal chaos will erupt, at women's voices, in cries of bewilderment and fury.

"Why do you always have to *label* yourself? We're all just women here! Let's stress the *sameness* about ourselves, not the *differences!*"

"What makes you think you've cornered the market on pain just because you're *fill in the blank*, or a *fill in the blank?*"

THE FEMINIST IDEAL

Many of the women who come to Women's Voices, including myself, come from deep involvements in the women's movement. We have grown up with and helped determine the direction of feminism's second wave. We share a common language—consciousness raising, the personal is political, process, coalition—and we therefore sometimes mistake a shared lexicon with shared assumptions and perceptions about the world at large. But in the kind of pressure-cooker atmosphere that inevitably develops when women come together to explore their creativity and then *write* from the discoveries of those explorations, such assumptions can lead to serious complications and misunderstandings.

Every woman who attends Women's Voices, who enters this community of writing women, has at least some of her assumptions about the world challenged. For white women, this may be their first experience living in a world in which their assumptions are not automatically accepted as the truth of the way things are. They have been taught, in subtle or obvious ways, that women of color are their inferiors. But in this consciously constructed community, these supposedly "inferior" women have as much right to speak as anyone. Lesbians, about whom some women may know only stereotypes, are fully visible in their wide range of appearances, interests, occupations, family backgrounds, and politics.

Women of color learn that oppression is not a single, monolithic experience. Light-skinned women of color hear how the color line has oppressed their darker-skinned sisters. Middle-class women and wealthy women of all colors are confronted with their financial, educational, and social privileges. Lessons are presented, if not always learned, that not only must we claim and *use* the pain of whatever oppressions we live under, but we must also take responsibility for whatever privileges we may have as well.

It is now almost a cliché to say that the white women's movement in this country has been established on a foundation of dichotomy—women versus men—rather than one of plural or many-pronged issues and concerns, not always gender-related. Given the assumptions that support that foundation, it is no wonder that clashes occurred early on between white women who perceived The Struggle in terms of dichotomy, and women of color who considered those perceptions not simply narrow but simply impossible. In 1977 a group of black feminists, The Combahee River Collective, explained their position in "A Black Feminist Statement."

> Although we are feminists and lesbians, we feel solidarity with progressive Black men and do not advocate the fractionalization that white women who are separatists demand. Our situation as Black people necessitates that we have solidarity around the fact of race, which white women of course do not need to have with white men, unless it is their negative solidarity as racial oppressors. We struggle together with Black men against racism, while we also struggle with Black men about sexism.[1]

As a result of this and similar stances, women of color endured (and in some circles still do) accusations of being "male-identified" when they insisted that their struggles as women could not be separated from their struggles as women of color. Which is not to say that women of color all agree about *how* those two struggles should be integrated, or even *if* they should. What it does say is that from its inception, feminism has fought its own internal battles against *difference*. And for the most part, the luxury of ignoring, glossing over, or dismissing difference has belonged to those who are most like the holders and exercisers of ultimate power— the daughters, sisters, mothers, lovers, and wives of the white males in authority. And why should it be otherwise? The women who comprised the popularly portrayed "leaders" of the white women's movement grew up in the same culture and were taught the same intolerances for difference as were their white male counterparts.

Responses to these differences are sometimes brutal: Kill it, eliminate it. Often the murder is not direct but, ironically, is more "typically feminine." What is perceived as different is killed through subversion, inattention, or attempts at dilution by "including" the difference and trying to make it "fit," thereby rendering it powerless.

Women of color are hardly alone in their protests that the women's movement does not adequately represent their interests and concerns. Women who have no desire to climb the corporate ladder, to secure academic tenure, or to hold down "nontraditional" jobs have often felt excluded from the feminist club. Women who truly want to exercise the vaunted "choices" that feminism promises, making motherhood, for example, a freely *chosen* occupation, often feel that such choices invalidate their membership. Rural and older women have expressed their frustration with the narrow definitions that "the women's movement" seems invested in maintaining. But the mirror these women hold up to the media images of who is and who is not a feminist reflects back a picture of overwhelming *difference*. And failure to recognize that feminism is not the property of any single kind of woman means failure to forge a truly representative, and consequently enduring, powerful movement.

As a community, Women's Voices operates on the belief that each woman has a valid voice. Though we all bring with us from the outside world the baggage of racism, anti-Semitism, homophobia, ageism, and other bigotries and prejudices, inside the world we create that baggage is not acceptable. No woman, by virtue of whatever her privileged status may be, possesses a voice more valid than another's.

For women who are used to being given preferential treatment based on privilege, this comes as a shock. And they often experience being treated as equals to women they've been taught are their inferiors as a form of reverse discrimination.

At Women's Voices, white women are often confronted with women of color who tell them, "You have no authority to *grant* me acceptance. You are not in a position to *allow* me to speak and write about the world as *I* see it. I do so because I have as much right to do so as you do." To *grant* someone acceptance, to *allow* someone to speak automatically implies the power to *revoke* that permission. And that is not a relationship of peers.

This experience is perhaps most disturbing to the women who have had some direct exposure to feminism (not all the women have) and who consider themselves feminists. Many are from small towns, perhaps one of only a few "women's libbers" for miles around. They are accustomed to the role of the rebel; they are familiar with the position of the outsider. And that experience has made them hungry for making *connections* with other women, eager to *share* common struggles and common goals. So they become profoundly disturbed to find that they are now seen as the conformists, the conservatives, the ones against whom *others* rebel. They are told that it is not enough to be "liberal."

The reactions are as varied as the women themselves. Some quietly withdraw, privately seeking out support among those other women who *do* seem to be most like them. Others resist the pain by erecting the defense of "I came here to *write*, not to talk about politics and differences."

THE "ALL-AMERICAN" IDEAL

As a black *person* born and raised in the United States, I have never had a choice about dealing with difference. At an early age, I learned that it was more than my life was worth, emotionally and sometimes physically, to assume that my world view was universal. As a black *female* it became clear to me very quickly that what was considered "normal" was what was male. The world was run by white men who had access to and full use, if not personal possession, of vast wealth.

Under this system, issues of class, race, culture, ethnicity, sexual and affectional orientation, age, education, physical and mental ability are seen as divisive, messy obstacles to achieving that perfect specimen, the "All-American." The melting pot's recipe may utilize a host of different ingredients, but they are subjected to a homogenization process whose purpose is to produce that "All-American" product. And that product is certainly not dark-skinned, does not speak American Sign Language or with an "ethnic accent," is not poor, is certainly not lesbian or gay, and is not old.

The irony is, of course, that in one way or another, most people do not meet the criteria for making the "All-American" team.

PLANTING OUR FEET IN SOMETHING SIMILAR

> "We have only been taught three ways to handle difference; three ways only. If we think it is *dominant*, we want to *become* it. If we think it is *inferior*, we want to *kill* it. And if we're not really sure which it is, we want to ignore it. Well, if we are to survive, I think it is as women we must begin to examine alternatives."
>
> —Audre Lorde
> *Women's Voices*, 1983

It is in the best interests of those who comprise and control the power structure in this country to encourage permanent heats in the Oppression Derby. It is in the best interests of those in power to continue to feed the scarcity myth, that there is not enough to go around: not enough food, housing, medical care, child care, grants, contracts, jobs. It is in the best interests of everyone *except* those of us who have no power to define *feminist* and *American* so narrowly that those terms exclude as many people as possible, those who don't fit, those who are different. It is in the best interests of those of us who have been excluded to find and use alternatives to dismantle this system.

When we perceive difference as dominant, we want to become like it for two reasons. First, it is safer (or appears to be) to be like the person who holds power over your world. Second, occupying a position of dominance, or being accepted by someone who does, entitles you to privilege. Once possessed, privilege is not easily relinquished.

To remove this discussion from the abstract: Men have the entire world in which to roam. As soon as women label an event, a room, a publication, "women only," men scream "discrimination" and feel left out. The 99 $^{99}/_{100th}$ of the world that remains their province suddenly shrinks into the background, overwhelmed by the $^1/_{100th}$ that has been declared closed to them. (And, truth be known, even this exclusion is illusory. Men still have the power to reclaim that $^1/_{100th}$ if they choose to exercise it. They know it. The women know it. So perhaps it's the very fact of the declaration, the defiance of authority, that is so intolerable.)

Privilege, almost by definition, requires that someone else pay the price for its enjoyment. And when privilege is awarded on the basis of skin color, racial or cultural identity, religion, gender, economic or social status, it can become dangerous.

One of the most important lessons I have learned from my involvement with Women's Voices is that resistance to acknowledging one's own privilege, much less relinquishing it, often originates in fear. It is what makes a woman, in the face of another woman's pain, cry out, "But my pain is just as real, just as legitimate as yours!" This is particularly true if the first woman is a member of a traditionally privileged class and the other woman is not. The privileged woman is terrified of losing her privilege *and* her pain.

To acknowledge and respect another woman's difference, to acknowledge and take responsibility for one's own racism, homophobia, anti-Semitism, and so on does not mean that one's own oppression vanishes or becomes less painful or real.

Under these circumstances, it is very easy to fall under the spell of either/or thinking: In the face of my speech, you are rendered silent. If I talk about my anger, my hurt as a black woman, if you are white, then you must give up your own anger, your own hurt, from whatever source. Both cannot exist simultaneously. But that is a myth.

In the face of my speech you *should* be silent, but only for the moment, not forever. If you cannot listen, how can you hear what it is I am saying to you? I have asked that question over and over again. Often I am asked in return, "But what should I do after I've listened? I feel so guilty!"

There was a time when my answer, and that of many other feminists like me, would have been, "What you should *do* is go and educate yourself! Listening to me once, or even ten times, will not tell you all you need to know. And it is not my job to teach you about *my* oppression!" Those remain both true and untrue statements. The truth lies in the fact that as a black woman, as a black lesbian, I often grow weary of trying to fill in the abysmal gaps in the education of white and/or straight women who want to "understand" The Black Experience or The Lesbian Experience, as if either could be summarized or collected in a single woman's life. The truth lies in the fact that as not just a product of the educational system of this country, but a target of its daily infusions of culture as interpreted by or presented in movies, magazines, books, billboards, and television, I have spent untold hours being assaulted with information about white, Western culture, values, and world views. The *competition* in my brain to store information about my *own* history, heritage, and people is an exhausting one.

The untruth lies in the fact that unless I do know my own history and where I come from, I cannot tell the truth about my own afterimages. And if I cannot tell that truth to the woman who wants to know it, then she and I are both doomed.

At the same time, the white woman or the straight woman with whom I might share this knowledge must have her own context in which to put it. Without that context, I will be forever alien to her, she forever guilty to herself. And if my very existence continues to elicit only guilt, sooner or later she will simply tune me out. The association will become unbearable and intolerable. As an operative emotion, guilt becomes an excuse, an obstacle in the way of making any real change.

Like me, this woman must discover her own history, her own heritage, her own people. She must find the resisters, the fighters, the activists, the ones who refused to confuse things as they are with things as they should be. And she must find the power that comes from these discoveries within herself, her own family, her own community, her own culture.

But even before she can begin that discovery, she must first acknowledge her own privileged position in the world. For white women, no matter the other circumstances of their lives, are heir to certain basic privileges. Like everyone else raised in this culture, white women have been taught that to be white is to be superior to people of color. And while white women may not be responsible for the creation of systematic oppression, they do benefit from the system. White women must accept that those oppressions are real, that they influence and shape the way women of color see the world. Those are facts. They cannot be denied.

This recognition of, as white Southern writer Minnie Bruce Pratt says, "how *habitually* I think of my culture, my ethics, my morality, as the culmination of history, as the logical extension of what has gone before" is painful.

But even that recognition does not bring peace. More steps lie ahead. Acknowledging her own privilege may then make her plummet into a loathing of herself and where she has come from. She may experience the reverse of identifying with the oppressor and try to merge with the oppressed, not yet realizing that while she is not responsible for the privilege, she is responsible for what she does with that privilege, as we all are.

Few of us are without privilege of some kind. Few of us are innocent of using our privilege at someone else's expense. So most of us, when confronted with our behavior, with the knowledge that we have hurt someone else, feel lost in a foreign territory for which we have no map. Our difference becomes a danger to us instead of an advantage.

What we must face is that the differences between and among us are a source of power. We do not, nor have we ever had the luxury to, select which we will save and which we will discard of the many kinds of differences we may each embody. The complicated network of women's lives that weaves itself into the community tapestry that is Women's Voices, for example, is, in the end, all of a piece.

In answer to the self-posed question, "To whom do I owe the woman I have become?" Audre Lorde answers in the introduction to her biomythography, *Zami, A New Spelling of My Name*:

To the white woman I dreamed standing behind me in an airport, silently watching while her child deliberately bumps into me over and over again. When I turn around to tell this woman that if she doesn't restrain her kid I'm going to punch her in the mouth, I see that she's been punched in the mouth already. Both she and her child are battered, with bruised faces and blackened eyes. I turn, and walk away from them in sadness and fury.

There will be no prizes awarded, no winners will be crowned in the false competition of The Oppression Derby. That "sadness and fury" must instead be used to fuel our mutual fight to win for every one of us, and those we love, our full measure of humanity. And that humanity can be achieved only if we embrace both what is different and what is the same among us.

BIBLIOGRAPHY

Bulkin, Elly, Minnie Bruce Pratt, and Barbara Smith. *Yours in Struggle: Three Feminist Perspectives on Anti-Semitism and Racism.* Brooklyn, NY: Long Haul Press, 1984.

Hull, Gloria T., Patricia Bell Scott, and Barbara Smith. *All the Women Are White, All the Blacks Are Men, But Some of Us Are Brave: Black Women's Studies.* Old Westbury, NY: The Feminist Press, 1982.

Lorde, Audre. *Chosen Poems, Old and New.* New York: Norton, 1982.

Lorde, Audre. *Zami: A New Spelling of My Name.* Watertown, MA: Persephone Press, 1982. (Reprinted by Crossing Press, Trumansburg, N.Y. 1983).

Segrest, Mab. Introduction by Adrienne Rich. *My Mama's Dead Squirrel: Lesbian Essays on Southern Culture.* Ithaca, NY: Firebrand Books, 1985.

Stalvey, Lois Mark. *The Education of a WASP.* New York: Bantam Books, 1971.

NOTES

1. The Combahee River Collective, "A Black Feminist Statement," in *Capitalist Patriarchy and the Case for Socialist Revolution*, ed. Zillah Eisenstein (New York: Monthly Review Press, 1978).

Anarchist Alternatives to Competition

MARTHA A. ACKELSBERG and
KATHRYN PYNE ADDELSON

In the women's movement of the 1970s, many feminists came to see competition as one means by which male dominance, and class and racial dominance, were created and maintained. They saw competition for positions according to "merit" and competition for power or influence within pluralist political structures to be ways of organizing institutions so as to preserve a social order in which some gained a lion's share of communal-social resources and others, only crumbs. When these feminists organized the women's unions, women's clinics, abortion referral and rape crisis centers, bookstores, magazines, and early women's studies courses, they attempted to put into practice collective, nonhierarchical, noncompetitive ways of organizing their work. Many of these feminists called themselves anarchist and consciously drew on anarchist principles.[1] Anarchists, decentralist socialists, and others who value worker control and participatory democracy have offered alternatives to competition which challenge the necessity of hierarchical work orders and question the rules by which pluralist political structures reward the few at the expense of the many.

As feminists examined the competitive structures and practices prevalent in U.S. society, they came to understand competition as a mechanism for justifying and legitimating an unequal distribution of social resources. Just as Plato conceived of a "myth of the metals," the so-called Noble Lie that, he believed, would explain to people the unequal distribution of roles and responsibilities in his ideal society (and, importantly, lead them to accept their places in it), so the prevailing political and social ideology in the United States insists that the existing distribution of resources is a result of "competition," or "the free market."

To explain social relationships in this way is, effectively, to treat them as the consequences of a game, with its rules more or less set. Such an approach masks relationships of power and powerlessness, and the particular ways in which existing rules benefit some at the expense of others. Many feminists recognized this in the early stages of the second wave of the U.S. feminist movement.

In this paper we argue, first, that this conceptualization of politics and social relationships is seriously misleading; and, second, that anarchism (and, in particular, anarchist-feminism) offers an alternative conceptualization which can incorporate a more complete vision of social reality and the process of social change. To show this, we consider two alternatives to competition as it is understood in the contemporary United States. One is drawn from feminist activism in Canada and the other from U.S. labor history. The Vancouver Women's Health Collective, a self-managed workplace, offered an alternative to hierarchically organized, management-run enterprise. In the Lawrence (Massachusetts) Textile Strike of 1912, anarchist methods of direct action worked as an alternative to competing interest groups in the pluralist political arena. In both cases, the contrast is not simply between competition and cooperation, but between different understandings of equality, justice, knowledge, and—importantly—the nature of social reality.

The dominant tradition in the United States is political liberalism—liberalism of a sort that insists upon liberty and "free" competition, both in the marketplace and among the citizens. Competition is intrinsic to liberalism in several ways. There is competition in the political sphere—often conceived as pluralist competition in which conflicting interest groups try to influence voters or their elected representatives. This kind of political competition appears as a fact of life in the United States, and many "liberal feminist" groups have tended to become interest-group organizations, trying to gain influence in this competitive struggle, using more or less established structures to attempt to win offices or influence policy.[2]

Other ways competition is intrinsic to liberalism in the United States have to do with the workplace and the economic marketplace. The capitalist "free enterprise" economy requires that businesses compete for a share of the market and that workers compete for jobs. This economic competition is overlaid with ideas about "survival of the fittest" and getting one's due for excellence and hard work under a meritocracy.

Many writers in the liberal tradition view hierarchy as a necessary condition of social life. They argue that coordination is necessary, and that the most efficient form of coordination is hierarchical organization. According to this liberal view, "competition"—based on skills, intelligence, or other "relevant" criteria, depending on the particular institution in question—is the most efficient, and the fairest, way to assign people to their places in hierarchical organizations. When the competition is held fairly (that is, when the rules are known to all, and when all appropriate competitors have an equal chance at playing the game), the result is a "meritocracy," in which positions go to the "most qualified."[3]

When liberals turn a critical eye toward U.S. society and see that the most highly rewarded jobs tend to be held by white, upper-class males, and that many highly qualified women and people of color never make it to the tops of the hierarchies, their explanation is that something has gone wrong with the competition. They attribute this "unfair" sorting to various kinds of discrimination on the part of those hiring, or those making up qualifying exams, and so on. Their proposed solution: end discrimination; adopt, as a goal, equal opportunity. Then, those few women and people of color who excel can join the few men who rise to the top and become vice presidents of banks, account executives, department managers, or full professors. (The numbers are few, of course, because the positions are few.)

Many writers and activists in the Marxist and other socialist traditions have criticized liberal individualism. They have seen pluralist political competition, and hierarchy and privilege, as problematic in themselves. They have invited us to look behind the story liberals tell, and to recognize that it is capitalism—a set of relationships of power and authority in the economic realm—that generates economic classes, the privileges (and relationships of domination and subordination) that go with them, and the need for claims about "competition" and "meritocracy" to justify these inequalities.

These Socialists treat class and and economic factors as the most crucial, deriving all other relationships of domination and subordination in society from those fundamental ones. They hold that people committed to social change must work together to overcome the economic structures of capitalism. Through such a struggle, they will make clear what claims about competition and meritocracy cover up, and will contribute to the undermining of all hierarchies, social, political, or sexual. Socialist feminists—noting the sexism of socialist movements and the fact that power based on gender and race often continues to be exercised even in socialist settings— have, in turn, challenged the classic socialist view and insisted that an analysis that locates the source of all oppression in economic relationships is incomplete.[4] While we agree with socialist feminists that the Marxist analysis, too, is inadequate, we believe that the Marxist framework itself is so flawed that it cannot be corrected through the simple addition of gender concerns.

While each of these approaches provides us with a particular "handle" on competition and hierarchies (particularly within the United States), each also leaves some important questions unanswered. We wish to argue here that instead of trying to modify these traditions, feminists would do better to turn to another—the anarchist tradition—which offers a different story about the nature and consequences of competition and the possibilities of cooperation.[5]

When we say *anarchist,* we mean to locate ourselves in the communalist-anarchist tradition of Bakunin, Kropotkin, Goldman, the Spanish anarchists, and grass-roots women's liberation groups in Europe and North America. The analyses of competition and hierarchy these groups have offered have varied, but all share a number of common perspectives: (1) a criticism of existing societies' focus on relationships of power and domination; (2) a vision of an alternate, egalitarian, nonauthoritarian society, along with claims about how it could be organized; and (3) a strategy for moving toward this alternate society. We shall see that the Vancouver Women's Health Collective and the Lawrence Textile Strike embody these perspectives in their organization and in their action.

What do anarchist theorists have to say about the nature and possibilities of cooperative, rather than competitive, social organization? Perhaps the most important point is that anarchism does not mean *lack* of but, rather, *different* structure. Human freedom is a social product: Freedom and community are compatible, but communities need to be structured in particular ways to support that freedom. In particular, they must be egalitarian: Society (including structures of work) should be arranged to foster relationships of reciprocity and cooperation (what anarchists have traditionally termed *mutualism*). Thus, there would be no need for economic inequalities or differential work incentives. The institutions in and through which people interact should encourage them to cooperate with one another, not to compete. Finally, people will come to recognize that the fulfillment of the self need not be achieved at the expense of others.

Freely organized groups, set up by people to meet their own needs, should replace centralized, hierarchical means of coordination. Leaders may well arise in some situations, but the right or authority to "command" a situation should not inhere in roles or offices to which some people have privileged access. Finally, instead of competing with nature—or even attempting to conquer it—people should orient themselves to finding new ways to live in harmony with our physical surroundings.

While this vision may not seem very different from one offered by Marxists and other socialists, anarchists have some important things to say about the process of social change. They insist that means be consistent with ends: that the process of revolution take place in and through structures that reflect the sorts of relationships in which people aim to live. Anarchism implies a concept of revolutionary practice which consists in creating new forms of communal-social existence, new ways to meet people's needs, forms through which people can struggle to overcome their own subordination. In the contemporary European and North American context, one of the most common manifestations of such new forms are collective workplaces (of which the Vancouver collective serves as an example). In 1912, this revolutionary practice guided the Lawrence Textile Strike. Not simply an action for higher wages or shorter hours, that strike was part of the anarchist process of social revolution.

COMPETITION IN A HIERARCHY
VERSUS COOPERATION IN A COLLECTIVE

The hierarchical work structures that many of us take for granted are quite recent creations. The reorganization of work in the Industrial Revolution involved changes in social arrangements as well as in technology—the division of manufacturing jobs into small tasks, bringing workers together under one roof in a factory, and separating the planning of work from its execution. These changes often had the effect of denying workers effective control over their work and of removing satisfaction from it.[6] In the twentieth century, the social revolution continued, and hierarchy extended, with managerial as well as manual work increasingly specialized. Over time, the deficiencies of rigid hierarchies have been widely recognized[7] and new models and practices have been developed which modify them to varying degrees. Nevertheless, the basic hierarchical structure, the assumptions it rests upon about the inferior intellectual and creative capacities of those farther down in the hierarchy, and its function as a mechanism of social control remain characteristic of most industries and many offices.

It is precisely such assignment of roles and rewards by competition that is problematic in the view of feminists, anarchists, and others. Hierarchical and collective methods of organizing work are not simply different ways of doing the same thing. They are based on different conceptions of knowledge, understanding, and rationality—and of right and justice.[8]

The Vancouver Women's Health Collective was established early in 1973 when women from a variety of local feminist health services (abortion referral and self-help among them) joined together.[9] The collective offered abortion counseling, contraceptive advice and diaphragm fitting, a health information phone line, and drop-in service. The members engaged in community education—for the public as well as for medical and nursing students—part of which took place through collective women's study groups. They also ran a self-help clinic, which aimed to empower women so that they could take responsibility for their own health.[10] Out of their roots in the women's movement, the members were determined to use feminist principles in a collective workplace structure.[11]

The collective operated on the premise that the more information one has in a given situation, the more power she has and the more responsibility she can take for her own actions. To withhold information is to keep people powerless. As a result, the collective was structured so that information, power, and responsibility were distributed as equally and as widely as possible. Instead of vesting authority in particular individuals who held managerial positions and controlled information, the collective rotated all coordinating and administrative positions among its members. Decisions concerning matters that touched on policy, whether large or small, were made by consensus at weekly meetings. Members rotated through all jobs, and taught one another the information they needed to perform them. The sharing of coordinating positions and consensus decision making were also major methods of information exchange. The group engaged in self-criticism at their weekly meetings, avoiding the situation where "the boss" is the only one with authority to criticize workers or the workplace. In theory at least, all members of the collective were equal participants in running the organization and in making and carrying out decisions. In practice, as in any collective, some members had more time to contribute, some had been around longer and knew more, some were newcomers who needed to learn more before they could fully take part.[12]

This collective had a "rational" structure, in the sense that positions and procedures were clearly set out.[13] However, the decision procedure in this collective reflected an understanding of rationality different from that characteristic of hierarchical work situations: Rationality derived from firsthand knowledge of the situation. Those making policy decisions knew every aspect of the work because they had done it. Because of the way work was organized, they could bring their own experience, rather than the expertise of managers, to the decision process.

Finally, while hierarchically organized workplaces assume that inequalities in both power and material rewards are necessary to provide incentives for workers, this collective was based on the assumption that people do their best not when they feel they must compete with others, but rather when they can work cooperatively with them.[14] Linda Light and Nancy Klieber, for example, distinguish between what they term "social power," or the power to dominate or control others, and what they refer to as "personal power" or "autonomy." Personal power is associated with independence, self-reliance, self-actualization, and confidence.[15] They state that hierarchically organized groups differentially distribute the two kinds of power so that there is competition among individuals for both sorts. By contrast, they argue, collectively organized workplaces *increase* personal power for all involved. The *sharing* of social power seems to generate personal power. People feel better about themselves, and they act more creatively and responsibly, when they work with others toward a common end. In collectives, workers' freedom and autonomy on the job is greater than it is in hierarchical work organizations. There is some evidence that benefits carry over to the nonwork lives of the participants. Carole Pateman, for example, has argued that increased opportunities for taking responsibility in the workplace affect people's sense of self-confidence and what is termed "political efficacy" *outside* the workplace.[16]

However, increased feelings of efficacy are not by themselves sufficient to assure that workers will have more autonomy and personal freedom in their lives. Collective workplaces as we know them exist in a larger society that is characterized by competition and hierarchy. Members of collectives often try to change those larger competitive structures, but they are not always successful—certainly not to the degree that their members are assured of achieving full autonomy or experiencing their full personhood in their nonwork lives. Members of the Vancouver Collective did try to work for broader political change by taking a self-help orientation and by working to educate the women who used their services. Yet, like any collective in contemporary North America, the group had to operate within larger competitive structures. Neither the collective as a unit nor its members as individuals had much social, economic, or political power within that larger context—power either to change it or to stave off its impacts on them.

The Vancouver collective operated in the context of a mass political movement in which many groups were working for more democratic workplace structures. There were also major efforts to change the nature of the health care system and a free clinic movement. Those groups denied the appropriateness of "competition" as a method of distributing goods and services. But this is where many collectives confront and have confronted their most difficult challenges. Food co-ops offer alternatives to supermarkets that must attract members/shoppers if they are to survive. Health care collectives offer alternatives to medical practices that must attract patients. Paradoxically, collectives committed to cooperative, noncompetitive modes of working must engage in competition even to survive. This struggle is particularly difficult when there is no strong mass movement to support their efforts.

PLURALIST POLITICAL COMPETITION VERSUS
DIRECT ACTION

Anarchists provide alternatives not only to competition in the workplace but also to "political competition" and struggles for "power" as ways of organizing the distribution of resources and control over policy making in political communities, large and small.

"Interest-group liberalism," which views political life as a series of competitions for power among groups of people representing different interests, provides the dominant understanding of politics in the United States. The assumptions underlying it are that most people know what their interests are, and are more or less capable of articulating and organizing around them. Politics is the competitive battle for preeminence among groups: The group with the most clout has its preferences enacted into policy. The system can be called democratic because it is formally open to the formation of new groups, because no one group wins every time, because there is apparent consensus on the "rules of the game," and because it seems that anyone who cares enough has a chance to influence policy. The role of politicians, and of laws, is to keep the competition fair—that is, played according to the rules.[17]

Although many women's organizations have learned to organize to be "effective" within this system, the shortcomings of the pluralist perspective ought to be evident. Most simply, those who already have access to power because of money, class, race, sex, age, or the like are able not only to keep it but to enhance it. More specifically, in treating interests as characteristics of individuals, the pluralist perspective masks the power of corporate groups to define the agenda of politics. Furthermore, it denies people the opportunity to think about or act upon our goals as members of communities. It encourages us to think about politics as a game in which there are winners and losers, rather than as an activity in and through which we can discuss and act on issues of common concern. More generally, the particular ways in which interests, groups, and competition play in this story virtually guarantee the continuing disadvantage, if not exclusion, of significant numbers of people from the competitive process, and the continuing advantage of those who, by virtue of corporate or other economic power, effectively "play" by very different rules.[18]

There are other modes of thinking about politics and engaging in political activity that avoid some of these pitfalls and challenge the notion of politics as a competitive game. Anarchists have developed other approaches quite self-consciously; feminists have as well—although not always so self-consciously. The theory and practice of direct action provide one such alternative.

Direct action methods have been used in many different movements in the United States to bring about social change. Freedom schools, sit-ins, health collectives, food co-ops, and industrial strikes are all examples of direct action methods to effect change by *creating new realities*, on however small a scale, rather than by attempting to influence decision makers through a pluralist bargaining process. Anarchists have argued explicitly that direct action can empower people by providing opportunities for them to learn about the realities of power in their societies and to recognize their own abilities to effect change. Through direct action, that is, people can come to understand their own interests and to learn how to create a society that better suits them.

Historically, in the United States, Canada, and western Europe, women have tended to be more centrally involved in direct action struggles than in more traditional "political" movements.[19] Many contemporary feminists have also adopted direct action methods, although often without any theoretical self-consciousness.

Early in this century, the anarcho-syndicalist Industrial Workers of the World (the IWW, or "Wobblies") used direct action methods in two major strikes: the Lawrence Textile Workers' Strike and the Paterson Silk Workers' Strike. Syndicalists were dedicated to revolution not by violent overthrow of the government but by nonviolent "industrial warfare." They believed that workers, if united, could effectively shut down the capitalist system, and replace it with a form of social coordination structured by worker syndicates rather than by a political state with its elected officials, courts, police, and armies.

The Wobblies were activists, and their theorizing was done through their practice.[20] The perspective they developed about human knowledge, individual interests, and rational decision making was very different from the pluralist one. Specifically, they argued that people's social positions affect what their interests are, their awareness of those interests, and their ability to forward them. Political/social action must be a continuous process of changing reality: both to educate workers and to empower them, enabling them to recognize their own powers, their own ability to create new realities.

According to their anarcho-syndicalist perspective, when workers reach the point of striking, they have come to recognize, at least to some extent, that their interests as workers are not being served. A more complete understanding of their interests, however, requires an analysis of the social, economic, and political system in which they live and work. This, according to the Wobblies, was not a matter of studying Marx but of acting—and then learning from the action and from other people's reactions. The Wobblies' best-known success was in the Lawrence Textile Strike.

The Lawrence strike began in January 1912, when workers walked out after a wage cut. It was an unusual strike. First, it began spontaneously, and only later was it shaped by IWW leaders. Second, it broke down the traditional divisions between workers and community members, men and women, and united all in a remarkable display of unity. As one participant summarized,

It was a new kind of strike. There had never been any mass picketing in a New England town. Ten thousand workers picketed. It was the spirit of the workers that seemed dangerous. They were confident, gay, released, and they sang. They were always marching and singing.[21]

One of the ways this strike was "new" was the degree to which it involved women and children, who constituted over half the textile workers at the Lawrence plant. The mass picketing involved men, women, and children in an endless parade around the strike zone. There were women delegates elected to the strike committee, and one of the Wobblies' star organizers, Elizabeth Gurley Flynn, helped to guide the strike. But to place the Lawrence strike solely within labor movement history is to misunderstand both the place of women in it and the nature of anarchist politics. For the Lawrence strike was *not* simply a workers' strike; it was a revolutionary community effort that engaged the women and children at home as well as those who worked. It was a community move toward anarchist revolution, and it was quite different from the strikes led by unions such as the American Federation of Labor, in which women were, with few exceptions, supports for their men's efforts at getting higher wages within the capitalist workplace.[22]

The Wobblies used strikes as a means to gain advantages in wages or work conditions, but also as direct actions through which workers and their families and communities educated themselves about the nature of capitalism and the state and transformed themselves into a working class capable of changing the economic and political structure of the society in which they lived. As Melvyn Dubofsky has summarized,

> Wobblies hoped that simple ideas would lead to action, and that action in turn would transform the strikers' originally simple concepts into more complicated revolutionary principles. In other words, the simple concept that employers mistreated workers would result in a strike, the nature of which would teach the strikers about the realities of class, the viciousness of employers, and the depravity of the capitalist state, and from this, the strikers would derive a sense of class consciousness and revolutionary principle.[23]

This view of education and injustice contrasts sharply with that of competitive, meritocratic perspectives. *Injustice* refers, here, not to discrimination or bias in applying the rules but to unfairness in the rules themselves and in the basic social and economic arrangements.

Once the Lawrence strike began, workers and members of the community took action on their own initiative.

> The strike committee organized an elaborate system directed by a relief committee composed of representatives of all nationalities caught up in the struggle. Each ethnic group also had its own special relief committee. These committees investigated the needs of applicants, provided soup kitchens for single men, and furnished food or store orders for families. The committees provided for fuel, shoes, medical assistance and, in some cases, even rent. Although loosely organized and administered by uneducated immigrants, the committees operated with remarkable efficiency.[24]

The underlying assumption here is that personal power and knowledge come from acting on one's beliefs, and testing and changing them through action. The result is knowledge of the existing society and its injustices, as well as knowledge of how to change it. For the period of the strike, at least, direct action methods enabled women, men, and children to experience their own power and to exercise some influence over others in the absence of formal "social power."

CONCLUSION

While this article can provide only a brief overview of some of the anarchist alternatives to the competitive structures so many of us take for granted in the contemporary United States, we hope we have demonstrated that alternatives do exist. Even though the prevailing belief system in the United States insists that competition is the one best way to understand the process of sorting people into jobs and of distributing scarce resources, anarchist alternatives make clear that there is more than one way to tell the story.

From the anarchist perspective, competition serves to justify vast differentials of power, authority, resources, and even human dignity in society. The ideological dominance of the competitive model leads most people to believe both that hierarchy is fair (because it is efficient and necessary) and that their own place in it is, somehow, deserved. Such understandings both contribute to individual and communal disempowerment and discourage any efforts at social change in the direction of a more cooperative, less competitive society.

To the extent that feminists accept the liberal/competitive story and challenge existing practices only on the grounds of discrimination (or meritocratic fairness), we contribute to the perpetuation of social hierarchies and to the disempowerment of all people who find themselves disadvantaged by those structures. Conversely, to the degree that we recognize the empowering potential of cooperatively structured institutions and practices, name them, validate them, and support them, we can participate both in enabling people to recognize their own abilities and in creating institutions and practices that are, in themselves, the building blocks of a new society. Feminists of the women's liberation movement in the 1970s acted out of such an understanding. We must not lose that understanding.

This perspective takes on particular urgency when we consider it in the light of recent works on moral decision making that suggest that meritocratic orientations are compatible with (white, middle-class) male modes of operation in the United States.[25] However problematic those studies may be in other respects, they do raise the possibility that women and members of minority and working-class groups may be disadvantaged from the start in any competitive structure, no matter how "fair" its rules or how fairly they are applied. In addition, they suggest that members of nondominant groups (whether women, working-class people, or people of color) are more attuned to cooperative orientations and may even perform better in situations of cooperation than of competition. From this perspective, too, maintenance of competitive structures disadvantages those already disadvantaged, and severely limits the range of human experience reflected in social institutions.

All this is not to say that the process of creating a society based on cooperative, rather than competitive, principles would be a simple one: The experiences of both the Vancouver Women's Health Collective and of the Wobblies should make clear that the opposition to such alternatives is severe.[26] It is to say, however, that such alternatives have existed historically and continue to be developed in our own day. We must recognize that competition is not the only way to play, and, more important, that competitive structures need to be opposed not only by cooperative structures but in cooperative ways.

NOTES

1. See, for example, the journals *Quest, The Second Wave,* and, more recently, *Social Anarchism.* For an overview of women's liberation see Sara Evans, *Personal Politics* (New York: Vintage, 1979); also Kathryn Pyne Addelson, "Moral Revolution," in *Women and Value,* ed., M. Pearsall, (San Diego: Wadsworth, 1986).

2. NOW, for example, has come to adopt such strategies, although in the late 1960s and early 1970s it participated in the more broad-based collectivist movement.

3. See, for example, Max Weber, "Bureaucracy," in *From Max Weber: Essays in Sociology,* ed. H. H. Gerth and C. W. Mills (New York: Oxford University Press, 1958), 196–244 and John Rawls, *A Theory of Justice* (Cambridge: Harvard University Press, 1971).

4. See, for example, Zillah Eisenstein, ed., *Capitalist Patriarchy and the Case for Socialist Feminism* (New York: Monthly Review Press, 1975); and Kate Young, Carol Wolkowitz, and Roslyn McCullagh, eds., *Of Marriage and the Market* (London: CSE Books, 1981).

5. Alison Jaggar omits anarchist feminism and "black feminism" from her typology of feminisms in her recent book, asserting that they do not constitute positions separable from other feminist theories (see *Feminist Politics and Human Nature* [Totowa, NJ. Rowman and Allanheld, 1983]). As we shall argue, this belief constitutes a serious misunderstanding of anarchism and a mistaken view of "theory." It may result from an overemphasis on the work of academic feminists. We hope that this article will serve to challenge her claims.

6. See S. Marglin, "What Do Bosses Do?" *Review of Radical Political Economics* 6, no. 2(Summer 1974): 33–60.

7. See, for example, Michael Crozier, *The Bureaucratic Phenomenon* (Chicago: University of Chicago Press, 1964).

8. As we noted earlier, liberal social theory analyzes this hierarchical division of labor as both necessary and rational—necessary in that it guarantees efficiency, and rational in the special sense that officeholders secure the right to command under a legally established, impersonal order which clearly defines their authority in terms of the offices they hold. Formal rules define relations among workers and regulate both competition and cooperation. To the extent that the hierarchy is characterized as a "meritocracy," competitors are said to win out on grounds of their qualifications, defined by their job descriptions and judged in part by standardized tests. According to the liberal story, the fair and impartial application of these procedures defines justice and efficiency, in the operation of both the workplace and the economy.

9. Information on the Vancouver Women's Health Collective was taken from Nancy Klieber and Linda Light, *Caring for Ourselves: An Alternative Structure for Health Care* (Vancouver, B.C.: School of Nursing, University of British Columbia, 1978).

10. Women's self-help groups differed from some others, for example, Al-Anon, because members consciously shared a relation to a sexist society and health care system. Their goal

was not simply to provide services (or even to help women help themselves) but to change the way the women related to the health care system and society as a whole, so as to challenge that sexism. *Our Bodies, Ourselves*, by the Boston Women's Health Collective (New York: Simon & Schuster, 1971), is probably the best-known product of the women's health movement.

11. Their place in the women's health movement led them to be concerned with health care delivery, and they made efforts to treat their patients with respect and to give them power over their own health—for example, through their self-help clinic. In this article, we limit ourselves to discussing the workplace structure.

12. Initially, the Vancouver collective was staffed entirely by volunteers. Over time, however, there was a marked increase in funding, so that many workers could be paid. Being staffed by paid workers is rarely a problem for collectives, but being staffed by a combination of paid and volunteer members often is. See Klieber and Light, *Caring for Ourselves*, chap. 15.

13. We should note that clearly stated rules and procedures are not necessarily present in all collectives—and that their absence is often problematic. See, for example, Joreen, "The Tyranny of Structurelessness," *The Second Wave* 2, no.1, and Jane Mansbridge, "Town Meeting Democracy," *Working Papers* 1, no.1 (Spring 1973): 5–15.

14. See, for example, Georgia Sassen, "Success Anxiety in Women: A Constructivist Interpretation of its Sources and Significance," *Harvard Educational Review* 50, no. 1 (February 1980); 13–24; also Carol Gilligan, *In a Different Voice* (Cambridge: Harvard University Press, 1982), especially chap. 3. Anarchist writers and activists have also addressed these issues directly. See, for example, Peter Kropotkin, *Mutual Aid*; Colin Ward, *Anarchy in Action* (New York: Harper & Row, 1974); and Martha Ackelsberg, "Revolution and Community: Mobilization, De-politicization and Perceptions of Change in Civil War Spain ," in *Women Living Change*, ed. Susan C. Bourque and Donna Robinson Divine (Philadelphia: Temple University Press, 1985), especially pp. 94–99.

15. Klieber and Light, *Caring for Ourselves*, 18.

16. Carole Pateman, *Participation and Democratic Theory* (Cambridge: Cambridge University Press, 1970), especially chaps. 4 and 5.

17. For a particularly clear presentation of this perspective, see Edward C. Banfield, *Political Influence* (New York: Free Press, 1960); and Joseph Schumpeter, *Capitalism, Socialism, and Democracy* (New York: Harper & Row, 1974), especially chaps. 19–23.

18. See, in particular, Michael Parenti, "Power and Pluralism: The View From the Bottom," *Journal of Politics* 32(1970): 501–530; Lewis Lipsitz, "The Grievances of the Poor," in *Power and Community*, ed. Philip Green and Sanford Levinson, (New York: Pantheon, 1970): 142–172; and, on the issue of community, Michael Sandel, *Liberalism and the Limits of Justice* (Cambridge: Cambridge University Press, 1983); and Michael Taylor, *Community, Anarchy and Liberty* (Cambridge: Cambridge University Press, 1982).

19. Temma Kaplan was one of the first to notice this relationship, though she adopts a somewhat different terminology and analytical framework. See, for example, "Female Consciousness and Collective Action," *Signs* 7, no. 3 (1982); 545–567. See also Paula Hyman, "Immigrant Women and Consumer Protest: The New York City Kosher Meat Boycott of 1902," *American Jewish History* 60 (1980): 91–105; and Dana Frank, "Housewives, Socialists, and the Politics of Food: The 1917 New York Cost-of-Living Protests," *Feminist Studies* 11, no. 2 (Summer 1985): 255–285.

20. It is characteristic of anarchist theory that the theorizing be done through practice, rather than in abstract writings by "intellectuals" or political leaders. If Marxist or liberal theory is taken as a paradigm, then anarchists appear to have no theory (or to be simplistic

or naive theoretically). But to apply that paradigm is seriously to misunderstand anarchist theory and practice.

21. Mary Heaton Vorse, cited in R. D. Boyer and Herbert M. Morais, *Labor's Untold Story* (New York: Radio and Machine Workers, 1972), 175. Melvyn Dubofsky's discussion of the strike is thorough and helpful; see *We Shall Be All: A History of the Industrial Workers of the World* (Chicago: Quadrangle Books, 1969). See also Elizabeth Gurley Flynn, *The Rebel Girl: An Autobiography, My Life (1906–1926)* (New York: International Publishers, 1973).

22. Important exceptions to this generalization are those women who organized women workers in what was to become the International Ladies Garment Workers' Union. See, for example, Alice Kessler-Harris, "Organizing the Unorganizable: Three Jewish Women and Their Union," *Labor History* 17 (Winter 1976): 5–23. But even this exception is partial: The union was fighting for better wages and hours, not for a reorganization of the economic and social system. For another view of the *community* nature of the strike, see also Ardis Cameron, "Bread and Roses Revisited: Women's Culture and Working Class Activism in the Lawrence Strike of 1912," in *Women, Work and Protest: A Century of United States Women's Labor History*, ed. Ruth Milkman (Boston: Routledge and Kegan Paul, 1985).

23. Dubofsky, *We Shall Be All*, 284, reporting Elizabeth Gurley Flynn's analysis.

24. Ibid., 250. Participants reported very similar experiences with anarchist-sponsored committees to organize the distribution of basic necessities in Republican Spain during the Spanish Civil War. See, for example, Ackelsberg, "Revolution and Community," 85–115.

25. See, for example, Georgia Sassen, "Success Anxiety in Women"; Carol Gilligan, *In a Different Voice*; and Sue J. M. Freeman, "Women's Moral Dilemmas: In Pursuit of Integrity," in *Women Living Change*, ed. Bourque and Divine.

26. The Syndicalists and Anarchists faced persecution and imprisonment in the wave of patriotic fervor that carried the nation into World War I. After the war, there were deportations and the severe repression of the 1920s "Red Scare" that saw the notorious executions of Sacco and Vanzetti. When the unions finally came to the textile industry they came through the AFL-CIO and labor and capital became competing interest groups under a liberal ideology.

Competition, Compassion, and Community: Models for a Feminist Ethos

MARÍA C. LUGONES and ELIZABETH V. SPELMAN

INTRODUCTION

One of the ways to explore the meaning of any version of feminism is to ask what it says or implies about how people ought to treat one another. After all, feminism is something to be lived; it is not merely an assent to a string of statements about the oppression and liberation of women. For example, feminists presumably consider it desirable not to think or say sexist, racist, homophobic, or classist things about one another; presumably we ought to rejoice in one another's good fortune and not be envious of it; presumably we ought to be willing to help each other out. Ought we to compete with one another? Are competition and competitiveness useful and desirable, from a feminist perspective, or are they harmful and to be avoided as much as possible?

In what follows we begin to lay out answers to these questions through (1) examining what competition and competitiveness are; (2) considering a strong statement about the importance of a competitive ethos to a vibrant political community; (3) thinking about the desirability of what would appear to be a contrasting ethos— an ethos of compassion; and finally (4) bringing forth our own observations about the way competition and competitiveness function in communities. Both of us are philosophers who are feminists; our reflections here grow out of the courses we teach in ethics and in social and political philosophy, as well as out of our experiences in the feminist and nonfeminist communities in which we live, work, and play.

We wish to thank Marilyn Frye, Helen Longino, and Valerie Miner for their careful attention to earlier versions of this essay.

A CASE FOR THE VIRTUES OF COMPETITION

We now turn to the philosopher Hannah Arendt, for we have found her work to be both helpful, in enabling us to define competition, and provocative, in its enthusiastic endorsement of the virtues of competition.

Some of Arendt's work provides by implication a sustained argument for the idea that feminists have made a mistake if we have scorned competition as a possible virtue. According to Arendt, something very much like the desire to compete (in at least one of its senses) ought to be at the center of any revolutionary activity that has a hope of culminating in the establishment of an enduring political community. Arendt's position emerges while she is in the process of comparing what she takes to have been the ethos of the French Revolution with that of the American Revolution. The French Revolution failed where the American Revolution succeeded, according to Arendt, because the leaders of the French Revolution conceived of themselves as compassionate beings intent on freeing the suffering masses from deep poverty and misery. The American Revolution was much more successful, according to Arendt, because it was led by, and in behalf of, people who wished to be freed not so much from poverty but from obscurity: They wished to create a political community in which there existed the possibility (though presumably not the guarantee) of satisfying the desire to excel, to distinguish oneself in the eyes of one's fellow citizens. They did not think of themselves as overwhelmed by the forces of "necessity," that is, as engaged in a desperate struggle to be fed, to be sheltered, to survive; the freedom they fought for was not freedom from exploitation and want, but freedom to be engaged in the activities constitutive of the public realm— "the discussion, the deliberations and the making of decisions." What moved them, Arendt says, is what John Adams called "the passion for distinction," which is a "desire to be seen, heard, talked of, approved and respected by the people about [one] and within [one's] knowledge."[1]

Arendt notes, quoting Adams again, that such desire to excel and passion for distinction are incompatible with the longing to dominate others systematically: "It is precisely because the tyrant has no desire to excel and lacks all passion for distinction that he finds it so pleasant to rise above the company of all men; conversely, it is the desire to excel which makes men love the world and enjoy the company of their peers, and drives them into public business."[2]

Arendt's account thus implies that there are concepts of oneself and of others that are characteristic of the ['desire to excel":] When you have such a desire, you don't see the other as suffering or as subject to your domination; when you have such a desire, you don't see yourself either as coming to the aid of others or simply as vanquishing others. The desire involves, instead, wanting to avoid obscurity both for yourself and for others. One is obscure insofar as one is not distinct from others, and insofar as this distinction is attained by excelling, one becomes free from obscurity by proving oneself to be better than others in some respect. So *excelling*, in Arendt's sense, seems to require a conception of an individual's participating in public affairs as a matter of making her mark, a mark that can be clearly attributed to her and to her alone. She contributes to the public good through the process of becoming distinguished from and by the public; and the public world is good for her just because it is the place, the space, in which such attainment of distinction is possible. Arendt seems to think that a better society and better people will result from this process of avoiding obscurity through excelling.

Arendt thus can help lead us to a particular understanding of competitiveness, inasmuch as the desire to excel, the desire for distinction, and the desire to avoid obscurity appear to be part of a competitive attitude. But these desires are not by themselves definitive of a competitive attitude.

Competitiveness

The desire to excel, the desire to avoid obscurity, and the desire for distinction become definitive of a competitive attitude in a context of opposition and they come, in their turn, to be shaped by this context. For at the heart of the desire to excel in the context of opposition is the desire to excel not merely in some non-comparative sense, but to excel over others, to better them. If one competes successfully in a context of opposition, one has excelled over others, whether or not one has excelled in some noncomparative sense as well. Though excelling over others does include a willingness to have one's limits tried by the performances of others, and though such trials may result in excellent performances, the overriding preoccupation is with standing out against the performances of others. Thus the desire for distinction is of a piece with the desire to excel in the context of opposition: One desires to stand out against a background of one's opponents by bettering them. The desire to avoid obscurity which, in other contexts, may be a desire for recognition that is not a desire to be distinct from others, can be transformed in the context of opposition into a desire to stand out against a background of one's opponents by bettering them and to be witnessed by those one has bettered; only then is the desire to avoid obscurity constitutive of a competitive attitude. Where before I looked for appreciative attention, now, when placed in a context of opposition and treated as having distinguished myself, I come to long for such distinction (for example, my beautiful singing is described by others as "the best," and I experience myself as coming to long for the glow of distinction).

In the context of opposition one avoids obscurity only through this standing out and through this standing out being witnessed. The satisfaction of these desires in the context of opposition requires scarcity since it requires a background; not everyone can stand out. To better another competitor is to turn her into part of the background through which comparative excellence acquires meaning: a background of others that see her excellence through their being excelled. This witnessing of the background gives the successful competitor a solid sense of her separateness.

Through striving, the successful competitor acquires a claim to comparative excellence, one that she did not have prior to the competition. In this she is different from the one who desires to dominate, since the latter has a belief in her superiority which precedes her attempt at domination, and she claims dominion over others based on this superiority. She does not strive to *better* others, she believes herself to *be* better than others. The successful competitor also differs from the one who struggles against those who attempt to usurp that over which she has a claim prior to the struggle. For example, to demand one's civil rights is not to proclaim one's desire to compete.

Though the Latin *competere* means "to come together," the English *compete* means "To strive against." One is engaged with others in competitive striving, but such striving is essentially self-centered. During the competition each competitor can think of the others only by way of measuring her own performance. She aids them in performing well only by way of concentrating on outdoing them. If someone is ready to give up, she must ignore her. If someone was not ready to begin with, this cannot be a matter of her concern. She pays attention only to those ready, enduring, excellent performers by way of acquiring a measure of the worth of her own performance.[3]

A competitor qua competitor sustains quite a different conception of herself and others than she would if she were in engaged in activities in which it is appropriate to think about other humans as needy or as collaborators. (If some of what we have said so far strikes the fan of team sports as wrong, it is because team sports are double-faced: they are competitive and collaborative. In attempting to analyze the competitive attitude, we are analyzing only one of the attitudes appropriate in team sports.) The competitor's attempt to distinguish herself can only be sabotaged if she presents herself to others as burdened by need or suffering (unless, of course, her attempt to distinguish herself is in terms of degrees of suffering[4]). Competitive competitors will not want to reveal whatever vulnerabilities they have, lest that knowledge give any edge to their fellow competitors. At the same time, one may not even want to be made aware of certain serious vulnerabilities in one's opponent, for fear that one's own compassion or concern for the other will get in the way of one's steady determination to overcome one's competitor. (Indeed, competitive athletes often remark on just such difficulties: They don't want to think about their opponents' sore ribs or turned ankles lest, out of compassion for them, they cease playing their hardest.) The competitor, even if needy, does not face her opponents as needy nor does she conceive of them as needy as she stands alone among them. Excelling over them requires that she stand alone. (Even if a host of others made her competing possible, she is the one competing, not them. She is the one who is going to excel over others, to distinguish herself.) If successful, she will stand out alone while the attention of those she has bettered shapes her aloneness as separation, distinction.

Individual and Communal Excelling
The self-centered desire to stand out alone against a background of others by having excelled over them and to be seen by them as having excelled over them emphasizes an individualistic conception of excellence and of the one who excels. This can be readily seen when one thinks of someone engaged in a communal project who is motivated by this self-centered desire. This is not an uncommon occurrence. Such a person will desire to be seen and to see herself as solely responsible for the success

of the project or as the most important contributor to its success, or will work to give rise to a sense that the project is only hers. She will attempt to obscure the participation of others, to minimize the extent to which their imaginations formed the project, to minimize the importance of their work in the realization of the project. Unless she is self-deceived, a person who has this self-centered desire to stand out alone through excelling over others in their eyes cannot conceive of the project as a communal one except in the sense in which all competitors have a project in common: Each individually strives to stand out against a background of others. She vies for leadership; for example, she competes with others for the distinction of the project's author and most important contributor. She attempts to make the project solely her own. Authoring and carrying out the project become the scarce goods for which she is striving against others. One should note that in such cases there is an attempt both at competition and at domination: She vies for leadership and attempts to appropriate the work of others.

There are contexts in which the desire to avoid obscurity and the desire for excellence are not only compatible with but necessary ingredients of projects that are properly communal. In those cases these desires are incompatible with an individualistic conception of excellence and of the participants in the project. In a truly communal project my goals and the carrying out of them are not separate from those of others in the community. The integrity of my project and my integrity as one of the authors are inseparable from the community. My project and myself are in community.

Here it may be helpful to move, by example, from the sociality of one's work and one's self to a fuller sense of being and doing work collectively. Suppose you make 15 jars of your very own tomato marmalade by yourself and have no one to "show off" to. No one to see all your jars lined up, no one to taste the marmalade and find it delectable. Your imagination and care have gone into the making. All by yourself with your marmalade, you may miss recognition, appreciation. Your sense of lacking reveals the sociality of your conception of your project and of yourself in the production. It isn't that you want your marmalade to be the best in the neighborhood, better than other people's. You do not want to show off to be recognized as having bettered others. It is rather like being all dressed up with no place to go. The project involves others (though not in the making). It is made to be seen, tasted, handled by others. The little jar in the dark pantry is one's work waiting to come out for the social unveiling, the appreciation that completes it. If in the pantry forever, your work remains obscure, pointless, incomplete. If you take it out all by yourself, there is no celebration of its sociality. You are alone in having worked.

When our work is constantly obscured by lack of careful appreciation, it seems pointless (even when it is consumed, especially in a taken-for-granted way). We move through our days not quite substantive to ourselves, as if people could walk through us. One can aspire to do something well in honor of oneself and of those others who are indispensable to the full achievement of the social meaning of one's creations. But in order to be able to appreciate our work, others must understand it and they must be attentive and careful so as to exercise this understanding. Notice the similarities between the description of this example and what Arendt says about freedom from obscurity, but also notice that nothing in the example exemplifies a passion for distinction. The marmalade maker has a passion for recognition, for counting, for appreciation, and we can see that the very value and meaning of her work are at stake in this recognition; it is not a frivolous desire. Notice also how familiar we are with children's asking for this recognition when they perform cartwheels, for example, and they tell us, "See how well I do this!" They are not asking for recognition of comparative excellence, but they desire recognition of their achievements.

It is important that in our example she makes the marmalade by herself in a world where the project is conceived as a social one. It is because she is alone in the making, because it is not a communal project in its conception and production, that it is so easy to see the similarities with the competitor. She, like the competitor, stands alone in her work. But now let us think of a project whose conception, production, and direction are truly communal; for example, the decisions about the planting, the harvesting, the cooking, the canning, and the distribution are made not by the woman by herself but by all those who are going to consume the product of this labor, and the work is carried on together. In such a case we are much less likely to think of obscurity as important. We will tend to ignore this important aspect of one's work because, in a truly communal project, it will be realized. In much work that is truly communal in conception, production, and direction, we can still think of each person as striving to do her part excellently in the noncomparative sense and we can see her excellent performance from the point of view of the larger task. Her work is social in more ways than is the work of the solitary marmalade maker. She is free from obscurity when her work is appreciated, recognized with careful attention by the collectivity. As with the marmalade maker, she is not competing; the meaning of her task and of its excellence does not lie in its being better than others. It is also important to notice that recognition does not have to be of the "being awarded distinguished status" kind; recognition can be demonstrated in the careful way in which one's work is treated.

It should be clear than excelling in the noncomparative, "doing excellent work," sense is not only consistent with communal projects but is an important attitude for working on the group's project. Yet sometimes one finds groups putting down those who excel in this sense—indeed what appears to be a feminist taboo against competition may emerge on this kind of occasion. This may be due to a confusion between the two senses of excel: the doing excellently sense, and the excelling over sense. In the doing excellently sense, to keep people from excelling or not to acknowledge excellence harms the group. To be told that one has done an excellent job in this sense is confirming, reassuring, pleasing. Moreover, when one is doing hard work against high odds, one needs one's work to be celebrated. Celebration provides a respite from continually facing the high odds against the group's success. It is also important to note, again, that to recognize excellent work does not necessitate thinking of the work as better than the work of others. To strive for excellence in this sense is quite consistent with a serious concern for the excellence of the work of others that is not a self-directed concern (in an individualistic sense of "self"). The excellence of the work of others is not under these conditions a measure of the worth of one's work. One needs to be preoccupied with her work and to have a moving desire for the excellence of it because it is necessary for the completion of the group's project and not just for its own sake. (And note that the group's project may be aimed at, and in any event have the consequence of, the group's no longer being obscure or invisible.)

Though being celebrated for doing excellent work does not necessitate comparisons with others, deciding that someone does a job better than others is sometimes important in a communal project—for example, in thinking about task allocation. Sometimes it is best not to have the person who does the best job perform the task, because others need to learn or that person is already too visible in the eyes of the enemies of the group as that task's performer, and so on. Thus that someone does something better than others is something to be recognized only when matters of practical decision require it. At other times it is beside the point. To confuse celebrating someone's excellence with thinking of her as superior to others is to confuse the two senses of *excel.* As we have seen, celebrating someone's excellence (noncomparative sense) satisfies the desire to avoid obscurity within the communal context by giving her work a solid sense of recognition which sustains her integrity and the integrity of her work in community.

It is undeniable that when one is engaged in a communal project that is conceived of by every member of the group as the group's project (one they have collectively defined, that requires collective effort), and the bad times come, it is more difficult to give up the project, to abandon one's commitment, in the presence of other members of the group. Rather, one feels egged on by the presence of other members into continuing and doing better, giving up despair, trying to find some other course of action, thinking of alternative strategies. The presence of other members of the group works to rekindle the sense that giving up is not quite one's decision, that one is—unlike the competitor—not alone in carrying out the project.

In its being communal, the group's project is indistinguishable from my own; the group's success or failure is indistinguishable from my own. One feels like doing more, giving it one's best by being reawakened to the integrity of the group and to one's lack of integrity without it. In the group one counts for more than by oneself because the task can be accomplished only if the group works together. The possibility of failure is more useful than the possibility of success in bringing clearly to one's mind how important the group is to the possibility of success. Being one of many necessary contributors becomes clear when things are not going well, precisely because then the necessity of one's contribution becomes more pointed while at the same time it is clear that one's contribution alone is not enough.

FEMINISM AND COMPETITIVENESS

One reason why the examination of competitiveness is an important and fruitful process for feminists is that crucial to such an assessment is our becoming very clear about what the feminist project is, or what the feminist projects are. If we think of competition—as joint striving in opposition to one another—as compatible with the feminist project(s) and part of of the feminist ethos, then we cannot think of ourselves as engaged in a communal project except in a very special sense; for the only sense in which we have a shared project is that each of us needs the other as someone in distinction from whom we see and measure ourselves, in the process of making our mark on the world. We all presumably have, on this conception, some of the same values—for if you do not value the same activities I do and rank them in accordance with the same scale, I should hardly care whether I excelled in your eyes—hence presumably we also see each other as persons whose assessments of ourselves and our activities we honor and trust.[5] But we do not have a communal project in any other sense, because my excelling, my being better, requires that you or someone else do worse; if our project were truly a shared one, my doing well could not posssibly be *incompatible* with your doing well.

This very feature of competition reminds us of why feminists have had reason to regard competition as vicious—despite the fact that for some people being called a "vicious competitor" is a term of praise. One of the things wrong with competition is that it requires that there be fewer slots than people who need or desire to fill them; it requires that one's own success and well-being are impossible without someone else's failure and/or misery. At the same time the world of competition is not self-sustaining—the possibility of it rests on there being a correlative world of nurturance, support, love, and compassion. Feminists have been suspicious of the world of competition not only because of what goes on in it but because of what has been expected of those in the correlative world to keep the competitors in fighting shape.

Focus on the inhabitants of the other world, the world of the Other, and their lives, points to crucial features of the world of competition: It is a world in which people who enjoy privileges based on sex, race, class, sexual orientation, and soon are more likely to "win" precisely because those who do not enjoy such privileges are slotted for positions in that other world which makes the world of competition possible. A better way to ensure systematic self-deception in those who "succeed" in the world of competition could hardly be imagined. The people who are in a position to be most acutely aware of what it takes to keep those "competitors" even in the race are the very same people whose job it is to provide a cushion against the harshness of the warriors' world: maids, wives, secretaries, nurses, chauffeurs, shoeshine boys, waitresses, waiters, prostitutes. How would our "fierce competitors" do if there were no one to perform all the services and functions these others perform for them (at unconscionably low wages, or none at all), including the crucial function of being at one and the same time deferential and compassionate? Those who service the competitors' world[6] have the knowledge, and their lives represent the fact, that that world is hardly what its inhabitants would like to believe it is; but their job is to attend to (or prevent) the wounds the warriors endure, not to add to the wounds by laying bare the many big and little lies the "competitors" need to believe (for example, that there was a competition to become competitors, that of course they got to the competition by their own steam, that without doubt the judges are fair).

So feminists have been quite distrustful of competition. Competitiveness has often been seen as the ethos of a world the maintenance costs of which have been high, though varied, for women of all races and classes. Insofar as women have been seen as competitors it has not, for the most part, been within that world but for the attention of those within it. Women have been seen not so much as the subjects of competition but as the objects of it; for among the means, and marks, of success among those in the world of competition is having "won" the "most attractive" women. The kind of attractiveness depends on the kind of competition: white slaveholders in the United States, for example, bid for ownership of the black women they thought most likely to be "good breeders," while perhaps competing for husband rights over white women with "good breeding." In *The Republic* Plato promised the most successful warriors the right to breed with the women of their choice.[7]

Competitiveness, then, has not been seen as a promising model for a distinctively feminist ethos—to such an extent that there is a sense in which competitiveness has been seen as antithetical to "real sisterhood." It may be that in certain versions of feminism—for example, its liberal varieties—an important goal for women is to be able to join the competitive world. Liberal feminists seem to be saying that the serious political problem is obscurity, not the absence of satisfaction of basic needs, and that obscurity can be avoided only through competition. But even in this view, women are not explicitly portrayed as competing with one another prior to the time when the competitive world will open to women at large. An attitude of competitiveness toward a fellow member of an oppressed group appears to be both harsh and counterproductive—harsh, because you don't fight against someone with one or two or three strikes already against her; and counterproductive, because women need to be unified in order to bring about the wanted changes in the world, and if we compete among ourselves, that only amounts to performing for the oppressors the task of keeping us divided and weak.

RACISM AND COMPETITION

But we must examine not only the desirability but the possibility of competition among women. One aspect of racism involves seeing oneself as superior to others because of one's race. However that is spelled out, it is worth noticing that such a view of oneself and others has important consequences for the possibility of cross-racial competition, and that includes of course cross-racial competition among women. In the eyes of the one who takes herself to be racially superior, competitive striving with those she takes to be racially inferior is not possible in any realm

FEMINIST TRANSFORMATIONS

where racial superiority is assumed to be tied to superiority in the performance of tasks constitutive of that realm. Competitive striving is not possible in such cases precisely because the attitude guiding her in her striving, the competitive attitude, requires that one establish superiority through the striving and not that one presuppose superiority. The competitive attitude requires that one strive to excel others in a context of opposition and that one desire to be witnessed by one's opponents in having excelled them. This desire is incompatible with seeing oneself as racially superior to start with, for that claim to superiority precedes any encounter. From the point of view of the desires constitutive of the competitive attitude, the judgment that those who she takes to be her racial inferiors have of her cannot be taken seriously.

Those of us who are not white Anglo are seen as inferior in the eyes of the white racist, and in such eyes the best we can do is to "pass" through assimilation. But since the one who passes is not the real thing, one can be thought of as a competitor only to the extent that the racist is successfully deceived and to the extent that one is successful in falsifying oneself.

Among Hispanics in the United States competitiveness is not seen as a virtue; the Hispanic ethos does not include competitiveness as valuable. But competitiveness is ruled out also because vis-à-vis Anglos, Hispanics have been slotted for positions of servicing them. A refusal to service white Anglos (some Hispanics can afford such refusal some of the time; others cannot) cannot be understood as competing with them. As suggested above, resistance is not a form of competition. But Hispanics cannot afford to compete among themselves either, if they are to change their situations. To the extent that the struggle to claim themselves and to change their situations is or has to be a communal project, competing among themselves is incompatible with the project for reasons made evident earlier. But as discussed there, the communality of this project does not preempt but rather enhances the possibility of noncomparative excellence and the avoidance of obscurity.

COMPASSION

Because the perception of women as an oppressed group has been a central part of feminist theories, *compassion* may have appeared or may appear to be an important, even a defining, element of a feminist ethos. By definition those who are oppressed suffer, in ways that are as varied as the various modes and means of oppression. The appropriate attitude, it may seem, toward one's sisters' suffering, toward one's sisters as sufferers, is compassion: a sensitive and sympathetic awareness of their suffering along with the desire to do something about it. Indeed compassion sometimes seems to be the feminist virtue par excellence; we are even encouraged to be forgiving of behavior in a woman that we'd readily condemn in a man (or anyway in certain men under certain circumstances), precisely on the grounds that compassion for that woman requires us to see that behavior as occurring in extenuating circumstances and hence ought to be forgiven. Compassion also is a likely candidate, or so it seems, for being the feminist virtue just because being compassionate is something women presumably have known how to do—so we don't have to search for some *new* attitude, all we have to do is change our ideas about who is the appropriate or most needful object of our compassion: women, instead of men.

We also are encouraged to think of compassion as the feminist virtue, or anyway the white feminist virtue, by those accounts of the origins of the white women's movement according to which the antecedent of white women's concern for their own oppression is their concern and compassion for black slaves (in the nineteenth century) and effectively disenfranchised black citizens (in the twentieth). On these accounts, it was white women's compassionate attitude toward U.S. blacks that led naturally to their taking up a similar attitude toward themselves. Much better that a feminist movement be based on a model of female virtue than on one of male vice.

If we think, for the moment, of feminism as in part a response to the destructiveness and self-deception of the world of competition and its insidious relationship to the correlative world of nurturance and compassion, then we might also think of feminists as having chosen, or drifted toward, the second of two possible responses: (1) creating a world in which women cease to be the objects, and start becoming the subjects (or agents), of competition; or (2) creating a world in which women cease being merely the subjects, and start becoming the objects, of compassion. One understanding of a "woman-identified woman" is that she is a woman who chooses to give to other women the kind of compassion and support that men have expected women to give to men. The feminist ethos that emerges thus is not one in which women are to imitate how men act toward each other in the world of competition, but rather one in which women imitate, in their relationships with one another, certain aspects of how women are supposed to act toward men. (That is perhaps one reason why feminism feels so threatening to some men—"Who is going to take care of us, if the women don't? Lord knows we can't deal with each other compassionately and still succeed in the world of competition.")

Nevertheless, there are a variety of reasons for being cautious about the picture of an ideal feminist community as infused with an ethos of compassion. To understand this we need to recall that compassion is a noteworthy and honorable emotion precisely because the person who feels it is *not* in the same situation as the person who is suffering. There is a difference between the case of people as co-sufferers in the sense of both being subject to the same suffering and in the sense that one is subject to a particular suffering and the other, while not subject to that suffering (not at the moment, and perhaps never at all), imagines what the other is experiencing and is pained by it. As Lawrence Blum reminds us, "compassion does not require even that its subject have experienced the sort of suffering that occasions it."[8] In short, compassion is other-directed: it is concern for *another's* situation, not one's own.

The history of feminist thought and activity is rich with lessons about the other-directedness of compassion. The image of women as given to compassion and hence just naturally good at nursing and tending to the poor and downtrodden is a dandy

FEMINIST TRANSFORMATIONS

device for ensuring that both men and women will think that women always should put the needs of *others* before their own. (It also, of course, obscures the fact that among the poor and downtrodden are women.) It is a piece of the popular history of the nineteenth- and twentieth-century women's movement in the United States, as mentioned earlier, that many of the women who were at its forefront began to think about their own situations through their activity in behalf of *others;* that is, there were white women who were moved, by a sympathetic awareness of the situation of blacks who were slaves (in the nineteenth century) or disenfranchised citizens (in the twentieth), to engage in political activity aimed at bettering the conditions of blacks' lives. Indeed, these white women were unwittingly testing the limits of the stereotype of women as compassionate beings, for while they may have been encouraged by such a stereotype to feel compassion, they were discouraged by a conflicting stereotype from acting on that compassion in public spaces. They also exhibited the *other-directedness* of compassion, for they did not see any of the problems black people had as problems they themselves suffered from, as was shown when they defined their own suffering as women in terms that effectively excluded the suffering to which black women (and working-class white women) were subjected: concern about suffrage and the conditions of marriage did not include concern about racism or working conditions in the factories.[9] There is no denying the fact that being moved by the suffering of others, and being moved to do something about it, were influential in the early stages of the nineteenth- and twentieth-century white middle-class women's movements; but white women's attitudes toward the suffering of those they did *not* identify as "one of us" did not and could not serve as the models of attitudes they took up toward their *own* suffering—if that had been the model, the white women could not have conceived their oppression and liberation in terms that effectively excluded black women and other women of color.

So we can see just how *other-directed* compassion works, by noting the extent to which it involves the identification of the needs and situation of others as distinct from one's own. There is no *logical* room for compassion between one person and another when their situation is in relevant respects the same: "Compassion . . . is an act of imaginative entrance into the world of another's pain, and is proper on the part of those who do not themselves bear the same kind or degree of suffering."[10]

If, then, compassion for one another were an important virtue *within* feminist communities, it could only be so to the extent that the women (and men) in them did not see their situations as similar. But if they don't see their situations as similar at least in relevant ways, in what sense are they members of a community bound together by shared concerns and goals? Insofar as I feel compassion for another person, I do not have, or have not made, her problem my problem, nor have I seen her problem as mine in any significant way.

CONCLUSION

There are at least two alternative conceptions of communal projects and both are compatible with the "doing excellent work" sense of excelling. In one conception, everyone's doing excellent work matters to the extent that completion of the project requires it, but the project's goal is distinguishable from the members becoming excellent performers. The excellent performance is seen as instrumental rather than as constitutive of the project. So if it is not necessary to the attainment of the goal that everyone perform excellently, it is not important to enable everyone to perform excellently. In the other conception, the excellent performance by any member is desirable for her own and the group's good, and the group's project is constituted, at least in part, by the *enabling* of the members to excel. In both cases it is good for the group if all members excel, and it is important for the group to recognize excellent work. But it is only given the second conception that the group *must*, as a matter of the definition of its task, be concerned with enabling all members to excel. If this latter task is to be accomplished, an attitude of compassion toward the members of the group who are not doing good work is inappropriate. Compassion is too passive, easy, disrespectful. For what one needs if one is to be enabled by others is to be understood by them (one's position, one's difficulties, one's present limitations), to have others work with one from one's starting position with care, and to be brought out of that by them without discontinuity to the excellent performance of the relevant tasks.

Hence compassion, no less than competition, will not be characteristic of a feminist ethos if feminism is defined as a communal project. It is true that both competition and compassion typically involve one with others in some sense: you cannot really compete unless there are others around, indeed others with whom you share similar skills, values, and interests; and compassion by definition involves an attitude about others. But in neither case are others conceived of as people whose seeking, struggling, or feeling are one's own or significantly tied to one's own: in the case of competition, one works *against, in opposition to,* others; in the case of compassion, one struggles or feels *for,* or *in behalf of,* others. Communal projects, in which one's self, one's projects, one's sorrows, and one's joys are not so easily distinguishable from the selves, projects, sorrows, and joys of others, hence have no room for either competition or compassion.

NOTES

1. Hannah Arendt, *On Revolution* (New York: Penguin, 1963). See especially chaps. 2 and 3. Quotes on p. 120.

2. Ibid., 120.

3. See in this connection Friedrich Nietzsche's *Beyond Good and Evil* (Baltimore, Md.: Penguin, 1973), para. 258. Speaking about a "good and healthy aristocracy," he says:

> Its fundamental faith must be that society should *not* exist for the sake of society but only as foundation and scaffolding upon which a select species of being is able to raise itself to its higher task and in general to a higher *existence:* like those sun-seeking climbing plants of Java—

they are named *sipo-matador*—which clasp an oak-tree with their tendrils so long and often that at last, high above it but supported by it, they can unfold their crowns in the open light and display their happiness.

4. It is a bitter irony indeed that one of the few competitions at least some feminists have been willing to engage in openly is the striving to establish their group as the "most oppressed."

5. There is an interesting paradox here, however: on the one hand, if I need your high evaluation of me I must respect your ability to evaluate, and agree with your scale of evaluation; on the other hand, it seems that competitiveness fosters a disregard for another person except insofar as that person is someone against whom my own progress or excellence can be measured. But perhaps it is not so unusual to respect another person enough to want to have her think highly of you, but otherwise show little respect for or interest in her.

6. Unfortunately we cannot discuss here whether those in the service world compete among themselves in the same sense as do those in what we've called the world of competition.

7. Plato, *The Republic*, 460b (Book V) (New York: Pantheon, 1961).

8. Lawrence Blum, "Compassion," in *Explaining Emotions*, ed. Amelie Oskenberg Rorty (Berkeley: University of California Press, 1980), 510.

9. See, for example, Angela Davis, *Women, Race, and Class* (New York: Random House, 1981); Eleanor Flexner, *Century of Struggle* (New York: Aetheneum, 1973).

10. Terence Des Pres, *The Survivor* (New York: Pocket Books, 1977), 173.

The Ideology of Competition

HELEN E. LONGINO

In the early days of the current wave of the women's movement, we thought "sisterhood" would overcome an imposed competitiveness among women. Sisterhood was powerful—powerful enough to help us transcend the rivalries and petty jealousies that characterized relations between women and reinforced the isolation of women from one another. United, we could undo the male power structure and reshape society; individually, isolated from one another, we could only do our best to find a niche for ourselves working for "the man" as wife or paid employee. The Miss America Pageant protest in 1968 was an expression of rage against the universal beauty competition that was every woman's daily experience. (Many of us must remember the terrifying and painful awakening to that reality in sixth, seventh, and eighth grades.) The protest was a rejection of a system of judgment that focused on qualities that had nothing to do with our capacities to carry out our real tasks in our varied lives and which thus perpetuated the trivialization of women. Sisterhood meant relief from participation in this demeaning race.

The various transformations of the concept and ideal of sisterhood since the coining of the slogan "sisterhood is powerful" are traced elsewhere.[1] I want to focus on a theme that runs as an undercurrent through much feminist writing and talking—the rejection of competition as incompatible with the ethics of sisterhood. I think that this rejection is based as much on our *idea* of competition as it is on our experience of it. Feminists, along with other left and radical groups who see power in unity and collectivity, are in opposition to liberal and conservative thinkers on the issue of competition. This polarization both clouds our understanding and limits what we perceive to be positive forms of social relations. There is probably a psychological issue here as well: Women, it is said, are socialized to avoid conflict and, to the degree competition and conflict overlap, our socialization must lead us to avoid or to think we are avoiding competition. Some feminist psychologists go so far as to claim that even after discounting and eliminating sexist research there is reason to think that there is such a thing as a female personality which unsuited women for participation in the competitive world of work.[2] Whatever we may make of this idea, certainly the traditional feminine virtues, for example, gentleness and compassion, put women at a disadvantage in competitive pursuits.

We are discovering, however, that we engage in competitive behavior even while espousing ideologies that condemn it. Those ideologies lead us to reconstruct our behavior in false, misleading, and sometimes self-serving ways. Under their influence we deny the reality of competition and of our own competitive behavior. The condemnation of competition is at least in part a reaction to the equally unsound idealization of competition by social Darwinists and their fellow travelers. I intend in this essay to start unraveling this complex weave.

TWO MODELS OF COMPETITION

I shall begin conceptually. I wish to distinguish from each other two models of social behavior to which we give the name *competition*. Both models are realized in sports.

One is that of the race. Let's just think of a simple hundred-yard dash. The competitors simultaneously break from the starting point one hundred yards from the finish line—a tape stretched across the track. Whoever traverses that one hundred yards in the least time breaks the tape and wins the race. Now, given a well-matched group of entrants, there is no a priori reason why all nine, or however many of them there are, should not hit the tape at the same moment. Such an outcome is unheard of; even ties are rare. This is because people—even in well-matched groups—differ. The differences in the runners—in how they prepared for the race, in their psychological and physical states at the moment of the race, in the shoes they wear, and in the food they ate for breakfast—will show themselves in the runners' times. The more well matched they are, the more challenged and stimulated to run her best each entrant will be. Inequalities (differences, however momentary and transitory) in the relevant qualities of the competitors make for winners and losers.

The other major model is that of a game whose rules make more than one winner impossible: a zero-sum game. In baseball, the team with the most runs after nine complete innings wins. If after nine innings the teams are tied, they must continue to play complete innings until at the end of one, one team leads the other in runs. A tie is impossible in baseball and in similarly structured games, like tennis. In *this* model, the rules and structure of the competitive situation itself make for winners and losers: the game cannot end until it is won. This is the sporting analogue for the scarcity model of competition in which limitations on the availability of the object sought make for winners and losers. In sports this limitation is imposed by rules. In contexts less structured by convention, the limitation is also less conventional, for example, the number of people who can claim to be the first to reach the top of some peak by some route is limited by the number of bodies that can be accommodated in that space at the same time.

The point of this excursion into athletics is to get concrete examples of two quite distinct sets of conditions for competition. Competition always involves a contest among individuals seeking the same thing when not all can obtain it. The two models help us distinguish the mechanisms preventing the goal's general accessibility. In one model, the challenge, or differential abilities, model, inequalities or differences, however subtle, among the contestants are the presumed mechanism restricting access to the prize. Depending on the context, the challenge or the differential abilities aspect of this model is stressed. In the other model, the scarcity and/or indivisibility of the goal restricts general access. In any given instance of competition, one or the other of these factors may be operative. What judgments are appropriate must be in part a function of which mechanism is in play and whether it is appropriate to the goals of the competitors. A footrace over a predetermined course is a good way to find out who is fastest over that course, a good way, other things being equal, to stimulate the runners to run their best. It's not a particularly good way to determine who should sit in the Senate, or even who should judge other races. A sudden-death tiebreaker is a good way to settle the winner of a match. No one would suppose that the outcome of one tiebreaker could determine who of two competitors is the better tennis player overall. Even the World Series in baseball is decided by a minimum of four games, played in the home cities of both contending teams. The blanket condemnation of competition as well as its uncritical idealization ignore the distinctions suggested by these examples. I shall use these models in the analysis of some social and political thinking about competition in the following section.

COMPETITION IN SOCIAL AND POLITICAL THOUGHT

The attitudes and unreflective judgments expressed by many white, middle-class feminists in the United States are formed in part by the history of the idea of competition in modern Western social thought. Much of the culturally formative thinking about social issues in Europe and European America has been done by men. Competition is no exception. Both the malign *and* the benign roles competition has been assigned by social thinkers since the seventeenth century influence our conceptions and our moral appraisals.

Competition and human nature were first and most dramatically yoked in the work of the seventeenth-century philosopher Thomas Hobbes:

> So that in the first place, I put for a general inclination of all mankind, a perpetual and restless desire of power after power, that ceaseth only in death. And the cause of this, is . . . that a man . . . cannot assure the power and means to live well, which he hath present, without the acquisition of more.[3]

Hobbe's state of nature is a grim world (and a male world) in which each individual is driven by fear of every other and by a consequent impulse to amass as much of life's necessities as possible. Hobbesian men are fundamentally of equal capacity and thus capable of equally desiring and pursuing their ends. In the absence of the sovereign, the "common power to keep them all in awe," men are in a constant state of war against all. Hobbes is working with a scarcity model of competition. But scarcity of the object is created by our own insecurities. We all desire the same things, and our fear of having those gods we have already acquired taken away pits us against each other in the accumulation of more. He may simply have been laying the groundwork for the necessity of the sovereign, but Hobbes's depiction of the state of nature seems to us today an extremely prescient description of life in a capitalist economy. The antagonistic individualism built into his account has become a fairly common view of human nature and social life. Competition is not a game but the solvent of spontaneous social relations in the state of nature.

The naturalizing of competition begun by Hobbes resurfaced in the work of the late-eighteenth-century thinker Thomas Malthus, to be taken up by Charles Darwin. In his essays on population, Malthus formulated laws of increase which built scarcity into the natural world. The earth's population increases geometrically while its capacity to feed that population increases only arithmetically. There is consequently a struggle for those scarce and (calculated per capita) diminishing resources.

These notions of Malthus provided both the essential clue to Darwin's question about the mechanism of speciation and a quantitative understanding of biological change.[4] Given random variation among individuals and differing environments to which different variations are suited, only those individuals possessing variations suited to the environments in which they find themselves will survive to reproduce and, hence, to pass on their (heritable) characteristics to their progeny. Malthus's model of improportional rates of increase assured that some variations would be eliminated and others would persist. Darwin's description of natural selection itself implicates only the scarcity model of competition. In his chapter on the "Struggle for Existence," however, he invokes the striving-to-win characteristic of athletic contests even as he discusses the complex relations of interdependency. "But a plant on the edge of a desert is said to struggle for life against the drought, though more properly it should be said to be dependent on the moisture."[5] While the interactions he describes are as well examples of interdependency as of competition, it is the language and imagery of struggle and of striving to best others that is used to summarize interactions among living things. The climate of thought in which Darwin's theories of biological evolution were launched supported their hardening into an even harsher picture of nature.

For the classical economists of the nineteenth century, competition was an engine of progress. For Adam Smith and John Stuart Mill, competition—among sellers and among buyers—was the most effective regulator of supply and demand, of prices and wages.[6] Any interference with competition in the market created imbalances and inequalities in the system. Free and unrestrained competition promoted the division of labor and increased efficiency, technological innovation, and the wealth of nations. It created, in a word, Progress. Why did competition have this function?

The model of competition assumed by Smith and Mill and that is reflected in the supply and demand curves of classical economics seems to be the challenge model. As small-scale producers and buyers all strive to maximize their returns relative to their investments or expenditures, they provide standards of efficiency, productivity, marketing, and so on, for one another not to meet but to better. Many small firms, thus, compete to provide the best items at the lowest price, and those whose productivity falls enough below the average will have to drop out. The assumption that all participants in an economic situation are self-interested maximizers of material advantage provides the dynamics to drive the system. Smith and Mill seem to have assumed that new producers would move in and replace those thus eliminated. Marx, on the other hand, argued that unrestrained competition on this model would inevitably lead to monopoly.[7] As soon as a firm acquired an advantage, simple marketplace survival would dictate that it strengthen and consolidate that advantage. Eventually, one firm or small group of firms would emerge with a controlling share of the market. This consequence of the assumptions of classical economics still seems to escape the notice of contemporary advocates of the free market.

Social Darwinism, which applies evolutionary thinking to society, combines the uses and models of competition found in nineteenth-century economics and biology. Some Social Darwinists saw moral and social progress as the result of evolutionary processes operative in society. Moral and social progress was, of course, exemplified for them by the upper and middle classes of Victorian England, contrasted with the alien cultures of Asia and Africa. Others emphasized the application of the biological categories within their social world and saw society and social structure as the outcome of a social struggle in which each could succeed only at the expense of others—the most fit are those perceived as industrious, thrifty, inventive, and ruthless, who rise rightfully to the top and to positions of leadership, while the idle and infirm are selected against. Social hierarchy is thus seen as a natural phenomenon brought about by natural forces. The scarcity model of competition is used to structure thinking about the relations of the members of society to the necessities of life—because those necessities are scarce, all must compete in a struggle that only some can win. The differential abilities model is used to develop explanations of success and failure: the poor are poor because they are less fit.

Ruth Hubbard has exhibited the expression of Victorian sexual stereotypes in Darwin's thinking about and observation of sexual behavior.[8] Darwin describes sexual selection, for example, as a process involving males engaged in various forms of contest for access to females, while the females wait to be claimed by the victorious males. This image fed back into social theory in Herbert Spencer's view that strongly differentiated sex roles (in particular, those characteristic of the English middle class: active, enterprising men and passive, receptive women) were a manifestation of evolutionary advance.[9] Darwin himself thought that sexual selection explained the superiority of men over women in intelligence, creativity, and other traits.[10] There is evidence that as Darwin's *Origin of Species* went through several editions, his thought became progressively more pervaded by Spencerian ideas. The phrase "survival of the fittest," for example, which captures for many the spirit of evolutionary

FEMINIST TRANSFORMATIONS

theory, was coined by Spencer, not Darwin, and does not appear until the third edition of *Origin*.[11] Many contemporary biological theorists use the economic model of self-interested maximizers to provide the dynamic basis of biological change.[12] The scarcity and the differential models have been thoroughly intertwined, competition and economics both naturalized, and the natural world made over in the image of patriarchal capitalism.

Social Darwinism provided the bourgeois classes with the legitimating social theory they needed.[13] In feudal society hierarchical structure had been justified by concepts of nobility—one's birth determined one's station in life, and in particular one's position in the distribution and structure of power in society. In the modern world, the rising middle class needed a new system of legitimation that acknowledged their economic power and integrated it with the rightful exercise of political power. Names and offices were changed but the fundamentally pyramidal structure of society was not. Control of resources is still in the hands of the few—but now the notion of merit rather than birthright is used to legitimate membership in the ruling elites. And merit is, of course, determined by competition. How else?

This, I think, is the ideology of competition—*ideology*, because it's not really descriptive of how power and control and access to resources are distributed and because our belief that it is descriptive does function to legitimize inequalities of distribution. As long as it does so it makes the task of enforcing those inequalities that much easier. It does this in two ways: (1) It reduces the number of seekers after power and resources by eliminating those who are "naturally unfit" for competition. Laziness and delicacy have been thought to be characteristics that disqualify their bearers from competitive activity. And we know who's been called lazy and who's been called delicate. (2) If access to power and resources is determined competitively, then if we have them it's because we were successful and if we don't it's because we failed. Either way we deserve what we get. If we get tenure at our university teaching job, it's because we are the best qualified. If we don't get it, we just weren't good enough. The fact that our educational system is producing many more highly qualified scholars than it has room to employ or that U.S. institutions have a history of discriminating in favor of white, middle-class males is generally ineffective in combating the sense of personal failure and inadequacy that losing in such a contest can bring about. In contemporary jargon, the ideology of competition functions as mystification. The emotional response I've described is testimony to its power.

WOMEN ON COMPETITION

Women have responded to the idea of competition in a number of ways. Each of the three ways I will mention seems to fasten on one aspect or model of competition which then provides the basis for judging competition generally. Both feminists and nonfeminists are among those who have rejected competition or competitiveness as unwomanly or unsisterly, as unbefitting a female identity.

The nineteenth-century cultivation and idealization of female domesticity and "true womanhood" carved out a sphere of activity for middle-class women that was untainted by the aggressive struggles that characterized the public world of the male sphere.[14] Catharine Beecher was one of the most eloquent spokeswomen for this view. Writing on education and the benefits of education for women, she said:

> Though she may not teach from the portico, nor thunder from the forum, in her secret retirements she may form and send forth the sages that shall govern and reno-vate the world. Though she may not gird herself for bloody conflict, nor sound the trumpet of war, she may enwrap herself in the panoply of Heaven, and send the thrill of benevolence through a thousand youthful hearts. Though she may not enter the lists in legal collision, nor sharpen her intellect amid the passions and conflicts of men, she may teach the law of kindness, and hush up the discords and conflicts of life. Though she may not be cloathed as the ambassador of Heaven, nor minister at the altar of God, as a secret angel of mercy she may teach its will, and cause to ascend the humble, but most accepted sacrifice.[15]

Not all nineteenth-century women agreed. The Grimké sisters, whose public activism against slavery came in for Beecher's condemnation, took great exception both to Beecher's criticism and to her vision of womanhood.[16] The exact role and influence of the ideal of "true womanhood" has been explored at length by contemporary feminist historians. Belief in women's passivity, nurturance, and dependence was widespread and a mainstay of arguments both for and against their participation in public life. Even Darwin's nineteenth-century feminist critic, Antoinette Brown Blackwell, accepted the idea that males and females were by nature fundamentally different and rejected only the idea that women were thereby inferior or deserving of fewer rights than men. Many of the women in the anti-ERA campaign are heirs to the contrasting view of Catharine Beecher, believing apparently that participation in the public world would corrupt their moral purity and, hence, their moral authority.

That rejection of competition—as "unwomanly"—is quite different from its condemnation as "unsisterly." Feminists who protested the beauty pageants understood that restricting women to the domestic realm did not protect them from a competitive environment. It just changed the rules and the prizes. Feminist separatists have advocated withdrawal not just from the male world, but from the sphere allocated to women by patriarchy and to which women will always be restricted in a patriarchal system. Outside that system, in nonoppressive, nondistorting environments, women can develop fully as the human beings we are. Sisterhood means being supportive of one another, cooperative, nurturant, not trying to outdo one another, which is what men typically do. In our creation of a different, separate world, we can be different. Radical feminist organizations with all kinds of projects and goals have sprung up—with ideals of sharing and collectivity and mutual support. We have networks of organizations focused on preventing violence against women—shelters and rape crisis centers; on health—clinics for body and soul; on education—

bookstores, presses, and alternative learning centers. We have art projects like Judy Chicago's "The Dinner Party" and "The Birth Project," and rural living projects like the communes in Oregon and California. These have provided vital channels for women's energy and creativity. Radical feminists and socialists alike have sought to build anti-hierarchical, cooperative structures. Yet, in my experience, even here we've been beset by struggles for leadership, conflicts over "political correctness," and so on. Not exactly the haven we expected or intended.

Other women have insisted that women can compete as well as men if given the chance. They've taken men on with their own rhetoric and demanded equal opportunity to compete, to engage in the pursuit of power, position, prestige, or "just" a job. Liberal feminists insist that the key to undoing women's oppression is to legally banish discrimination on the basis of sex and to enforce equality of opportunity. Such women are often condemned by their more separatist sisters (and their more separatist selves). They for their part can retort that by entering the public world they will change it. Academia again offers a good example. Women who wish to teach must compete on the academy's terms: publish, get good teaching evaluations and good recommendations, and cultivate the right connections. If their research is feminist, in content or orientation, it must still meet (nay, exceed) traditional standards of scholarship. In a pamphlet entitled "Academic Feminists and the Women's Movement," academic feminists were roundly denounced as coopters and diluters of feminist theory and analysis originating outside the university.[17] Such dilution, some might say domestication, is perceived by the authors of the pamphlet as necessary for successful competition on the academic turf. It is also seen and condemned as betrayal. There is certainly a vast difference in political analysis and political commitment to be found in the ranks of academics researching "women's issues": from careerists in Women's Studies to activists attempting to integrate community and scholarly concerns. Still, feminist scholars are beginning a transformation of the academy and academic disciplines. There *are* more women (a few more), and curricula do include more information and analysis by and about women.

Each of the responses I have described has been associated with vigorous, thoughtful, and courageous engagement. As responses to competition, each is also, however, conceptually both limited and limiting. The rejection of competition as unwomanly combines a belief in essential sex differences with a reaction against a public world idealized as brutal, ruthless, struggling, "red in tooth and claw." The concept of competition at work here is that touted by the Social Darwinists in their defense of the class system and European imperialism. Scarcity is unquestioned, and the assumption of differential individual ability is unquestioned. Women are simultaneously necessary to the continued existence of the class and species but inevitably losers if they participate directly in the struggle for existence. The retreat to domestic virtues of nurturance and compassion, to "true womanhood," is a solution to the resulting puzzle of women's role in society. The position, at least as articulated by Catharine Beecher, however, is inconsistent: Beecher was, and twentieth-century conservatives are, actively defying their own ideas, exercising virtues other than those recommended to other women.

The radical and socialist rejection of competition is at bottom a rejection of the postulate of scarcity. The visions held out by both camps include the exercise of the various socially necessary and personally gratifying occupations without the competitive struggle that is characteristic of the male and capitalist world. The radical feminist tends to understand competition as a masculine craving for domination (which by definition can't be shared, requiring as it does a class of the dominated). Whereas Hobbes attributed competition to human psychology, the scarcity that fuels competition in the eyes of the radical feminist is an artifact of masculine psychology. For radical feminists, consensual decision making by collectives whose members are equally engaged in a project eliminates domination as an object of desire. The socialist, on the other hand, understands scarcity (at all levels) as an artifact of the requirement of individual (or private) accumulation in a capitalist economy. For socialist feminists, social ownership and control of the means of production eliminate the need for private capital accumulation.

In focusing on competition as a hallmark of masculine or capitalist behavior rather than on the scarcity of power or capital that fuels it, theorists have conflated the scarcity and differential abilities models. As a consequence, both radical and socialist feminists have failed to see pitfalls for ourselves as conflicts over ideas, leadership, and the allocation of resources have emerged. Often such conflicts are born when effective spokespersons for particular proposals exert themselves on behalf of those proposals. Such assertiveness, valued when directed externally, has often been perceived as domineering and condemned as competitive when directed within the group. By labeling the phenomenon as that competitiveness forbidden by ideology, we refuse the implicit challenge to develop comparable strengths. Absent an alternative way to understand these conflicts, they *are* transmuted into competitive struggles for power between individuals. This sea change makes the organization vulnerable to the same pressures at work in the surrounding culture. Either our purposes and goals get lost or collectivity is sacrificed to those goals and replaced by hierarchical forms of organization. Our conceptual linking of competition with domination, hierarchy, and scarcity prevents us from appreciating the value of competitive challenge in developing skills and talents and ultimately undermines our potential to change ourselves and our worlds.

The equal opportunity theorist and activist, on the other hand, seems to see competition solely on the challenge/differential abilities model. This focus prevents her from seeing that the contest is unfairly set up from the start, and that the system within which she competes or advocates that others compete does not have the openness presupposed by the challenge model. And so, some (a few) will always have much more than most, no matter how many of us enter the race, no matter how many of us are competent. A hierarchical social structure guarantees that we cannot all break the tape at once. Not only is it not possible for all those who are equally qualified to acquire equal degrees of power and access to resources, but the distribution of resources also guarantees that members of certain classes will not succeed in the attempt to gain power and resources. Youngsters who are poor, working and/or not white are chronic victims of inadequate schooling. Young women of all classes and races are discouraged from pursuing interests in math, sciences, and other abstract subjects. To understand competition solely on the challenge model is to ignore the fact that the competitions that matter the most to the equal opportunity theorist are, in our society, zero-sum games from which some are excluded at the outset. Competition in limited dimensions for limited and defined goals is simply different from the competition for places of power in a hierarchical meritocracy. In liberal capitalism, competition has burst the boundaries of specific athletic contests to become the arbiter of value generally. Our equal opportunity rhetoric often blinds us to this fact.

FINAL REMARKS

None of the responses to competition I have discussed is adequate in itself. Each does us a disservice in some way—by proscribing actions and activities we might find fulfilling and rewarding, or by confusing us, or by leading us on in a reward system that perpetuates scarcity and inequality. I do not want to be understood as urging that all competition on the challenge model is morally permissible. While I am confident that there are alternative ways of coping with scarcity, I feel that they need to be spelled out. In addition, competition on the challenge model requires that we develop more fine-grained distinctions and more complex understandings of the function of competition in different circumstances. Incentive-driven speedups in the workplace, for instance, which employ the challenge model, are damaging and divisive to those who must participate in them. What I do hope to have done in this essay is to have shown the necessity of such distinctions for moral and political argument. The radical and socialist feminist arguments against competition are directed at one mode, while liberal feminist arguments that are supportive of competition presuppose quite a different one. This result does not minimize the differences between these political positions. It should help us to clarify what they are.

NOTES

1. Redstockings, *Feminist Revolution* (New York: Random House, 1978).
2. Judith Bardwick, *Psychology of Women* (New York: Harper & Row, 1971).
3. Thomas Hobbes, *Leviathan* (New York: Collier's, 1964; originally published 1651), 80.
4. Sylvan Schweber, "The Origin of the *Origin* Revisited," *Journal of the History of Biology* 10, no. 2 (Fall 1977): 229–316.
5. Charles Darwin, *Origin of Species* (New York: Modern Library Edition, n.d.; originally published London, 1859), 63–66, 52.
6. Adam Smith, *The Wealth of Nations* (New York: Modern Library Edition, 1937; originally published London, 1776); John Stuart Mill, *Principles of Political Economy* (London: Longman Green, 1909; originally published London, 1848); Robert Lekachman, A History of Economic Ideas (New York: Harper & Row, 1959).

7. Karl Marx, *Capital,* vol. I (Moscow: Foreign Languages Publishing House, 1961; originally published Hamburg, 1867).

8. Ruth Hubbard, "Have Only Men Evolved?" in *Discovering Reality,* ed. Sandra Harding and Merrill Hintikka, (Boston: D. Reidel, 1983), 45–69.

9. Janet Sayers, *Biological Politics* (London: Tavistock, 1982); J. D. Y. Peel, ed., *Herbert Spencer on Social Evolution* (Chicago: University of Chicago Press, 1972).

10. Charles Darwin, *The Descent of Man* (New York: Modern Library Edition, n.d.; originally published London, 1871), 873–875.

11. Many scholars have remarked on this fact. Diane Paul (The University of Massachusetts, Boston) corrects some misconceptions about Darwin's use of the phrase in "The Selection of the 'Survival of the Fittest' " unpublished ms.

12. The most notorious example is to be found in Richard Dawkins, *The Selfish Gene* (New York: Oxford University Press, 1976). Michael Gross and Mary Beth Averill discuss the stretching of the concept of competition to accommodate a huge variety of biological interactions in "Evolution and Patriarchal Myths of Scarcity and Competition," in *Discovering Reality,* ed. Harding and Hintikka, 71–95.

13. Paul, "The Selection of the 'Survival of the Fittest' "; Schweber, "The Origin of the *Origin* Revisited"; R. M. Young, "The Historiographic and Ideologic Contexts of the 19th Century Debate on Man's Place in Nature," in *Changing Perspectives in the History of Science,* ed. M. Teich and R. M. Young (London: Heineman, 1972).

14. Barbara Welter, "The Cult of True Womanhood: 1820–1860," *American Quarterly* 18 (Summer 1966): 151–174.

15. Catharine E. Beecher, "Suggestions Regarding Improvements in Education" (originally published 1829), reprinted in *Up from the Pedestal: Selected Documents from the History of American Feminism,* ed. Aileen Kraditor (Chicago: Quadrangle Books, 1968), 85–86.

16. Angelina Emily Grimké, "Letters to Catharine E. Beecher" (originally published 1838), in *Up from the Pedestal,* ed. Kraditor, 58–66.

17. Ann Leffler et al. "Academic Feminists and the Women's Movement" (Iowa City: Iowa City Women's Press, 1973).

The Open End

HELEN E. LONGINO and VALERIE MINER

We end this forum as we began—with questions. The following queries have been raised by our contributors in various ways. We trust this anthology of different voices will stir even more questions among readers regarding their own ideas and feelings about competition. We look forward to more forums and conversations and books and panels on the subject. To that end, or rather to that continuance, here are few provocations.

• Can we create a cooperative sociality within which competitions would be limited, contained, and subordinated to communal prospering?

• Can cooperatively organized groups and projects survive within the competitive context of capitalist culture? How best can they be shielded from its transformative power?

• Can we broaden our concept of the self from that of the maximizing monad of Western political theory to that of a dependent and depended-upon organism?

• Where is it possible to replace ideas of scarcity with those of plenitude? And can we develop noncompetitive ways of apportioning resources when scarcity is a reality and not a politically convenient construction?

• Do any contemporary cultures or subcultures succeed in balancing competition and cooperation? Can they serve in any way as models?

• Does our ability to cooperate depend on our ability to acknowledge and accept our differences? How do we distinguish between "different" and "opposite"?

• Is competition possible among nonequals?

• How can we apply the lessons learned as mothers and daughters and sisters to more public contexts?

• How can women raised as Euro-American imperialists learn from the female cooperation in many Third World cultures?

• How can we distinguish between appropriate and inappropriate competition? Should some ends or activities be precluded from competitive action? Is there a point beyond which competitively fostered development is harmful rather than beneficial?

• Must we choose between acting to change the system and trying to succeed within it? Are both simultaneously possible?

The *Feminist Press at The City University of New York* offers alternatives in education and in literature. Founded in 1970, this nonprofit, tax-exempt educational and publishing organization works to eliminate sexual stereotypes in books and schools and to provide literature with a broad vision of human potential. The publishing program includes reprints of important works by women, feminist biographies of women, and nonsexist children's books. Curricular materials, bibliographies, directories, and a quarterly journal provide information and support for students and teachers of women's studies. In-service projects help to transform teaching methods and curricula. Through publications and projects, The Feminist Press contributes to the rediscovery of the history of women and the emergence of a more humane society.

NEW AND FORTHCOMING BOOKS

Carrie Chapman Catt: A Public Life, by Jacqueline Van Voris. $24.95 cloth.

Daughter of Earth, a novel by Agnes Smedley. Foreword by Alice Walker. Afterword by Nancy Hoffman. $8.95 paper.

Doctor Zay, a novel by Elizabeth Stuart Phelps. Afterword by Michael Sartisky. $8.95 paper.

Get Smart: A Woman's Guide to Equality on Campus, by S. Montana Katz and Veronica Vieland. $29.95 cloth, $9.95 paper.

A Guide to Research on Women: Library and Information Sources in the Greater New York Area, compiled by the Center for the Study of Women and Society of the Graduate School and University Center of The City University of New York, and the Women's Resources Group of the Greater New York Metropolitan Area Chapter of the Association of College and Research Libraries. $12.95 paper.

Harem Years: The Memoirs of an Egyptian Feminist, 1879–1924, by Huda Shaarawi. Translated and edited by Margot Badran. $29.95 cloth, $9.95 paper.

Leaving Home, a novel by Elizabeth Janeway. Afterword by Rachel M. Brownstein. $8.95 paper.

Lone Voyagers: Academic Women in Coeducational Universities, 1869–1937, edited by Geraldine J. Clifford. $29.95 cloth, $12.95 paper.

My Mother Marries, a novel by Moa Martinson. Translated and introduced by Margaret S. Lacy. $8.95 paper.

"Not So Quiet . . .": Stepdaughters of War, a novel by Helen Zenna Smith. Afterword by Jane Marcus. $8.95 paper.

Sultana's Dream and Selections from The Secluded Ones, by Rokeya Sakhawat Hossein. Edited by Roushan Jahan and Hanna Papanek. Translated by Roushan Jahan. $4.95 paper.

Turning the World Upside Down: The Anti-Slavery Convention of American Women Held in New York City, May 9–12, 1837. Introduction by Dorothy Sterling. $2.95 paper.

With Wings: An Anthology of Literature by and about Women with Disabilities, edited by Marsha Saxton and Florence Howe. $29.95 cloth. $12.95 paper.

Women Activists, by Anne Witte Garland. Foreword by Ralph Nader. $29.95 cloth, $9.95 paper.

Writing Red: An Anthology of American Women Writers, 1930–1940, edited by Charlotte L. Nekola and Paula Rabinowitz. Foreword by Toni Morrison. $29.95 cloth, $12.95 paper.

FICTION CLASSICS

Between Mothers and Daughters: Stories across a Generation, edited by Susan Koppelman. $9.95 paper.

OTHER TITLES

Antoinette Brown Blackwell: A Biography, by Elizabeth Cazden. $24.95 cloth, $12.95 paper.

All the Women Are White, All the Blacks Are Men, but Some of Us Are Brave: Black Women's Studies, edited by Gloria T. Hull, Patricia Bell Scott, and Barbara Smith. $12.95 paper.

Black Foremothers: Three Lives, by Dorothy Sterling. $9.95 paper.

Complaints and Disorders: The Sexual Politics of Sickness, by Barbara Ehrenreich and Deirdre English. $3.95 paper.

The Cross-Cultural Study of Women, edited by Margot I. Duley and Mary I. Edwards. $29.95 cloth, $12.95 paper.

A Day at a Time: The Diary Literature of American Women from 1764 to the Present, edited and with an introduction by Margo Culley. $29.95 cloth, $12.95 paper.

The Defiant Muse: French Feminist Poems from the Middle Ages to the Present, a bilingual anthology edited and with an introduction by Domna C. Stanton. $29.95 cloth, $11.95 paper.

The Defiant Muse: German Feminist Poems from the Middle Ages to the Present, a bilingual anthology edited and with an introduction by Susan L. Cocalis. $29.95 cloth, $11.95 paper.

The Defiant Muse: Hispanic Feminist Poems from the Middle Ages to the Present, a bilingual anthology edited and with an introduction by Angel Flores and Kate Flores. $29.95 cloth, $11.95 paper.

The Defiant Muse: Italian Feminist Poems from the Middle Ages to the Present, a bilingual anthology edited by Beverly Allen, Muriel Kittel, and Keala Jane Jewell, and with an introduction by Beverly Allen. $29.95 cloth, $11.95 paper.

Feminist Resources for Schools and Colleges: A Guide to Curricular Materials, 3rd edition, compiled and edited by Anne Chapman. $12.95 paper.

Household and Kin: Families in Flux, by Amy Swerdlow, Renate Bridenthal, Joan Kelly, and Phyllis Vine. $9.95 paper.

How to Get Money for Research, by Mary Rubin and the Business and Professional Women's Foundation. Foreword by Mariam Chamberlain. $6.95 paper.

In Her Own Image: Women Working in the Arts, edited and with an introduction by Elaine Hedges and Ingrid Wendt. $9.95 paper.

Integrating Women's Studies into the Curriculum: A Guide and Bibliography, by Betty Schmitz. $9.95 paper.

Käthe Kollwitz: Woman and Artist, by Martha Kearns, $9.95 paper.

Las Mujeres: Conversations from a Hispanic Community, by Nan Elsasser, Kyle MacKenzie, and Yvonne Tixier y Vigil. $9.95 paper.

Lesbian Studies: Present and Future, edited by Margaret Cruikshank. $9.95 paper.

Mother to Daughter, Daughter to Mother· A Daybook and Reader, selected and shaped by Tillie Olsen. $9.95 paper.

Moving the Mountain: Women Working for Social Change. by Ellen Cantarow with Susan Gushee O'Malley and Sharon Hartman Strom. $9.95 paper.

Out of the Bleachers: Writings on Women and Sport, edited and with an introduction by Stephanie L. Twin. $10.95 paper.

Portraits of Chinese Women in Revolution, by Agnes Smedley. Edited and with an introduction by Jan MacKinnon and Steve MacKinnon and an afterword by Florence Howe. $10.95 paper.

Reconstructing American Literature: Courses, Syllabi, Issues, edited by Paul Lauter. $10.95 paper.

Rights and Wrongs: Women's Struggle for Legal Equality, 2nd edition, by Susan Cary Nichols, Alice M. Price, and Rachel Rubin. $7.95 paper.

Salt of the Earth, screenplay by Michael Wilson with historical commentary by Deborah Silverton Rosenfelt. $10.95 paper.

These Modern Women: Autobiographical Essays from the Twenties, edited with an introduction by Elaine Showalter. $8.95 paper.

Witches, Midwives, and Nurses: A History of Women Healers, by Barbara Ehrenreich and Deirdre English. $3.95 paper.

With These Hands: Women Working on the Land, edited with an introduction by Joan M. Jensen. $9.95 paper.

The Woman and the Myth: Margaret Fuller's Life and Writings, by Bell Gale Chevigny. $8.95 paper.

Woman's "True" Profession: Voices from the History of Teaching, edited with an introduction by Nancy Hoffman. $9.95 paper.

Women Have Always Worked: A Historical Overview, by Alice Kessler-Harris. $9.95 paper.

For a free catalog, write to The Feminist Press at The City University of New York, 311 East 94 Street, New York, NY 10128. Send individual book orders to The Feminist Press, P.O. Box 1654, Hagerstown, MD 21741. Include $1.75 postage and handling for one book and 75 cents for each additional book. To order using MasterCard or Visa, call: (800) 638–3030.